CHALLENGING LEGAL CORE VALUES

Consent-Based Rape Legislation in Practice

Åsa Wettergren, Moa Bladini and Sara Uhnoo

BRISTOL UNIVERSITY PRESS

First published in Great Britain in 2025 by

Bristol University Press
University of Bristol
1–9 Old Park Hill
Bristol
BS2 8BB
UK
t: +44 (0)117 374 6645
e: bup-info@bristol.ac.uk

Details of international sales and distribution partners are available at bristoluniversitypress.co.uk

British Library Cataloguing in Publication Data
A catalogue record for this book is available from the British Library

ISBN 978-1-5292-3753-5 paperback
ISBN 978-1-5292-3755-9 ePub
ISBN 978-1-5292-3754-2 OA PDF

Cover design: Liam Roberts Design
Front cover image: iStock/kupritz
Bristol University Press uses environmentally responsible print partners.
Printed and bound in Great Britain by CPI Group (UK) Ltd, Croydon, CR0 4YY

Bristol University Press' authorised representative in the European Union is:
Easy Access System Europe, Mustamäe tee 50, 10621 Tallinn, Estonia,
Email: gpsr.requests@easproject.com

Contents

PART III   Autonomy and Rationality of Legal Subjects

List of Abbreviations

AC	Appeals Court
Brå	Brottsförebyggande rådet (Swedish National Council for Crime Prevention)
DC	District Court
NJA	Nytt Juridiskt Arkiv (New Legal Archive)
SCC	Swedish Criminal Code
SCJP	Swedish Code of Judicial Procedure
SvJT	*Svensk Juristtidning* (*Swedish Law Journal*)
SOU	*Statens Offentliga Utredningar* (Swedish Government Official Reports)

About the Authors

Moa Bladini is Associate Professor at the Department of Law, University of Gothenburg. Her research engages in criminal and criminal procedural law, particularly gender-based violence and courtroom studies. Previous publications include *I objektivitetens sken* [*In the Semblance of Objectivity*] (Makadam, 2013), 'Silenced voices. online violence against women as a threat against democracy', *Nordic Journal of Law and Society* (2020); 'Swedish rape legislation from use of force to voluntariness', *Bergen Journal of Criminal Law and Criminal Justice* (2020); 'It sounds like lived experience – on empathy in rape trials', *International Journal of Law, Crime and Justice* (2023); *Rethinking 'Anti-Gender Hate Speech'* (Routledge, 2025).

Sara Uhnoo is Associate Professor in Sociology at the Department of Sociology and Work Science, University of Gothenburg. Her current research interests are feminist criminology, courtroom studies and youth studies. Previous publications include 'It could be my son! "Himpathy" and the male fear defence in rape trials', *Journal of Law and Society* (2024), 'The wave of consent-based rape laws in Europe', *International Journal of Law, Crime and Justice* (2024); 'Negotiating access', in L Flower and S Klosterkamp (eds) *Courtroom Ethnography* (Macmillan Palgrave, 2023); 'Emotion management of disaster volunteers: The delicate balance between control and recognition', *Emotions and Society* (2020).

Åsa Wettergren is Professor in Sociology at the Department of Sociology and Work Science, University of Gothenburg. She is an internationally recognized scholar in the Sociology of Emotions. Current research fields are Law and Emotions, and Emotions in the Environmental Movement. Previous publications include *Professional Emotions in Court* (Routledge, 2018); 'Comparing culturally embedded frames of judicial dispassion', in S Bandes et al (eds) *Research Handbook on Law and Emotion* (Edward Elgar, 2021); 'Epistemic emotions in prosecutorial decision-making', *Journal of Law and Society* (2023); and 'Emotionalising hope in times of climate change', *Emotions and Society* (2024).

Acknowledgements

We thank Riksbankens Jubileumsfond, which made this book possible by funding our research project *Rape or consent? Effects of the new rape legislation on legal reasoning and practice* (Project ID: P19-0515:1) and also for funding the costs of Open Access. We are deeply grateful to all the legal professionals participating in our study, admitting access, and sharing their thoughts and emotions on the 2018 rape law and its implementation. Our study would not have been possible without you, and we sincerely hope this book makes sense to you. We also thank the complainants of our 18 cases, for admitting access to their rape trials. We are deeply indebted to Zentrum für interdisziplinäre Forschung) (ZiF) at the University of Bielefeld, which granted us one month as a visiting group in November 2023. Thanks to their generosity and extra-ordinary hospitality we were able to work together, intensively and focussed, on the analysis of all our data, and to plan the outline of the book. We enjoyed comfortable accommodation, free access to all the facilities, all the working materials and administrative support we could wish for, as well as a swimming pool, a sauna, and a beautiful forest. We also greatly enjoyed the city of Bielefeld with surroundings, not least for its music and art scenes. Last, but not least, we thank the five anonymous reviewers, whose enthusiasm and support for the book proposal and the first draft of the manuscript was a great encouragement when the writing, at times, felt overwhelming.

Preface

In 2021, following a lecture on the emotive-cognitive judicial doing of objectivity delivered to a District Court, one of us engaged in a conversation with a judge about rape cases. The judge remarked that these cases were not after all particularly challenging, as there was always corroborating evidence. He then paused, wrinkled his eyebrows and added: 'But it's true that the corroborating evidence are often witness stories, and they only say what the complainant has said. I have to give this a second thought'.

Our project, which we started in 2020, investigates the implementation of the Swedish consent-based rape law. At the time, the legislation was only a year and a half old, and our first interactions with the legal community revealed widespread professional frustration. The common question was 'How can we ascertain whether a crime has been committed within a closed setting?' One appellate court judge frankly told us the task was like fortune telling from coffee grounds. Judges who expressed certainty noted that it was not *only* the complainant's story but also the corroborating evidence. However, such evidence was often of testimonies relaying what the complainant had shared or detailing her reactions and behaviour after the alleged rape. Moreover, we found that even forensic and technical evidence – what we refer to as 'hard evidence' – was frequently interpreted in light of the credibility ascribed to the complainant's account, and therefore remained tied to their narrative.

Claiming that this posed no challenge to judicial judgment seemed a vast oversimplification, especially since, through previous research, we knew that judges frequently employ leaps of thought to reconcile their situated and embodied decisions with disembedded and abstract core judicial values – rationality, autonomy and objectivity.

This dynamic is true for all criminal cases, yet rape cases under the new consent-based law vividly reveal the disjunction between the theoretical ideals of legal discourse and the actual practice within courtrooms. A tacit professional consensus seems to exist around discursively ignoring this gap, if not denying its existence entirely.

This book explores the gap through systematic empirical analysis of the legal practice surrounding the crime of rape in the courts. In doing so, we acknowledge that we are entering an area that remains psychologically sealed for many legal professionals. The gap is a black box to be unpacked if we want the new rape law to achieve its objective. The main objective is to strengthen the legal protection of sexual and personal integrity and sexual self-determination. Despite appearing straightforward, this objective is, in fact, profoundly challenging to realize given deeply entrenched stereotypes around male and female sexuality.

That said, the carceral aspects of the law are debatable. Although following a general pattern from a rehabilitation ideal towards a more punitive justice model in the current Swedish context, the three-year minimum sentence for rape (as of 2022) is severe, especially in comparison to crimes like gross assault, which carries a minimum sentence of 1.5 years.

However perfect or imperfect the consent-based rape law may be, our analysis suggests that it offers significant potential for the development of the entire legal system towards a more critically reflexive, versatile and just system, mindful of its role in defending contemporary democratic societies.

Åsa Wettergren, Moa Bladini and Sara Uhnoo
8 November 2024

PART 1

Introduction

1

Background and Outline

Introduction

This book offers an in-depth, empirically grounded qualitative analysis of the new Swedish consent-based rape law, which entered into force in July 2018, and its implementation by legal professional actors from the combined theoretical framework of feminist legal critique and the sociology of emotions. Based on our results, the aim of the book is to demonstrate how the implementation of the new rape law in practice challenges core legal values. The new rape law explicitly opens up the possibility of transformation of the legal values of rationality, autonomy and objectivity, and the procedures attached to these. During our data collection, however, it soon became clear that the most fundamental source of resistance is structurally embedded in how the legal system understands the meaning of its core values. Regardless of the enthusiasm, or lack thereof, about the new law among legal professionals, most of them clung to ordinary procedures. Our analysis goes in-depth in search of the sources of resistance to the implementation of the new law.

Combining a feminist legal perspective with the sociology of emotions, we argue, allows to see how the legal system, although inherently autopoietic (Teubner 1993), evolves slowly, due to both external and internal change. In this book, despite the many obstacles to an effective implementation of the 2018 rape law, we remain optimistic about the possibility of change. As stated by Carol Smart (1995:154–156):

> The idea of the uneven development of law […] perceives law as operating on a number of dimensions at the same time. Law is not identified as a simple tool of patriarchy or capitalism. To analyse law in this way creates the possibility of seeing law both as a means of 'liberation' and, at the same time, as a means of reproduction of an oppressive social order. Law both facilitates change and is an obstacle to change […] Hence the law is not the mere instrument of an omnipotent state. Its effects are uneven in all dimensions, and the aims of legislators

and even governments may be thwarted by the relative 'independence' of law and the judiciary.

Consequently, the implementation of the law in our study can be seen both in the larger perspective as a case of reforming a legal system and, in a narrower sense, as a case of reforming its legal handling of the specific crime of rape in response to changed socio-legal norms of gender and sexuality. It is worth mentioning that our critique of the core legal values addresses the meaning and implementation of these concepts in practice. We do not argue that ideals of rationality, autonomy and objectivity are irrelevant to the legal system. Rather, we want to problematize how the meaning of these values is made neutral and given. We seek to deconstruct rationality, autonomy and objectivity by studying how they are put to work in legal practice, demonstrating how they are in fact contingent on situated context. This way, we want to open critically reflexive discussion of the legal core values in relation to a changing society and the moral question of what justice is and can be.

As a backbone of the liberal democratic state, the legal system derives its public legitimacy from its pursuit of legal justice in an objective and transparent manner. The rule of law guarantees equality before the law and that no person shall suffer the curtailment of their civil rights (for example, freedom of movement) without a proper defence or fair trial. Since the emergence of the current legal system in the heyday of nineteenth-century modern capitalism, it has been debated whether 'fair and equal treatment' is, or even should be, the same as justice and social equality. Classical sociologists, notably Emile Durkheim and Max Weber, proposed opposing views. While Durkheim (1997) viewed the modern law as an expression of the collective moral consciousness, and its function to be restorative and achieve social integration, Weber (1978) perceived the emergence of modern law as deeply entwined with the process of rationalization and bureaucratization (see also Bergman Blix and Wettergren 2024). To Weber, there was a marked difference between substantive law, governed by ethos (and thereby by emotion), and formal law, governed by objective instrumental reason. The latter refers, above all, to the legislation and legal procedure, which is bureaucratic and treats everyone equally, 'without regard for persons' (Weber 1998:214). With regard to power and the state, Weber noted that the emergence of formal law served the objective interests of 'the propertied classes' to facilitate market transactions. Therefore, objectivity and the rule of law had nothing to do with justice to the people (most were not property-owning or allowed to vote in political elections). The origin of modern law, as described by Weber, is arguably open to the feminist legal critique of the purported 'objectivity' of modern law as a black box concealing male (and capitalist) interests (for example, MacKinnon 1989; Rifkin 1980). However, it also opens the question whether legal 'objectivity' serves the interest of the (changing) powers-that-be.

Given that liberal democracy today includes all citizens, and to some extent denizens, laws have changed, along with the rest of society, since the nineteenth century. Women, workers and minority groups, once excluded from the civil rights granted to white, middle- to upper-class men, have gradually become included, largely thanks to social movements pushing social norms. New laws also protect the interests of groups that used to be the 'others' of 'property-owning men'. Yet, if liberal democracy in the past century has pushed legislation more towards the substantive end, justice and equality, actors in the legal system struggle with this development, or resist it, because the implementation of some new laws seem to clash with the purportedly neutral values at the heart of 'the rule of law', such as objectivity, autonomy and rationality. Based on our study, this book explores this inner conflict of the legal system in the case of the new rape law in Sweden. Considering that the core values and the challenges associated with the enforcement of rape laws appear to be universal across judicial systems in democratic states (for example, Bitsch 2018; Hörnle 2017; Lovett and Kelly 2009; Mardorossian 2014; McGlynn 2010), Sweden serves as an intriguing case study, albeit distinguished by the unique aspects of Scandinavian legal traditions (Wong and Bogdan 2022) and a comparatively high level of gender equality[1] (Uhnoo et al 2024b). The legal framework of the new law will be discussed in detail in Chapter 2. Below, we briefly describe the context and origin of the law and its statistical impact.

The new rape law in facts and numbers

In 2018 Swedish rape legislation changed profoundly, replacing the requirement of the use of force as the decisive criterion of rape, with an explicit requisite of (non)voluntariness (popularly 'consent'). The law envisaged a norm shift; from the perception of the other's (usually female) body as available until they forcefully resist, to unavailable until they say yes (Andersson et al 2019). It sought to address problems such as victim blaming (Sutorius and Kaldal 2003), secondary victimization (Törnqvist 2017) and a high rate of acquittals in rape cases: around 35 per cent compared with 7–8 per cent in other general cases (of all crimes) (Prop 2017/2018:177). In Europe at the time, Germany, the United Kingdom, Ireland, Belgium, Luxemburg and Montenegro already had consent-based rape laws, while Malta and Iceland changed to consent-based rape laws at around the same

---

[1] https://eige.europa.eu/modules/custom/eige_gei/app/content/downloads/factsheets/ EU_2023_factsheet.pdf (Accessed 10 October 2024).

time as Sweden. Many more European countries have followed suit: Ukraine, Greece, Portugal, Croatia, Cyprus, Denmark, Slovenia, Spain, Finland, Greenland, Switzerland and the Netherlands (Uhnoo et al 2024b).

Uhnoo et al (2024b) identified three reasons for this 'wave of consent-based rape laws' sweeping Europe:

1. the European Union's 2011 Istanbul Convention (art 36), requiring states to criminalize non-consensual sexual acts, currently monitored by the Group of Experts on Action against Violence against Women
2. the impact of the global #MeToo movement in 2017, which seems to have propelled states' implementation of the EU regulation
3. local socio-cultural factors as revealed by the EU Gender Equality Index, on which most countries having adopted consent-based rape laws score highly. They also score highly on confidence in the justice system and rejection of rape myths

Reform of the Swedish rape law had been underway since the 1970s and followed after several gradual amendments to the previous coercion-based law (Bladini and Svedberg Andersson 2020; Leijonhufvud 2015). It was arguably facilitated in terms of public opinion by the #MeToo movement. However, even before that, the Social Democratic government had declared itself a 'feminist' government,[2] similarly to other governments in the Nordic region (Heinskou et al 2020). Several objections and concerns were raised in the debate about the new law, some from the judiciary itself, that the new legislation would result in (an even larger) focus on the complainant and their behaviour (Council on Legislation,[3] Swedish Bar Association[4]). Around the time of launching the new law, newspaper opinion and debate articles aired outrage about the law for undermining the rule of law, reversing the burden of proof, lowering the standard of proof, and sending innocent young men to prison (cf Carroll 2021).

From available statistics, we observe that there was a steady rise in reported rape cases of persons aged 15 years or older (from 5,236 in 2017 to 6,549 in

---

[2] https://www.svt.se/nyheter/inrikes/lofven-en-feministisk-regering (Accessed 4 April 2024). The present right-wing government's wholly dependent collaboration with the extreme-right-wing party, Sweden Democrats, has scrapped this designation.

[3] Council on Legislation answer to Prop 2017/18:177 En ny sexualbrottslagstiftning byggd på frivillighet, Bilaga 8, https://data.riksdagen.se/fil/A2A4407F-B114-4368-A233-80FFF FB4D50F (Accessed 28 May 2024).

[4] Swedish Bar Association answer to Prop 2017/18:177 En ny sexualbrottslagstiftning byggd på frivillighet, https://data.riksdagen.se/fil/A2A4407F-B114-4368-A233-80FFFFB4D 50F (Accessed 28 May 2024).

2022).[5] It is also evident that the new rape law had a decisive impact on the number of indictments.[6] During the five-year period from July 2018 to June 2023, there was a 41 per cent increase in rape prosecutions.[7] On average, 500 more rape charges were brought each year across the country compared to the period before the new law. This increase is due to the extension of criminalized acts. It should be noted, however, that in our interviews with prosecutors, they unanimously declared that the new law made it much easier to proceed from preliminary investigation to indictment.

A criticism of the old Swedish rape law concerned high attrition rates. The rate of convicted cases in the District Court (DC) increased by an impressive 75 per cent in 2019 as compared with 2017 rates, from 190 cases in 2017 to 333 in 2019 (see note 5). However, this was an effect of the increase of indictments rather than of a higher propensity of courts to convict. The rate of convictions as compared with indictments actually decreased from 68 per cent the year before (2017) to 51 per cent the year after (2019). In 2022, this rate returned to 65 per cent. This could signify that, over time, the implications of the new law have settled more broadly. We know that in our interviews with judges, conducted in 2020–2021, an implicit or explicit distinction between 'real rape' (coercion-based rape) and rape under the new law was often made. The fact remains that, while more people are indicted for rape, the likelihood of individual conviction has not increased because of the new law.

The absolute number of convicted cases has continued to rise slightly; in 2023 the number was 377 cases. This also includes a slow increase in convictions for negligent rape (28 in cases in 2023).[8] It should be noted that in 2022 the minimum penalty for rape was raised from two to three years' imprisonment.

The clearance rate for rape cases (rape of persons aged 15 years or older) remains low, at around 12–13 per cent in 2022, and only 4 per cent in negligent rape cases.[9] In Sweden, a rape offence is considered cleared once

---

[5]   The figure from 2022 includes the new crime of negligent rape. See also Brå, *Den nya samtyckeslagen i praktiken: en uppföljning av 2018 års förändringar av lagreglerna rörande våldtäkt* (2020), at https://bra.se/publikationer/arkiv/publikationer/2020-06-15-den-nya-samtyckeslagen-i-praktiken.html (Accessed 31 October 2024).

[6]   Source: Swedish National Council for Crime Prevention (Brå) statistics. Obtained by contacting Brå October 2023.

[7]   https://www.aklagare.se/nyheter-press/aktuellt-pa-aklagarmyndigheten/fler-atal-for-valdtakt-med-sexualbrottslag-som-bygger-pa-frivillighet/ (Accessed 31 October 2024).

[8]   Lagföringstatistik 2023: https://bra.se/download/18.667e8ab318fa42b86e6467b/1716885583202/Statistikrapport_lagforda_2023.pdf (Accessed 31 October 2024).

[9]   Brå, *Bifallna åtal: utveckling 2015–2020* (2022), at https://bra.se/download/18.137f5428182e8ddc63a27d/1662377357995/2022_Bifallna_atal.pdf (Accessed 31 October 2024).

the police or the prosecutor's investigation have tied a perpetrator to the offence by deciding to prosecute. The statistics further show that the number of suspects of Swedish ethnic origin increased by almost 45 per cent following the new law. This seems to be echoed in our interviews – some expressed concern over the increased number of previously unpunished 'ordinary men' before the court (Uhnoo et al 2024c).

Core legal values

The core legal values of objectivity and autonomy rest on modern Western ideas of rationality, according to which rationality is purposeful, goal-oriented, calculative, cognitive and masculine. In contrast, emotion is viewed as rationality's opposite, belonging to the realm of the private, the sentimental and the feminine (for example, Barbalet 1998; Gustavsson 2011; Svensson 1997; Wettergren 2019). The bifurcation of emotion and reason was perceived by Weber as a process of rationalization, leading to the demystification of society in which the role of charisma, religion and tradition in premodern societies lost its meaning (Weber 1998). Classical sociologists were generally quick to realize that modernity, along with industrialization and urbanization, released the individual from their mutual bonds of 'mechanical labour division' and from socially and spatially constraining and tradition-determined futures (Durkheim 1997; Koselleck 2004). Migrating to cities, living among strangers, the opening of educational opportunities, the standardization of the value of money and the standardization of time and space (Asplund 2022; Elias 2007; Simmel 1971) enabled social mobility and what some sociologists later termed the 'disembedding of the individual' (Giddens 1991).

In social science, and in line with emerging ideas about the 'economic man', rational choice theory appeared as a viable model to explain the action choices of these 'free-floating' and self-modelling individuals (Flam 1990). As noted by historians and emotion sociologists, the era between the 1930s and 1970s was marked by a declining interest in the role of emotions for humans and rational action, while these exclusively cognitive theories gained ground (Kemper 1978; Scheer 2021; Stearns 1994). In effect, the individual was considered rational (in their own interest) and autonomous, while the masses (collectives) were viewed as emotional and contagious (Le Bon 2010). As we observed previously, the modern legal system, particularly modern continental law, was born of this development, incorporating the idea of the pure rationality of the autonomous individual.

Today, following various cultural, affective and emotional 'turns' since the 1970s and the postmodern intellectual movement in the 1980s (Kleres 2009), the view of rationality as unemotional or strictly instrumental has been nuanced and largely discarded within social sciences. However, in the practice of public institutions, liberal democratic politics (Mouffe 1999) and the legal system, it has lingered. Being 'professional' remains the antithesis of being emotional. Repression of legal actors' own embodied being in the world is one side of this coin; the other side is the projection of the disembodied, calculative rationality, the individual acting in their own interest, onto legal subjects.

Objectivity and autonomy

> The court may not base their evaluation [of the evidence] on a complete subjective opinion, but the assessment must be objectively based and supported by reasons acceptable to other reasonable persons. (NJA II 1943:445, travaux preparatoire)

This quotation, concerning judges' evaluation of evidence, from the early preparatory works of Swedish procedural law, indicates taken-for-granted objectivity in the twentieth century. It is arguably presumed that a judge can evaluate the evidence correctly, based on their own rational minds, but the evaluation should also be motivated in ways that are accepted by other rational persons. It is a given that in the 1940s, 'other rational persons' primarily refers to the '*bonus pater familia*' or the rational man.[10]

The meaning of legal objectivity is taken for granted as inherent in being professional (see Chapter 5), involving 'the fair and equal treatment of everyone before the law' by formal procedure and judicial display of impartiality. This is the bureaucratic doing of objectivity, '*sine ira et studio*', as described by Weber (1998). The individual is presumed to be autonomous, capable of making independent decisions based on their rational mind, unencumbered by concerns for others (Gunnarsson and Svensson 2009; Gustafsson 2011; Svedberg 2016). The objective legal professional should have no affiliation to those involved in the case, nor any personal, political or other stake in the outcome; they should be free from any felt or otherwise external pressure. Judges are thus presumed to be rational beings who can

---

[10] In Sweden, as in most other European countries, the juridical professions, as all state offices, were closed to women at the turn of the nineteenth century, on the grounds that women were 'emotional and impulsive' and therefore unfit for such work. The much debated Competence Act of 1923 allowed women in Sweden to hold a number of state offices, such as the offices of lay judges, court clerks and presiding judges in low courts. However, the final text of the law contained several exceptions made for the bill to pass in parliament, in which opponents held a strong position. The first female DC judge, Maja Britta Oldin, was appointed in Stockholm in 1961. The first female judge in the Supreme Court, 1968–1977, was Ingegärd Gärde Widemar: https://domstolenshistoria. se/kvinnliga-pionjarer/#1632406147580-9616f8a2-d4ef (Accessed 11 April 2024).

ensure the objective evaluation of evidence. In this lies the fallacy of 'fair and equal treatment'; if the powers-that-be perceive themselves as the 'objective' source of laws, legal procedure enacting the laws will contribute to shape the world, through practice, to fit the power perspective. Procedure may be 'neutral', but its effects will be systematically biased in favour of the powers-that-be (cf Fricker 2007; Lacey 1998).

In reality the positivist ideal of objectivity consists in practice of a continuous approximation by situated doing (Bergman Blix and Wettergren 2019; Bladini 2013). Broken down to the different situations of judicial objectivity, an *impartial* presiding in court requires empathic imagination to view one's own comport from the perspective of others, mindful of what might be perceived as bias, for instance, from the perspective of the defendant (Bergman Blix and Wettergren 2016; Wettergren and Bergman Blix 2016). The judge's 'objective mind' during the trial process is sustained by the wilful effort to uphold a state of 'not yet knowing' – that is, the emotion work of summoning active interest and curiosity in learning and the oscillation between certainty ('now I know') and doubt ('I still do not know enough'). An empathically sensitive impartial display, together with this 'certainty-doubt spiral' (Törnqvist and Wettergren 2023) and the epistemic emotions of interest and curiosity, constitute the emotional underpinnings of judges' objectivity during the trial and deliberations (Bergman Blix and Minissale 2022; Minissale 2023a).

From this perspective, and in today's social context, the formulation 'the assessment must be objectively based and supported by reasons acceptable to other reasonable persons' can also be read as a way of *doing* objectivity. If we consider its meaning today, it harmonizes with the social scientific concept of intersubjectivity, referring to collegial consensus on the transparency and reasonableness of interpretations made, and conclusions drawn, from qualitative data (for example, Alvesson and Sköldberg 2009). The quote also points to the interdependency (as opposed to autonomy) of doing objectivity. It is through collegial review and consensus that claims to objectivity are made.

The legal system has been described as an autopoietic (self-referring) system (Teubner 1993; see also Luhmann 1996) of meaning-making with an internal logic that upholds the distinction between the legal and non-legal. The system thus is not entirely closed off from the rest of society, but transforms social influence to legal matter dictated by its own legal logic. The system is partially 'cognitively' open, but operationally closed (Björling 2017; Teubner 1993). One example of this, relevant in the context of rape legislation, are the criteria established by the Supreme Court on credibility assessments, originating in witness psychology research, The criteria are used to facilitate legal evaluation of the quality of complainants' stories. When comparing the criteria with the research it is based on, there are significant overlaps; however, when used in practice, crucial parts concerning how to use the criteria were omitted because these complicate the legal adoption of the criteria (Hauch et al 2017). As discussed in Chapters 4 and 8, the criteria were used by legal professionals as 'objectivity lifebuoys' to discursively construct an oral testimony as (un)credible.

The autopoiesis of the legal system cements its conservatism and tardiness with regard to changing norms and values of both society and other social science disciplines. Throughout this book, we assert that, despite the legal practical awareness of interdependence (as opposed to autonomy) in the doing of objectivity (as opposed to objectivity as a stance), and even the intuitive understanding of emotions' role in legal work and rationality ('we are only humans' as legal professional often say), legal professionals discursively reproduce early twentieth-century positivist ideals, orally and in text (Bladini 2013). This points to what we call 'the emotive-cognitive judicial frame' (see further Chapter 3). The emotive-cognitive judicial frame is a set of tacit behavioural norms and feeling rules that informs legal practice and role performance in line with the autopoietic production of meaning. Although practice needs to be flexible and negotiable, the emotive-cognitive judicial frame informs actors about the doable and the undoable, the sayable and the unsayable, in terms of changing legal practice. This partial closure ensures the boundaries of law and its exclusive 'autonomous' social and academic position.

Previous research and the contribution of this book

The overwhelming amount of rape cases involve a male perpetrator and a female victim. Therefore, not disregarding the fact that same sex rape occurs, in line with previous research we approach rape as, primarily, a traditional heteronormative crime. Feminist research on rape legislation and legal practice, and feminist jurisprudence, are well-established international fields (Brooks and Burman 2017; Burman 2009; Dowds and Agnew 2022; Heinskou et al 2020; Houge and Laugerud 2023; Hörnle 2017; Lees 1996; MacKinnon 1989; Maier 2014; Mardorossian 2014; Martin 2005; McGlynn and Munro 2010; Smith 2018; Spohn and Horney 1992; Temkin et al 2018). Their valuable contributions can be summarized as 'what we know'. We know that the legal systems in democratic Western countries, whether common law, continental law or the 'Scandinavian hybrid law', have largely failed to implement rape legislation, whether coercion-based or consent-based, in the ways intended by legislators.

The failure is clearly observed when compared with other crimes: attrition rates in rape cases are remarkably high; the rate of convictions as compared with the number of indictments is remarkably low (except for in Norway;

cf Jacobsen and Skilbrei 2020); there are few other criminal trials that centre on the complainant's credibility and the truthfulness of their testimony, or story, comparable with the way it is done in rape cases (Andersson 2004). Consequently, the complainant's integrity and social standing as a citizen deserving of respect and recognition is routinely violated (Antonsdottir 2020) and they are often directly or indirectly blamed for the crime (Bitsch 2018; Randall 2010; Smith and Skinner 2017). In terms of the mechanisms behind such failures, we know that the legal perspective has been convincingly deconstructed as patriarchal. In other words, the purportedly objective gaze of law is a male gaze (Martin 2005). Proceedings and decision-making in rape cases are informed by rape myths, cutting across society and the legal system (Daly 2022; Orrbén 2024; Smith 2018; Temkin et al 2018; Wallin et al 2021). This is to say, in rape cases, legal professionals, for some reason, risk drawing on diehard social norms about sexuality and gender, hidden behind the semblance of objectivity and legal logics (Bladini 2013).

Previous research has identified central rape myths:

1. 'She lies' and 'she cries rape' basically because of disappointed expectations of the sex or the relationship, because she is ashamed of adultery or because she has any other interest in smearing the defendant (for example, Wheatcroft and Walklate 2014).
2. The rape in question is not 'a real rape'. Even if rape is defined by law as lack of consent and extended to established relationships, the iconic 'real rape' is an assault by a stranger in a public place, involving so much force or violence that the victim cannot be blamed for failing to defend herself (for example, Estrich 1987; Ryan 2011).
3. A 'real rape victim' screams and shouts and fights back (for example, Ellison and Munro 2009). Further, they have in no way 'induced' the crime committed – they have been subject to bad luck and are preferably randomly selected by the rapist. Hence, they cannot in any way be considered responsible (for example, Christie 1986).
4. A 'real rapist' is a socio-economically disadvantaged, or otherwise deprived, male loser with a record of previous violence or documented misogyny (for example, Lees 1996). Alternatively, it is a frustrated man from a different culture in which, unlike our own culture, women's gender-equal integrity is not respected (Bitsch 2019).

Knowing that the legal system changes slowly some feminists have advanced the argument that changing the legal construction of rape and its focus on the victim rather than the perpetrator requires a total reconstruction of the legal system (MacKinnon 2016), while others argue that change *within* the given legal system is crucial (Smart 1995).

Our book seeks to contribute to previous feminist research by also drawing on a different field, research on law and emotions. International research in this field, informed by the psychology and philosophy of emotions and mainly focused on common law countries, has approached the legal system by bracing itself against the 'script of judicial dispassion' (Maroney 2011; Maroney and Gross 2014) dominant in Western legal systems. Findings demonstrate the centrality and usefulness of empathy (Booth 2012; Darbyshire 2011), the skilled strategic emotion management of the judiciary (Bosma 2019; Roach Anleu and Mack 2017) and the use of various discrete emotions as resources in legal professional work (Maroney 2012; Scarduzio 2011).

A substantial contribution to this field is made by extensive ethnographically inspired studies of the Swedish legal system, drawing on the sociological perspective on emotions (for an overview, see Bergman Blix and Wettergren 2024). Importantly, the sociology of emotions questions the bifurcation of emotion and rationality as opposite phenomena and demonstrates how emotions are not just useful complementary resources in rational legal work, but inherent to legal work, providing the energy, motivation and orientation of professional action. Emotions are also the ideological anchor of legal 'rationalist' ideology (Lange 2002) motivating conformity with the feeling rules governing the reproduction of the 'dispassionate' emotional regime or, put directly, the passionate defence of dispassionate rationality (Barbalet 1998; Wettergren 2019).

The sociology of emotions has, to our knowledge, previously only been applied to rape proceedings in a few cases. In Norway (Bitsch 2018, 2019) it was used to pinpoint systematic bias against defendants with a foreign ethnic background and to defence lawyers' adaptation of their strategies when faced with complainants who evoked their sympathy (see also Smith 2018). Gunby and Carline (2020) explored rape barristers' emotion work when managing and distancing themselves from clients' emotions, striving to maintain objectivity while also leveraging these emotions to persuade a jury. In the broader research field of law and emotions, the sociology of emotions has been used to analyse the professional emotional profiles of judges (Bergman Blix 2019; Bergman Blix and Wettergren 2016, 2018), prosecutors (Törnqvist 2017; Wettergren and Bergman Blix 2016, 2022) and defence lawyers (Flower 2018, 2020). It has also been used to analyse epistemic emotions in the decision-making of prosecutors (Törnqvist and Wettergren 2023) and judges (Bergman Blix 2022; Bergman Blix and Minissale 2022; Törnqvist 2021).

Based on this research, we concur that emotion and cognition are intertwined phenomena and mutually dependent. Legal professionals' adherence to the core legal values of rationality, objectivity and autonomy *as if* they were exclusively cognitive phenomena is monitored by the 'emotive-cognitive judicial frame' and the master emotions of shame and pride (Scheff 1988, 1990). Shame and pride markers govern conformity with feeling rules that above all stipulate that core legal values and the rationality of the legal system should appear and be discursively reproduced as unemotional. The implications of this perspective on the emotions in and of legal work will be further detailed in Chapter 3, in which we also define the main concepts used in the analysis.

The emotion-sociological perspective contributes to feminist legal studies with the potential of understanding the mechanisms behind the legal system's 'uneven development' as *emotionally anchored*, not in the individual psyche, but in the structures of the legal system tacitly communicated by the emotive-cognitive judicial frame that both informs and is continuously negotiated in legal practice. The silencing of emotions inherent in this frame systematically underestimates the influence of subjective beliefs and common sense in legal procedures. The combined feminist and emotion-sociological law and emotions perspective, we argue, allows a more dynamic understanding of the, willingly or not, support function of contemporary rape myths and stereotypes for scaffolding the legal doing of objectivity and rationality. The combined perspective opens up the possibility of understanding legal discrimination as part of how processes of silencing emotions, understood by legal professionals themselves as vital for the legal system's legitimacy, interact with gendered power structures.

Consent-based rape legislation has been studied recently (Adler 2022; Hlavka and Mulla 2021; Horvath and Brown 2023; Hörnle 2017; Jordan 2022) but the new Swedish rape law, and thus the very recent turn to consent-based rape legislation in Scandinavia, has never been studied in its *implementation* before (but see recent work from a Nordic perspective by Andersson et al 2019; Bladini and Svedberg Andersson 2020; Heinskou et al 2020; Wallin et al 2021). The feminist legal field has begun to incorporate an emotion perspective as part of the power dynamics between victim and perpetrator (Wegerstad 2021), but not as part of its critique of core legal values (but see Bladini 2013). Thus, this book contributes theoretically and empirically to the international fields of both feminist legal studies and law and emotions.

Relevance to other legal systems

The analysis and results presented in this book are based on the Swedish legal system, sometimes called a 'mixed' or 'hybrid' legal system as it builds on codified law combined with case law as a complement, but also due to its combination of an inquisitorial preliminary investigation (continental law) and adversarial process (common law). In Chapter 2, the Swedish legal system will be explained in detail.

The particulars of national legal systems and their legal cultures obviously influence research findings. In so far as abstract theoretical concepts inform the research and are developed through empirical research, however, there is what we may call a theoretical or analytical possibility of generalization (Alvesson and Sköldberg 2009; Halkier 2011). Our empirically grounded conceptual development of the interpretive theoretical framework (combining feminist and emotion-sociological law research) is transportable to other countries and other legal systems. This means that the implications for practice may differ due to local legal systems or practices, but, in so far as the local legal system is premised on the same judicial core values, our results will be of use for enhanced understanding of the legal handling of rape in other countries.

For instance, legal objectivity as a construct that excludes emotionality and blinds legal professionals to the import of embodied experiences through emotions and common sense, is a modern Western phenomenon shared across nations and legal systems in the Western world (cf Latour 2010; Nedelsky 2011). Likewise, concepts we draw on from the Anglo-Saxon studies of common law rape case procedures are highly useful for understanding, in the local Swedish context, the problems attached to effective implementation of the new Swedish rape law. The individual professional emotional profiles of the different legal actors may vary between common law and continental law. For instance, the objectivity requirement of prosecutors as state employees takes different expressions in these various legal systems, but prosecutors in common law countries are also concerned with such a requirement (for example, Bandes 2006; Mack and Roach Anleu 2010). As demonstrated by Maroney (2011, 2012), Roach Anleu and Mack (2017) and others (for example, Dudek and Stepien 2021; Jeuland 2020; Minissale 2023a) the role of the judge remains, across different systems, to impersonate and radiate the authority and comport of the legal system and the rule of law. While the Swedish (and the Finnish: for an overview, see Antonsdóttir and Laugerud 2024) system stands out in both continental and common law in allowing the complainant to be party in the procedure, in other countries their stories are heard as witness testimonies, and as victim impact statements (for example, Schuster and Propen 2010). In addition, in Sweden, the victim is supported throughout the criminal procedure by a victim counsel.

We argue that, in this context of Western democratic legal systems, Sweden is to be viewed as a case of, first, advanced consent-based rape legislation mirroring the historical emergence of social values attempting to break with a traditional patriarchal heteronormative regime of sexuality; and, second, a case of how such legislation challenges the modern construction of the rule of law in theory and practice (cf Burman 2007).

Our general approach to the way that national culture affects legal culture, and thereby opens up the opportunity for context-bound national versions of the shared phenomena under study, follows that suggested by Wettergren and Bergman Blix (2021) in their discussion of comparing culturally embedded frames of judicial dispassion. Thus, we argue that the general judicial regime of dispassion and the way it integrates a gendered power order transcends national cultures and is a feature common to all Western countries following shared roots in Western modernity. However, the national emotional regimes differ. Sweden's national emotional regime is exceptionally subtle compared with most European countries, which means that a dispassionate display for Swedish judges appears much more rigid than the corresponding in, say, Italy (Minissale 2023b). The same can be said of the gendered power order, for which Sweden boasts its vanguard position as a gender-equal country, obscuring the ways that pockets of patriarchal domination linger largely undisturbed. One such pocket is the legal system.

The international regime of judicial dispassion intersects with the local emotional regime through the negotiation of behavioural norms and its feeling rules in the previously discussed emotive-cognitive judicial frame. This concept is applicable to legal systems in all Western countries, and thus opens the way to understanding the national legal systems' various ways of adhering to the nation-transcending judicial regime of dispassion.

Conclusion and presentation of contents

In this chapter we have presented the aim of this book, to demonstrate, through in-depth, empirically grounded qualitative analysis, how the implementation of the 2018 Swedish consent-based rape law challenges core legal values, that is, the legal meaning of rationality, objectivity and autonomy. We briefly discussed the history of the modern legal system, the context of the new law and its impact, as well as our approach to the core legal values under scrutiny. The study itself was put in context of previous research, including a section where we argued for the relevance of our results, on the Swedish consent-based rape law, to other countries and legal systems.

The book is divided into five parts. Part I 'Introduction' includes the present Chapter 1 'Background and Outline'; Chapter 2 'Legal Framework', in which we present the Swedish legal system, its fundamental principles, and the details of the rape law; and Chapter 3 'Theory and Method', where we explain our theoretical framework and main concepts, our study design and data, and discuss our method of analysis.

Part II 'The Making of Legal Objectivity' focuses on legal objectivity-making in practice. Chapter 4 'The Feeling of Not Knowing' offers an overview of legal professional opinions about the new law and their use of 'common sense', followed by evidence in rape cases and how 'soft' evidence itself challenges legal professional expertise. Chapter 5 'Professional Roles in Objectivity Making' delves into the doing of objectivity as a collective achievement and how the different legal roles reason about potential role adaption to achieve procedural justice in rape cases. Chapter 6 'The Making and Breaking of Objectivity' follows up with an in-depth analysis of three cases, highlighting how conventional vs adapted legal roles can impact on the collective doing of objectivity.

Part III 'Autonomy and Rationality of Legal Subjects' focuses on the projection of the legal understandings of the core values onto legal subjects. Chapter 7 'Autonomy and Action Rationality of Non-Voluntariness' has a focus on the legal assessment of the complainant's behaviour. Chapter 8 'The Burden of Explanation' clarifies the focus on the defendant and how the new law provides them with a standard alternative hypothesis (voluntary sex), and what happens if they chose to remain silent or deny. Chapter 9 'The Making and Breaking of Consent Defences' explores the autonomy and action rationality ascribed to the defendant and the complainant in the majority of cases where alternative hypothesis of voluntariness have been used.

Part IV 'Rationality and Autonomy in Legal Decision-Making' focuses on judgments and the legal evaluation of evidence performed by presumably rational and autonomous judges. Chapter 10 'Navigating Reasonable Doubts in the Judgments' discusses the structure of judgment and different methods of evaluation of evidence. Chapter 11 'Pathways to Knowing' delves into three cases, for an in-depth analysis of the legal evaluations in each of them.

Part V 'Conclusion' consists of Chapter 12 'Core Judicial Values and Beyond', in which we sum up the results from previous chapters and discuss them in the context of the legal system as a slow-changing autopoietic system. A large part of the chapter discusses how legal professional roles need to evolve and adapt to meet the intentions of the new rape law, as well as to follow and protect the evolved social norms of equality, democracy and inclusion.

2

Legal Framework

Introduction

The aim of this chapter is to explain the Swedish legal system and the legal framework of the consent-based rape legislation. We begin by a brief introduction of the main characteristics of the Swedish legal system, including a description of the courtroom setting where rape trials take place, and the actors involved. This is followed by an overview of the criminal procedure and fundamental principles. The chapter ends with a description of the criminal legislation of rape. This exploration will provide the necessary legal context for the empirically grounded analysis of the Swedish consent-based rape law in the rest of the book.

Main characteristics of the Swedish legal system

The Swedish legal system is often regarded as part of the Nordic legal family, which includes Denmark, Finland, Iceland, Norway and Sweden. The Nordic countries have collaborated on legislation in various fields since the end of the nineteenth century, although to a lesser extent in criminal and procedural law. Nevertheless, the criminal regulations exhibit similarities, with the Swedish system being closest to that of the Finnish. The legal systems in the Nordic countries are often characterized as mixed systems, based on codified law with elements of preceding case law. They are positioned between the continental and common law systems, historically and in terms of content leaning more towards the continental law tradition (Wong and Bogdan 2022:10). As will be further developed in this chapter, other distinctive features of the Swedish criminal procedure include the inquisitorial nature of the preliminary investigation and the adversarial format of the trial. Additionally, the division of labour and the objectivity requirements for prosecutors and judges, as well as the complainant's role as a party in court, are key characteristics of the system (Edelstam 2001).

Sweden's legal framework comprises four constitutional acts and additional legal acts enacted by the Swedish Parliament. The country has two main types of courts: administrative courts, which handle administrative and public law, and general courts, which deal with criminal and civil law cases. The latter are organized in a three-tier hierarchy consisting of 48 District Courts (DC), six Appeals Courts (AC) and one Supreme Court. A DC judgment may be appealed to the AC, and the appeal must be submitted in writing in general within three weeks of the DC's ruling. The primary function of the Supreme Court is to establish legal precedents in civil and criminal cases. Additionally, the Swedish court system includes several special courts and tribunals.

The stage – the courtroom setting and actors

The emotional regime that legal professionals must adhere to in a Swedish court does not permit strong expressions of emotion, with many judges exhibiting what is known as the 'stoneface' (Bergman Blix and Wettergren 2018). In other words, the emotional norms within a legal setting are designed to ensure that proceedings are 'protected from emotion's pernicious influence' (Maroney and Gross 2014:143).

The norms requiring legal professionals to set aside their emotions often result in trials characterized by a calm and quiet atmosphere, especially in the AC, in which laypeople are seldom present. The calm and quiet atmosphere is also more commonly observed in small towns than in bustling cities (Bladini et al 2023). However, both the public spaces outside the courtrooms and the courtrooms themselves are generally tranquil, although individuals called to court as witnesses, complainants or defendants may not feel at ease (Bladini 2019). This observation is noteworthy, as the atmosphere in other legal cultures can be markedly different.

Additionally, punctuality is crucial. Cases are typically meticulously planned by the court in collaboration with the defence and prosecution. When a witness is called, it is usually for a specific day and time. If the trial is delayed and a witness is left waiting, the chair of the court typically ensures that the witness is informed in a timely manner and often apologizes for the delay upon their entry.

A fundamental principle in the Swedish justice system is the principle of transparency, ensuring the openness of judicial proceedings to public attendance (Edelstam 2001; Instrument of Government 2:11; SCJP 5:1). The public is allowed to attend any criminal trial. Trials are publicly announced on the website and at the court entrance. Information on the ongoing trial, the charges and the parties are posted outside each courtroom. However, trials in rape cases typically take place behind closed doors due to the sensitive nature of the proceedings from the perspective of the complainant (SCJP 5:1; Public Access to Information and Secrecy

Act 35:12). Consequently, there are often no relatives, journalists or other representatives of the public present in the courtroom during rape trials.

In the courtroom

Criminal cases, including rape trials, are typically adjudicated in the two first instances within the Swedish legal system: in the lower instance, the DC and in the higher instance, the AC. The Swedish criminal procedure is notably informal relative to other legal systems. Judges and other legal professionals do not wear traditional judicial robes or gowns, which contributes to a more relaxed courtroom atmosphere (Flower 2018).

When the trial begins in DC, the case is called, announced via the public address system, and the prosecutor, defence lawyer, victim's counsel, defendant, the complainant, if present, and the public are permitted to enter the courtroom. At this time, the judges, one legally trained and three lay judges, sit in a row at the back of the courtroom; their seats are often slightly elevated. The actors involved in the case take their seats on opposite sides in front of the judges. The prosecutor, complainant and victim's counsel are seated on the left-hand side of the court members, while the defence lawyer and defendant are on the right-hand side, opposite the prosecutor and complainant. In the middle, in front of the court, is a chair designated for witnesses. There are seats for the public, along the wall opposite the judges, directly upon entering the courtroom. When the defendant is in custody, which is the standard procedure in rape trials, security guards are stationed at one end of the public seating area, normally two to three security guards for each defendant.

It should be emphasized that this is a description of the trial in the DC. The courtroom in the AC is arranged similarly, but typically neither the complainant nor the victim's counsel is present during the hearing, and, post-COVID 19, the prosecutor often participates via video link. Consequently, the room typically comprises the judges, three legally trained judges and two lay judges, along with the defendant and their defence lawyer. In the AC, testimonies from the DC trial, including those given by witnesses and the complainant and defendant, are usually presented through video recordings.

Defendants in rape cases have the right to a defence lawyer, who can be a public defender appointed by the state or a private lawyer chosen by the defendant.[1] Given that the system of victim counsels is unique to the Nordic context, it is important to address their role in more detail. This legal support for complainants was introduced in 1988, largely due to advocacy from women's movements and critiques of the treatment of complainants in

---

[1] SCJP Chapter 21.

rape trials (SFS (1988:609), see also Antonsdottir and Laugerud 2024). In serious offences, including rape, the victim counsel is state funded, which is uncommon in other jurisdictions (Brienen and Hoegen 2000). According to the Swedish Code of Judicial Procedure (henceforth SCJP), the complainant may also participate as a party to the prosecution. The support includes legal advice, assistance with evidence, and advocating for compensation (Prop 1987/88:107). Emotional support is also crucial throughout the trial and in helping complainants navigate the justice system. However, the role of the victim counsel is somewhat unclear in relation to the prosecutor, particularly in rape cases under the new law (see Chapters 5 and 6).

As mentioned above, complainants are rarely present at the AC hearings. Testimonies from the DC are video-recorded and reviewed by the AC, sparing the complainant from undergoing further questioning. This practice prioritizes the complainant's mental well-being while preserving the integrity of the process. Following this line, when the new rape legislation entered into force in 2018, the right for the victim's counsel to be present in the AC was changed as the complainant was seldom present; it now requires special reasons for the victim's counsel to be allowed to participate (Prop 2017/18:86).[2] In this book we will argue, contrary to what has been laid out here, that the absence of the complainant and of the victim counsel may turn out to be unfair for the complainant in rape cases.

The lay judge system

In criminal trials, excluding minor offences, the DC's judging panel consists of four members: one legally trained judge, who serves as the chair, and three lay judges. Each member of the panel has equal voting rights in both the determination of guilt and the sentencing decision. The composition shifts in the AC, in which the panel comprises three legally trained judges and two lay judges, thereby altering the judicial dynamic (SCPJ).

The system of lay judges in Swedish courts dates back 800 years, and their role and purpose has shifted over the years. Initially, the lay judges consisted of 12 individuals selected from peasants present at the time of the case's hearing. The chief judge decided on matters of law alone, while the lay judges typically addressed the factual questions – a system somewhat similar to the jury system. However, by 1442, the members of the lay judge panel were appointed on a permanent basis. The current system, in which lay judges have equal voting rights, has been in use since 1983. They are

---

[2]   On the right to a victim's counsel in the AC, see case law from the Supreme Court, NJA 2021 s 964. It should be further noted that the regulation is under review and may be changed into the former order.

politically appointed for a term of four years, but, as lay judges, they hold a non-political position of trust. In addition to meeting formal eligibility requirements and suitability assessments, the lay judge corps is thus intended to be representative of the population and embody a general sense of justice. The purpose of this system is to provide the public with insight into the workings of the courts. Lay judges are expected to contribute common sense and experience from various fields, thereby enhancing public confidence in the judiciary. Despite being a non-political position of trust, the system of lay judges has often been criticized because many lay judges who are selected are members of political parties. This has led to concerns that the system introduces political opinions into the judicial process (Anwar et al 2015; Diesen 2011/2012).

During the deliberations in the DC, the legally trained judge typically presents the case according to the applicable law and casts their vote first. Following this, the lay judges vote. In the AC, the voting order is structured such that the least experienced legally trained judge votes first, followed by the more senior judges, with the most senior judge voting last. After the legally trained judges have voted, the lay judges then cast their votes (SCJP 29:1). Depending on the nature of the case, voting may occur in several rounds, with each round addressing a distinct legal issue (SCJP 29:2).

Previous research has indicated that approximately 1 per cent of all criminal court verdicts are so-called 'lay judge decisions', meaning that the lay judges outvote the legally trained judge in the DC (Diesen 1996). In our material on the rape cases, we observed a significantly higher proportion of lay judge decisions in the DC overturned in the AC. A recent report on rape cases also highlights how legally trained judges increasingly disagree on the outcomes of rape trials (Strindlöv 2024).

The criminal procedure

The Swedish criminal procedure is regulated and structured to ensure the rule of law and the right to a fair trial. Built on key principles such as the principle of legality, transparency and public access to judicial proceedings, the process consists of several stages: the preliminary investigation headed by the prosecutor in collaboration with the police, the decision to prosecute, the main hearing in the DC and potential appeals to and hearing in the AC (Ekelöf et al 2016). Fundamental principles surrounding the trial include orality, immediacy, legality and the presumption of innocence, ensuring that all individuals have the right to a fair trial and that no one is convicted without being heard (Ekelöf et al 2016).

The main source of law is the Code of Judicial Procedure (SCJP), which is the principal statute regulating criminal procedure. The code covers civil and criminal procedure and, when it entered into force in 1948, it marked the change from an inquisitorial to an adversarial procedure. The code is complemented by other laws. In addition to the codes, there is prevailing case law from the Supreme Court, which, while not binding, serves as guidance for the courts on matters not clarified in codified law, such as the evaluation of oral witness statements, which will be discussed below.

A criminal case starts with a police report. A crime can come to the attention of the police through a report made by the victim or another individual. The police are also obliged to file a report on-site if there is reason to suspect that a crime subject to public prosecution has been committed. It is crucial that a police report is made as soon as possible, as this increases the chances of gathering evidence, which in turn improves the ability to investigate, link a suspect to the crime, and subsequently bring charges (Swedish Prosecution Authority). In rape cases, the time elapsed between the rape and the police report is often highlighted by the parties during the trial.

A preliminary investigation must be opened as soon as possible (SPCJ 23:1). The investigation serves two primary functions: to ascertain the identity of potential suspects and to evaluate whether there is sufficient evidence to warrant prosecution (SPCJ 23:2). A prosecutor leads the investigation in rape trials. Throughout the investigation, the prosecutor provides directives to the police, ensuring that all relevant evidence is gathered. Prosecutors are bound by the principle of objectivity, which obliges them to consider not only evidence indicating the suspect's guilt but also any circumstances that suggest the suspect may be innocent. This obligation extends into the adversarial trial itself (SCPJ 23:4 and 45:3a).

The prosecutor decides whether to press charges, ensuring that the evidence is sufficient to take the case to court (SOU 2016:78). If the prosecutor deems there is enough evidence to convict, charges are filed. This involves submitting an indictment to the DC, outlining the nature of the crime, circumstances and evidence (Ekelöf et al 2016). The indictment contains a statement of the criminal act as charged, which is the only procedural act that binds the court (SCPJ 30:3) and sets the framework for the trial. It outlines the act for which the defendant is charged, including the time and place of the incident. Regardless of what emerges during the proceedings, the court cannot convict for anything outside the scope of the statement of the criminal act as charged. This said, the legal interpretation of 'the criminal act as charged' has been debated.[3]

---

[3] In a debated case, that is the Supreme Court decision in Case B 1937-23, 17 November 2023, this question was at stake. In this case, the AC acquitted an adult man who had his finger in or around the genital of a small child because it could not be determined from the child's story and use of the term 'snippa' (a common non-offensive word for the female genitals in Swedish) that his fingers had actually penetrated her. The Supreme Court

Fundamental principles

As mentioned earlier there are some principles of a fundamental character in criminal procedural law. One of the main principles is the principle of orality, meaning that all evidence and other material must be presented orally during the main hearing in court. From this principle, it also follows that all testimonies must be given orally and without the use of notes. The testimony should be given spontaneously, as if it were being recounted for the first time, despite the fact that most individuals being heard – complainant, witnesses and the defendant – have already been interviewed by the police multiple times regarding the same event. This applies to all kinds of cases, but has a particular impact in rape cases, as the testimonies are key pieces of evidence (see Chapter 4). However, police officers are allowed to use notes, as they cannot be expected to remember all the similar incidents they have experienced during their service over time.

The principle of orality stems from the principle of immediacy requiring that the court bases its decision solely on what has been presented directly during the main hearing. Another related principle is that of concentration. It means that the trial should be concentrated in time (Ekelöf et al 2009; Wong 2012) and preferably not spread out over weeks or months. The Swedish criminal procedure is founded on negotiation and adversarial principles, which means that the procedure is constructed around two acting and contradictory parties and is mainly accusatory, although the judge may take an active role to ensure the case is thoroughly investigated (Ekelöf and Edelstam 2002).

The principle of free admission and evaluation of evidence

The evidence in rape cases, as described in greater detail in Chapter 4, consists, as in many other cases, of both technical (including forensic) evidence and oral testimony. In the book we will also refer technical evidence as 'hard', 'factual', or 'objective' evidence, contrasting the 'soft' evidence of oral testimonies (stories) in rape cases. This distinction is routinely made by the legal professionals themselves.

The technical evidence can include DNA, documented injuries, statements about blood alcohol content, text messages and so on. What distinguishes rape cases and makes the evaluation of evidence particularly difficult is that the technical evidence often concerns whether intercourse has taken place

---

referred the case back to the AC, ruling that it had the duty to also assess the alternative offence of sexual assault although the prosecutor had no such secondary offence included in the charges.

or not, and, to some extent, issues of intoxication and injuries. However, the most challenging questions, which can mainly be answered through oral testimony, are the issues of voluntariness and intent.

The law of evidence in Swedish criminal procedure is governed by the principles of free admission and free evaluation of evidence (Ekelöf et al 2009; Fitger 2014). The rules concerning the evaluation of evidence are stipulated in Chapter 35 of the SCJP, and the principle of free admission and evaluation is codified under 35:1: 'After evaluating everything that has occurred in accordance with the dictates of its conscience, the court shall determine what has been proved in the case'.

The principle of free admission suggests that there are no strict regulations regarding the admissibility of evidence, thereby allowing parties to present any evidence, even if it has been obtained illegally. This differs from many other jurisdictions. However, the principles of orality and immediacy interact with the principle of free admission of evidence. These principles aim to ensure that judges have access to the best possible evidence (Wong 2012). The principle of orality does not entirely exclude written evidence; written statements may be admitted under certain circumstances, as specified in 35:14 and 46:6 SCJP. Furthermore, the court retains the discretion to dismiss evidence based on its relevance and associated economical costs.

The principle of free evaluation of evidence signifies that judges are not constrained by legal rules; however, there are certain limitations. Evaluating the evidence entails that the court determines the probative value or weight of the evidence as part of assessing whether the standard of proof has been met in the case. In criminal trials, the prosecutor bears the full burden of proof (Bolding 1989; Ekelöf at al 2009). The standard of proof in criminal procedure is expressed as 'beyond reasonable doubt'. This is in line with the presumption of innocence, as established in ECHR art 6. The same article establishes a right for the defendant to remain silent during the whole procedure. This right will be discussed further as some defence lawyers argue that the way the new regulation is applied violates this right (Chapters 8 and 9).

According to SCJP 30:2, the judgment must be based solely on the material presented during the hearing. This implies that judges may not consider any information from sources external to the trial. Restrictions on free evaluation are further delineated in the preparatory work; it is not allowed to base the judgment on entirely subjective opinions. The preparatory work stipulates that the assessment 'should be accepted by other sensible persons'. As argued in Chapter 1, this can be interpreted as an expression of validity in terms of intersubjective consensus. As will be further illuminated in this book it can also be extended to empathetic interpretation (NJA II 1943:445). Additionally, the judge must not base the judgment on the entirety of the case without first evaluating each piece of evidence individually and subsequently assessing them in the context of the totality of the evidence (NJA 2015 s 702).

Evaluation of evidence

> Evaluating evidence is not at all about the logical connection between cause and effect in the form of legal facts and legal consequences, but solely about the establishment of facts in the case [...] however, the assessment is empirical in nature. It is through our, that is, the court's, collective experience that the relationship between one or more pieces of evidence and the prosecutor's theory is tested. (Diesen 1996:15)

As this quote suggests, a crucial but complex and contentious aspect of a judge's duties involves the evaluation of evidence presented before the court. The process of evaluating evidence is intended to be a rational procedure characterized by objectivity and neutrality (Bladini 2013). On the other hand, as the quote also implies, it is not all about logical connections, but assessing empirical facts and a lived reality (cf Bladini 2013) through individual and collective experience.

The evaluation of evidence must be grounded in general principles of experience and logical rules of inference, with expert knowledge consulted when necessary (SOU 1926:32, p 255, SOU 1938:44, p 377 ff, see also NJA II 1943 s 455). The judiciary's task is to determine whether the prosecutor's account of the offence aligns with the actual events. This requires anchoring the evidence in a broader reference framework – an understanding of reality (Diesen 1996:8). In this context, the maxims of experience, as articulated in the preparatory works, are of particular importance. According to procedural regulation (SCJP 35:2), no evidence is required for facts that are commonly known, so called notorious facts. This principle applies both to facts and maxims of experience and is relevant to evidentiary and auxiliary facts, though not to legal facts.

The preparatory works describe notorious facts as those immediately observable by judges in the exercise of their duties (NJA II 1943 s 490). Examples include the understanding that a glass will fall if dropped or that visibility decreases in fog – phenomena that are universally acknowledged without the need for further evidence. Such circumstances form part of the implicit knowledge we rely on to navigate and interpret the world around us. However, what constitutes common knowledge is not static; it evolves over time and varies across cultures and historical periods. Questions regarding what is notorious and not, will be further discussed throughout the book, for example in relation to frozen fright and intoxication. In the context of rape, individual and shared experiences intersect with culturally ingrained notions of rational behaviour, common sense, and, by extension, beliefs about sexuality and gender (for example, hissense, hersense). The conceptual framework for analysing these aspects is presented in detail in Chapter 3.

Methods of evaluation of evidence

We will now briefly outline the foundations for evidence evaluation in Swedish criminal procedure, as described in doctrine and Supreme Court case law, none of which is binding but rather guiding, but is used to a large extent in practice. Traditionally, the Supreme Court in Sweden has primarily engaged with legal rather than evidential issues (Ekelöf et al 2009). However, since the 1980s, the Supreme Court has contributed to the development of evidence law by establishing general guidelines on handling common questions regarding the evaluation of evidence (Holmgård 2019). The Supreme Court has emphasized that principles and recommendations concerning the sifting of evidence should be used with caution and discretion (NJA 2004 s 176).

There are several theories on methods for evaluating evidence developed in legal doctrine. These methods are often categorized into mathematical and non-mathematical approaches or, alternatively, into probability-based and psychological/cognitive methods (Ekelöf et al 2009).[4] A method proposed by Diesen (2015), known as the method of alternative hypotheses (*hypotesmetoden*), has held a significant position not only in legal doctrine, but also in practice (Holmgård 2019). As we shall see, the method of alternative hypothesis has a particular meaning in rape cases.

Rape cases are recognized as complicated to evaluate, and the most complicated evidentiary question in rape cases is the assessment of oral testimonies. Historically, guidance was provided by a Supreme Court case from 1980 (NJA 1980 s 725), which stated that a victim testimony that was coherent, clear and detailed was a sign of truth. The court noted that there was no reason to doubt that the statement reflected the actual event, and that the victim had no motive to falsely accuse the defendant. Under these circumstances, the victim's testimony alone was deemed sufficient to establish the defendant's guilt beyond reasonable doubt.

In more recent cases, this position has been revised. In a case from 2005,[5] the Supreme Court discussed the necessity of corroborating evidence, which

---

[4]   For a long period, probability-based methods were predominant. However, during the early part of the twenty-first century, the prominence of mathematical and frequency-based methods began to wane (Ekelöf 2009). Currently, there is renewed interest in mathematical-based evidence theory, which aligns with international trends (Dahlman 2018). This resurgence may be attributed to the rapid advancements in artificial intelligence within society at large, and within the judiciary in particular (Bladini and Bergman Blix 2022).

[5]   NJA 2005 s 712.

led to a marked decrease in the proportion of convictions in sexual offence cases (Brå 2019). Furthermore, in NJA 2010 s 671, the court addressed criteria for assessing testimony, recommending greater attention be paid to inadequacies, such as lacunas, contradictions or errors. In this case, the Supreme Court asserted that merely finding the victim's testimony more credible than the defendant's is insufficient for a conviction. Recent case law (2017 s 316 I and II) also incorporated findings from witness psychology research, positing that a statement that is clear, lengthy and rich in detail may indicate veracity. However, these cases emphasized the need for caution in applying these criteria, acknowledging that individuals' abilities to articulate themselves orally can vary significantly. Furthermore, these cases mark a deviation from previous practice by asserting that a lack of consistency is not necessarily indicative of falsehood, contrary to previous case law. It should be noted that, in our analysis of judgments in Part IV, we observe that judges frequently adhere to these guidelines from the Supreme Court. However, almost all of them omit the aspects that introduce complexity (that is, the individuals' ability to articulate themselves orally). Following the discussion in Chapter 1, this can be seen as an example of how the law as an autopoietic system effectively integrates facts and influences from outside the legal system (such as witness psychological research) into the legal framework, yet transforms these, or select parts of them, to reproduce its own self-image and self-referential logics (Björling 2017; Teubner 1993). Another obvious example of this partial integration is the legal encoding, the translation into legal language and logics, of the messy and lived reality of an offence (Bergman Blix and Minissale 2022; Bladini et al 2023). This translation is performed by the prosecutor before indictment.

A final and significant case from the Supreme Court that has gained substantial influence in practice is the case NJA 2015 s 702, commonly known as the *Balcony Case*. In this case, the Supreme Court reiterated that the principle of free evaluation of evidence does not permit judges to make arbitrary assessments; only rational reasons may be used, and the analysis should be conducted objectively and in a structured manner. The Supreme Court suggested a method for structuring the process of evaluating the evidence presented before the court. Even though the Supreme Court emphasized that the suggested method might not be applicable in all types of cases, it appears to have gained considerable influence, particularly in the DCs (Agnafors 2019/2020; Mellqvist 2019/2020) and in rape cases, as we shall see in Part IV. It should be noted that a recent case from the Supreme Court addressed and aimed to adjust the huge impact of the case (see NJA 2023 s 29 I and II).

The *Balcony Case* model, as we will refer to it, proposed that the process of evaluation of evidence should follow four steps. The method recommended in the case implies that the court should initially consider only the evidence that strengthens the prosecution (Step 1) and assess whether this evidence is sufficient to prove the defendant's guilt beyond reasonable doubt (Step 2). Only then should the evidence presented by the defendant be considered (Step 3). Finally, the court should make an overall and final assessment (Step 4). At each of the previous three stages, an overall and final assessment of all the evidence should be made.

The criminal legislative frame

The criminal law is founded on several fundamental principles and assumptions designed to ensure justice and efficiency within the criminal justice system, while recognizing the intrusive and disruptive nature of punishment. Historically, Swedish law has emphasized the necessity of confining criminal law to the most severe situations, thereby upholding a principled approach to legal intervention (Asp et al 2013). The doctrine of criminal law underscores the principle of *ultima ratio*. This principle posits that criminal law should serve as the last resort in addressing societal issues (Asp et al 2013). However, recent trends in criminal policy represent significant breaks from the principles of humanity and *ultima ratio*. Contemporary legislative developments and policy shifts increasingly favour more stringent and punitive measures, reflecting a broader societal and political response to rising concerns over crime and public safety (Anderberg et al 2022).

The criminal policy on sexual violence has been part of this development, raising concerns and debate about the feminist movement contributing to carceral feminism, which emphasizes punitive measures over rehabilitative or preventative approaches (Boyle 2019; McGlynn 2022; Terwiel 2020). The implementation of Sweden's new rape law, characterized by an expanded definition of the criminal offence and increased penalties, should be recognized within this context. This development may influence judges' perceptions of their autonomy, a topic that will be explored in detail further on.

Another crucial principle is the principle of guilt, which requires that only a person who demonstrated guilt should be subject to criminal punishment. An accident is not ground for criminal liability. In rape cases the question of guilt, in relation to intent and negligence, is crucial.

There are three levels of intent and two levels of negligence in Swedish law: 1) *Direct intent* (*avsiktsuppsåt*), which is the most deliberate form of intent, where the perpetrator acts with the explicit purpose of causing a particular outcome; 2) *Oblique intent* (*insiktsuppsåt*), where the perpetrator does not directly aim for the specific outcome but is fully aware that it will almost certainly occur as a consequence of their actions; 3) *Recklessness* (*likgiltighetsuppsåt*), the lowest form of intent and that involves a two-step assessment. The first step is to establish that the perpetrator recognizes the risk of a certain outcome occurring. The second step is to establish that the perpetrator is indifferent to whether the outcome will actually occur (Asp et al 2013). In Swedish law, this corresponds to a situation where, for example, the perpetrator is fully aware that the other person does not consent to a sexual act but proceeds regardless, showing indifference to the lack of consent. This lowest form of intent closely borders the most severe form of negligence, described below, which means that prosecutors often prefer to charge for an intentional crime and only invoke grossly negligent rape as a secondary option (cf Brå 2020:6).

There are two forms of negligence in Swedish criminal law: conscious negligence and unconscious negligence. The first requires that the perpetrator was aware of the risk of a certain consequence (in this case that voluntariness was lacking) but believed that this was not the case, that is indifferent to the risk but not to the fact (regarding voluntary participation). The second, unconscious negligence, implies that the perpetrator did not realize the risk (did not realize that she did not participate voluntary) but had reasonable grounds to assume or should have realized it. The requirement for negligence in rape cases requires gross negligence. This refers to the most blameworthy cases.[6] This is most often the case of conscious negligence but can also apply in cases of unconscious negligence (cf NJA 2019 s 668) in situations where the perpetrator has not made an effort to, for example, verify the specific circumstances, despite strong reasons to do so, such as in the situation where the other party is highly intoxicated (cf Prop. 2017/18:177).

Specifically on rape

The criminalization of rape and sexual violence may be the part of criminal law that has been subject to changes most often in Sweden (Träskman and Wennberg 2019). The question of how best to prevent and regulate rape to offer victim/survivors the strongest and most effective legal protection, including respectful trials, has been discussed and debated for decades across the world, including in Sweden (Leijonhufvud 2015; McGlynn and Munro 2010). The are several consent-based models of rape, including 'no means no', 'only yes means yes' (that is, affirmative consent) and the consent-plus model suggested by McGlynn and Munro (2010) and freedom to negotiate. Most consent-based legislation in Europe build on the 'yes means yes' model (Uhnoo et al 2024b). The Swedish model falls under the affirmative consent model and was built on the idea that rape is a problem about sex, choice and communication (Wegerstad 2021).

---

[6]   What this entails has been examined by the Supreme Court, which has raised the standard to require 'remarkably blameworthy' conduct; cf NJA 2022 s 237.

The Swedish consent-based law introduced the explicit requirement of voluntariness, which broadens the scope of criminalized conduct, thereby encompassing a wider range of actions now classified as rape. Additionally, negligent rape was introduced as a new crime, whereas previously only intentional rape had been subject to criminalization. The requirement of lack of consent is articulated as non-voluntariness in Swedish law, to avoid confusion with the general ground for freedom from liability due to consent (SCC 24:7). In this book, we alternate between the terms 'voluntariness' and 'consent', and use them synonymously.

Prior to the enactment of the new law, several concerns and expectations were raised within both legal and academic circles. A primary concern was that the law might lead to increased focus on the victim, potentially subjecting them to heightened scrutiny regarding their behaviour and actions throughout the legal proceedings, thus exacerbating issues of secondary victimization (see Chapter 7).[7] Additionally, critics argued that the law's provisions lacked sufficient clarity, particularly concerning the meaning of voluntariness, raising concerns about legal certainty and leaving open questions about its interpretation and application in practice. Another significant apprehension related to the burden of proof, often discussed as a burden of explanation, whereby the accused might be implicitly required to demonstrate their innocence, thereby challenging the rule of law and the presumption of innocence (see Chapters 8 and 9).[8]

Conversely, proponents of the law expressed optimism that it would lead to a higher conviction rate in rape cases and expand the range of criminalized conduct, providing more comprehensive protection for sexual autonomy. They also anticipated that the legislation would contribute to a normative shift in societal attitudes, fostering a deeper understanding of consent and reshaping public perceptions of what constitutes rape, thereby aligning legal standards with contemporary values of personal and sexual integrity.

However, several critical issues remain unaddressed in the preparatory legislative process and necessitate clarification in practice (Prop 2017/ 18:177). The new regulation of the offence, in SCC 6:1, is defined in its entirety as follows:

> A person who performs *vaginal, anal or oral intercourse* or some *other sexual act, comparable in the severity* of violation to intercourse, with a person

---

[7] Cf prop 2017/18:177; Lagrådet; Advokatsamfundet. However, it should be noted that the law also seeks to address the problems of victim blaming and secondary victimization that has been highlighted and critisized in previous research (for example, Sutorius and Kaldal 2003; Törnqvist 2017).

[8] Cf prop 2017/18:177; Lagrådet; Advokatsamfundet.

who is *not participating voluntarily* is guilty of rape and is sentenced to imprisonment for at least three and at most six years. The same applies to anyone who compels a person who is not participating voluntarily to perform or endure such an act. *When assessing* whether participation is voluntary or not, *particular consideration* is given to *whether voluntariness was expressed by word or deed* or in some *other way*. A person <u>can never be considered to be participating voluntarily</u> if:

1. Their participation is a result of assault, other violence or threat of a criminal act, a threat to bring a prosecution against or report another person for an offence, or a threat to give detrimental information about another person; or
2. The perpetrator improperly exploits the fact that the person is in a particularly vulnerable situation due to unconsciousness, sleep, grave fear, the influence of alcohol or drugs, illness, bodily injury, mental disturbance or otherwise in view of the circumstances; or
3. The perpetrator induces the person to participate by seriously abusing the person's position of dependence on the perpetrator.

If, in view of the circumstances associated with the offence, the offence is considered less serious, the person is guilty of rape and is sentenced to imprisonment for at most four years.

If an offence referred to in the first paragraph is considered gross, the person is guilty of gross rape and is sentenced to imprisonment for at least five and at most ten years. When assessing whether the offence is gross, particular consideration is given to whether the perpetrator used violence or a threat of a particularly serious nature, or whether more than one person assaulted the victim or took part in the assault in some other way, or whether, in view of the method used or the young age of the victim or otherwise, the perpetrator exhibited particular ruthlessness or brutality. (Act 2022:1043, emphasis added)

This new legal construction of rape establishes that the boundary between a legal and illegal act is determined by whether participation in a sexual act is voluntary. Specifically, the law criminalises the act of engaging in 'sexual intercourse or similar' with a person who does not participate voluntarily. This encompasses two scenarios:

1. A person has not decided by free will to participate in 'sexual intercourse or similar', meaning that someone has not expressed a 'yes' by word or deed or in some other way.
2. A person has decided by free will not to participate in 'sexual intercourse or similar', meaning that person said 'no' (Wennberg 2018/19).

The evaluation of voluntariness must consider the situation in its entirety, referred to as 'the situation as a whole'. This concept is a key issue for the analyses we make throughout this book. Critics argue that this framework blurs the line between voluntary and non-voluntary participation, making it difficult to determine until after the act. Furthermore, a person's internal reluctance to engage in a sexual act, despite having consented, does not suffice for criminal liability. This suggests that someone might show apparent voluntariness even if they were not genuinely willing to participate. Also, a situation when the active party successfully pesters about sex ('nagging sex') is mentioned in the preparatory works as an example that falls outside the scope of rape (Prop 2017/2018:177 p 33). The crucial factor is whether the individual could freely make their decision. The government has posited that this perspective aligns with the concept of sexual self-determination, allowing individuals to opt for actions they might otherwise avoid. This notion, which ties closely to the idea of autonomy, will be explored further in Chapter 7 (see also Bladini and Svedberg Andersson 2020). It is essential that participation remains voluntary from the moment the sexual act occurs and throughout its duration (Prop 2017/2018:177). Each new act also requires new consent. As will be seen in Parts III and IV, sometimes the line between a new act and the same act seems blurred, and different courts may construct the sexual act differently, as one single sequence or in several isolated pieces.

The regulation highlights that, in determining whether participation was voluntary or not, special consideration must be given to expressions of voluntariness through words, deed or in other ways. The preparatory work offers examples of such actions, including facial expressions or body language. This implies that a key aspect of the legal evaluation involves examining what the complainant has, or has not, communicated (Prop 2017/2018:177). The government asserted that sexual self-determination encompasses the right to decide whether to engage in sexual activities and the right to respond to sexual advances in any manner, including passivity. Therefore, the government concluded that the legal framework should not impose any specific requirements on *how* individuals express their voluntary participation in sexual activities, leaving it to the judiciary to assess each case individually (cf Wegerstad 2021). However, the main rule, therefore, is that passivity is not an expression of voluntariness (Prop 2017/2018:177). The Swedish Supreme Court ruled that the scope for interpreting passivity as voluntary participation is very limited. This decision emphasizes that consent must be explicit and cannot be inferred from passive behaviour (NJA 2019 s 668).

The government emphasized that it is the perpetrator's responsibility to ensure that the sexual act is mutual, particularly if the complainant is passive (Prop 2017/2018:177). This is an important change, normatively and in the application of the law. However, as we shall observe, the courts are not yet used to such an understanding of the situation. In determining whether participation is voluntary from the perpetrator's perspective, the victim's inner will is deemed irrelevant; what matters is the victim's communicated intentions. This means that what the victim expressed or failed to express is made crucial in evaluating the perpetrator's criminal liability.

The last part of the rape regulation states that a person can never be considered to be participating voluntarily if the perpetrator 1) has used force through violence or threat, or 2) improperly exploited the fact that the person is in a particularly vulnerable situation, due to, for example, intoxication or 3) by seriously abusing the person's position of dependence. The first and second situation has most frequently occurred in our study. In particular, the issue of intoxication has been complicated and raised questions about what constitutes 'notorious facts', as well as what conclusions can be drawn from memory gaps or blood tests.

The principle of guilt is fundamental for criminal liability. This means that, even if the prosecutor has been able to prove all the factual circumstances that fulfil the elements of the rape provision, it is still required that the crime was committed with intent. If the crime was not committed with intent but gross negligence, there is now a possibility to apply the negligent rape offence that entered into force as a new crime in 2018. The offence gross negligent rape follows the same construction as intentional rape, with the same objective criteria, that is factual circumstances. The question of intent and negligence is a more complicated one to prove.

Intent and negligence should be assessed based on the individual abilities and experiences of the defendant in the particular case. In other types of assessments regarding what can be considered reasonably careful, different standards have been used throughout history. For example, in tort law the standard of *bonus pater familias* (the rational and prudent family father) has been applied (Påhlsson 2005). Regarding the expectations of awareness and negligence, and what is expected of the individual defendant in rape cases, this will be discussed further in our analyses.

Conclusion

We have now outlined the main characteristics of the Swedish legal system, a 'mixed' system that combines codified law with case law and is part of the Nordic legal family.

Most rape cases are handled in the DC and AC. In the DC, the majority of judges are laypersons, while in the AC professional judges dominate. Although the principle of transparency applies, rape trials are typically conducted behind closed doors, with the complainant usually present in the DC but rarely in the AC. Swedish criminal procedure emphasizes legal certainty, transparency and immediacy, moving from preliminary investigation to trial, with prosecutors required to present both inculpatory and exculpatory evidence. The principle of orality mandates that evidence be presented orally – a particularly important feature in rape cases, where oral testimony is often central.

A 2018 reform shifted the emphasis in rape law from force to voluntariness and introduced grossly negligent rape. This consent-based framework has sparked debate, challenging traditional principles like the presumption of innocence, particularly through increased scrutiny of complainants and potential shifts in burden of proof. These implications are explored further in subsequent chapters.

3

Theory and Method

Introduction

In this chapter, we first outline the theoretical framework and key concepts in our analysis. In the second part of the chapter, we describe the methodology and data collected in our 18 rape cases. Throughout this book, we return to a critique of the juridical method and argue that legal professionals need to understand how to treat and interpret narratives, akin to the hermeneutic method of interpretation in social science. We spend a few lines on this in the 'Note on methods of analysis' section.

Theoretical framework

One contribution of this book is that the framework combines feminist legal theory and emotion-sociological theory. This combination, we argue, opens new ways to understand the surreptitious continued impact of stale patriarchal values on an otherwise proud-to-be (almost) gender-equal society. It contributes to feminist legal critique by adding the analytical lens of emotions and contributes to the sociology of emotions by furthering the empirically grounded theorization of the entwinement of rationality and emotions (see, for example, Barbalet 1998; Damasio 1994; Feldman Barrett 2017; Flam 2000; Reddy 2001; Scheer 2021; Scheff 1990). In the following discussion, feminist and emotion-sociological theoretical perspectives will be integrated to detail main analytical concepts.

Feminist legal theory has analysed the patriarchal foundation of the legal system and demonstrated its reliance on gendered stereotypes involved in rape offences (for example, Lacey 1998; MacKinnon 2016; Naffine 2002; Smith and Skinner 2012; Temkin 2000). Drawing on this research, concepts of structurally embedded patriarchy, power, sexuality, gender and rape myths are central theoretical tools used in the analysis. To understand how legal professionals come to enact stereotypical thinking, often unwittingly and in many cases despite their best endeavours not to do so, we draw on the sociology of emotions. Here, a key distinction is made between 'background emotions' and 'foreground emotions' (Barbalet 1998, 2011); foreground emotions are those also commonly perceived as 'emotions' and experienced as 'being in an emotional state'. In line with the Western modern tradition of separating emotions from reason, the emotional self is considered an irrational self. Hence as discussed in Chapter 1, it is a pervasive idea within the legal system and state institutions in general to conflate professional or bureaucratic rationality with an 'unemotional' state of mind. When emotions do surface in the awareness of the emoting professional actor, it appears as a breach of professional feeling rules. This foreground emotion is also experienced by the emoting subject as disturbing because it needs to be controlled in line with existing feeling rules. Such conscious emotion work takes cognitive energy and focus from other (professional) tasks (Hochschild 1983).

In contrast, 'background emotions' conceptualize the barely conscious emotion conducive to rational action (for example, Burkitt 2012; de Sousa 1987; Helm 2009; Lantz 2021; Morton 2013). Background emotions motivate and orient professional work. Calm and entwined with the ongoing action, they often go unnoticed by the emoting subject. Background emotions constitute the focal point of our interest in professional legal emotions because they inform and orient legal practice. Be it the feeling of comfort and pride in juridical expertise, the interest and curiosity in acquiring knowledge (about a case), the certainty and feeling of knowing when it is time to take a decision, or the slight annoyance that helps to discern relevant from irrelevant information and adequate from inappropriate action. Conscious reflection on background emotions is unwarranted unless propelled by the need to reflect on past actions and decisions (Barbalet 1998; Burkitt 2012; Holmes 2010; Wettergren 2019, 2024).

Hochschild (1979) elaborated the sociological concept of feeling rules and the emoting subject's need to work on emotions to adapt to the social order. She distinguished between emotional labour – when work explicitly demands the production of certain emotions (often in service or care work) – and emotion work of everyday life when different social situations, including formal and informal rituals, come with their own sets of tacit feeling rules. In line with previous research on law and emotions in the legal system (for example, Bergman Blix and Wettergren 2018), we use the terms 'emotion work' or 'emotion management' for the continuous and by time habituated emotional adaptation to tacit feeling rules pertaining to professional performance. In the legal context, we use the concept 'emotive-cognitive judicial frame', a set of implicit feeling and behavioural rules for legal practice, motivating and orienting the reproduction of established ways to feel and do core values of objectivity, autonomy and rationality. In this frame, professional background emotions habitually pass as 'non-emotions' because they do not conflict with the feeling rules of rational action. In contrast, the concept 'emotive-cognitive', highlights rational action as *simultaneously* emotional and cognitive. The most imperative feeling rule of the emotive-cognitive judicial frame however, is that emotions are private and personal and must not be allowed, nor seen, to interfere with legal work (for a discussion see Wettergren 2019).

That said, professional emotionality and skilled emotion work is a collective endeavour central to the emotive-cognitive judicial frame. Within the emotive-cognitive frame, each professional role is furthermore equipped with its own emotional script: judges should display impartiality, interest, seriousness and authority, and often are the least visibly 'emotional' in (the Swedish) court. Prosecutors should display confidence and certainty in their investigation and in the guilt of the defendant, sometimes also moral indignation and disbelief in the defendant (and sometimes the defence lawyer). Defence lawyers should display unwavering loyalty to the client and their rights and interests, but with respect for the legal procedure (Flower 2020).

Previous research has observed professional irritation and moral indignation directed by both judges and prosecutors at defence lawyers who seemed to confound professional loyalty with sincerely felt conviction of their clients' innocence (Bergman Blix and Wettergren 2018; Flower 2020). Such lawyers were viewed as potential troublemakers because they could be unpredictable and sometimes disrespectful towards the prosecutor, questioning the objectivity of their investigations. Interestingly, in rape trials defence lawyers seem to be allowed greater leeway in this regard without evoking the irritation of judges and prosecutors. The legal roles, their 'professional emotional profiles', and their respective part in the making of legal objectivity is further discussed in Chapter 5 (see also Bladini et al 2023).

The tacit rules of the emotive-cognitive judicial frame inform the legal professional collective and its perception of and solidarity with shared ideas of what the legal system is and should be, while also shaping professional roles in staging objective justice in the eyes of the public. Important in this context is that the assumption that emotions are separate from legal work suppresses the influence of emotions instead of rendering them transparent and part of professional reflexivity (cf Barbalet 2011).

The emotive cognitive judicial frame obscures the influence of social norms and values in legal professional work and thereby ignores the influence of sensed information about legal subjects conveyed by their bodily appearance and behaviour in court. This becomes particularly problematic in criminal offences for which information brought by emotion is accorded importance, as in rape cases. Legal professionals have little experience in critically reflecting on information brought to them this way. On the contrary, professional habit is to suppress the emotional origin of such information, thereby omitting the 'feeling' from 'knowing' in 'the feeling of knowing'.

In line with the view of emotion as orienting and informing human rationality, emotions have an epistemic function. The philosophy of emotions has theorized about the importance of emotions for fact-finding and gaining new information (for example, de Sousa 2009), highlighting the emotionality of what are often presumed to be 'cognitive drives' like interest, curiosity, certainty and doubt, as well as pinpointing manifestly background no-name 'evaluative feelings' (Helm 2009), such as the 'the feeling of knowing' or 'the feeling of not knowing'. In previous research (Bergman Blix 2022; Törnqvist and Wettergren 2023; see also Bladini et al 2023) the paramount role of doubt and certainty for the 'objective mind' and decision-making of judges and prosecutors have begun to be investigated, furthering the case for emotions as crucial in the emotive-cognitive judicial frame (Lange 2002; Maroney 2011).

The import of the theories of epistemic emotions in our analysis strengthens our argument regarding the widespread 'feeling of not knowing' experienced by legal professionals when faced with the evidence of rape cases, expressed and named as frustration, irritation, uncertainty and so forth (see Chapter 4). Conversely, we use it to understand how judges move from the feeling of not knowing to 'a feeling of knowing', expressed in terms of 'reasonable doubts' or 'beyond reasonable doubts' in their judgment (see Chapter 11). We use the 'certainty-doubt spiral' term coined in previous research (Törnqvist and Wettergren 2023) to name the feeling of doing objectivity as an intellectual capacity; certainty is counteracted by doubt in a spiral of accumulated knowledge that drives knowledge-seeking to a point at which certainty feels satisfactory and forecloses further knowledge-seeking (de Sousa 1987). The certainty-doubt spiral keeps premature and 'irrational' conclusions away from the legal decision-making process. Background emotions are typically experienced and communicated vaguely as 'feelings' or 'a feeling of' something, revealing of the entanglement of a range of emotions, or emotional compounds, that have not (yet) been cognitively retrieved and subjected to emotional reflexivity (Burkitt 2012; Holmes 2010; Reddy 2001).

In our analysis, we pinpoint instances in which backgrounded emotions of sympathy or antipathy against one or the other legal subject were sensed in the emotional climate of the courtroom or communicated between the lines in the wording of judgments. Feelings of sympathy and antipathy do not need to be very strongly felt or expressed to tip the balance of certainty of the legal decision 'beyond reasonable doubt' or 'not beyond reasonable doubt' in rape trials, in which all the value of the evidence hinges on the credibility of the complainant's story.

Sexuality and the micro-politics of emotion

Sexuality is understood in this book as imbued by historical gendered power relations, contrasting the narrow legal view that sexuality is about decontextualized erotic attraction between individuals. The legal preparatory works of the new rape law encourage heeding the context of the sex act when evaluating the requisites of voluntariness and intent ('the situation as whole'; see Chapter 2). This suggests a potential interest in context-dependent power dynamics. One central argument in this book is that 'the situation as a whole' is key to evaluating the evidence in rape cases.

Emotion originates in social interaction; it both motivates and informs interaction and is the outcome of it. Constant emotional exchange occurs between bodies in the social sphere (Goffman 1990; Hochschild 1983). Helpful to understand the complex interactional dynamics of a sex act and its relation to 'the situation as a whole' is Candace Clark's theory of the micro-politics of emotion. According to Clark (1990; see also Ahmed 2004), emotional exchange is 'political' by communicating 'place claims' (situated status) and social proximity (intimacy or distance) to the other. Emotions received and emotions given signal the social place claimed and accorded and inform about the 'subjective' and 'objective' place of the actor. A mismatch between subjective and objective place may give rise to happiness (if the subjective place is much better than claimed), fear or anger (if the subjective place is much worse than claimed), while either mismatch may also evoke shame (for not meeting the standards expected) or consternation (uncertainty regarding the motives of others or trust in them, including trust in one's own capacity to read the situation correctly, cf Barbalet 1998; Kemper 2001).

With this in mind, a hypothetical interaction between a hypothetical couple of friends, A (male) and B (female), might evolve as follows. A and B are long-time friends, but A is secretly in love with B. After a party, they decide to share a bed and B trusts A, who is a friend, to go to sleep next to her. Drunk as they are, A dares to make advances to B. B is already half asleep and wakes up in a state of confusion. She does not know if she feels right but moves a little more to the side and tries to go back to sleep. But soon, A's advances are repeated and now B, annoyed, says 'stop, we're just friends and we're just going to sleep'. A asks if B does not like him; B says 'yes, but now I want to sleep'. A becomes annoyed: 'why should we be in the same bed then?' B agrees to hug a little but then says 'no' again, and so forth.

Being in love or feeling attracted to someone often comes with a claim to intimacy, a claim that is intrusive and potentially abusive if the other person does not feel the same. In the hypothetical scenario, B is consternated by discovering an unexpected mismatch between her subjective place (friend) and objective place (lover). She may feel many emotions at once: anger/annoyance, unpleasant surprise, guilt (for not reciprocating), shame (for having invited him), uncertainty (for the broken trust) and fear (of losing his friendship or of his anger).

We need not dwell on the possibilities in detail to understand that, in the situation, B might not simply react by telling him off and leaving the bed. The relationship between them as friends harbours a bundle of entangled emotions and emotive-cognitive considerations of various possible actions and action outcomes. Gender matters because it is more likely that B, as a woman, will try to remain kind and navigate the situation to avoid hurting her friend's feelings, either because she is afraid of losing a dear friend or because she is afraid of his anger. These emotions are likely still backgrounded but informing and orienting her immediate responses. In retrospect, she might think that she should have told him off at once because their friendship would be ended anyway. The emotive-cognitive rationality of this hypothetical scenario is, arguably, well known among women, and its emotion-action complexity common sense from a female everyday life perspective (Bladini and Svedberg Andersson 2020). Linked to the emotive-cognitive rationality of this situation is the well-established concept of 'female fear' (that is, women's ever-present fear of rape):

> Most women experience fear of rape as a nagging, gnawing sense that something awful could happen, an angst that keeps them from doing things they want or need to do, or from doing them at the time or in the way that they might otherwise do. Women's fear of rape is a sense that one must always be on guard, vigilant and alert, a feeling that causes a woman to tighten with anxiety if someone is walking too closely behind her, especially at night. (Gordon and Riger 1991:2)

The main theoretical idea is that women's fear of rape, their lived experiences of being constructed as 'sexed and embodied subjects' and 'rapable, vulnerable and victimizable' (Smart 1995:221–222), limits their opportunities, makes them adjust their actions and self-images accordingly, and thereby affects their rationality, how they behave and the choices they make (Cahill 2001; Wendt-Höjer 2002).[1] Stefansen (2020:63) used the concept of a gendered 'phenomenology of fear' to explain why even 'micro-transgressions' may

---

[1] According to Smart (1995), the fear of rape and experiences of sexual offences has a disciplining effect on all women and is viewed as 'constitutive of gender power relations, in that they confirm the lack of bodily protection and women's lack of the right to be left alone, in contrast to men' (Stefansen et al 2020).

function as 'constant reminders that girls must take into account that their right to bodily integrity is less protected than it is for boys' (see also Young 1990). Thus, feminist scholars have used the concept of female fear to explain women's situated experiences, behaviour and rationality: in other words, what is understood to be reasonable course of action for a woman in particular circumstances to avoid rape.

From the male perspective, it appears from our analysis in this book that the previously described situation between A and B is unclear and frustrating. Expecting, believing or hoping that B felt for him as he felt for her, he interpreted her decision to accept to share a bed with him as confirmation of his secret place claim. Gagnon and Simon (1973) introduced the notion of 'sexual scripts' as a metaphor for the social patterning of sexual desires, practices and interaction. In a general sense, a script 'defines the situation, names the actors, and plots the behaviour' (Gagnon and Simon 1973:19). Following the stereotypical male script, A understood that he was expected to take the initiative, which he did because alcohol boosted his self-confidence. Following the stereotypical female script, B understood that she should not hurt his feelings. According to these gendered scripts, the expected emotional reactions to the described mismatch between subjective and objective place is that A becomes disappointed or angry, and B feels afraid or sad. From the male perspective, it appears difficult to understand why B did not recognize his love for her or understood what her decision to accept to share a bed meant to him. This situation would be recognized by many men.

Power and empathy (see later in this chapter) are linked in that those who belong to a social group that does not have the general privilege to define the situation must be prepared to read the situation from the perspective of those who belong to a category that has this privilege (Goffman 1990). The new law, we argue, demands a change in the gendered power balance and forges the same empathic sensitivity in the masculine emotional script as there is in the female emotional script. We observe that the banality of the hypothetical scenario, at first glance, is deceptive. The situation, although it is probably unclear to the interactants, is structured by a historically sedimented gender power order and associated scripts of gendered emotions.

Rape myths

The same intriguing banality is apparent in how rape myths are activated through the rule of law. The traditional patriarchal view of heterosexuality ascribes initiative and activity as properties inherent to male sexuality (Muehlenhard et al 2016), while female sexuality is passive and romantic. Men desire sex while women desire love and romantic relationships. Women are positioned as gatekeepers, inherently responsible for their virtue by protecting their sexuality (Jozkowski and Peterson 2013) and its strategic distribution with the aim to achieve a romantic relationship and male protection. This responsibility includes behaving in virtuous ways to be respectable and to avoid provoking male sexual desire. Men, while expected to respect the virtuous woman, are allowed to seduce her with or without the promise of a romantic relationship; it is presumably part of their 'game'.

As dated and fantastic as this view of male and female sexuality may be, its common-sense logic informs the rape myths still at work in the legal system. Thus, we find myths like 'the real rapist', a man who does not respect a virtuous woman but 'takes' her as he pleases. Such reckless behaviour is habitually associated with foreigners/strangers or men at the lower end of the social status ladder (Burt 1980; Estrich 1987). Correspondingly, the 'real victim' – an ideal analysed in all its aspects by Christie (1986) – is a woman who fulfils the virtuous requirements and is raped through no fault of her own, that is, without provoking male sexual desire.

While the 'real victim' myth is evolving and explicitly counteracted by the new rape law, we demonstrate in our analysis how some related myths (for example, 'she lies') is a naturalized starting point of the taken-for-granted procedure in rape cases. Correspondingly, male fear of false accusations 'naturally' informs the logic of so-called consent defence strategies (Uhnoo et al 2024c). From an emotion-sociological perspective, the 'she lies' myth is a projection of proverbial female romantic expectations. These expectations, as it were, are bound to be disappointed, given their clash with the proverbial male sexual desire.

Based on the generalizing stereotypes of male v female sexuality, the male collective is structurally predisposed to guilt, just like any social category (for example, class) is collectively predisposed to certain emotions depending on their position in the social hierarchy. This can be inferred by the power/ status theory of emotion (Kemper 2006). Although the theory offers heuristic tools to understanding what is happening in terms of emotions and action motivations between social groups, it is not deterministic and must be used with caution. Structurally embedded (in social power/status relations), collective emotions are not reducible to the micro level (Barbalet 1998). In other words, just because men are structurally predisposed to feel guilty about their power over women, every man need not feel powerful or guilty in their relationship to women. Rather, structurally embedded power/status emotions should be viewed as emotional resources useful for political and mobilizing purposes because they provide a starting point for evoking collective identification through shared emotions.

Thus, rape myths like 'she lies' are a logical response to the structurally embedded emotions of male guilt, sensing the structurally embedded emotion of female vengeance (Barbalet 1998; Kemper 2006). This is not to say that every woman resents her structural subordination (on the contrary, most women have learnt to deal with it, for instance, through the evolving female emotional script) but that the structurally embedded emotions of subordination, potentially shared by the collective of women, are anger and vengefulness. This, in turn, makes men as a collective structurally predisposed to fear and resent women, especially when the collective of women appears to move upwards on the social ladder (cf Barbalet 1998).

Guilt is a feeling of irresponsible (misused) power (Kemper 2001). Fear is the emotion of losing power, which in this context is the expected outcome of being accused of rape. Consequently, in a society with gender-equal ambitions reflected in its rape legislation, men fear that women may accuse them of rape to seek revenge for disappointed expectations and abuse. While the gender roles are changing and the suspected reason for crying rape evolves into, for instance, disappointed sex expectations ('bad sex'), the idea of the disappointed romantic relationship is also surprisingly enough still used in the explicit or implicit argumentation of defence lawyers.

Interestingly, and as will be further observed in the analyses of this book, the 'she lies' myth appears relevant from the juridical perspective as an 'alternative hypothesis' (Chapter 2). Thus, it is from the juridical perspective not a general distrust in women's motives but the rule of law that makes it necessary to probe the possibility that she might have 'other motives' for reporting rape. 'She lies' is then based on the presumption of innocence and the protection of the defendant's rights. Against this we argue that, while the suspicion of false accusation as an alternative hypothesis may arise in every reported offence, it is extremely unlikely to have the consequences that it has for the offence of rape. This reveals an overlap of the 'she lies' myth with the presumption of innocence in the rule of law.

The new law firmly refutes stereotypical views of female sexuality. However, the way the law is applied continues to rely on an understanding of masculine sexuality as active and rationally motivated to follow the desire to pursue and complete sex if a man perceives that a woman has indicated by word, deed or otherwise her willingness to have sex with him. The reason for this is, we argue, that the modern legal system was built by men and for men at a time when inequality, be it gendered or classed, was perceived as motivated by the obviously inherent intellectual capabilities of the educated white man – '*bonus pater familia*' (see Chapter 2; Bladini and Svedberg Andersson 2020).

Broadening the picture, the lingering presumptions about gendered sexuality and connoted rape myths have interesting emotive-cognitive consequences, observed for instance in the concept of himpathy, short for sympathy with him (Manne 2018). Himpathy is the sympathy felt and/ or expressed by understanding of the male fear of false rape accusations, actualized whenever a rape law is debated in terms of making it 'easier' for women to report rape. It has been prevalent for as long as rape laws have existed, but was particularly explicit in the 1960s in Sweden when rape within marriage was criminalized (Leijonhufvud 2015) and today when the new law criminalized sex that occurs without ensuring voluntariness. Uhnoo et al (2024a) demonstrated that himpathy, as the expressed understanding of male fear of 'taking the initiative', as it were, was present among legal professionals the first three years after the new rape law. Himpathy further relates to the 'real rapist' myth, as research suggests that it grows stronger when the defendant has good social standing within society or at least has a 'ruinable' future (Uhoo et al 2024c).

Power discomfort and autonomy

The power to deprive someone of their civil liberties is not taken lightly in the rule of law in democratic societies (for example, Sterzel 2001). Previous research (for example, Bergman Blix and Wettergren 2018) observed that judges think a great deal about this power of their professional position, either taking a 'personal responsible' or 'bureaucratic cog in the wheel' approach to it. Any which way, the degree of judicial reflexivity about power demonstrates background sensitivity to feeling guilty should the power be wrongly used. It should be noted that reflexivity regarding their power and the possibility of feeling guilt is a derivative of the rule of law, which is expressly focused on the rights of the accused and their protection against being wrongfully convicted. It is observed in the oft-cited saying among judges that it is 'better to acquit 10 guilty ones than convict one innocent' (Ekelöf et al 2009). When this sensitivity to the potential of guilt is experienced consciously enough to be expressed in interviews, we call it 'power discomfort'. This can be, for instance, expressed through hesitant and ambivalent reasoning regarding the new law or expressed unease with the 'type of evidence' of rape cases or an expressed understanding of male fear (himpathy). In our analysis, we demonstrate how background power discomfort may orient judges' assessment in rape cases, especially in those featuring defendants with ruinable futures.

An interesting finding in this book is that many legal professionals expressed discomfort with calling 'the sex act' rape when no violence was involved. Here, power discomfort points to the 'real rape' myth, which equates rape with violence (Burt 1980; Estrich 1987). As will be discussed, although in all our 18 cases the charges included the statement that sex was not voluntary, both judges and prosecutors were disposed to look for and lean on some sort of violence or force by the defendant.

The juridical concept of voluntariness was defined and discussed in Chapter 2. From the feminist legal perspective, we approach 'voluntariness' through a critique of the liberal idea of the autonomous subject, the subject as free to make perfectly rational choices. We argue that this understanding of autonomy obscures the way that sexual interaction is embedded in context-dependent micro-power structures (Andersson 2011; Bladini and Svedberg

Andersson 2020; Clark 1990, Lacey 1998; Naffine 2002). As a core concept in the criminal legal system, the autonomous legal subject is understood as intentional and free to make their conscious choices regardless of context or relational bonds (Gunnarsson and Svensson 2009; Mackenzie and Stoljar 2000).

Conversely, the liberal notion of autonomy is also an idea applied to legal professionals (notably judges) regarding their free and uninfluenced interpretation and application of the law. As we noted in Chapters 1 and 2, the judge, by virtue of their appointment and office, may evaluate the evidence in any way they find suitable if their assessment is recognized by other judges as reasonable. This trusted capacity of judges includes the ability to distinguish between 'objective' and 'subjective' considerations and between 'rational' and 'emotional' ways of reasoning. Consequently, the idea of the meaning of legal autonomy makes it difficult for legal professionals to recognize the *felt* intersection of structural inequality with micro-power relations and their effect on the action rationality of legal subjects. Conversely, it obscures the influence on legal professionals of relational bonds, particularly bonds of collegial solidarity and loyalty to the core values of the legal system.

Empathy

We view empathy as an emotive-cognitive tool that allows one to imagine what it would be like to be 'the other' person and thus to experience a situation from their perspective (see Cuff et al 2016). The empathizer acquires insights in a range of different aspects of being the other. The more aspects that are considered and the more attuned they are with the other, the more accurate the perspective-taking of the other, the 'empathizee', will be (Morton 2013); feeling the emotions that inform the other's perspective and thereby gaining understanding of the other's thinking and action. Importantly, the imaginative work required by the empathizer is facilitated if the other already shares significant perspectives with the empathizer, for instance if both empathizer and empathizee are highly educated middle-class women (Clark 1997). Empathy is partly an acquired capacity; the reading of fiction, for instance, has been demonstrated beneficial for enhancing empathic capacities (Oatley 2009). In professional contexts like state institutions, empathy is often used instrumentally to facilitate communication and legitimacy with clients/customers (for example, Goodrum and Stafford 2003; Jacobsson 2008; Larsson 2014). Instrumental empathy is limited to the understanding needed for pursuing the professional goals of the empathizer and does not take a deeper interest in understanding the other.

In this vein, in the legal context, previous research has demonstrated empathy as fundamental for judges presiding in court (for example, Bergman Blix 2019; Glynn and Sen 2015; Roach Anleu and Mack 2017) for the collective professional doing of legal objectivity (Bergman Blix and

Wettergren 2019) and for increasing the legitimacy of the legal system (for example, Bladini and Bergman Blix 2022; Mack and Roach Anleu 2010; Maroney 2012; Maroney and Gross 2014). Here, empathy is used to take the perspective of the legal subjects' apprehension of what is happening in court and how the professional actors are perceived by them. It is also used to anticipate and prevent foreground emotional disturbance of the smooth and efficient court procedure. In this book (Chapter 11) we also see that judges employ empathic attunement in the writing of rape case judgments.

Wettergren and Bergman Blix (2016) further demonstrated that prosecutors use their empathy instrumentally in the translation of real events to legally encoded offences presented to the courts. Empathy enables prosecutors to imagine the intent of the offender and the size of the damage to the victim to determine the precise charges. Prosecutors also use empathy to anticipate how the presentation of evidence would appear from the judges' and defence lawyers' perspectives, helping them select 'good' evidence and plan the presentation of evidence. Empathy used by prosecutors was thus shown to be a matter of degree, contingent on the professional instrumental need to know enough to be able to prosecute. In other words, prosecutorial empathy was limited to the aspects sufficient for knowing how to translate lay narratives into legal codes (Bladini et al 2023; Wettergren and Bergman Blix 2016). Oriented by a commitment to the legal encoding and pride in legal expertise, professional empathy shielded prosecutors from excessive perspective-taking that might evoke foreground emotions of anger and sadness, and thus the risk of becoming too emotionally involved in a case.

If professional empathy is instrumentally used by prosecutors to tune in with the actors involved in a criminal incident, judges go by the legal encoding as presented by the prosecutor when preparing the case and need not engage in much empathic imagination themselves. In rape cases, however, the main evidence being the complainant's story, we argue that judges need to use empathic imagination to gain insights into the emotive-cognitive motives and action rationality of the parties. We demonstrate in the analysis that this can be facilitated by prosecutors complementing their legal encoding work with 'empathic translation' of the evidence. Empathic translation means the prosecutors dwell on explicating their own empathic insights in the complainant's emotive-cognitive action rationality, that is, the way it makes sense to the prosecutor.

Whether judges admit their need for empathic attunement in rape cases or not, their empathic imagination is strategically targeted by the legal actors' 'empathy negotiation' for their respective clients (Bladini et al 2023; Uhnoo et al 2024c). Empathy negotiation is defined in this book as the strategic conveyance of the complainant's or the defendant's situated emotive-cognitive action rationality, enabling judges to tune in with the crucial aspects of their perspectives to determine (non-)voluntariness and intent. It invites the court to *feel* the legal meaning of the story, holistically, and not just approach it instrumentally. Empathy negotiation involves 'temporal boundary work', a concept emerging from our analysis, denoting the legal actors' efforts to strategically define the beginning and end of 'the situation as a whole' (see Chapter 2). By extending or contracting 'the situation as a whole' they can highlight select interactions between the parties in the argumentation for or against expressed voluntariness or criminal intent. Our analysis demonstrates that the prosecution, but foremost the defence, also use temporal boundary work to place 'empathy hooks' and what we simply call '*Things*' (cf Zizek 1989). Empathy hooks can be anything that aims to prompt the judges' perspective-taking imagination, such as '[imagine:] the complainant is sitting in my client's lap moving her hips – how was he supposed to understand that?' or '[imagine:] the complainant is alone in her home at night with an intoxicated stranger – how is she supposed to deal with that?' Empathy hooks facilitate 'the feeling of knowing' (Chapter 4).

We define *Things* as any 'unexplainable' element in the parties' stories that can be marked as irrational or paradoxical and that therefore obstructs empathic attunement. In the analysis, we see that defence lawyers routinely identify an abundance of (potential) *Things* in the complainant's story. In the name of doing objectivity, prosecutors usually reveal what they consider to be elements in the complainant's stories that need to be highlighted for them *not* to be left unexplained. In so doing prosecutors unintentionally aid the defence in selecting the *Things* to mark as crucial for doubt. In the judgments, we recurrently saw *Things,* advanced by the defence, turned into 'objective' reasons for acquitting. *Things* thus serve as ontological anchors to give off the impression that legal logics are neutral, and that the verdict is based on facts alone.

Prosecutors' empathic translation may include both temporal boundary work and empathy hooks, but this is presented as evidence 'to speak for itself' and their own in-depth understanding of the meaning of the evidence is rarely conveyed to the judges. Nor do prosecutors actively negotiate empathy for the complainant during the trial, for fear of compromising the objectivity requirement. In the analysis we show that, in the trial, the victim counsels can instead successfully take on the role as empathy negotiator for the complainant.

Common sense

In the analysis, we demonstrate how common sense and personal experience are drawn upon to make sense of the evidence in rape cases. We understand common sense as the background emotions of the obvious and the normal (see discussion of the legal discourse on this in Chapter 2). Common sense is thus not the same for everyone but differs depending on social group belonging and experience and we may also distinguish professional from private common sense. Professional common sense, we argue, originates in work experience and the feeling of knowing the ropes of the profession. It may be common sense among surgeons how to operate on a broken leg and it is common sense among judges how to perform legal logics. This means that legal common sense rests on core legal values and habituated ways of doing objectivity and autonomy in legally rational ways, governed by the emotive-cognitive judicial frame. We use the term 'legal logics' to denote this professional legal common sense.

'Private common sense' refers to the life experience of belonging to a certain social category or group, and the norms and feeling rules shared with other people from the same group (cf Smith 1987). Two fundamental social categories are women and men. Although common sense varies inter-sectionally between social groups within the gender categories, in the context of rape legislation and its practical implementation it appears that a *gendered* common sense shared by the majority female or male experience cuts across different social backgrounds and informs the judgment. We use the term 'hersense' and 'hissence' for these kinds of generic and gendered common sense. Given that, as argued previously, the emotive-cognitive judicial frame originates from the viewpoint of nineteenth-century privileged white men, whose gaze on the world was believed to be the neutral and rational one (cf Haraway 1988, 1992), it is no wonder that hissensical reasoning and legal logics easily coincide. The generic element is seen in how rape myths structurally embedded in the legal system, on the one hand, provide a resource for *all* rape accused men (for example, the 'she lies' myth; see Chapter 4). The privileged element, on the other hand, is seen in the fact that some of these structurally embedded rape myths (for example, the 'typical rapist' myth; see Chapters 8 and 9) only serve as a resource to *some* men.

The same can be argued about hersense. As we will show in the empirical chapters, the new rape legislation opens up the opportunity for generic hersensical reasoning, notably by stating the active party's responsibility to seek consent/voluntariness. In other words, the law legitimizes hersense to blend with legal logics and, by inference, to challenge the bond between legal logics and hissense. As radical a potential as this may be, we must also keep in mind that hersensical legal logics also contain both generic and privileged perspectives. Further, the concepts of hissense and hersense are not to be confounded with the sex of the legal professional. Educated and trained within the emotive-cognitive judicial frame, both women and men who go by the conventional and habituated doing of objectivity, rationality and autonomy are likely to reproduce hissensical legal logics in rape cases. This was seen in the majority of cases, regardless of the sex of the legal professionals. It is, however, interesting to note that skilled defence lawyers in our cases explicitly and repeatedly 'reminded' the court that rape cases should be handled as 'any other criminal case' in terms of standard of evidence. These 'objectivity rule reminders', as we call them, worked as a strategy against the intention of the new law, invoking the critique of the new rape law for potentially violating of the rule of law. Objectivity rule reminders thus pressed the fear of professional failure potentially attached to exploring the new law's hersensical dimensions (Uhnoo et al 2024c).

We now leave the theoretical part of this chapter and proceed to the last part in which we present our research design and provide an overview of the data collected.

Methodology

Our method was qualitative, inspired by ethnography. In line with the theoretical framework, our interest was to study how background emotions of legal professionals facilitated the import of common sense, sexual stereotypes and rape myths. Importantly, because background emotions operate in ongoing everyday (rationality of) action, they are unlikely to be reported in interviews inquiring about emotion. Therefore, investigating background emotions requires the combination of observations and interviews. Previous research on background emotions of legal professionals used the technique of using detailed notes from court observations to prompt judges and prosecutors to recall and reflect on specific sequences of emotive-cognitive exchanges in which they had been involved (for example, Bergman Blix and Wettergren 2018, 2019). The method of shadowing (Czarniawska 2007; McDonald 2005), which allows quick validations of the researcher's interpretations of what is happening was also fruitfully used.

Apart from this, observations and shadowing are great tools in the study of background emotions because they enable the researcher to interpret emotional expressions (mimics, gestures, body movements) in context (cf Kleres 2011) by relating the expressions to what was said and done in that moment. Context is crucial for understanding the meaning of emotive-cognitive behaviour and expressions. Comparing the parts (for example, expressions) to the whole (the context) is also a classical way of doing qualitative 'hermeneutic' analysis (cf Scheff 1997). The method reappears in narrative emotion analysis where verbatim and linguistic parts are compared to dramatic structure of the story (Kleres 2011) and in discourse analysis where the meaning of signifiers are revealed through analysis of the emerging network of signs and the discourse as a whole (Jörgensen and Philips 2002). In qualitative analysis, parts and wholes are related and compared in several steps at several levels of analysis, from the descriptive to the interpretative (Wolcott 1994), which eventually allows for theorizing and theoretical development by relating to extant theory (Halkier 2011). In previous studies of emotions in Swedish courts, this is how the theory of professional legal emotions and the concept of the emotive-cognitive frame were originally generated (for example, Bergman Blix and Wettergren 2018, Wettergren and Bergman Blix 2021). In this study, as previously described, this theory was developed with feminist legal studies to understand the implementation of the new rape law.

Methods of data collection

We collected three types of qualitative data; *field notes* from observations of 20 live court hearings (six trials in the DC, 14 in the AC), one detention hearing and five observations of deliberations; *written judgments* (DC and, if appealed, AC) from all our 18 cases; and *tape-recorded and transcribed interviews* including in total 62 interviews with legal actors (for more detail, see next sub-section).

With findings of previous research as a point of departure, in the present project our interest was in the emotive-cognitive handling of a particular offence, shifting our focus from general legal emotive-cognitive work to the specific one enacted in rape cases. Since shadowing is a time-consuming method, in the present project we shadowed only a few participants involved in our cases, prioritizing a broader scope of interviews with as many as possible legal professionals involved in each case.

Shadowing in most of the cases was restricted to meeting the legal actor who was our first contact in each case, be it a lawyer, judge or prosecutor, before the trial, spending the breaks with them, and a short debriefing or follow-up interview after the trial. In three cases, we shadowed the preliminary investigations, involving some detention hearings, reading the case files and inviting continuous feedback face-to-face or via telephone from the prosecutors. Notes were taken of these conversations.

The interviews were semi-structured using thematic interview guides, including general questions about the new law and/or specific questions about a case followed where the interviewee had been involved. The general interviews included reflections on the new law and its norm-changing intentions, the evidence and the assessments, reflections on the criterion of voluntariness and its legal meaning, and so on. We also asked about reflections on the role of social status, impressions, eloquence and common sense, all significant for analysing background emotions in rape cases. The general interviews unfolded as conversations and left plenty of room for the interviewees' own associations and follow-up questions, while the case-specific interviews were more focused on probing what we had observed during the trials and questions about the wording or logics of the judgments.

It should be noted that in the empirical chapters we use 'follow-up interview' to denote an interview that followed upon observation of a case in which the interviewee was involved. Due to time constraints, this was not always separated from the general interviews. In a few cases, the general interview was conducted before and a follow-up after the observation. In most cases, general and the specific interview themes were merged in an interview guide divided in two parts. Only general interviews were conducted with individual and focus groups of legal actors who were not involved in specific cases. Focus group interviews are marked as 'GI' (group interview) in the empirical chapters, but without pseudonyms (for example, 'DC judge, GI').

As for the observations, we aimed to observe cases live in the DC and follow through to the AC to observe the trial there too and to interview as many of the legal actor involved as possible. As we collected our data during COVID-19, with periodical restrictions concerning both travel and people present in the courts, we sometimes had to make do with the AC trials. As described in Chapter 2, in 2008 the AC began to use video records of all hearings in DC trials instead of redoing the hearings live. This means that attending an AC trial also provided satisfactory information of the DC trial. We collected all written judgments from the DC and AC of our 18 cases. In Sweden, judgments are made public in full for all criminal trials, but the personal details of the complainant are omitted from rape judgments.

Recruitment, data and access

Data collection took place between June 2020 and June 2022. Recruitment was initialized by presenting the project at four strategically selected District Courts and two appeals courts, and thereafter based on self-selection and snowballing. We followed 18 rape cases and made 58 audio-recorded in-depth interviews with individual legal professionals, and an additional four focus group (three in each) audio-recorded interviews with female and male lawyers respectively, and one focus group interview with three District Court judges. Three interviews with appeals court judges involved in our cases were made with two judges in each to save their time. In total we interviewed 23 AC/DC judges, 15 prosecutors and 24 defence lawyers/victim counsels. The gender ratio was 42 per cent men. For all 18 cases we observed and took field notes of the trials, collected indictments, judgments and appeals. In five cases we were allowed to observe AC and/or DC deliberations, and in two cases we followed the preliminary investigation. Table 1 describes the data collected in our 18 cases.

As seen in the table, we managed to secure interviews with the prosecutors in all but two cases. In the rest of our cases, we interviewed the DC judges in seven cases and the AC judges in 15 cases. In two cases, 5 and 12, we could only conduct interviews with one of the legal actors, the prosecutor, but in both we followed the preliminary investigations. To cover up for missing data, we conducted a few supplementary individual and focus group interviews (not included in the table). AC judges involved with a case were interviewed together to minimize their time, but also given pseudonyms (for example, 'Petter and Lisa, Case 7').

We also see in the table that four cases were not appealed, while two cases withdrew their appeals after the AC trial but before conviction, presumably because the defence anticipated conviction and a longer sentence than given by the DC. In the remaining 12 cases, six were changed by the AC from acquittal to conviction or the reverse. Three of these were so-called lay judgments (see Chapter 2). Together with the two withdrawn cases, this renders a changed verdict rate of 43 per cent (six out of 14 cases). As will be seen in the empirical chapters, AC judgments confirming the verdict of the DC sometimes also contained significant changes, but in terms of the evaluation of the evidence, and thus the reasoning, motivating the verdict. Noteworthy is that there are two cases included in our material that deviate from the vast majority of the rape cases in terms of the gender of the victim or the offender: one involving a male victim and female offender (Case 16), and another involving a male victim and male offender (Case 5).

Our initial interest was in cases in which a breach against voluntariness was the main charge. We were also initially keen to observe cases in which the new offence of negligent rape would be used either as the main or alternative charge. It soon became clear that, while a breach against voluntariness was routinely mentioned in most rape cases, other charges were often also added, such as the use of violence or force. However, this did not mean that voluntariness was not dealt with by the courts in those cases. As will be seen in the analysis, there was often confusion regarding the status of one prerequisite in relation to the other, which opened some interesting new issues, informative of the uncertainty surrounding the application of the new law. The use of the charge of negligent rape as a primary charge was extremely rare (see Chapter 1) and therefore we dropped it.[2]

Collecting data during COVID-19 entailed that we occasionally missed out on observing cases in the DC due to travel and physical presence restrictions. Additionally, in a couple of cases, access to the live trial in the DC was denied by the professional judge. In other cases, already in the process of appeal, we were asked by the lawyers or prosecutors to follow, as they thought they would be of particular interest to us. All these situations meant that we could only observe the DC proceedings played back in the AC (for an in-depth discussion of our access to the court proceedings, see Uhnoo et al 2024a).

---

[2] Elsewhere, we have analysed a small number of cases using this charge (Wallin et al 2021), indicating some interesting implications such as the 'remorse defence', which calls for further research if negligent rape becomes more common.

Table 1: Overview of the data in the 18 cases followed

Case no.	Observation DC	Outcome DC	Observation AC	Outcome AC	Interviewed legal professionals
Case 1	Observation, incl. deliberation	*Convicted, rape*	Not Appealed		P, DCJ
Case 2	Observation, followed PI	*Acquitted, rape*	Not Appealed		P, DL, VC, DCJ
Case 3	–	Convicted, rape	Observation	*Convicted, rape*	P, VC, ACJ
Case 4	–	Convicted, sexual assault	Observation	*Convicted, sexual assault*	P, DL, ACJ,
Case 5	Followed PI, observation of remand hearing	*Convicted, rape*	Not Appealed		P
Case 6	–	Convicted, rape	Observation, incl. deliberation	*Convicted, rape*	P, DL, ACJ1, ACJ2
Case 7	–	Convicted, rape	Observation	*Acquitted, rape*	P, DL, ACJ1, ACJ2,
Case 8	–	Acquitted, rape	Observation	*Convicted, rape*	P, DL, ACJ1, ACJ2,
Case 9	Observation	Convicted, rape	Observation, incl. deliberation	*Acquitted, rape*	P, VC, DCJ, ACJ1, ACJ2
Case 10	Observation, incl. deliberation	Acquitted, rape	Observation	*Acquitted, rape*	DL, VC, DCJ
Case 11	Observation	*Convicted, rape*	Observation	Appeal withdrawn before final court decision	P, VC
Case 12	Followed PI	*Convicted, rape*	Observation	Appeal withdrawn before final court decision	P
Case 13	–	Convicted, negligent rape	Observation, incl. deliberation	*Convicted, rape*	P, ACJ1, ACJ2

Table 1: Overview of the data in the 18 cases followed (continued)

Case no.	Observation DC	Outcome DC	Observation AC	Outcome AC	Interviewed legal professionals
Case 14	Observation	*Acquitted, rape*	Not Appealed		P, DL1, VC, DCJ
Case 15	–	Acquitted, rape	Observation	*Acquitted, rape*	P, VC, DCJ
Case 16	–	Acquitted, rape, Lay judgment	Observation	*Convicted, rape*	DCJ, ACJ
Case 17	–	Acquitted, rape, Lay judgment	Observation	*Convicted, rape*	P, DL, DCJ,
Case 18	–	Acquitted, rape., Lay judgment	Observation	*Convicted, rape*	P, VC, ACJ,
	In total: 6 observations and 1 remand hearing. Deliberation observed in 2 cases.	Conviction: 10 Acquittal: 8	In total: 14 observations, deliberation observed in 3 cases	Conviction: 8 Acquittal: 4 AW: 2 Verdict changed: 6	P in 16 cases DL in 7 cases VC in 8 cases J in 15 cases (DCJ 8, ACJ 15)

Notes: PI = Preliminary investigation; AW = Appeal withdrawn before final court decision in AC; P = Prosecutor; DL = Defence lawyer; VC = Victim counsel; DCJ = District Court judge (professional judge); ACJ = Appeals Court judge (professional judges).

As mentioned, the primary selection criterion for interviewees was that they represented one of the legal professional categories involved in each case, and initially we aimed to cover all categories. A second selection criterion was a general interest in discussing the new consent-based rape law. While we succeeded in securing at least two of the categories of judge, prosecutor and lawyer involved in most cases, we accessed more AC judges than we did DC judges and more prosecutors than lawyers. Missing lawyers typically said they would be willing to do interviews when we met during the trial, but did not return our emails afterwards. The lack of lawyers in our material prompted a search for more lawyers interested in discussing the new rape law, which resulted in the two focus group interviews with lawyers unrelated to our 18 cases. It should be noted that several victim counsels also worked as defence lawyers and in their interviews drew on their experience of both. The 'missing' interviews with lawyers giving their perspective on the specific case were also compensated by field notes from the small talk, during breaks in the trial observations, in which lawyers were often keen to share their view on the case.

Noteworthy in this project is the interest that the AC judges took in our project. In our experience, AC judges are more difficult to engage in research than DC judges. One reason for this is that, because the AC is the last legal resort (in Sweden it is very rare that the Supreme Court accepts cases appealed to them, see Chapter 2), judges feel a pressure to sustain the emotive-cognitive judicial frame and to 'get the decision right'. In the present project, they were keen to communicate their views on the new law, whether asserting what they believed to be the correct way to apply it or conveying their carefully formulated critique and uncertainty about it. Given that access to AC judges is rare, we prioritized these over the interviews with DC judges.

The fact that the DC judge interviews are fewer is also due to some of the DC trials being observed from the AC trial, as mentioned previously. We deemed it likely to render rather limited information if we were to secure the DC judge for an interview about a case they had presided over months ago. In our experience, given the number of cases they handle, follow-up interviews needed to be conducted soon after the trial for judges to remember them, and especially for them to be able to recall background emotions. Instead, to learn more about their general view on the new law, we organized a group interview with DC judges.

From the theoretical perspective laid out previously, it may appear odd that, although our selection involves a fairly equal share of women (58 per cent) and men (42 per cent) we have only raised the issue of the gender of the legal professionals in a few particular cases analysed in the empirical chapters. There are several reasons for this. First, our qualitative method does not include a quantitative analysis of the correlation between the gender of the different legal professionals in each case and the particulars of the proceeding and of the judgment. The sample is too small for such an analysis to be meaningful. Second, a gender perspective saturates our theoretical framework and is observed in how we dig in-depth into the analysis of aspects of reasoning or judging of relevance for this perspective. We have only raised the gender of the particular professionals involved in cases when this can be related to a particular finding indicating, for instance, if female legal professionals seem to draw on hersense to inform their empathic imagination, or male professionals draw on hissense (for example, Chapter 5). The dominant pattern, however, is that the legal professional role performances, regardless of gender, adhere to the conventional understanding of the core legal values as embedded in the emotive-cognitive judicial frame. The fact that traditional legal logics blend with hissense, as previously argued, means that female legal actors are not, per se, more inclined to favour a female perspective than are their male colleagues.

Ethical considerations

The project was approved by the Swedish Ethical Board (Dnr. 2020–02205). All participants were informed both orally and in writing about the conditions of participation and the storage, treatment and use of the data before accepting to participate. All geographical and personal identifiers were removed and, in some cases, particular details were changed or omitted. All place and person names in the analysis are pseudonyms.

In Sweden, rape trials are closed to the public to protect the integrity of the complainant. Given our focus on legal professionals, and for ethical reasons, complainants and defendants were not included as participants in the project. They were, however, always informed, verbally and in a written document, via their respective lawyers. We always began by informing and asking the complainant for permission to attend before we decided to follow a case, since the closed doors are meant to protect them. When granted permission from the complainant (in all the cases) permission to attend still hinged on the presiding judges (for details, see Uhnoo et al 2024a), except in cases where we followed the judge.

Lay judges were not included in the study because they are not legal professionals. Previous research, observed that lay judges tend to go by the professional judge's assessment. If this is not the case, the judgment is always appealed by the legal professionals. In the AC, the division between professional judges and lay judges is three to two, hence the verdict of the lay judgment from the DC is transformed into a professional verdict, which most often means that it is changed (Bergman Blix and Wettergren 2018). Lay judges have limited influence on the application of the law (see, for instance, Chapter 8).

Note on methods of analysis

All transcripts from observations and interviews were imported into the qualitative data program ATLAS.ti and read and coded thematically; codes were processed into categories and subcategories. As is very common in qualitative analysis, we used an abductive approach (Alvesson and Sköldberg 2009; Halkier 2011; Wolcott 1994), drawing on both existing theoretical concepts (for example, 'empathy') and new themes derived from the data (for example, 'empathy negotiation', 'empathy hook' and 'empathy translation') as codenames for patterns identified in the analysis. We worked together during the main part of the coding process to ensure an intersubjective agreement on the patterns emerging in the data, and their interpretation, and how the patterns and empirically grounded concepts (for example, empathy translation, empathy hooks, *Things*) linked to the broader theoretical framework.[3]

In Chapter 12 we call for developing a legal method of evaluating the qualitative character of the evidence in rape cases. Here, we will merely highlight a few things of importance both for our own method of analysis and for the discussion in Chapter 12.

First, there is really no such thing as objective factual data or evidence. Whether the evidence consists of stories, numbers or physical artefacts, its meaning is dependent on social interpretation. Interpretation is in turn contingent on previous experience and knowledge, that is, a lay or professional 'theoretical' framework. The correctness of the conclusions drawn through interpretation must be intersubjective to claim extra-subjective relevance. Hence, all interpretations must be communicated and consciously reflected upon to gain intersubjectively corroborated status. The factual correctness, applicability and generalizability of intersubjective conclusions is tested by using these conclusions, or the 'theory' on the next set of data, and, again, the intersubjective reflection on the results. Proceeding this way is arguably the closest we can move to objective status of any knowledge about the world.

Second, when working with human stories, which is something we do all the time in social science, we are aware of interpreting interpretations (double hermeneutics; for example Alvesson and Sköldberg 2009). The stories conveyed through interviews or observations are not imprints of 'the real' but are always already tainted by social, cultural, linguistic imaginaries and delimitations and by personal histories and perspectives. When we conducted interviews with legal professionals, we were obviously aware

---

[3]   This was done in one month as a visiting group at the Centre of Interdisciplinary Research in Bielefeld (November 2023).

that we co-produced their stories by asking particular questions, and that the interviewees adapted their answers to who we were and the topic in question, and that they may think, feel and share differently with others about the same topic. Thus, we do not pretend that our data reflect the only or, in the individual case, most real story of legal professional approaches to the new law. Given the number and in-depth quality of interviews, and comparing the interviews with our observations and our reading of the judgments (part-whole analysis see below), and finally comparing our findings with our own and other's previous research, so-called analytical generalization (Halkier 2011), we feel confident that our results render a reasonably correct view of the application of the new law by legal practice, during the first three years of its implementation.

Third, and in line with the second point, qualitative inquiry targets commonalities and patterns in human behaviour that delve beyond research participants' own understanding by comparing *talk*, conveying the subject's own interpterion's, to *doing*, observing actions, and the *outcomes* of action and interaction. The main approach in qualitative analysis, often referred to as a 'hermeneutic spiral' (Alvesson and Sköldberg 2009), can be applied as an umbrella concept to the above to denote how the generation of robust understanding of the social is a matter of comparison. Comparison occurs both between different sets of similar data (interviews) and different kinds of data (interviews, observations and written judgments). In the hermeneutic interpretive process, each coded segment is thus compared with the broader set of emerging codes and categories, or the parts are compared with the whole. Through this, qualitative research digs into the mechanisms and rationales of human action that are not necessarily the same as their own interpretation or understanding of it. While legal professionals reading this book may not agree with all our interpretations, we hope that our study will inspire them to reflect on their own understanding of what they do at work.

Conclusion

In this chapter, we described our theoretical framework and main concepts, including concepts derived from the empirical analysis. We described and argued for the integration of feminist legal theory and the theory of the sociology of emotions to enhance understanding of the matters at stake when legal actors apply the new rape law. We thereafter explained our methodology and provided an overview of the data in our 18 cases. We concluded the chapter with a brief discussion of qualitative interpretation, double hermeneutics and how knowledge about the social world necessitates collective and intersubjective critical reflexivity.

PART II

The Making of Legal Objectivity

4

The Feeling of Not Knowing

Introduction

This chapter investigates the professional uncertainty and ambivalence/discomfort associated with rape cases, particularly after the implementation of the new rape law. Following on from Chapter 2, describing the legal framework of the new law, we begin with a brief overview of emotive-cognitive reflections of the professional legal actors about the law, and a discussion on how types of common sense are involved in their reasoning. Thereafter, we focus on the production of evidence to scrutinize the most common professional legal concern with rape cases, invoked as the reason for the high attrition and the relatively low conviction rates: the 'bad' evidence and the risk of lowering the standard of proof. Prosecutor Sandra (Case 8) reasoned about this:

> In these [rape] cases, we have no, there are no eyewitnesses. There is, of course, sometimes technical evidence. The technical evidence is only relevant if there are people who didn't want to lie in that bed at all. Usually there are no injuries to the victims either because it's not that kind of violence. And when it comes to the genitals, it's actually the case that even if you have bruises and such in the genitals, not bruises perhaps, but sometimes you can have such cases, because you always do this kind of rape kit. Then it may be that the complainant actually has redness and perhaps bruises, but it can … the professional medics often say that it can arise during voluntary sexual intercourse, so that doesn't say anything. Instead, the evidence we have is really the complainant, how she talks and how she acts plus uh … like this circumstantial evidence. That's what's important because we don't have any other evidence and there aren't many other offences that can be judged on the basis of a complainant's story with a little … the complainant's reaction afterwards and some other things … You could say. So it's like … it's a special … I'm not going to say that the standard

of proof has been lowered, but it is a different type of evaluation of evidence. Because otherwise it wouldn't be possible to handle these offences. The legislator and the public have implemented this in some way, for better or worse.

As we see in the quote, the problem with the evidence seems to be rooted in the lack of eyewitnesses and the assumption that, without them, it is impossible to know what happens in a closed room where people have sex. What remains then is the complainant's story and 'how she talks and how she acts'. That this makes Sandra ambivalent is seen in how she first asserts that 'there aren't many other offences that can be judged on the basis of a complainant's story', but immediately goes on to refute allegations that this would lower the standards of evidence. The quote ends with her saying that, in order 'to handle these offences', this is how it has to be 'for better or for worse'.

We conceptualize the concern regarding the 'bad evidence' as a 'feeling of not knowing', which, contrasting other criminal offences, seem to linger in the handling of rape cases. Central in Sandra's quote, however, is the statement that 'it is a different type of evaluation of evidence' required in rape cases. We thus argue that it is not only the character of the evidence but perhaps even more the legal approach to the evidence that is the root of the uncertainty and discomfort reported by legal actors. The legal approach, in conformity with the emotive-cognitive judicial frame, rests on collectively reproduced established understandings of objectivity, rationality and autonomy as neutral and socio-culturally isolated phenomena. The evidence in rape cases shakes and destabilizes the common understanding of these values and thus the habituated legal approach.

Destabilization is due to the evidence centring on subjective narratives, something that is normally an object of professional legal irritation. In the emotive-cognitive judicial frame, irritation usually carries several important epistemic signal functions that help sort out the irrelevant from the relevant information in juridical assessments (Bergman Blix and Wettergren 2018, 2019; Törnqvist and Wettergren 2023). That stories and impressions, in rape cases, instead move to the centre stage as main evidence constitutes a break with established ways of doing things. This further requires legal professionals to consciously reflect on background emotional information, which they do not normally do. In short, focusing on others' and one's own emotions as relevant information conflicts with the emotive-cognitive judicial frame's rule to 'put emotions aside'. The asserted feeling of not knowing thus targets both the evidence and how to make sense of it.

This chapter focuses on the emotive-cognitive reasoning of all legal professionals and thereby prepares for analysis of the professional legal roles (the doing of objectivity, rationality and autonomy) in the book. The particulars of the judicial decision-making and judgments will be treated in depth in Chapters 10 and 11.

Emotive-cognitive reasoning around the new law

Each legal professional role has a pattern in their way of answering the question of whether and, if so, how the new law has changed their work with rape cases. Defence lawyers generally express anger at the law for undermining the rule of law. One reason is the unpredictability of rape case trials. For instance, defence lawyer Svante (Case 8) stated:

> Well, it [the new law] has significance in the sense that I … am considering quitting that type of case. Actually … I think it's, I probably won't stop anyway because I think that my – you … should do the best you can. You should do what is possible to do. Even if … well, I have never [engaged in predictions like] this will go this way or that way. It's the court that decides. But I have been able to make a reasonably … balanced judgment and, most of the time, I think I have been quite right. Uh … but … I feel that's basically impossible today. So that, I'm thinking of … to … to let go of that area, but at the same time … well, who should then do it?

Svante says he can no longer make 'a reasonably balanced judgment' and therefore is considering quitting rape cases. Suggesting that different judges diverge too greatly in how they evaluate the evidence, the unpredictability undermines the rule of law in terms of legal certainty. This concern is shared by some prosecutors. A claim made exclusively by defence lawyers is that the law makes their work harder. Svante continued:

> And then there's … a huge number of unreported cases. Who are not … who are not convicted. Or yes, many acquittals that should have been convicted. They – that's how we've perceived [the meaning of] legal certainty, until now. You could say that. There isn't the same legal certainty in these cases anymore.

What Svante was trying to communicate in this quotation is that legal certainty under the rule of law used to mean that many 'who should have been convicted' were acquitted because the evidence was not enough to convict beyond reasonable doubt. That this has now changed, he seemed to suggest, means that something has changed in the evaluation of the evidence. He did not go as far as some other defence lawyers, who explicitly claimed that the burden of proof has shifted from the prosecution to the defence. According to this reasoning, if the court believes the complainant's story, the defence must provide counterevidence to refute the charges (see Chapter 8). However, some defence lawyers stated that many innocent men are now sent to prison. For instance, defence lawyer Ulla (Case 6) outlined two of her recent cases, in which she was stupefied when her clients were convicted. The researcher asked if she experienced that more people were innocently convicted of rape today: 'Yes, I have to think so because I believe that these two are innocently convicted and I don't have that experience from before … uh … to have that feeling, no. Whether it's true or not I don't know, but that's my opinion'.

For lawyers also acting in the role of victim counsel, the answer to the question about their view of the new law seemed to vary depending on the role perspective from which they were speaking. This was the case with Ulla, who was equally upset by the cases in which she represented the complainant and equally stupefied by the acquittal of the defendant in those. This alone is arguably indicative of the lack of legal certainty. In her role as victim counsel, Erika (Case 9) expressed her view of the new law:

Researcher:	Have things changed in your opinion? With this new law?
Erika:	Yes, I think we've moved away from those details about outfit and so on. […] Now it's more on, like around the sex act and the sex act itself, which is good if you can get a lot of details about it. Then of course there's the person. Is it a credible person? It may have to do with personality. But any other improvement as it is, I think there is more … focus now than before on … the suspect's responsibility to explain how he perceived this consent … Well, there are more detailed requirements on him, if you like, or on the perpetrator. You could say that. And I think I can see that. How was this consent expressed? Not just [*makes groaning sound*] but, it's, there are a lot of questions about it … And why? I think it has to do with the fact that the legislator has said that there must be consent in every single step. It's not enough at the beginning of a sexual act, or when you're making out, that you think, 'Now we're both in on this', but when we make new decisions during the actual sex act, we both must be in on it.

Erika expressed a rather ideal view on the new law, as it might work, or works in some cases. Meanwhile, as reflected in the quotation, both lawyers and prosecutors expressed concern about the high demand on the legal subjects' ability to talk, their eloquence and ability to provide detailed descriptions. Defence lawyers said that this makes it even more difficult to defend foreigners or migrants, while prosecutors (as we will discuss later) were concerned about the eloquence of the complainants.

A common pattern concerning the role of prosecutor exclusively was the opinion that the new law made prosecution and indictments easier. We discussed this in Chapter 1, in which we observed that indictments had increased by 41 per cent (between 2017 and 2019). Interestingly, it was common to begin the answer like prosecutor Jan (Case 6), with the very low expectations he had for the new law:

> I was a little sceptical when this change in the law came about because I thought that it is still the same difficulties with evidence, we may not get what they are looking for. But I have changed my mind. I think that we have caught quite a few cases that could not be prosecuted in the old way and where it is actually possible to obtain a conviction. When it is the case that the complainant has not put up the slightest resistance … In the past, when rape was reported, it was often … objectively speaking, rape was not … there had been no violence, there had been no threat, it had just been against their will, so I think the new change in the law wasn't so bad.

As mentioned, prosecutors also worry about the legal uncertainty concerning court decisions and the required eloquence of the complainant. Another view sometimes expressed was an unease with the minimum penalty of two years (since 2022, three years). Jan continued:

> I can think that the actual rape legislation is a bit … blunt in that it becomes so incredibly serious right away. Either it's nothing or it's two years in prison, and you feel that sometimes it would … objectively speaking, it might not be worth two years in prison if a friend insists on having sex, but it might be a lower prison sentence; one year might have been adequate. If you look at types of offences, if we take aggravated assault, to get two years, you basically have to have stabbed someone in the stomach. It takes an incredible amount [of violence] … I think the whole rape legislation is a bit unbalanced.

The quote reflects a particular idea about what should render two years in prison (the 'real rape'), accentuated by juxtaposing aggravated assault and rape. This and similar expressions of power discomfort are more commonly expressed by judges than by prosecutors. The latter are usually confident about the case and the defendant's guilt when they prosecute and, in the end, the decision is not theirs but the judges'. Thus, it says something about the new law if some prosecutors question its proportionality. Elsewhere, we have analysed this power discomfort as an expression of structurally embedded himpathy (Uhnoo et al 2024c). However, comparing the penalty value of rape with crimes like aggravated assault does raise seemingly reasonable questions.

One such question is why prosecutors, if they feel that two years' prison is too high in some cases, do not use the possibility to instead charge for negligent rape (see Chapter 2). When we asked this question, prosecutors generally argued that the requisite of intent for negligent rape was too difficult to differentiate from the requisite of rape, so, if the evidence was sufficient to prove negligent rape, it was also good enough for rape.[1] Hence, the professional emotional profile of prosecutors – the display of confidence in the evidence and certainty about the defendant's guilt – makes them inclined to try the more serious charge. Following this way of reasoning, charging for negligent rape might signal a lack of confidence in the case.

That said, prosecutors above all displayed confusion vis-à-vis the new crime of negligent rape even when they used it as alternative ground for indictment. Prosecutor Barbro (Case 15) referred to a workshop in her prosecution office in which it was decided to always include negligent rape, as a safeguard, as a secondary claim. But she did not like doing so:

Researcher:	Is there something in the fact that [negligent rape] also radiates an uncertainty that … the offence of rape would not carry?
Barbro:	Exactly, that's how many times you think about secondary claims that it's like you're implying that it could be so … But you don't want to risk … that's always the case with all situations … you open a small possibility for the court to believe that even the prosecutor can believe that [negligent rape] is the case, but the prosecutor rarely brings any evidence or hardly raises the issue [of negligent rape] at all. This may be explained by the fact that … you are so determined that it is not negligence, but you want to cover it up because you don't want to risk that [the judges] write in the judgment that it is not … it must be included because otherwise they cannot convict [for negligent rape].

---

[1] See also Brå (2020:6).

Including the charge of negligent rape to avoid 'risk' refers to the fact that the handling of negligent rape causes confusion for judges. Some judges argued that they could go on to assess negligent rape even if the prosecutors did not include it in the charges; others argued they might have convicted for negligent rape instead of acquitting if the prosecutor had included it in the charges, and they were surprised they did not do so. In any case, the new offence, negligent rape, was not seen as a viable alternative charge among our interviewees (see statistics in Chapter 1).

Judges' opinion about the new rape legislation was very carefully expressed in most interviews, but the overall argument was, as will be observed later in this chapter, that the new law certainly did not change the 'problem with the evidence' that always had been present in rape cases. According to AC judge Bengt, evaluation of stories was 'a bit like fortune telling in coffee grounds'. Other judges argued that there was not any difference between rape case assessment and other criminal cases (see Chapter 5).

A few judges, exemplified by DC Judge Monika (Case 9), expressed understanding of the norm-changing intention of the new law and seemed to balance the power discomfort, by judges associated with the high penalty value, with trust that the law (and the norms) would eventually settle. Case 9 was Monika's first rape case under the new law, and she began by expressing that she was as sceptical of the new law as were her colleagues, but that she actually found the evaluation of voluntariness interesting and different from the assessments made before the new law. The only problem she had now with the law was the high penalty value. She clarified:

Monika:	[T]here are many in the general public who believe that you can stop sexual abuse just by changing the legislation. It's never going to happen, but you can send signals and you can hope that they will eventually get through [...] it's not the least bit difficult, I would say, for normal functioning men to know what is voluntary and what is not voluntary, but you choose whether you want to do something with someone who doesn't want to. There are exceptions to this – very young, very immature people. Maybe people who have some kind of ... disability in some way. But otherwise everyone knows where the line is. It's not difficult ... and it's something that involves ... work that has to be done outside the courts, but at the same time, it's important what we do as well. That's how it is with everything ... uh ... it's not fun for those who get involved to become a kind of ... what should we call it ...
Researcher:	First cases ... setting the markers.

Monika: No, it's not, for them personally it's not [fun], but I still think it's good to have such legislation, as long as you don't think it can stop all sexual abuse because that's not going to happen.

Here, we note that Monika, in contrast to some other judges, is open to the idea that the legal system and surrounding society take a shared responsibility for changing norms about sexuality, and that she basically agrees with this function of the new law, even at the cost of the suffering of young men during a transition period. Conversely, she counters potential power discomfort by expressing confidence in 'most men'. From this perspective, the issue is a non-issue, she seems to argue, since 'normal functioning men' *know* when sex is not voluntary and are able to choose whether to continue or not. While this argument is in line with the legal perception of individual autonomy, it does put self-disciplining responsibility on the active, and hence the more powerful, party.

To Monika, it is common sense that normal men know the line when they see it. Thus, DC Judge Monika used her own common sense (about normal men) to convict in Case 9 and felt reasonably at ease with that decision, as she was at ease with the norm-changing function of the new legislation. This is a vivid example of how hersense can harmonize with legal logics. In the sub-section below, we briefly focus on different types of common sense and the potentially problematic role of those in rape cases.

Common sense for good and for bad

As will be observed throughout this book, we argue that common sense, drawing on lived experience and being oriented by feelings of familiarity and comfort, is often surreptitiously decisive in rape cases precisely because judges are *not* supposed to involve their lived experience in their decisions. This means they cannot discuss it and reflect upon it without risking compromising their professionality. Common sense derives from taken-for-granted and tacitly (presumably) shared norms and values, and part of this is closely connected to rape myths – but not all. As explained in Chapter 3, a crucial distinction originating in our analysis is the one between professional legal common sense, legal logics, and the gender-specific private common sense we call hissense and hersense.

In Judge Monika's example, we observed an example of a hersensical view upon the new law, asserting that it just cannot be that difficult for men to tell the difference between voluntary and non-voluntary sex. In other words, we noted that she could blend a female and privileged (in terms of social group or class) common sense with the legal common sense asserted by the new law. What makes this legal logics so deeply controversial may be that it advances a female perspective on sex and sexuality as a (new) purportedly neutral legal perspective.

We note that, besides taking a hersense perspective in her legal reasoning, Monika explicitly expressed even if 'it's not [fun]' for the young men potentially setting the markers of the new law 'I still think it's good to have such legislation'. It was rare for judges to explicitly express such a gendered position-taking on the law, but some, both female and male, prosecutors and victim counsels also did so. Men taking a female-gendered perspective (expressing that they endorse both the pros and cons of the new law) is arguably a consequence of professional work experience as specialized on gender-related crimes. Interestingly, some men expressing this view do so from a hersense legal logics perspective that may harmonize with the new law, but in some cases was noted to conflict with their personal common sense. For both judges and prosecutors, as previously indicated, such a dilemma, resulting in power discomfort, was most clearly apparent when the defendant evoked himpathy (Uhnoo et al 2024c). In these cases, it may be convenient to follow the norms of standard legal logics justifying the argument about 'the bad evidence'.

If Judge Monika's hersense perspective made her express some hope in the new law, the opposite can be said about the hissense perspective. Characteristic for this, as we have already observed in Svante's case, is to argue that the law simply does not adhere to the rule of law. How this hissense argument blends with legal logics is observed in the quotation from an interview with defence lawyer Olof. He alternated between referring to the new law and to his own personal experience to illustrate what he considered 'obvious', thereby conveying an implicit critique of the law:

> And that, I mean, a … sexual intercourse that starts voluntarily and at any time, any of the parties can say no, and if you then continue, it becomes rape. But usually, you don't talk much when you have sex or … I don't know. […] [T]raditional evaluation of evidence in these cases is what the person concerned has said afterwards to friends and psychologists and so on. But … for those who have been young … uh, have, tried drugs, has never been my thing, but have been drunk and had sex with the wrong person and *regrets* … I would say.
>
> […] Well but regrets. And that can take many different forms. […] I've had a wife or girlfriend all my adult life, but it's obvious that you've been exposed to temptations, in some ways, right. And especially when you're young. And then maybe, some, little fling, that has … it's something that all people, uh, can be exposed to and … that people are unfaithful … sometimes.

The statement highlights how personal experience and emotional memories formulated as a common-sense understanding overlap with Olof's juridical reasoning around the rape law. He described how, in his experience, women (and men) may regret the sex, and implied that non-voluntariness claims might be motivated by such regrets. Generally speaking, given that the new rape law extends criminalization to ways of acting that were previously not illegal, some adults no doubt remember situations from their youth that would make them either perpetrators or victims under the new law. This makes rape cases different from most other criminal cases, in which legal actors are instead rather unlikely to recognize themselves in the criminal act under scrutiny or even identify with the defendant or the complainant based on gendered experience.

When hissense blends with the purportedly neutral legal values of rationality, autonomy and objectivity, drawing on rape myths like 'she lies' become rationalized, also in legal decision-making. In rape cases, the question whether she has a reason to lie is thus part of testing alternative hypothesis to decide if the evidence presented by the prosecution holds beyond reasonable doubt.

A clear example of how hissense can influence judgments was observed in Case 15, in which elderly DC judge Göran acquitted a man charged with abuse of a woman in a particularly vulnerable situation. The defendant himself had testified that the complainant was almost delirious, vomited and could barely stand straight, and the complainant herself did not even remember the sex act. Still, the defendant claimed the complainant had wanted sex. In the follow-up interview, Judge Göran commented on the judgment in Case 15:

> It's clear that ... had there been any expert evidence about ... prevalence of amnesia and how it affects and what is known about ... the ability to understand what's going on ... it could have ... it's always good to have expert knowledge. Then I think, if I think back to my youth when I have suffered from amnesia on various occasions, as far as I understand ... it never meant that I was not aware of what was happening in the moment. I didn't think about this so much [in my decision], but it's the things I've written about in the judgment that ... that's what became [decisive].

In this case, Judge Göran felt that he knew, based on his own youth experience, that people can act rationally even when so drunk that they suffer from amnesia afterwards. The reasons given in the judgment, arguing it was not beyond reasonable doubt that the sex happened the way the defendant said, were the lack of 'expert evidence' in support of the complainant's level of intoxication and amnesia. While Göran hastened to say that the decision was not influenced by his own experience, he may have ruled differently if his experience had instead been that such a level of intoxication indeed could lead to sexual abuse.

In rape trials, in which guilt must be proven beyond reasonable doubt, a particular complexity emerges where gendered interests clash (the male defendant being protected by a fair trial, the female complainant being offered legal protection against sexual violence) and intertwined with gendered experiences and fears (male fear v female fear). The high evidentiary standard – beyond reasonable doubt – a cornerstone of the rule of law, may inadvertently absorb male apprehensions concerning unjust accusations, especially against the backdrop of prevalent myths about false accusations. In other words, the emphasis on alleviating 'male fear' could potentially overshadow the quest for justice for victims, creating a judicial tension between protecting the accused and securing redress for victims. This legal balancing act necessitates ongoing critical reflexivity to ensure that both concerns are addressed and mitigated with due fairness.

Production of evidence

Researcher:	What are the special considerations regarding evidence in rape cases as a prosecutor? How do you prepare for a hearing?
Veronica:	You want a completely credible complainant's story as a starting point; you preferably want a long and vivid story from the complainant. That's the best thing, if you can have it, but you don't always have it … I think the most important thing … the best cases are when you have a good complainant's story, unless you also have technical evidence with injuries …
Researcher:	Mhm … right.
Veronica:	Then preferably that they tell someone and come across someone in an agitated state quite immediately afterwards and tell them what has happened.
Researcher:	Whether … she chooses to report directly to the police or not to report directly to the police, what significance can that have?
Veronica:	It's much easier to secure evidence if they report directly to the police, bruises and injuries and also that they examine themselves … undergo a gynaecological examination and trace evidence. (Veronica, prosecutor, Case 3)

It is the prosecutor's task before filing the indictment to ascertain that the requisite of non-voluntariness is in place and can be proven. To reach this point, several critical issues must be settled. As described by Veronica, superior evidence is a 'completely credible' complainant story (Wallin et al 2021), ideally supported by witness testimonies by people the complainant has engaged with 'immediately afterwards', and technical evidence. In this section, we discuss each of these kinds of evidence, with a focus on the complainant's story. We will start by highlighting the inherent credibility deficit of the complainant's story; the fact that the preliminary investigation of a reported rape begins by examining if the complainant has any reason to lie about being raped.

The credibility deficit of the complainant's story

Fricker (2007) discusses epistemic witness injustice, based on negative stereotypes held by a group in power who systematically exercises negative prejudiced identitarian power against another group. Witness injustice means that a person bearing witness who belongs or is believed to belong to a particular out-group is ascribed a credibility deficit – that is, they are denied privileged access to their own experience – by the group in power. In the legal feminist perspective, the routine scrutiny of the rape complainant's story at all stages, from report to final judgment, signals a systematic patriarchal injustice towards women reporting rape, conceptualized as the 'she lies' myth (Wheatcroft and Walklate 2014). We argue that this type of witness injustice against women who report rape is at least shared by the group of legal professionals and inherent to their juridical expertise and emotive-cognitive professional frame.[2] It is contingent upon the structure of the rule of law, which states that the defendant is always innocent before the opposite is proven, and, conversely, that alternative hypotheses must be ruled out before someone can be convicted beyond reasonable doubt. In other words, the rule of law in combination with the hissense rape myth about women's propensity to lie about rape sustains credibility deficit as a rational starting point for the investigation.

The presumption that the complainant may accuse the defendant of rape for motives other than seeking justice following sexual abuse is self-evident

---

[2] Identitarian power is power held by a group based on shared perceptions of social identity (Fricker 2007:29). This definition denotes a social group rather than a professional group, for whom it is probably better suited to speak of professional identitarian power. However, we argue that legal professional identitarian power is premised on a patriarchal, and thus social identitarian power, structurally embedded in the modern legal system.

for legal professionals (Uhnoo et al 2024c). Prosecutor Veronica (Case 3) said: 'We always ask that question, what is her reason for making this up?'. Prosecutor Sandra (Case 8) expanded on this:

> Then there are some complainants who may report rape carelessly, just like that, several times. Or maybe there are other things that make it not credible, maybe there's a custody dispute at the root of it. And you always have those things on your mind. So, the complainant's story, that's the be-all and end-all.

Here we see that the complainant's story is the 'be-all and end-all' evidence. If it is not trusted, it also jeopardizes the supporting evidence, 'soft' or 'hard'. Since there is often agreement that the accused and the complainant had sex, the new legislation, as it were, provides the defence with a default excuse; the parties had sex, but it was voluntary (a consent defence; see Chapters 8 and 9). This has the consequence that it is the complainant's claim to their own knowledge – that a crime has even occurred – that must first be proven, not just the defendant's guilt. Granted, the prosecutor must be convinced that the person filing the report is not lying about non-voluntary participation.

Once the police, the prosecutor and the victim counsel find the complainant's story reasonably credible, the investigation continues, but the complainant may be heard again several times before the prosecutor feels enough certainty to file the indictment (Törnqvist and Wettergren 2023). In comparison, the defendant's story, although also important, is not submitted to such scrutiny and such high credibility requirements. The credibility criteria will be discussed in a sub-section later.

At the trial, the complainant's credibility deficit is addressed anew, notably by the defence – and rather relentlessly so. This given, the prosecutor addresses it again to clarify why 'weaknesses' in the complainant's story do not compromise it. They do so to demonstrate to the judges that the prosecution is confident about the credibility of the story, and to prevent attempts by the defence to undermine it. This prosecutor strategy is, as we will observe in Chapter 5, rather problematic in rape cases.

It is worth noting that defence lawyers argue that, provided their client is charged, *they* begin the trial with a credibility deficit, given the systematic witness injustice that may be attached to the 'rapist stigma' (Uhnoo et al 2024c). However, judges' keen observation of the presumption of the defendant's *innocence* makes most of them predisposed to be more wary of potential witness injustice on behalf of the defendant than on behalf of the complainant. This appears reasonable in criminal trials in which systematic credibility deficit attached to the complainant is less likely to influence the objective observation that a crime has occurred. On the other hand, the 'typical rapist' myth (contingent on the defendant's social and ethnic background) also implies a credibility deficit, which may tip the balance to the complainant's advantage (for example, Lovett and Kelly 2009).

Thus, the credibility deficit of the complainant results in an epistemic injustice, in which the complainant must have their own knowledge of the crime recognized before proceeding to determine if the evidence of the defendant's guilt is enough. The ontology of the rape is sometimes labelled the objective premise in written judgments, and it is confirmed only after the credibility deficit of the complainant has been thoroughly addressed. This makes the examination of the complainant an unusually long part of the trial. In our study, the examination could last for hours, while examining the defendant was considerably quicker (less than an hour).

That judges maintain a tacit assumption about the credibility deficit of rape complainants is apparent in the judgments (see further Chapter 7). Formulations like the one in the first sentence (emphasis added) in the example below are present in 14 of our 18 cases:

> *Nothing has emerged that has given the court reason to assume that the complainant would provide false information* in order to have [the defendant] convicted of a criminal offence. On the contrary, the complainant has self-critically questioned whether she could have acted differently in the long and short term to avoid the situation that has now arisen. She has also described that, despite major problems in the past, her life has been more difficult than ever before as a result of pursuing the current [rape] investigation. (DC judgment, Case 1, convicted)

Here, we also glimpse some of the implicit criteria for assessing the credibility of the complainant's story, namely modesty and self-criticism, and the lack of personal gain in pursuing justice. These sentences convey sympathy towards the complainant and even admiration of her perseverance – she has had 'major problems in the past' and now her life is even worse. In another excerpt from a judgment by which the defendant was acquitted, we sense a different set of discursively embedded emotions:

> Of course, it cannot be ruled out that [inexplicable elements of the complainant's story] have natural explanations, such as that the complainant was ashamed of what had happened. However, it is not possible to come to any other conclusion than that the witnesses' accounts indicate that, after the incident, the complainant gave false and exaggerated information about her non-voluntary participation in the sexual activities. (DC judgment, Case 8, acquitted)

In the wording of this judgment, the prosecution's rationale for weaknesses in the complainant's story are recognized but rejected, arguably (and paradoxically) based on the supporting witness stories. The dismissal of the complainant's story is phrased in rather harsh terms. By means of counterfactual reasoning it suggests that she likely participated voluntarily and that she may be guilty of false accusation.

Among our interviewees, the self-evident rationale for the 'she lies' presumption is associated with the nature of intimate relationships (Bladini and Svedberg Andersson 2020; Bladini et al 2023). Legal professionals, like most people, have experience of both intimate relationships and sexual interactions. As discussed previously, personal reflections often interact with their common-sense reasoning around matters of credibility and are reminders that intimate sexual relationships are complicated. Hence the alternative hypotheses that judges may weigh when they deliberate can be plenty: from *regret or shame* about the sex, especially in combination with infidelity, to *revenge* for disappointed expectations, partnership conflicts, custody conflicts or simply for bad sex. The personal experience of judges hardly includes the experience of having reported someone for rape due to those feelings. Yet, all these hypotheses belong to the standard repertoire of motives for the 'she lies' myth (Uhnoo et al 2024c). Since they circulate between legal professionals in the process of investigating rape and are repeatedly used by defence lawyers during the rape trial, it is no wonder they also figure in the background when judges deliberate and decide if a crime has even occurred and, if so, if the defendant is guilty *beyond reasonable doubt.*

Objections against the complainant's credibility deficit are sometimes voiced, arguing that lying about rape is rare because it is an all too emotionally costly and generally exhausting experience to report and pursue a rape case. This is primarily advanced by the victim counsel or prosecutor. The assumption that women file false rape reports is sometimes nuanced in terms of young women *misunderstanding* the new law. Jennifer, a lawyer (Case 11) with dire experience with both defence and victim counselling in rape cases, explained that many who report rape have missed that non-voluntary participation must be *expressed* in some way:

Jennifer: [The new law] has led to many more rapes being reported that by definition do not count as rape anyway […] After the interview with the complainant, you realize that no crime has been committed and I think it is very sad that there are many girls and women who believe that they have been raped when this is not actually the case according to the law […] It used to be easier for a complainant to understand what a rape was but now many people have the idea that as long as they think they don't want to, it's automatically a rape and that's completely wrong.

Researcher: I was going to ask what situations?

Jennifer: Those situations are pretty much that ... you have ... given in to nagging and consented by saying ... 'we'll do it then!'. And afterwards, you feel, 'why did I agree to it when I didn't really want to?'. But then you have in fact expressed your voluntariness both physically and verbally, and that's what many people find difficult to understand.

Jennifer, in this excerpt, seemed certain about where to draw the line between *expressed* and *not expressed* non-voluntariness, but her example is a case in which the complainant gave in to nagging. Giving in to nagging is positioned as *expressed voluntariness* in the rape law (Chapter 2). In other words, the line between *felt* (inner) non-voluntariness and *expressed* non-voluntariness is difficult to draw by both legal professionals and laypeople.

As hinted previously, the credibility deficit and systematic witness injustice directed at the complainant seems to be shifted towards the defendant in cases engaging the 'typical rapist' stereotype, in which the defendant, for example, has a previous conviction or is a foreign citizen (Bitsch 2019; Bitsch and Klemetsen 2017; Brå 2019; Manne 2018). However, in our data, although the patterns are only indicative, this shift seems to be contingent on the social status and gendered stereotyping of the complainant (see Chapter 8).

Tied in with the credibility deficit of the complainant are the explicit criteria that are supposed to guide legal professionals in their evaluation of whether the complainant's story passes the threshold to credibility. While the credibility deficit is a systematic witness injustice linked to the group (women) reporting rape, the criteria can be used to make legal assessments appear 'objective'.

Assessing the complainant's story

The meaning of 'credibility' in legal discourse is a floating signifier (Laclau and Mouffe 1985), usually stabilized by reference to reliability – the correspondence between a person's statement and controllable external circumstances (for example, 'hard' evidence). In rape cases, credibility and reliability tend to merge into the quality of the complainant's story, because the meaning of all supporting evidence, as we shall see, refer to the complainant's story. The courts commonly refer to guiding Supreme Court cases (NJA 2010 p 671; NJA 2017 p 316 I and II) on evaluation of evidence in sexual offences, suggesting that a credible story combined with corroborating evidence may be sufficient proof (Chapter 2 and Part IV). To assess an oral statement, the courts use both old and new criteria from case law, including criteria that have been withdrawn by the Supreme Court due to lack of support in psychological research. Repeatedly referred in interviews, final pleas and judgments, are the criteria 'long', 'coherent', 'clear', 'detailed' and 'consistent over time'. According to Willén and Strömwall (2012) these refer to the veracity of the story. Added to these are a list of control criteria: 'absence of inexplicable elements'; 'consistently high quality'; 'how the story is told' ('serious, spontaneous, thoughtful, relevant gestures and facial expressions'); if 'the story gives a credible impression'; if the story 'is characterized by self-experience'; and if 'no part of the story is weak'.

These criteria, included in the so-called Criteria Based Content Analysis (CBCA), have been questioned in legal and witness psychological research. For instance, in a study on police officers, judges and prosecutors, Strömwall and Granhag (2003) demonstrated that 'expert consensus' belief that truthful statements are consistent over time while less truthful statements are not, runs contrary to research findings. Non-truthful statements are instead more consistent than truthful ones, which can be explained by the 'repeat v reconstruct' hypothesis that 'assumes that liars try to repeat their initial statement, whereas truth-tellers try to reconstruct a previously experienced event' (Strömwall and Granhag 2003:34). In response to this research, the criterion of consistency was later modified by the Supreme Court (NJA 2017 s 316) and should no longer be viewed as a measure of credibility. Yet, the criterion is still used in some of our cases.

Strömwall and Granhag (2003:34) also warn against 'the detail criterion' because studies of the number of words used in a story showed that truthful statements contain fewer words than non-truthful statements, while more words tend to be confounded with 'richness in detail'. Furthermore, 'one person can judge a statement to be rich in detail, whereas another person can judge the very same statement to be poor in detail' (Strömwall and Granhag 2003:34).

The use of CBCA by non-experts has been addressed in more recent international research. In a large meta-analysis, Hauch et al (2017) measured the interrater reliability of the CBCA, arguing that the criteria *can* be applied to determine truthfulness, but only if done so by properly trained experts 'blind to other case materials to reduce bias' and, given 'the subjective nature of these evaluations', preferably by several experts to guarantee 'that other observers will come to the same conclusion'. Concerning the widespread use of the CBCA by courts to determine credibility, they conclude that incorrect use may lead to 'miscarriages of justice' (Hauch et al 2017:829): 'We are concerned that through the increased availability of various "criteria lists" in publications, workshops, and the Internet, more people may feel "qualified" to conduct credibility assessments. Without proper training, this is a bad idea'. Legal professionals in our study expressed awareness of the uncertain value of the criteria. Despite this, they still used them as default arguments in support of their assessment. Notably, the control criterion 'characterized by self-experience' is widely held by legal professionals to be dated and no longer in use, yet it kept appearing in our data (Bladini et al 2023). In final pleas it was often brought up by the parties in a 'better safe than sorry' manner, as noted during observation of the victim counsel's final plea in Case 1: 'The victim counsel emphasizes that the complainant's story was factual, detailed and *self-experienced*'. In the final plea of Case 10, the prosecutor argued:

> The complainant describes the details so that she [the prosecutor] herself gets stuck with the image of how [the complainant] is positioned face towards the water and wants to get out of there, into the water. This *is highly self-experienced,* the prosecutor argues. The complainant's story is, she continues, free from contradictions, exaggerations and unexplainable elements.

In interviews, the notion of self-experienced could be criticized and embraced simultaneously, as in the following quotation by victim counsel Per (Case 3):

> The character of the self-experienced is a juridical term for a feeling and it has been misleading sometimes because … what the hell does that mean? It deserves thinking about, but I usually think it's… a really good complainant who … the best they can be, is someone who, without too many controlling questions, tells you what happened, how it made her feel and how she felt afterwards, and then you talk about the character of the self-experienced, like … who the hell would make up such a story? So, it's more or less legal Swedish for that [feeling].

As Per stated, the character of the self-experienced is the legal term for 'a feeling' that makes doubt disappear. The quote may be read as a description of empathy, an emotional attunement with the complainant and, at the same time, a description of how to know 'the truth'. In the philosophy of emotions, this feeling can be grasped by the meta-cognitive 'feeling of knowing', bridging experience and present sensory inputs but 'bearing not on beliefs already acquired or on hypotheses currently being entertained, but rather on the existence of hidden knowledge: on whether we already know something, without knowing what it is we know' (de Sousa 2008:196). The feeling of knowing involves other meta-cognitive emotional cues like the 'feeling of familiarity' (Koriat 2000): that is, unconscious inference based on unknown memories. It can also be compared to the background emotion of scientific 'aesthetic pleasure'; 'the perception of characteristic organization or form in an apparent disconnection or even chaos of parts' (Barbalet 2011:7).

If we examine the totality of criteria to test the complainant's story, we observe that all of them speak to meta-cognitive feelings. The list can be viewed as an attempt to cognitively pin down what is in effect 'the subtlety and complexity of mechanisms which remain, precisely because they normally escape awareness, exceedingly hard to analyse' (de Sousa 2008:196). Judges can use the list to verbalize why they *feel* certain about their decision to convict or acquit. The following reasoning in a judgment elaborates on several of the criteria, including self-experience:

> The complainant is credible and her information is reliable. According to the court's assessment, the complainant's *spontaneous* account has been *long, detailed and coherent.* Her account has clearly described how she reacted and felt. The feelings and emotional reactions she described appear to be adequate and she has described what she thought and felt during the incident in a way that *appears to be self-experienced.* Her account has *not contained any obvious contradictions or unexplainable elements,* and she has provided *reasonable explanations for her behaviour.* Nor has the complainant *given the impression of exaggerating.* According to the court's assessment, the complainant has made *a very credible impression. Nor has anything emerged that gives reason to believe that the complainant has deliberately provided false or exaggerated information to falsely accuse* [the defendant]. (DC judgment, Case 4, emphasis added)

Besides the veracity criteria 'long, detailed and coherent', virtually all of the control criteria are mentioned in this excerpt: 'absence of inexplicable elements'; 'the way the story is told' (spontaneous, thoughtful, providing 'reasonable explanations for her behaviour'); and 'the story gives a credible impression' (no 'exaggerations' and no reason to 'falsely accuse'). The assessment of 'consistently high quality' arguably pertains to clarity and adequacy *and* to the explicit criterion of 'characterized by self-experience'. In other words, the story conveys *the feeling of knowing* what happened and of *certainty* about this knowledge.

In our material, similar use of the veracity and control criteria is a dominant intertextual pattern in judgments. Not all judgments list all the criteria, and, in some cases, the criteria adopted are less elaborated, as in the AC judgment of Case 18: 'Her account is clear, vivid, detailed, and coherent. Many of the details she recounts appear to be self-experienced'. In this quotation, we observe that the AC also uses the self-experience criterion. In contrast, AC judge Bengt (not involved in Case 18) reasoned around this and other criteria he uses:

Bengt: [T]he concept characterized by self-experience [...] in my opinion it is something to be avoided, but I think

<blockquote>

I can see that it is coming back now […] And the second thing you said was consistency, and my understanding is that the Supreme Court in its latest judgment from 2017 … I think the Supreme Court writes down the importance of the concept of consistency. It does not have such great significance.

Researcher: Right.

Bengt: On this checklist of whether a statement is acceptable or not, I think less attention should be paid to the concept of consistency.

Researcher: To what do you pay attention?

Bengt: I don't know, I was about to say, but it's … detailed, clear, whatever … the question of whether there are contradictions … uh… self-corrections … That seems to me to be a rather difficult point. There is self-correction if you tell the truth, but not if you lie … Yes … well, actually, it wasn't like that …

Researcher: Doubt … it could be … to doubt one's own story?

Bengt: I can imagine that even if it's not on that checklist, I would probably intuitively recognize it. Some specific details that are not needed when constructing a lie, but maybe it is just my own theory that it is important. But again, as I see it, it becomes more of a binary test. Does the story work or does it not work? If you have come as far as the court, then almost everything in the story is valid and the issue is really about supporting evidence. On the other hand, it may be that you still think that the story was so strong that you realize that this complainant is telling the truth. Then you only need a very small amount of supporting evidence.

</blockquote>

In this excerpt, Judge Bengt generously shared his confusion concerning the criteria and, although far from alone, this is rare. Bengt was informed about the research regarding the criteria and, as we see, he struggled to account for how and why he believed a story was credible. Interestingly, he ended with two ways to 'know': First, if the story was deemed strong enough by the prosecutor to proceed to indictment, it should reasonably live up to the criteria. This is a judicious argument, but not representative of the reasoning of the judges in our material. It arguably also refers the problem with the criteria to a problem of the prosecutor. Interestingly, in the same sentence, Bengt further transferred the evaluation of the complainant's story to the evaluation of the supporting evidence. This too is reasonable but, again, given that the supporting evidence also mainly consists of stories, it does not really solve the problem. In our material, as mentioned previously, we have observed that this transferral is often used when judges want to avoid discrediting the complainant but have decided to acquit (as in Case 8 mentioned earlier).

Second, Bengt stated that, in some cases, the story is so strong that the supporting evidence is really of marginal significance. After all, as he also stated, 'it becomes more of a binary test. Does the story work or does it not work?'. By not being able to confirm which of the criteria bear enough juridical weight to be properly followed, Bengt's reasoning instead confirms that all the criteria can be doubted per se, and that, knowing when a story is true or not is 'a feeling of knowing', which, we argue, is based on the totality of background emotional information retrieved, involving all the criteria at once (cf Barbalet 2011; de Sousa 2008).

One criterion often used, which appears both counterintuitive and juridically irrational, is the notion of the complainant's story as *spontaneous,* part of the control criterion *the way the story is told*. Spontaneity is associated with the legal principles of immediacy and orality (Chapter 2). In the following excerpt from a trial observation, we perceive an almost comical phrasing of these principles, signalling its believed significance for the truth value of a witness statement:

> The judge introduces the court to Witness 1, takes the oath and talks at length about the importance of criminal responsibility and that she must not take into account the interests of one or the other party [...] He goes on to say that 'your lips should reproduce the memories in your head. If you just have the ambition to tell the truth, it's all very easy'. (Field notes, Case 2)

The oft-used spontaneity criterion is clearly irrational because any story (by the parties or the witnesses) told in court has been told many times before. In particular, the complainant's story has been thoroughly dissected in the preliminary investigation. Still, the control criteria 'the way the story is told' (serious, spontaneous, thoughtful, relevant gestures and facial expressions) and 'the story gives a credible impression' signal that the story indeed should be told *as if* it was spontaneously told for the first time in court. It contradicts the criterion 'consistent over time', which implicitly admits that it is *not* told for the first time but rather remembered and repeated like it was told the first time. Several weeks or months may have elapsed since the first time the story was told. However, in cases in which the accused was not detained (for example, Cases 2, 15 and 10), more than a year may have passed. The ability to remember and repeat the same story of an event that moves further and further into the past is, in line with previous research (Strömwall and Granhag 2003), more likely to reveal that someone has memorized the story by heart. The ability to further convey the impression in court that the story is 'spontaneous' with relevant gestures and facial expressions is merely informative of someone's deep-acting emotion management skills (Hochschild 1983).[3] In the case of rape trials, these pertain to the parties' capacity to cognitively reframe a present situation by imagining the remembered past event to produce the impression of authentically felt emotions of that past event in the present courtroom. For the complainant, the authentically felt emotions should be adequate though suitably restrained, in accordance with the Swedish cultural emotional regime (Wettergren and Bergman Blix 2021). The criteria for assessing the complainant's story thus favour complainants possessing eloquence, sharp memory and deep-acting skills, and the confidence and calm to operate all this in a suitably spontaneous manner, in what is, for most people, a new and awe-inspiring environment. Moreover, they must answer repeat questions about every detail of the sex act.

Contrary to most popular perceptions and most defence lawyers' argumentation, rape trials are *not* word-against-word cases (Saunders 2018), which is also shown in our cases (see the coming chapters). The list of criteria is first and foremost designed to determine the complainant's story. As will be demonstrated in Part III and IV, in theory, the criteria could be applicable to the defendant's story, but as the prosecutor has the burden of proof and the defendant is allowed to lie, the criteria are seldom applied to their story.

As mentioned previously, the complainant's story needs support from 'circumstantial evidence'. There are two types of corroborating evidence: oral evidence (that is, witness testimonies) and hard evidence. In the next sub-section, we focus on oral evidence, namely the witness testimonies, which are believed to be crucial for establishing an outsider (objective) view of the complainant's actions and reactions after the sex act.

Supporting evidence – witness testimonies

As previously observed, there are seldom any eyewitnesses of the actual sex act. Nevertheless, witness testimonies are expected to detail what they were told – what the complainant said – about the sex act when they met the complainant (immediately) after. It is noteworthy that this part of their testimony is sometimes used against the credibility of the complainant's story, because details of this 'first', presumably most authentic, version of their story conflict with details in the story told in court (Part IV). Later in this

---

3   Hochschild's notion of 'deep-acting' as an emotion management technique, denotes the subject's cognitive reframing of the situation to produce emotions in line with feeling rules. Successful deep-acting makes the subject *feel* the desired emotion, contrasting 'surface acting' where the subject expresses the emotion but does not really feel it.

section, however, Case 3 will be discussed, in which the court considered that details may have been omitted in the complainant's first story because of the private nature of sex talk.

As explained in Chapter 2, the legal preparatory works address the necessity, in rape cases, to weigh in 'the situation as a whole', both before and after the sex act. This temporality of rape cases denotes the reconstruction of a more generous and flexible timeline than is normally admitted in the juridical encoding of criminal cases (Bergman Blix and Wettergren 2018). Consequently, defence lawyers often focus on the time *before* the reported rape to find expressions of voluntariness or reasons for their client to believe so. It should be noted that the rape act begins when the complainant no longer participates voluntarily. For instance, if voluntariness is not communicated when a change of position (from oral to vaginal) takes place, it may be rape. On the one hand, the party who no longer wants to participate needs to express this non-voluntariness. On the other hand, the active party is legally responsible for ensuring that the other party (still) participates voluntarily. Hence, prosecutors and victim counsels are usually only interested in what happened before the sex act in terms of expressions of non-voluntariness close to the actual rape act, or rather what the defendant did to assure that it was voluntary. The temporality of rape cases, and how it is used and negotiated by the parties in trials, will be analysed in depth in Part III. Suffice to say, it is tightly associated with the construction of typical victim and perpetrator stereotypes, and thereby also to the complainant's story in terms of recounted action rationality and (lack of) autonomy.

Pending the expectations of observed typical victim behaviour as something that may support the complainant's story, the prosecution's temporal focus turns to what happens in the time *after* the sex act, because it may have a decisive impact on the judges. In a group interview, Appeals Court Judges Lina and Petter (Cases 7 and 8) highlighted the importance of this through supporting witness testimonies:

Petter: There is rarely anyone who has seen the assault, you usually only have a man and a woman who tell you about a course of events and, if you are to find someone responsible for an offence, it is required that the complainant's information is credible and reliable and that they are supported by other ... simply have other supporting evidence in their favour. This also includes the witnesses who are heard, who [should] not only repeat what the woman has told them, but also what observations they have made of the woman. Their own observations of her.

Researcher: Behaviour and actions ...?

Petter: Exactly, in direct connection with the offence. It becomes quite important ... if it is consistent with what [the complainant] tells you.

As is apparent in the quotation, great value is ascribed to observations of the complainant's behaviour (preferably immediately) after the rape. Although there are no guiding legal principles nor sources regarding what qualifies as credible (victim-adequate) behaviour after a rape, crucial indicators often mentioned in interviewees are a state of shock or severe upset, crying, shaking, calling a friend or a parent, or – in the best case – directly calling the police. DC judge Mårten (Case 1) attempted to explain what reaction might count as 'enough' in slightly exaggerated terms: 'It's not enough to have told a neighbour two days later, but it might be enough to have told your mother and your sister right when it happened and then run out into the street screaming. [Then] there is some supporting evidence'. Prosecutor Jesper (Case 1) reasoned around both witness and digital evidence regarding behaviours after the rape that do not 'connect':

I had a case, someone who told me that she had been badly beaten and there was also a rape involved in that case and ... an hour later they had been shopping at [shopping centre] ... When I come up with these, when I think this sounds completely illogical and ... uh ... this rape is supposed to have taken place at a certain time and three hours later they have sent love texts to each other, for example ... If I can't understand it or make sense of it or if I think it's illogical, then the court will definitely think so when I have to explain it. It must be connected.

As observed in both these quotations, the complainant's behaviour after the sex act should resonate with tacit assumptions of an 'autonomous' and 'rational' typical victim behaviour (Wallin et al 2021). Cases such as those described by Jesper refer to intimate relationships that may be destructive and fraught by intimate partner violence, relationships in which abuse is normalized (Enander 2010, 2011; Moussion-Esteve 2022). Jesper's immediate suspicion of a false accusation may hence be illustrative of the social distance between him and some women, rather than of a temporal series of events that do not connect. The social distance makes it difficult for him to stretch his empathic imagination enough to fathom how someone can go shopping with their partner after being badly beaten and raped.

Valid witness observations of the complainant's behaviour after the sex act should, as noted above, also be *independent*, that is ideally uncontaminated by the complainant's own story or any other element. Among the latter, we infer a backgrounded suspicion of a sentimental bias, in our data typically ascribed to mothers, which is assumed to skew their autonomous assessment of a daughter's state of mind. One case, outside our 18 cases, described in the interview with Prosecutor Jenny, is particularly illustrative of the credibility deficit routinely ascribed to mothers. In this case, the complainant had reported a rape but, due to intoxication, had no memories of the sex act. However, the supporting evidence was considered strong by the prosecutor. There were laboratory reports on the level of intoxication, witness observations and psychiatric reports of her psychological breakdown after the sex act. The prosecutor's key witness of the actual rape was the complainant's mother, who was a professional nurse, a fact that would normally strengthen her status as witness. The mother's testimony regarding the daughter's level of intoxication in direct connection to the sex act confirmed her being in a vulnerable state.

In line with Jenny's assessment, the case was convicted in the DC, which argued in the judgment that 'it is evident that [the complainant] was in a particularly vulnerable situation due to intoxication and fatigue' and that the defendant 'improperly exploited the situation to have intercourse with her'. However, in the AC, the case was acquitted. Jenny commented on the AC judgment:

> The mother's testimony is just brushed aside … In that case, I think we should make the same assessment of [the mother/witness] story as we do with a complainant and look at the fact, that is, if it is a long, detailed story, and does not contain elements that are difficult to explain. The whole thing, all of [the criteria]. [Instead], they consider the fact that she is a relative and come to the conclusion that, because she is a relative, we can disqualify her … [a testimony] which is done by a professional woman.

In this quotation, Jenny highlighted the problem of the seemingly straightforward assessments of witness testimonies as compared with those of the complainant's stories: the veracity and control criteria are not used. Contrasting the way the mother's testimony was 'brushed aside', the AC's decision to acquit emphasized the testimonies of the police officers arriving at the scene after the mother. At this time, the complainant had come to life and was in a state of rage, screaming at her mother and police officers. The AC judgment concluded that this was a sign of an angry person: 'All in all, the police statements provide a picture that the complainant acted consciously and adequately in relation to the fact that she was angry and upset about the situation in the bedroom'. Besides an implicit assumption of the AC that anger is not a victim-adequate behaviour (Ask and Granhag 2007; Ask and Landström 2010), the judgment is arguably indicative of witness injustice against mothers, as combined with a routine trust in the quality of testimonies made by police officers.

In contrast, a case in which the totality of the supporting witness testimonies was considered 'good' is Case 3, despite the fact that it was the complainant's adult son (NN3) and partner (NN) who delivered the testimonies that were closest in time to the sex act. The convicting AC judgment (the case was also convicted in the DC) argued that they provided strong support to the complainant's story:

> They arrived at [accused]'s house shortly after the complainant had come out of the [room]. However, the purpose of their visit was actually to deliver cigarettes that the complainant had called them about earlier in the evening. *So they had no idea what had happened when they got there.* NN3 and [NN] *have both described* that they immediately realized that something was not right when they arrived. They have said that the complainant was sad when they arrived and that she said it was not good for her to be there. NN has said that the complainant looked completely destroyed. NN3 has said that the complainant told him that she [left the room], that [accused] came after her and tried to have sex with her but that she did not want to, that [accused] had put his fingers in her vagina and that [accused] had tried to get her to suck him off. NN said that the complainant told her that [accused] had raped her and that he had put his fingers in her vagina. NN has said that the complainant was very sad and cried when she told her story. NN3 and NN have said that the complainant had very painful genitals when they went to the hospital immediately after leaving [the accused]'s house. NN has said that this was also very evident in the way the complainant walked. (Case 3, emphasis added)

The testimonies referred in this quotation do not lose credibility although one of the witnesses is the complainant's son and the other is closely related to the son. They are constructed as independent observers ('they had no idea what had happened when they got there') and they described what they observed and were told in very similar ways – arguably because they arrived together but also because they live together. There were details missing in the couple's testimony of what the complainant had told them, details that were added when interrogated by the police. The judgment interprets this to the complainant's advantage *because the witness was her son*: 'It should be noted that NN3 is her son and that details of this kind are obviously sensitive to discuss'. Perhaps very crucial supporting evidence in this case was that the police officer, who was called to the hospital where the witnesses had taken her, partly supported *their* testified observations:

> Police officer John Doe said that, during the interview at the hospital in [town], the complainant said that she had pain in her genitals and

that she had difficulty walking. He also said that she stated that she had pain in her abdomen and that he saw her leaning forward when she went to pee.

As we observe in Case 3, the judgment considered all the witness testimonies as supportive of the complainant's story *despite* the fact that the witnesses mainly report what the complainant had said to them, and despite, or in this case rather *because of*, the fact that one of them is a close relative.

The contradictive conclusions that different judges draw from comparable witnesses is manifest in our data. We argue that the way the judgments are written benevolently or malevolently, as it were, with regards to the value of the supporting evidence reveals a feeling of (not) knowing, discussed previously, from the hearing. The judgments are then formulated in accord with certainty or doubt regarding the credibility of the compliant. Case 3 will be further discussed in Part III, in which we expand on how the legal parties, during the trial, work on the judge's feeling of knowing to the advantage of the complainant's or defendant's story.

The overall problem with the supporting evidence in terms of witness observations of the complainant's behaviour after the sex act are several: first, these witnesses are, for quite obvious reasons, often close friends or relatives, and second, it is commonly presumed that the closeness to the complainant makes them emphasize or even exaggerate the state of upset and distress of the complainant (as victim-adequate behaviour is a rather widespread trope; see for instance Bosma 2019; Rose et al 2006; Törnqvist 2021), especially when the complainant and witnesses are young people (under 18 years). As in Jenny's case, mothers' testimonies are often treated with suspicion (Bladini 2013). Jenny's case is exceptional in that the mother is also a professional and was the first to enter the scene of the crime when the complainant was passed out; thus her testimony was truly independent of the complainant's story. Fathers, although they tend to be angry in court, tend to be met with greater respect, though they are usually less informed than mothers. This may be associated with the fact that (privileged) male anger is historically coded as rational (Kemper 2006; Lively 2008; Shields 2002). A special category of witnesses that are routinely accorded a high degree of credibility are police officers. The third problem is that consistency between different witness testimonies is used to corroborate or refute the reliability of the complainant's story concerning specific details of movements in space and time, positions and interactions in specific places, time stamps, outfits and so on. Finally, it is interesting to note that witness testimonies, regardless of their relative importance, are *not* systematically subjected to credibility tests but rather are received as informative statements of a more or less dubious kind, used ad hoc to support or refute the credibility of the complainant, to align with the court's view of the case. They appear to be trusted or distrusted for various implicit reasons or used selectively to *do objectivity* in the judgments by retroactively justifying the decision. This retrospective cherry picking in judgments is arguably done in all criminal cases, given that no judgment can possibly refer to all evidence presented during a trial, and therefore must choose the 'best parts', sufficient to demonstrate the juridical logic of the decision. However, in rape cases, this method reveals in an unfortunate way how similar evidence can lead to completely opposite evaluations.

Supporting evidence – hard evidence

Hard evidence includes technical and forensic evidence, and other 'factual' supportive evidence external to the subjective oral testimonies in court: medical reports, chat messages, film sequences and photographs, emergency calls, telephone records, global positioning system markings and time stamps. While these types of evidence have an objective existence, their impact and meaning in rape cases is not obvious, especially not when both parties (which is most often the case) agree that the sex act happened. Hard evidence in rape cases, thus, does not have the same direct impact on the assessment of the defendant's guilt as it does in other criminal cases. In the meantime, scientific advancement has led to an increase of the availability, and thus use, of forensic evidence. Houge and Laugerud (2023:4–5) argue that this development has

> led to a shift in legal arguments in Norwegian rape cases, from proving or disproving sexual contact to disputing whether the forensically established sexual encounter was consensual [...] Thus, despite proliferating forensic technologies, rape and sexual violence are still particularly challenging crimes to prove, often at its core dealing with questions of credibility and reliability, of words against words, rather than proving facts through physical or expert evidence. Particularly relevant to our study, research suggests that rape myths and forensics overlap in their impacts.

In line with these findings in Norway, our results demonstrate that it rarely matters if the medical examination reports DNA or semen when the defence opts for the strategy of consent defence (Chapters 8 and 9). The hard evidence confirms that sex has occurred but not that it was non-voluntary. Evidence of marks and bruises can result from normal sex, as can vaginal irritation. The meaning of hard 'objective' evidence is thereby referred back to the parties' stories and has to be understood in the light of these stories.

As will be demonstrated in subsequent chapters, the status of hard evidence depends on the framing and argumentation of the prosecution and the counter-framing of the defence. It is not uncommon that a text message containing an apology is argued by the prosecutor to be an indirect confession. In one of our cases (Case 9), that strategy was successful in the DC but not in the AC, in which the defence lawyer's framing (men tend to apologize at random to keep women satisfied and happy, and his client was dead scared; see Uhnoo et al 2024c) was instead successful.

This said, hard evidence is not unnecessary. On the one hand, the mere existence (and proliferation – see quote above) of forensic evidence increases expectations on such evidence to be presented. This was seen in Case 15: oral testimonies of the complainant's severe intoxication (making her particularly vulnerable) were not considered sufficient without support from a blood test. On the other hand, in cases in which the defendant denies the sex, hard evidence like semen or DNA might be crucial as it disproves the defendant's denial. Yet, as will be developed in Part III, such a lie does not necessarily impact on the verdict. In most cases, hard evidence creates expectations on the defendant's story, that is, a 'burden of explanation'. In our study we also see that hard evidence, like photos of, or filming, the sex act, sometimes seemed consequential for the verdict. Hard evidence thus seems to be both necessary and is sometimes effective, but in complex ways, and still dependent of the context/the rape/the story.

Consequently, from our 18 cases, we infer that hard evidence that can be interpreted in support of the complainant's story plays an important, sometimes decisive, role in the preliminary investigation and in the decision to prosecute. It strengthens the prosecutor's feeling of a good case and thereby their professional self-confidence (Törnqvist and Wettergren 2023). However, the influence it receives in the hearing and for the court's decision is contingent on the emotive-cognitive framing and counter-framing of the parties. In Chapter 5, we will demonstrate that the main problem of the evidence in rape cases is not the lack of 'hard' evidence – as this must be translated and framed anyway – but prosecutors' default way of doing objectivity, according to which the 'evidence talks for itself', directly to the judges.

Conclusion

In this chapter, we have argued that the legal handling of rape cases under the new law is haunted by a pervasive *feeling of not knowing*. That feeling refers above all to not knowing how to handle the matter of qualitative evidence (that is, stories) as the main evidence. This type of evidence is called 'soft' evidence, implicitly, and sometimes explicitly, aligning it with 'subjective' evidence. 'Subjective' evidence in the realm of the emotive-cognitive judicial frame and its default understanding of objectivity and rationality, is no real evidence without firm support by tangible factual evidence, the objective existence of which is 'seen' by everyone. It is this latter type of evidence that the legal system traditionally intends by the concept of evidence. Therefore, the purportedly habituated sense of rationality of legal expertise is *irritated* by the referral to soft evidence, irritation here being an epistemically oriented emotion marking such 'evidence' as irrelevant. In rape cases, and especially under the new law, making (non-)voluntariness the main requisite, legal professionals are expected to put this habituated way of doing legal objectivity and rationality aside, and to instead take an active interest in the quality and reasonableness of stories. They are asked to assess the credibility of mainly the complainant's story to determine, first, whether an offence has been committed, and, if so, they continue to assess the criminal intent of the defendant. As we have observed in this chapter, the main evidence of the complainant's story is reinforced by supporting evidence, but this consists mainly of other stories (that is, witness testimonies). Moreover, the factual evidence often presented in rape cases rarely 'speaks for itself' because bruises, semen, DNA and the like, take on different meanings if it is believed that the sex act was voluntary or that it was not. Viewed from this perspective, the professional confusion and feeling of not knowing when faced with rape cases, and the resulting irritation and power discomfort evoked, is understandable. All of this is packaged in the default notion of 'the bad evidence' in rape cases.

We suggest calling the 'soft' evidence qualitative evidence, akin to the qualitative data of social science, and argue that it is not 'bad' evidence but a different type of evidence that requires a different method of evaluation than the one usually adopted by legal professionals. In this way, the new rape law seriously challenges the emotive–cognitive judicial frame by implicitly requiring legal professionals to learn new ways of doing legal rationality. However, the law and preparatory works do not offer much assistance. As we discussed, the criteria for assessing the credibility of stories, established by the Supreme Court, are controversial and contested by witness psychological research, especially when adopted by courts. Yet, they are used in an almost ritualistic manner, as objectivity lifebuoys.

In this first empirical chapter, we have begun to highlight what will become increasingly clear in the subsequent empirical chapters – that the lack of knowledge of how to handle and assess the evidence in rape cases opens to background emotions of familiarity, recognition and 'comfort in sense', feelings that orient in the direction of different types of common sense. As argued in the first part of the chapter, the new law opens up the opportunity of hersensical reasoning to blend with legal logics, but this is rare. Hissenscial legal logics is the conventional and habituated way of reasoning, consistent with the norms and values of the existing emotive–cognitive judicial frame. It is also here that stereotypes regarding female and male sexuality and exaggerated female emotionality (making women cry rape) become most active.

The credibility deficit of the complainant, we argue, because it is explicitly voiced and present in all phases of the process from report to final judgment, is first and foremost an outcome of how the legal system and the rule of law is constructed, and how juridical knowledge is internalized and operationalized by legal actors: in other words, the emotive-cognitive judicial frame. The reluctance to recognize the new knowledge required to handle the evidence in rape cases is anchored in the frame. In so far as it constructs a shared professional identity, the legal system, we argue, exercises identarian power, producing systematic witness injustice against women reporting rape.

Allowing the sense of discomfort and irritation to spark interest in exploring what practical changes and changes in approach to knowledge are required to manage rape cases in a legally secure manner would be one way of addressing the reluctance to change. A less successful way, which may give the legal actor the security and comfort of having acted within the existing framework, is to try to approach rape cases as one would any other criminal case. In subsequent chapters we will take a closer look at how legal actors work in practice with rape cases.

We now shift focus from the evidence to the doing of the objective and impartial trial as a collective achievement (Bergman Blix and Wettergren 2018, 2019). Through Chapters 5 and 6 it will be clear that argumentation, which includes the framing of the evidence – the complainant's story, the witness stories and the objective evidence – and the negotiation of empathic imagination, is crucial in rape trials. We will begin by discussing the respective legal roles.

5

Professional Roles in Objectivity Making

Introduction

Objectivity is one of the overarching principles and core values of modern law and modern bureaucratic institutions (Bergman Blix and Wettergren 2019; Bladini 2013; Lange 2002; Maroney 2011). It is not just a matter of how jurists perceive their own and their colleague's professional stance, but also of how the legal system presents itself to the legal subjects (and the audience) in courts. As a theoretical concept, it is often associated with *tabula rasa* – a blank slate – tied in with the notion of legal autonomy, including impartiality, the absence of personal emotional bonds, preferences and attitudes. The blank slated mind also includes the absence of knowledge of and insights in lived experiences of different social groups because such knowledge could compromise objectivity (Bladini 2013; Vermeule 2001). As a *legal* concept, it has mainly been explained as an obligation of impartiality and neutrality inherent in the role of judge and prosecutor (Bladini 2013; SCJP 23:4 and 45:3a §). Judges and prosecutors *are* objective at work. It means that when they cross the line from private to professional being, they presumably put emotions aside and step out of their embodied being in the world.

In contrast, previous ethnographic court research has shown that, contrary to this ideal, objectivity in legal practice is really striving towards an approximation to the ideal (for example, Jakobsson 2008; Minissale 2023). Objectivity is a mode of acting and thinking that is situated and continuously *made* in relation to particular issues and particular people. In this chapter, and Chapter 6, we focus on the legal objectivity made in relation to people, that is, procedural justice or 'Justice [...] seen to be done' (Lord Chief Justice Hewart, 1924).[1] Doing objectivity 'seen to be

---

[1]   The origins of "Justice must be seen to be done" (accessed 7 February 2024).

done' is essential for the legitimacy of the legal system (Tyler 2003). This image of an objective judiciary is a collective 'doing', a continuous work in progress achieved by tacit collaboration between the different legal professional roles, in relation to the structural (state, organizational and material) and the interactional (legal roles and procedures) levels of the legal professional arena.

In this chapter, we discuss the different legal roles in *the collective doing of objectivity* in rape cases. Doing objectivity, we argue, requires situated inter-professional attentiveness and adaptation: if the defence lawyer fails to fulfil their loyal role, for instance, the prosecutor may leave their confident antagonistic approach, or the judge might leave the sternly impartial one, to compensate and make sure the defendant understands their rights (Bergman Blix and Wettergren 2018, 2019).

As briefly discussed in Chapter 3, there are habituated ways of performing each legal role and its professional emotional profiles, leading to routinized or default understanding of one's role and its part in doing objectivity in court. An overview of the traditional roles is represented in Figure 1.

In this chapter, we discuss why this default way of doing objectivity counteracts its purpose in rape cases. It is only the defence lawyers' role that is not challenged in rape proceedings. On the contrary, skilled defence lawyers may actually 'win' a rape case by their loyalty performance. As they have never 'been objective', skilled lawyers can draw freely on structurally embedded hissense, and on their intuition about the role of background emotions in court.

Figure 1: Traditional professional roles

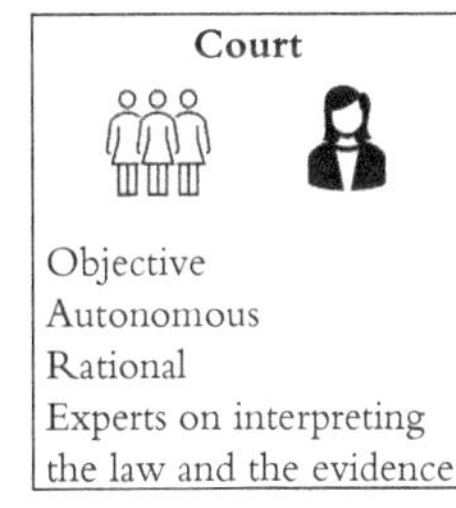

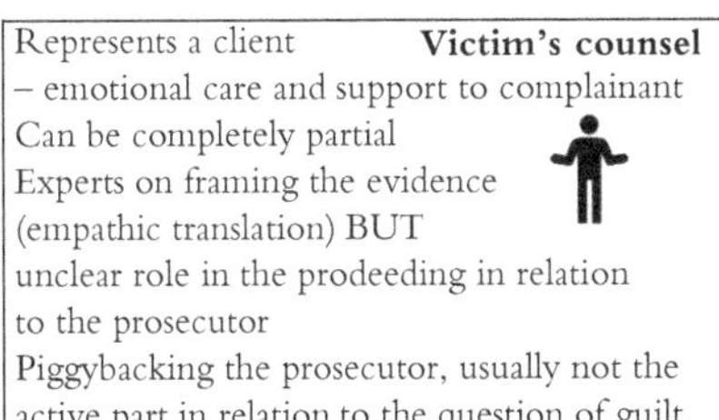

In this chapter we focus on each of the legal actors' professional roles separately, pinpointing for each of them the default doing of the interactional objectivity and providing examples of flexible adaptation observed in our data. In Chapter 6 we will continue to analyse three of our cases in-depth.

Professional roles

The judge – power discomfort and impartiality

Judges' professional emotional profile is distinctly tied in with power and status, impersonating the rule of law (for example, Mack and Roach Anleu 2010; Minissale 2023). The duty of wielding authority, entailing the sentencing of citizens to penalties on behalf of the state, is intrinsically tied to the obligation of being objective (ECHR art 6; RF 1:9). This burden of power in turn entails that the judges carry the weightiest burden of the ideal of objectivity. In the accusatorial trial they usually assume a passive role as stone-faced yet attentive listeners (Bergman Blix and Wettergren 2018). Thus, they rely on the groundwork of the other legal actors, for the collective achievement of objectivity (that is, the image of justice). For instance, to maintain a passive (impartial) stance regarding the investigation of guilt, the prosecutor's presentation of evidence must be comprehensive and clear, the defence lawyer must perform their loyal defence, and the questions that need to be answered to clarify the case must be posed. Judges take two ideal-typical stances regarding the power to decide over defendants' freedom: either considering their personal responsibility to ensure wise decisions, or by considering themselves a cog in the wheel of (state) power through which they only exercise the will of the lawmaker. Either way, there is a *discomfort of power* underneath, explaining why judges are concerned about the defendant's perspective and perception of justice in the trial proceedings (Bergman Blix and Wettergren 2018). Judges are often reluctant to intervene and ask questions themselves because it might tip the case against the defendant and hence be viewed as compromising impartiality (Bergman Blix and Wettergren 2019). As demonstrated in Chapter 4, the rule of law focusing on the defendant's rights and presumed innocence makes the complainant's credibility deficit a structurally embedded precondition of rape proceedings, as guilt must be proven beyond reasonable doubts. Furthermore, rape cases tend to exacerbate judges' discomfort of power, based on the feeling of not knowing.

The feeling of not knowing can be managed in different ways. The most common method is to maintain the standard doing of objectivity, holding the prosecutor responsible for proving the defendant's guilt:

> Above all, it is the prosecutor who wants to present the evidence that he or she thinks will support the charges, and then it is up to the prosecutor

> to ensure that [the relevant] questions are put on the table. The court can also ask questions if we think that something is unclear, but we must be careful not to ask questions so that we convict someone of a criminal offence because it is not our … we should not push the case forward but … questions are raised, and we have to relate to what we have got [when we decide]. (Lina, AC judge, Cases 7 and 8)

As seen in the quote, judges may ask questions but prefer to refrain from it. The standard approach is thus likely to lead to acquittal if the prosecutor's argument has gaps in it. Realizing the need for a different approach to the evidence in rape cases, some judges also add their expectations on the prosecutor to explain what the evidence mean, what we call empathic translation of the evidence, as expressed by DC judge Rut (Case 14):

Rut:	It varies quite a lot between different prosecutors, sometimes you can be downright surprised that the prosecutors are so careful to say that I think this has happened and then describe what has happened. I have sometimes not been able to avoid asking the question, how does the prosecutor think this has happened and actually received an answer that the prosecutor cannot say anything about it … in an astonishing way. I think you should be clear about that when you bring a prosecution, but it varies.
Researcher:	Why do you think the prosecutor answers like that?
Rut:	Well, I've thought about … sometimes they might be afraid that the court will say that it probably wasn't like that [acquit]. But maybe there are other things that mean the charge should be approved, but because the prosecutor doesn't say this … I don't know.

In this quotation, Judge Rut recognized that she needed the prosecutor to facilitate her empathic imagination of the crime and that she was frustrated both by having to request clarification (departing from her passive role) and by the answer from the prosecutor. Presumably (see next section), this prosecutor did not consider empathic translation part of their role but expected the judge to understand without translation. Hence, extending Rut's position, one could also argue that judges may take a more active and responsible stance vis-à-vis empathic imagination. This need to enhance their own empathic ability was expressed in a group interview with DC judges:

DC judge 1:	In other cases, you don't need to have a well-developed empathic ability to be able to judge in them. You don't

> need to be able to understand the other person to judge in an assault case. But you sure as hell need to be able to understand the motives and motivations and understand the person [in a rape case], because that's what empathy is all about, not to sympathize but to understand the other person. And that's also an ability and we're not really trained in that, you could say.

DC judge 2: And this is put to the test ... actually, by reading into the relationship. Have they met before? ... And then somehow find a way to understand how the other person works.

Judges in this excerpt argue for the need to stretch their own empathic ability beyond the ordinary to be able to make sense of rape cases. The problem is that judges lack training in this sort of empathy-taking and are inclined to fear that it might compromise their objectivity, reflecting an objectivity ideal in line with Rawls 'veil of ignorance' (Vermeule 2001). The challenge with this assumption is that the use of common sense, and backgrounded sympathy and antipathy for the legal subjects, risks to become heuristic tools in the assessment of the credibility of the complainant's story.

Judges embody their own experiences, both as private persons and as professionals, a practical knowledge conveyed by background emotions. Professionally, these guide the delineation between relevant and irrelevant information, legally correct and incorrect evaluation and decision-making. Lacking knowledge and insight into human behaviour and the action rationality of socially remote others when put to the task of empathic engagement with a complainant's story, it lies close at hand to draw on the background emotions of personal experiences and common sense, as noted by DC judge Mårten (Case 1):

> That's how it is, and I'm sure you also reflect on the fact that we notice ... how can there be such a difference [regarding the outcome of rape cases]? It must mean that, although we may not think about it ourselves, we also reason differently. Therefore, it is even more important to think about why we reason the way we do. I'm sure [own experiences] can have an influence; I don't know. It is very difficult to be objective in relation to yourself.

The difference in reasoning highlighted in this excerpt is arguably also tied in with the fact that judges are not trained to critically examine and reflect on their background emotions, but are simply told to 'put them aside'. In the Swedish context, a few professional judges sometimes use lay judges to reflect on their own background emotions. DC judge Mårten explained how his advice to lay judges also heightens his own awareness about forming 'ideas about what happened':

Mårten:	[I tell the lay judges] 'You will notice that it is not like it is at home … every time but it will vary. You can have a very strange and difficult background, but it won't be like your home every time'.
Researcher:	Is it a kind of prejudice management that you do as chairman, when you talk to the lay judges that way?
Mårten:	I think … we need to do that, both for ourselves and for others. By saying it out loud, I also point out to myself that this is how it is. It's not uncommon to think and sometimes say that you may have an idea about how you think this has happened, but that's not what it's about and it's that idea that becomes difficult to move away from. It is so easy to sit and think, what really happened? That's not what we're supposed to say; we're supposed to say what is proven to have happened. We want to know, but we can never know.

When Judge Mårten here referred to what is proven, he discussed the evidence presented by the prosecutor, but he also mentioned keeping one's mind open for empathizing with socially remote others ('it's not like it is at your home'). Interestingly, 'we can never know' seems to suggest that the feeling of not knowing should linger with regards to what happened (*the* truth) but not to what is proven (legal truth). This distinction is very common among judges in criminal trials (Minissale 2023). In rape cases it is not a fruitful one, because the complainant's story, if deemed credible, is in fact taken to be 'the true' story, as discussed in Chapter 4. Rape cases thus seem to collapse the construction of truth vs legal truth.

Moving on to the role of the prosecutor, it becomes clear that, unlike ordinary criminal cases, there is a somewhat unclear perception between prosecutors and judges of each other's roles in rape cases, because both these legal roles are preoccupied by doing objectivity. While judges typically expect the prosecutor to present the case in a way that conveys an idea of what happened, prosecutors typically expect the judges to make their own sense of the evidence.

The prosecutor – adapting the objective-partial argumentation

The prosecutor is legally bound by the objectivity principle (that is, an obligation to be objective, not only during the pre-investigation, but also during the trial) (SCJP 23:4 and 45:3a §). This demand of being objective and representing the state affects prosecutors' view of their professional role and tasks. For example, it means that the prosecutor must conscientiously heed potential new evidence presented in court that raises doubts about the defendant's guilt (see Törnqvist and Wettergren 2023), although the presence of an (engaged) defence lawyer lightens this burden. In criminal trials with a great deal of hard 'objective' evidence, it is rare that any new evidence appears of the kind that entirely undermines the certainty about the defendant's guilt.

The professional emotional profile of prosecutors in court is characterized by the display of confidence and certainty (Törnqvist and Wettergren 2023; Wettergren and Bergman Blix 2021). Confidence and certainty signal that the individual prosecutor, after an objective preliminary investigation and filing of the indictment, knows the case and is certain that the accused is guilty beyond reasonable doubt. Given this confidence and certainty, the prosecutor can perform as a party in court. How they perform in court is not only dependent on their view of their own role, but also on their view of the judges. As Julia (prosecutor, Case 14) termed it, 'Facts speak for themselves, and judges are experts of interpretating evidence'.

No evidence does in fact speak for itself but requires legal encoding first. Thus, translation from fuzzy real life to the clean and ordered version of it makes real events comprehensible within a legal framework. This translation is done by the prosecutor during the preliminary investigation, in the formulation of the charges, selection of the evidence and preparation of its presentation (Bladini 2013; Ekelöf et al 2009; Wettergren and Bergman Blix 2016). The presentation of the evidence is structured as a legally encoded narrative with its own internal consistency and reliability-tested logics, clearly arguing for the action rationality and criminal intent of the defendant. Hence, the presentation of the evidence is the part of the trial that prosecutors generally consider most important and prepare for the most. The standard approach to the presentation of the evidence versus the final plea was illustrated by prosecutor Julia (Case 14):

> The pleadings, I think it's, it's very much just a show ... When I was a court clerk and involved in these deliberations, it was always decided, in principle, beforehand, because [judges] have their opinion ... You will never persuade the judge if you haven't done so during your presentation of the case and your evidence. And with the witnesses you have produced you won't change your plea, because my ... I mean, the plea has a very little value ... For example, in the AC, they hardly want you to plead and the DC, they don't really want any pleading ... I know that they have experimented, in some [courts] you are not allowed to plead more than 15 minutes because you don't have the energy to listen so ... You have to wrap it up ... yes – I absolutely

believe in that, but I do believe that you gain a lot by getting a good presentation of the evidence and make that a good story because it's me who tells what's happened, and what my claims are, and if I am clear and concrete and can show that in my evidence and you can follow what I say … I think you gain much, much more from that. Rather than the plea, it … I really think you neither gain nor lose from the plea.

Julia's argument regarding the value of the plea is consistent with our previous research on ordinary criminal cases, indicating that prosecutors do not expend much effort preparing the final plea (contrary to defence lawyers – see later) (Bergman Blix and Wettergren 2018). If the presentation of the evidence is well done, the expectation is that the court will convict and the final plea is 'just a show'.

In rape trials, this strategy is flawed because of the character of the evidence. First, the main evidence is the complainant's story. Second, the supporting evidence most often consists of a) witness testimonies and b) technical and forensic evidence, both depending on the complainant's story for their meaning.

Additionally, these cases differ from others because the defendant may more easily impose reasonable doubts by presenting a consent defence (see Chapter 8). Consequently, the prosecutor cannot build confidence in the case in a manner akin to criminal cases in which facts and evidence speak for themselves once legally encoded. Instead, the translation of the evidence from fuzzy reality to legally encoded reality must be done by means of empathic translation interweaved in the presentation of evidence, and of empathy negotiation in the final plea. In our study, a few prosecutors seem to have grasped this. For instance, prosecutor Nina (Case 18) said that, contrary to other criminal cases, she 'put[s] in extra energy' in the final plea of rape cases:

That is why I like this job, there is nothing more engaging than sexual offences. There I try to … leave my … once I have filed the indictment, then I'm no longer objective; I've taken a stand. I can let go of my objective robot role and become more involved. I often don't want to say much about what the complainant has to say because I don't want to put words in her mouth. I usually make that clear. I usually tell the complainant that it should be seen as a conversation between me and her, even if we don't know each other, not as an interrogation. I have a strategy before I go into the courtroom and then the plea, that I raise … I usually ask rhetorical questions, and I hope that the court reacts to that. For instance, 'I know you are sitting here thinking, why didn't she report?'. I try to make an incendiary speech at the end. I feel like a spin doctor; if the complainant has not reported … then it is an advantage, and if she has reported directly, then that is an advantage. If she has left discrepancies in her story, it's because she is traumatized, if she has given a [long and detailed] story, then that's great. She is consistent. I win no matter how I set it up.

As argued by Nina, to properly frame the evidence and confidently proceed with the charge of rape, the prosecutor must take more of an advocacy role and leave 'the objective robot role'. They need to enhance their empathic ability already inherent to their professional emotional profile to embrace the lived experience of the complainant's perspective. In our 18 cases, the pattern is that prosecutors feel awkward taking this step because it disturbs their feeling of being objective, representing the state not the complainant (cf Goodrum 2013; Goodrum and Stafford 2003). In some cases, moreover, they have not empathically grasped the lived experience of the complainant's situation. Hence, they are unable to convey it to the court, for example by using empathy hooks (such as vivid descriptions of the situation from the complainant's perspective; see Chapter 7).

By default, prosecutors tend to balance the duty to be both partial and objective by anticipating questions from the defence. According to their reasoning, when these questions are posed to the victim by 'the friendly party' (that is, the prosecutor), the complainant can address them and explain in peace, while the defence is denied some of their ammunition. In rape trials, this tactic is either just not successful or, worse, it helps the defence to identify *Things* (for example, inexplicable elements in the complainant's story that the prosecutor considers crucial to sort out) useful to forge doubt in the judge's mind. Clever defence lawyers are aware of this, as observed in the following statement by an experienced lawyer, Elvira, in regard to her role as victim counsel (Case 11):

> The prosecutor wanted to prevent certain things by asking questions and then I could see with my experience as a defence lawyer that some things don't even need to be brought up because then the defence will find out. It was a bit unnecessary, so I took it up with the prosecutor and said that you can forget about asking these questions because it's not ... the defence will never find out if you don't bring it up ... I think that many [prosecutors] want us to raise everything that may be sensitive now [before they can be used by the defence]; it's just that sometimes it may be better to leave things that may be sensitive now because then no one knows that it even exists.

What Elvira points out is that the prosecutor's ordinary tactic is counter-productive in rape trials. By 'sensitive things', she means weak spots and inexplicable elements in the complainant's story. This naturally brings us to the role of the victim counsel.

The victim counsel – covering the prosecutor's back

In criminal cases in which a complainant has been involved and has suffered from the consequences, a victim counsel is assigned to support – inform and care for – the complainant and make the damage claims (Carroll 2022). In the standard way of doing legal objectivity as an interactional achievement, this role is important because it advances the prosecutor as the objective representative of the state, free from potential emotional attachment to the complainant. Moreover, it clarifies to the complainant that the prosecutor is not 'their representative' in court. This ordinary role as victim counsel is not juridically challenging and often assigned to juniors by the law firm. However, in our study it seemed to be more common that lawyers dedicated to these cases alternate between the role of defence lawyer and victim counsel. We also perceived them as more engaged than in other criminal cases. Victim counsels with experiences also in the role of defence lawyer possess in-depth knowledge about the defence's typical strategies, which makes them an important resource in rape cases.

That said, extending their role as victim counsel in rape cases to that of an active party in court is not common. Defence lawyer Mattias, who also worked as victim counsel, seemed to not have given this a thought. As defence lawyer in Case 10, he objected to the presence of the complainant's parents in the DC because, as he said, 'either the doors [of the courtroom] are opened, or they are closed'. However, he was well aware of the effect of parents and in the AC (where the complainant was not present), he instructed his client's parents to follow their son into the courtroom and hug him before leaving:

Mattias:	I had instructed them, as you understand, that 'now we go in together as a family'.
Researcher:	Mm.
Mattias:	'You show … you hug' … and they like 'well, uh yes'. I think that *that aspect is… is extremely important* what you show the court. That, even if it shouldn't have any significance, we are human beings.
Researcher:	Mm.
Mattias:	Here they see a mum hugging her son.
Researcher:	Do you try to …when you are a victim counsel, do you think in the same way?
Mattias:	No, much less. […] To a much lesser extent I think about it then.

In this excerpt, we observe that clever defence lawyers have a professional feel for the significance of background emotions brought by impressions made by those present in court. With their experience as defence lawyers, victim counsels potentially carry this in-depth knowledge about viable strategies against the opposed party to the prosecution. Like Mattias, however, most seem to overlook the possibility of adopting these strategies as victim counsels.

One reason may be the delimited task ascribed to the victim counsel in ordinary criminal cases. While their role is open to step up as a more active 'victim-lawyer' (Carroll 2022), the extent of communication with the prosecutor, about a potentially enhanced and collaborative work division, varies. The victim counsel Maria in Case 15 was aware of her potentially enhanced role, but seemed hesitant to take the initiative:

> So, sometimes it can be a bit difficult when you are in that role and you think, why doesn't the prosecutor ask this question? Does he or she have a reason for not asking this question? I don't want to ruin a plan that the prosecutor may have, but at the same time I feel that now that I've been involved for so long it's easier to realize that this question has just been missed. I will take it. I know that how we do this differs among lawyers. Some don't want to interfere at all, but let the prosecutor handle the question of guilt entirely, both during questioning and pleading. I don't do that. That's my view on my role, that I want to do everything I can to close any gaps. The prosecutor should be in charge of the whole thing, and you have a pretty good starting point when you listen in and can constantly note that I should follow up with an additional question. The prosecutor missed this; he said something different in the police interrogation. It is obvious that you should use that, I think.

In the excerpt, Maria clearly describes her task as following up on the prosecutor, filling in the gaps, but is mindful of not encroaching on the prosecutor's territory. The prosecutor in Case 15, as will be clear later, likely did not even consider how collaboration, inviting Maria to use the full potential of her knowledge and experience, might have benefitted the case.

Case 11 was an altogether different matter with regard to the interaction between the prosecutor and victim counsel. Victim counsel Elvira took an active role, both in the examinations and final pleas. She did not just fill the gaps, but did everything the prosecutor could not do, including foreseeing and disarming the defence's potential *Things*. She also drew on her own experience as a woman to negotiate empathy for the complainant in her final plea. She explained:

Researcher: Speaking of your plea, in general I think that … there will be a lot of reasoning about … unreasonable, reasonable, normal, abnormal, logical, illogical behaviour. You highlight, I thought, very clearly … female experience. I could really identify with what you described as a reasonable reaction … do you see that kind of argumentation as a matter of gender difference?

Elvira: Yes … uh … it was a rather difficult question actually because I try to plea the same way also when I represent a male defendant on the basis that *his* behaviour might actually be the most reasonable based on the circumstances of the situation. I don't see that … and then I might not raise it from a female experience. I can do that if I represent a woman, but I can hardly do it any other time, but then you can still deal with what is reasonable and unreasonable … and probable in a given situation.

Noticeable is that Elvira does not differentiate between her role as victim counsel and her role as defence lawyer in terms of pleading strategies. Drawing on hersense to explain the complainant's seemingly irrational behaviour, when she acted as a victim counsel, was an effect of her professional engagement and loyalty to the client. Saying that she concretizes her strategy depending on who she is representing and the way the trial develops, she also highlights the flexibility and opportunism of lawyers, contrasting the procedural formalism that regulates the prosecutor's role. Victim counsels can either diminish their role to such a formally partial role (damage claims) or enhance it to perform as they would in their role as defence lawyer.

Sophia (Case 14) was yet another engaged victim counsel who placed great emphasis on the final pleas. Comparing her own role with that of the prosecutor, she expanded on her pleasure to find her argumentation reflected in the judgment and the crucial importance of the final plea:

Sophia: How to explain and make things understandable, that's what is … I would say that it's by far the most fun part of my job, when it comes to pleading. Not only that you have to make it understandable during the course of the case, during the presentation of the evidence, so that you keep a common thread and it is clear what the focus should be, but when you tie up the loose ends and actually have to give explanations and comments on what the complainant has said, why she says that and

<table>
<tr><td></td><td>why it is natural that you might react that way, that is what is so damn fun. I love that. I would say … if I had to say what is the most fun thing about this job, that's it. That's what determines whether I should work as a lawyer or not, actually.</td></tr>
<tr><td>Researcher:</td><td>I understand. The prosecutors don't have that. I also think it's clear that the prosecutors often … they also said that the plea doesn't matter.</td></tr>
<tr><td>Sophia:</td><td>I don't agree with that at all. I won't say that because I'm not … a judge so I don't know … and, as I said, I haven't served as a clerk, I haven't sat in a deliberation, but I … and it's not because I'm the world's best lawyer who has always been successful, but I often think when I read judgments that I can see … they listen to exactly what I said when it comes to that thing. How nice that they embraced that. I don't think the pleading doesn't matter.</td></tr>
<tr><td>Researcher:</td><td>So, you can read the judgment and see that they have picked up different sentences that you have formulated?</td></tr>
<tr><td>Sophia:</td><td>I had a trial, I was in the defence, and when I … read the reasons for the judgment … I almost felt that I was reading my plea. It was absolutely wonderful. But often in cases, I mean, there are things that can actually be directly decisive that you see that here they listened to this thing and maybe they hadn't … they can also miss things in a hearing, something that is said … It's clear as hell that it [the final plea] is important, but it may be that there are both … there are certainly both lawyers and prosecutors who think it doesn't matter and therefore don't get directly involved in it. I think that's a shame, a real shame. One should take the time.</td></tr>
</table>

Sophia's experience of influencing the judgment with her final plea is shared by many skilled defence lawyers (see, for instance, Mattias, cited earlier). Noteworthy in the first part of the excerpt is that she is equally engaged with the final plea in her role as victim counsel and that she is aware of it as complementary to the prosecutor's more restricted role.

We can observe from the above that the role of the victim counsel is unclear (Antonsdottir and Laugerud 2024); whether they serve primarily as a supportive guide throughout the legal procedure or take on a more active role in court is basically up to their own initiative. This is particularly problematic in rape cases, in which there is an urgent need for an advocate who can actively engage in empathy negotiation. This need arises especially because prosecutors often treat rape cases similarly to other criminal cases, as previously discussed.

The complainant is not allowed to take part in the trial in the AC unless there are certain reasons to allow it (Chapter 2). Based on the limited 'minimal' role of the victim counsel as presenting damage claims and providing care and support for the complainant, the AC therefore does not consider it necessary for the victim counsel to be present either. In the AC, the prosecutor merely confirms the damage claim from the DC. Consequently, in the AC, the discrepancy between the loyal and engaged defence lawyer and the dryly objective prosecutor is exacerbated. Clever defence lawyers use this uncontested space to refine and improve their final pleas, including other strategies for activating background emotions by means of impressions in the courtroom.

The defence lawyer – partially emphasizing objectivity

Defence lawyers are not expected to be objective but to be *loyal* to their clients (Flower 2020). That said, defence lawyers play an important role in the interactional legal doing of objectivity. As mentioned in Chapter 3, from the perspective of judges and prosecutors, loyalty should be expressed in an appropriate and balanced way. Lawyers who are too engaged are known to make a show of their defence and the adversarial game, causing unnecessary disruption and confusion in the proceedings. Too little engagement is viewed as a failure in the collective doing of objectivity because the defendant will not receive a proper defence in line with the rule of law. This, as mentioned earlier, prompts prosecutors or judges to compensate, which creates more work for them. The ideal defence, from this objective state employee perspective, does not dispute the prosecution's objective evidence of their client's guilt but places greater emphasis on negotiating the sentence (by means of empathy negotiation) than on arguing their client's innocence. Hence, the 'non-objective' defence lawyer role is crucial for the collective legal doing of objectivity, particularly for this 'to be seen to be done' (Bergman Blix and Wettergren 2019).

From the perspective of the lawyers, loyalty and care for the client are part of their professional emotional profile and they must produce it, whether they like or believe in their client or not (Flower 2020). Thus, 'being loyal' primarily requires placing personal emotions aside, akin to the objective state of mind performed by prosecutors and judges.

That said, noteworthy in the rape cases is that defence lawyers can really have an impact on the outcome of these trials. In these cases, they are also allowed to excel in defending their client's innocence. They do this through the creation of *Things* that forge doubt in the judges' assessment and empathy negotiation that strikes the chord of their background power discomfort and evokes himpathy (Bladini et al 2023; Uhnoo et al 2024c). Due to the status of the complainant's story as main evidence, they also gain greater leeway in attacking the credibility of the complainant. As demonstrated in Uhnoo et al (2024c), they are wary of remaining within accepted boundaries, but they often know how to draw on rape myths and activate stereotypes without being too obvious.

The defence strategies in terms of advancing the client's perfectly normal and innocent behaviour will be analysed in Chapter 9. In this excerpt from the interview with defence lawyer Rikard (Case 7), we observe how he expresses pride and satisfaction in his rhetorical skills, which included insisting on holding his final plea inside the AC courtroom during COVID-19:

Researcher:	Is it good or bad for your client to sit in another room? What do you think about that? It's hard to say.
Rikard:	Well, yes, it's hard to say. But you can see, although that's a completely different matter, that it's not appropriate to process from another room in general, as a lawyer. They – as I said, it works in the AC when you just sit and watch films, but when it comes to pleading, it was a requirement, or requirement, it was a desire on my part to actually come in and plead. Well, because it's very difficult to talk to people in a wise, good way when you don't see any reactions and so on.
Researcher:	Mm, but the prosecutor did not. Is there, is there an imbalance there between you?
Rikard:	[*laughs*] Yes, yes! ... Then you just have to say thank you and accept that. No, no, but yes – I don't think it's ... but then it's true that – the prosecutor may plead in a slightly different way. Usually with slightly different ... they should be objective and so on. They have [a different] role in this so that, it is possible.

A remarkable observation we made is that, in rape trials, defence lawyers champion as *objectivity rule reminders*. Almost all lawyers include in their plea a reminder to the court that the evidence of rape cases should be treated in no way differently than in other criminal cases. This works in essence as a reminder of both the oft-claimed 'bad evidence' in rape cases (see Chapter 4) and the oft-debated notion that in rape cases 'the standard of proof' is 'lower' than in other criminal cases. It is important to note that the rule reminder draws on traditional hissense legal logics. It can thus also be seen as an attempt to foreclose the hersense dimension of the new law. Skilled lawyers in rape cases sometimes override the prosecutor's task to set the agenda and drive the case. This is arguably because rape cases upset the strict order of doing objectivity and the ordinary division of labour between the legal roles. Partial framing and argumentation are the lawyers' waters, not the prosecutors'.

Conclusion

The chapter presents and discusses the notion of objectivity making as a situated and interactional process, producing the image of objective justice, reflecting professional efforts to approximate the objectivity ideal of legal logics; a non-emotional and disembodied, blank-slated mind. To do objectivity, all legal roles must play their part in the trial. We discussed the conventional role scripts, stemming from the emotive-cognitive judicial frame, and how they may conflict with the procedure in rape trials. We saw that some research participants have begun to reflect on role adaptations, proposing enhanced empathic ability for judges; empathic translation of the evidence for the prosecutor; and a more active advocator role for the victim counsel negotiating empathy.

In the next chapter we proceed to the in-depth analysis of three cases, which each in their own way demonstrate how various combinations of legal roles, and their adaptation or lack thereof, has effects for the doing of objectivity in rape offences.

The tacit feeling and behavioural rules of emotive-cognitive judicial frame regulates the understanding of objectivity, as a value and a practice. It presumes that evidence is 'factual' and speaks for itself and that the judge can make sense of the evidence and evaluate it by their own rational minds (Chapter 11). In rape cases, however, the main evidence being *a story*, new ways to do objectivity and a fair trial, particularly for the judge and the prosecutor, are needed.

6

The Making and Breaking of Objectivity

Chapter 5 discussed objectivity making, as a collective achievement based on the labour division of the legal roles and their respective scripts when doing objectivity. The judge and the prosecutor are required to 'be' objective while the lawyers (defence and victim counsel) are partial but their loyalty to the client is nevertheless crucial in the collective objectivity making. In this chapter we investigate how the understanding of objectivity, as inherent in the emotive-cognitive judicial frame, primes for a focus on the legal rights of the defendant. In the rule of law, this focus is warranted by the fact that the defendant (in most criminal cases) is likely to be convicted and deprived of their civil rights. Consequently, in conventional collective objectivity making it is the perspective of the defendant and their perception of a fair trial that is in focus when justice is 'seen to be done' (cf Tyler 2003). Doing objectivity in the legal procedure is part of procedural justice, argued to be crucial for the legitimacy of the legal system and the public's compliance with the law. We argue that, especially in rape cases, procedural justice also includes the perspective of the complainant. By analysing, in-depth, three exemplary cases (Cases 2, 11 and 15), we demonstrate how the conventional doing of objectivity ignores the perspective of the complainant and possibly exacerbates the violation of their privacy. While this is manifestly not the intention of the new law, we also show how role adaptations can address this problem. We begin with Case 2, which provides an example of the interactional failure of doing objectivity in rape cases, through the combination of the judge's focus on the defendant, the prosecutor's conventional role performance, the victim counsel's uncertainty, and the defence lawyer's extensive empathy negotiation.

Doing objectivity as collective failure – Case 2

In Case 2, three women around 20 years old picked up a man in his late 30s on their way home from a party. They had all been drinking, they were all going to sleep in one of the women's flat and they were all flirting with the man. When they arrived home, they put on a film. The complainant, who was the youngest, fell asleep on the couch and the man went to the bedroom where he had voluntary sex with the two other women. When later he was about to leave, he also had sex with the complainant on the couch. He claimed it was voluntary. She said it was not, that she woke up when he penetrated her. In court, the defendant had the appearance of a standard white middle-class man in his 30s. He was a mid-manager at a company and a father of small children. He was well dressed and eloquent, but clearly devastated, crying a great deal. He claimed that he had never had such a shock in his whole life; the stress, fear and pain he had felt since the arrest was the worst he had ever experienced.

The defendant's story was very close to the complainant's story, except for the voluntariness of sex act. The complainant was under 18 years of age, of minority background, whose appearance in court was calm and contained. Her friends were called as witnesses. Illustrative of the focus on the complainant's story, the examinations of it lasted three hours while the examinations of the defendant's story lasted 35 minutes.

The judge, the prosecutor, and the victim counsel

At the beginning of the trial, when the prosecutor read the charges, he was unexpectedly interrupted by the presiding (professional) judge. This is uncommon, not only because judges are usually reluctant to intervene but also because they cannot know the value of the presentation of evidence before they have heard it all (Bergman Blix and Wettergren 2018). Prosecutor Staffan was going through the psychologist's report about the complainant's story and mental state when presiding Judge Hans interrupted:

Judge: Excuse me, are you going to read everything out loud? I wonder if it's valuable because that's [the psychologist] no trained interrogation officer, and so on, it's difficult … I also wonder what the take away is for me and the lay judges?
[*Prosecutor Staffan answers calmly and insists that he wants to demonstrate on the evidence the theme that she has consistently told her story in a certain way and that he also thinks it is important because we will hear the psychologist tomorrow. The point of this evidence is the complainant's story.*]

Judge: It is more like a badly reported interrogation. I imagine that the psychologist's expertise is more about how rape victims *usually* behave in cases like this.

Prosecutor: If the chairman thinks it's more appropriate, we'll do it that way. (Field notes, Case 2)

The presentation of the psychologist's report is often used by prosecutors to support the complainant's victim-adequate behaviour. Here, it was also envisaged to support that the complainant's story had been consistent and stable over time. When asked in the break later, the prosecutor said the judge's intervention was 'expected' and this judge 'is like that'. Another judge would have let him continue with the presentation. In the follow-up interview, Prosecutor Staffan was asked to clarify:

Researcher: When the judge interrupted your presentation …
Staffan: Mm.
Researcher: You said that you knew and you had thought about that before, that he is like that. Did you ever … did you think that you could have … prepared your presentation in another way?
Staffan: No. Then I would just have done as I knew he wanted it, and that's how it turned out anyway. Those were the options that I had.

The two options suggested here by the prosecutor are either to try to forge his point with this particular piece of evidence (which he did) or to leave this part out (because he knew the judge 'was like that'; cf Wettergren and Bergman Blix 2016). Noteworthy here is that Staffan did not see a third option: explaining to the judge that each of the pieces of evidence presented were important parts of a whole, meant to convey insight into the complainant's perspective and her story. This attempt at empathic translation might have made it, at least, more difficult for 'this judge' to dismiss.

When the prosecutor was finished with the charges, it was time to hear the complainant. She had wished to be heard in the absence of the defendant. Prior to sending the defendant to an adjacent room in which he could follow the trial on video, the judge leaned towards the defendant and stated:

There is no judgment involved [in granting that you have to leave the room] on my part but only that [the complainant] has said that she cannot talk in a relaxed way if you are in the room. [*The judge then explains that the rule about this right of the complainant goes way back and that complainant's mere wish is enough to grant it. He then continues*]: A complainant who has been strong and stood her ground would perhaps not need this, but it is rather a matter of her being weak. [*The defence lawyer now intervenes and assures laughingly (palms turned towards the judge,*

he looks embarrassed) that he and his client have nothing against it. The judge smiles kindly at the defendant as he talks. He does not look at the complainant.]
(Field notes, DC, Case 2)

Noteworthy in this excerpt is not that the judge explained to the defendant why he was sent out, but the way that he did it. In this quotation, we observe how the judge's characterization of the complainant (weak, not standing her ground) could appear as a statement of the value of her story. She had not been heard by the judge yet but, having observed the parties for about half an hour, his way of explaining could risk being interpreted as sympathy for the (sobbing) defendant. The fact that the defence lawyer found it embarrassing confirms this.

The judge intervened a third time when victim counsel Ragnar examined the defendant and asked him why he had deleted the contents of his telephone when he was arrested. The defendant answered evasively and said it might 'have been a brand-new phone':

Judge [*interrupts*]:	Mr [name of victim counsel], there is no mentioning [in the case file] that the history has been deleted!
Defence lawyer:	Exactly!
Victim counsel:	The case file mentions that the history is gone, the phone is empty.
Judge:	It is important if you use a word like 'deleted' … the lay judges cannot see what's in the case file.
Victim counsel:	No, that's right, it does not say *who* has deleted everything.
Defence lawyer:	It is not at all clear that it has been deleted!
Judge [*interrupts DL with a dismissive, slightly annoyed face*]:	I've read that out loud now, so let's leave it at that. The examination is over, thank you! (Field notes, Case 2)

In this excerpt, we observe how Judge Hans virtually serves the defence a protest. Judge Hans may have become aware of it since the defence lawyer's enthusiasm seemed to irritate him. From the observer's (the researcher's) stand-point the situation was embarrassing for the judge and humiliating for the victim counsel, whose examination was abruptly cut off. In the follow-up interview, Hans said that he could not remember any of this from the trial, but that he found the victim counsel 'perhaps a bit inexperienced'. In the follow-up interview, Ragnar himself made the following reflection:

> Judges never like surprises … you might say … and … without going into further details about why I asked that question, so … you could say that the judge rarely likes it when things come into the case that they don't really know about. They want to know about it and have control over it … and then it is more understandable that you make that kind of comment.

Noteworthy in this excerpt is victim counsel Ragnar's attempt to justify Judge Hans's obstruction of his examination, which had been carefully designed to undermine the defendant's credibility. The justification can arguably be interpreted as face-saving (Goffman 1959, see also Flower 2020). On account of the assembled impression of all of Judge Hans's three interventions, Ragnar continued: 'Clearly, this type of, when there are several of these, these three things together as you say, how does it affect the experience for a complainant, for example? That, in contrast, that I think it's a good question.'

The role of Judge Hans in Case 2 appeared both partial and offensive from the perspective of the complainant, but also from the perspective of the observer. Yet, following the reasoning of the prosecutor and victim counsel, it was, strictly speaking, not breaking with procedural rules. On the contrary, the first intervention was in line with the principle of orality and immediacy, however awkward (Chapter 4). If the journal record from the psychologist was read aloud, it might risk contaminating the victim's story before she had a chance to share it herself. The second intervention, the long explanation to the defendant about the decision that he had to leave the room, was expanding the boundaries, but even so it was in line with the conventional focus on the defendant's rights. The third intervention, interrupting the victim counsel's leading questions to the defendant, was – despite that it might have revealed an 'inexplicable element' in his story – in line with procedural rules, according to the victim counsel himself.

Yet, the interventions deviate from common practice. Swedish judges are wary about intervening in the procedure unless they anticipate serious disturbance. They usually trust that the legal professionals might have a strategy and are curious to determine if the result will add to their knowledge and understanding of the case (Bergman Blix and Wettergren 2018). The presiding style of the judge in Case 2, his way of doing objectivity, might not have mattered much in a different type of criminal case. In a rape case, in which stories are the focus of the argumentation, and where there is a relatively high risk of acquittal, this style amounted to all but an empathic performance of impartiality. In other words, in terms of procedural justice, it can be seen to be a breach against neutrality (Bladini and Bergman Blix 2022).

In the follow-up interview, Hans explained that he had no experience with assessing voluntariness, but it was not an issue anyway because the prosecution claimed that the complainant was asleep when he penetrated her. This was, he reasoned, also rape before the new law. However, given that non-voluntary participation is the main requisite for rape, and prosecutors always include it in their charges, voluntariness should also be assessed. Hans, like many other judges in our data, focused on the charge of sleep as if it excluded the charge of un-voluntariness (see also Case 15, later). The following interview response indicates power discomfort related to rape cases in general and the new law in particular, based on the difference between assault rape and 'rape':

Hans:	It's always sad because, especially in rape cases … it's somehow a disaster, whichever way you do it. Well, I'm not talking about assault rape or anything like that.
Researcher:	No, no, exactly.
Hans:	But precisely in cases where … where there is an unpunished uh … offender. And then there is a … uh a raped woman. Who then seeks redress. And gets uh … such a setback, which, which makes it extremely hard. And the rule of law should then protect the alleged rapist from being convicted for a crime that he hasn't actually committed. Here it will be … here it will be very, eh, it eh, there will be huge consequences.
Researcher:	Right.
Hans:	When you acquit.

Power discomfort is expressed explicitly in the beginning and the end of this statement, in the terms 'disaster' and 'huge consequences'. It is also explicit in the wording 'which makes it *extremely hard*' and implicit in the reasoning around *previously unpunished* defendants and *raped women* seeking *redress* but experiencing *a setback* when the case is *acquitted*. Behind the argumentation lingers the 'real rape' myth. The 'real rapist' and 'she lies' myths are expressed in the discomfort of convicting previously unpunished defendants and by *the rule of law must protect alleged rapists* against *wrongful* conviction. Essentially, the quotation infers that it is very difficult to judge in cases in which the accused is previously unpunished yet may have committed a rape which is, in a way, not *a real rape*. Any way you try solving this dilemma will result in disaster for one of the parties (see also Uhnoo et al, 2024c).

As the interview continues, power discomfort is expressed in connection with a discussion on the reasons for acquitting in Case 2:

Hans:	You can't make the pieces [in the complainant story] fit together and the fact that I, uh, come back to this several times as …. you have to explain that … it's not that we are … the court has found … that [defendant] has not committed the offence.

Researcher:	No.
Hans:	That's very important, but the question answered is, has the prosecution proved the case beyond reasonable doubt?
Researcher:	Mm, exactly.
Hans:	Their allegation of offence. So, you may have come to the conclusion that she is considerably more credible than he is. As well as thinking that it didn't get all the way through, so to speak. Because you believed her. You have thought … this is a very, sort of a story that is coherent and gets some support. But you don't reach, uh, all the way through … and it is very important to explain that but here, I think it is enough. … And it is always a matter of judgment.
Researcher:	Exactly.
Hans:	And I can say, well … we [the professional judge and three lay judges] have agreed on this judgment, but then of course it is only me who formulates the reasons.

In this quotation, Judge Hans attempted to explain why the complainant did not receive redress. He used an impersonal pronoun (a general 'you') throughout, asserting the importance that the complainant understands that the court does not reject the credibility of her story but rejects the quality of the prosecutor's evidence. Here, Hans separated legal truth (what is proven) from *the* truth (what has really happened) (see Chapter 5). Ultimately, he assumed the first-person pronoun, to say that, in fact, this is not just his decision, but a decision taken by four judges (him and three lay judges). He only formulated and wrote the judgment. Distancing himself from personal responsibility, this is an argument that might be interpreted as a bureaucratic perception of power (Bergman Blix and Wettergren 2018).

The prosecutor and the defence lawyer

In this section we examine the relation between the prosecutor and defence lawyer, highlighting how prosecutors' standard doing of objectivity compromises the objectivity of rape cases by providing the defence with inexplicable elements used by the latter to forge doubt in the judges – what we call *Things*. *Things* can be used by judges as proxies for factual evidence to scaffold certainty about an acquittal.

In the following, two *Things* are created: how the complainant's jeans came off and the duration of the sex event. The question of who removed the complainant's clothes (notably trousers and panties) was addressed in all 18 cases, indicating that in legal logics this may be a sign of voluntariness (see Chapter 7). Starting in the prosecutor's questioning of the complainant in the DC:

Prosecutor:	When you fall asleep, what clothes are you wearing?
Complainant:	I fall asleep in my jeans, the same clothes as during the day.
	She was wearing jeans, and she was wearing them when she wakes up the first time, then she says quietly that she is 'pretty sure about it' [*repeats that twice*]. 'But it may have been that … but pretty sure of it'. When she wakes up the second time, her jeans have been removed but not her panties completely. She doesn't remember feeling him take them off.
	[*There is a noticeable pause. Silence.*]
Prosecutor:	You wake up to him having vaginal sex with you; that's the first thing you realize?
Complainant:	Yes.
Prosecutor:	How long does it last before it is interrupted?
Complainant:	One minute max. I didn't even have time to say anything, I was still shocked when he gets up and puts his clothes on.
	[*A noticeable pause. Silence. The judge looks in the prosecution's direction with an impatient expression, as if wondering if the examination is over now.*]
	[...]
Prosecutor:	Why do you think it ended?
Complainant:	Eh, I think because he ejaculated, I think so.
Prosecutor:	You said something about it ending so fast, that it therefore felt wrong, can you develop that?
Complainant:	No, but I mean, he was done, and then I think he gets up and puts his clothes on directly and yes, it felt wrong. That you wake up and find someone on top of you and then he gets up and gets dressed. (Field notes, Case 2)

In this excerpt from the field notes, two things are noteworthy: the long silences that mark potential inexplicable elements, which the prosecutor left without further questions. Since the prosecutor has been the leader of the preliminary investigation, he knew the different stories about both the clothes she was wearing (and how they came off) and about the duration of the sex act. The reason he did not ask questions to clarify was, as he explained when shadowed during the preliminary investigation, that he felt it was his duty to highlight 'some inexplicable elements' in the complainant's story. Prosecutor Staffan had been unsure about this case all along, he said, but decided to indict and then 'leave it to the judge to decide'. As we observed earlier in the quotation from Judge Rut, relegating to the judge to make sense of the complainant's story is not a wise thing to do.

If Staffan perceived his objective duty was to highlight inexplicable elements, it is strange that he did not push the complainant to try to explain. Allowing silence to linger provides no orientation regarding how the audience in the courtroom is supposed to understand what happened. Instead, it highlights the 'no-answer' and leaves room for questions: How can a pair of jeans be taken off without someone waking up? Or is her uncertainty because she *could* have taken them off herself during the hours she slept on the couch, without her remembering? Because it was very late, she was very tired, she had been drinking a great deal earlier that night and had a hangover?

Despite not receiving a straight answer, pushing the inexplicable elements would have provided potential empathy hooks and inspired imagination, making the uncertainty regarding the jeans feel more familiar to listeners who themselves experienced something similar. This would be to invite common sense, or experience based on messy lived reality, contrasting legal reality in which common sense (legal logics) refers to the autonomous rational subject. In the following, we observe how legal logics is put to work by the defence lawyer, as he picks up the inexplicable element of the jeans, and examines the complainant:

	[*The defence lawyer goes on, passive aggressive, calm but tense voice and indignant face, his questions are thrust out forcefully and articulately.*]
Defence lawyer [*asks about before they came to the apartment*]:	Was it flirty between you two?
	[*The complainant straightens her back before answering in a loud and clear voice, firmly.*]
Complainant:	We were nice to each other. But 'flirty' …?
Defence lawyer [*continues with questions about the sex act*]:	What was she wearing and how did the clothes come off? Was she wearing a bra? Jeans? [*His questions insinuate the scenario that contrary to what she calls 'dressed', she went to bed topless with the jeans on.*] And how could the jeans and any other clothes come off without you noticing?
Defence lawyer [*shifts to a new set of questions*]:	Did you have a boyfriend at the time?
Complainant:	No, but there was someone I had strong feelings for.
Defence lawyer:	Were you a couple?

Complainant:	Not officially a couple.
	[*DL stays silent for a long time.*] (Field notes, Case 2, researcher's interpretation emphasized)

Through temporal boundary work (see Chapter 7), the defence lawyer in the excerpt links what happened *before* the sex act, the 'flirting', with the inexplicable element of the jeans, and implicitly to what happened *after* (reporting rape). This way, the jeans turn into a *Thing,* a fact loaded with symbolic meaning. Contrasting the silence in the prosecutor's examination, the silence in this excerpt is intentionally rhetorical and long enough to give listeners time to imagine the potential boyfriend. It suggests that, regretting her infidelity, she would have invented non-voluntariness (rape). The inexplicable *Thing* with the jeans would then, from a legal logics' perspective, be explicable and rational. The boyfriend idea is a hissensical empathy hook orienting misguided empathic imagination of how it must have felt for the young girl when she realized that she might lose her boyfriend. The *Thing* with the jeans becomes significant through the linkage to before (flirting) and the after (regretting) and its rationality is supported by the 'she lies' myth, which is structurally embedded in rape proceedings and therefore intuitively recognizable by judges as an alternative hypothesis.

As the hearing continued, it became clear that there were disagreements on the duration of the sex act. This was implied already by the prosecutor's silence upon the complainant's statement that the sex act lasted only about a minute. The defendant had said ten minutes. One of the two witnesses from the evening were heard and significant emphasis was placed on the timing of the sex act, despite both witnesses' claims that they really did not remember well what happened when the defendant left their room. They knew they heard 'sounds from the couch' in the living room but were not sure exactly when or for how long they continued. The following excerpt is from the prosecutor's examination of Witness 1, who said the defendant had just left their room and then they heard sounds:

Prosecutor:	When you hear the sound, you were curious, do you talk about it?
Witness 1:	We were curious first. If we knew that [the complainant] was asleep we would have gone out to them, but we thought she wanted to. It was maybe 10–15 minutes.
Prosecutor:	That's a long time.
Witness 1:	Well, I don't remember. Maybe 10.
Prosecutor:	But longer than a few minutes?
Witness 1:	Yes, because we had time to talk for a long time, because we realized it was over when [the complainant] came in.

Prosecutor:	But do you hear when the sound stops?
Witness 1:	No.
Prosecutor:	Is it 10–15 minutes from when the sound starts to when [the complainant] comes in?
Witness 1:	Yes.

In this excerpt, prosecutor Staffan implicitly highlights the discrepancy between the time of the sex act as described by the complainant and the time that elapsed after the defendant left the room (and eventually the flat) and the complainant came into their room. His questions and the witnesses' answers can be interpreted as opening for uncertainty whether there had been a 10–15-minute-long sex act, in line with the defendant's story, or whether something else had gone on (for instance, a shorter sex act and then the defendant getting dressed and leaving). By not asking the witness to confirm this understanding, prosecutor Staffan again handed over an inexplicable element (time) for the defence to tweak as a *Thing*. The defence lawyer managed to do so, even when faced with the manifestly incoherent testimonies about time in his examination with Witness 2:

Defence lawyer :	How long did it take until he went home?
Witness 2:	An hour?
Defence lawyer:	How sure?
Witness 2:	30 per cent [*laughs*].
Defence lawyer:	Good, because in a police interrogation you have said 20 minutes.
Witness 2:	[*low voice*]: … but I went out …
Defence lawyer:	Okay, because in another police interrogation you said that you went to the door and listened and that it sounded like sex, you wondered 'how does he cope', and then he left after 35 minutes. How long did you stand at the door?
Witness 2:	Not long.
Defence lawyer:	What did you hear?
Witness 2:	I'm sure they had sex. Maybe a minute but we also fell asleep again.
Defence lawyer:	Did the complainant have a boyfriend?
Witness 2:	I don't know, we did not talk about that.
Defence lawyer:	What do you reckon the time was when the defendant leaves the apartment?
Witness 2:	6 or 7am, maybe 7?
Defence lawyer:	The defendant has a Google Maps where you can see where the phone has been. You arrived at the

	address at 04.35 and then he leaves at 09.58. What do you say about that information?
Witness 2:	When you're drunk, you don't know the time. For me, it felt like early morning.

Again, the defence lawyer interweaves questions about the *Thing* with questions about the boyfriend. The complainant had said there was no boyfriend but, at this point in the hearing, the imaginary boyfriend has been established as an empathy hook recurrently used by the defence.

The *Thing* is an empty signifier at first. A pair of jeans are taken off, but we do not know by whom. A sex event may have lasted one or more minutes, but no one remembers exactly. As the hearing evolves, things become weighed down with telling silences, connoted to other signs like boyfriends, and eventually surface as 'real' reasons for doubt. Skilled defence lawyers collect and create things at random, test them in the hearing, drop those that do not seem to resonate with the atmosphere in the courtroom and retain those that might work. In the process of selecting efficient things, the prosecution's own inexplicable elements, when these are revealed, are obvious indicators of *Things*. If the prosecutor does not even attempt to explain the inexplicable elements put forward, but leaves them for the court to decide, the defence lawyer will use them to forge doubt.

In the final plea, Staffan argued that the complainant's story was credible, consistent over time and supported by the witnesses. About the jeans, he said:

> There are some statements ... this statement that she is dressed, I imagine that the defence lawyer will bring this up and that it is strange. But it is for the court to evaluate. He adds that one might speculate of course. It could also be that she misjudged how much clothes she was wearing.

In the excerpt, an explanation of sorts is attempted, but it is no empathy hook. It rather raises new questions; what is 'misjudged' supposed to mean? About the time *Thing*, the prosecutor's plea simply stated that the witnesses more or less agreed on 'a timespan of about 30 minutes'.

The defence lawyer's final plea began by drawing on a common himpathy cue (Uhnoo et al 2024c), offering that 'these [rape]cases are extremely unpleasant' and his client's life 'would be crushed' if convicted. He went on with an objectivity rule reminder. The standard of evidence must be as high as in other criminal cases; there is no difference between rape cases and other cases. He then described the complainant's voluntariness, expressed in deeds, as told by his client: 'She caressed his back, they cuddled each other, and she moaned'. Eventually, he weaved together the *Things* (the jeans and the time) with the alternative scenario (boyfriend):

> The complainant wakes up, sees the defendant, they say good morning, he sits on the couch and she falls asleep. Then the defendant is said to have removed her jeans and panties. Here the court should use its common sense ... I think this is a consensual sex act that she later regretted. One could speculate. She's been dating a guy. The court needs to take this to heart and think about it. Is this beyond reasonable doubt? Witness 1 said the sound lasted 10–15 minutes. The complainant said about one minute. The defendant says 15 minutes, which is also correct. (Field notes, Case 2)

The defence lawyer in this excerpt confidently asks the judges to use their 'common sense' regarding the jeans, to take the boyfriend idea to heart and 'think about it', and argues that his client's version of the time is supported by Witness 1.

In the DC judgment (acquitted, not appealed), one of two main reasons for not finding the accused guilty beyond reasonable doubt was 'the unexplained fact that the complainant's account includes a claim that [the defendant] could take off her jeans without her waking up'. The second reason was 'the fact that Witness 1 and Witness 2 perceived that the sexual activity lasted considerably longer than the very short time reported by the complainant'. The judgment reasons that this timing 'confirms [the defendant's] rather than the complainant's statement'.

Case 2 is an exemplary representative of how *Things* make it all the way from the prosecutor, via the defence, to the judgment. Given the power discomfort of Judge Hans, observed earlier, it is understandable that he (and the lay judges) made use of these as objectivity lifebuoys, that is, as fact-proxies that raise 'objective' doubts.

This section has demonstrated how a prosecutor's standard doing of objectivity, presenting the evidence and their possible flaws, confident that the court can see that the evidence speaks for itself, creates an open door for the defence by: 1) revealing what the prosecution considers to be crucial inexplicable elements; 2) allowing the defence to turn those into *Things* to suggest alternative scenarios that cannot be ignored.

In Case 2, the defence lawyer performed this skilfully. The victim counsel however appeared to be ambivalent: on the one hand he seemed to be prepared to advance his role as a loyal advocator of the complainant, on the other hand he seemed unsure of his scope of action. The prosecutor in Case 2 exemplifies the prosecutors in our study who cling to their habituated way of doing objectivity in rape cases. When faced with a skilled defence strategy, they tend to perform weakly. Even more interesting is that they seem not to understand what they do wrong. In Case 2, we further observed a judge who arguably made objectivity the standard way, focused on the defendant's rights and perception of procedural justice. Through its extreme expression, clearly demonstrating empathy towards the defendant, it shows how the habituated legal logical way of doing objectivity is particularly ill-suited to rape cases. In this sense, and together with the performances of the prosecutor and the victim counsel, Case 2 demonstrates a failure of doing objectivity.

In the next section, we explore how collaboration between the prosecutor and victim counsel may look when they are both sensitive to how the evidence of rape cases requires adaptation of their respective roles and the work division between them.

Doing objectivity as collective achievement – Case 11

Case 11 is a one of our cases that represents an effective example of collaboration between the prosecutor and the victim counsel. Characteristic for these cases is mutual understanding of roles and willingness to adapt these to complement each other. As argued previously, adaptation means that the prosecutor refrains from highlighting weaknesses that may become *Things* and places greater emphasis on the empathic translation of the complainant's story, possibly by means of empathy hooks, while the victim counsel enhances their role from caretaker of the complainant to an active and loyal representative of their client throughout the trial, more akin to their role as defence lawyers.

In Case 11, the complainant had agreed with a friend/lover (witness-friend) that he and his friend (the defendant) should sleep at her place since they were passing though her town at night in their car. The condition was that they would not stay up but immediately go to sleep. During the evening, she video-called them from home as they were driving. She was drinking, was 'half-naked', and joked about sex. When the men arrived late at night, they brought two other women and lots of wine. It turned out that, in reality, they had been at a party in the same town. The complainant was sober and angry and wanted to go back to sleep, so she told them to leave. The defendant then tried to kiss her, but she told him off and he went to the toilet while the witness-friend and the two women left. The defendant, who was drunk, came out of the toilet naked. The complainant sent text messages and tried to call witness-friend to come to pick up the defendant but received no answer. She then offered the defendant to sleep in a guest room and gave him a pair of sweatpants to sleep in. He came out of the room and raped her while she was sitting on her sofa to calm down.

The complainant was a woman in her 30s with heavy makeup and wearing a black leather jacket. She did not show much emotion during the trial, nor did she give long and detailed answers. The defendant was a man of the same age, of minority origin. He had been making sexual advances at other women that night, and he was charged with two minor crimes at the same trial, to which he confessed. The defendant might thus seem to fit nicely with the stereotypical 'real rapist', but the complainant posed quite a challenge to the typical victim myth. The key witness – witness-friend – also figured as important in the trial. In court, he was well dressed, attractive and gave a self-confident impression, but expressed no sympathy for the complainant. He and the complainant had met on a dating application, but they were not a couple.

Prosecutor Jesper (Case 11) was worried because, before the trial, the defence had discovered proof of an old rape accusation made by the complainant. The defence lawyer was known to be sharp and for 'passing the line' in rape cases. The prosecutor's concern was that he would succeed in shifting the focus of the court from the actual rape to 'she cries rape'.

The victim counsel and the prosecutor

Here we observe how prosecutor Jesper examines the complainant's story on the inexplicable element that she did not simply make the defendant leave when she realized he was still in the house. Setting 'the situation as a whole' to begin at the point when the group entered the complainant's flat, Jesper aimed to include that she clearly expressed no wish to kiss the defendant. This said, this temporal boundary work also referred to the video call earlier the same evening, in anticipation of the defence's potential *Thing*. The excerpt begins when they discuss the kiss:

Prosecutor:	Tell me a bit more about it, how did it happen?
Complainant:	In the kitchen. I'm standing at the kitchen counter. No, I don't want him to kiss me.
Prosecutor:	Does it happen more or less directly? It makes me wonder, did you talk about anything sexual when you had this video conversation?
Complainant:	So, during our video call, he sees that I'm half-naked. But I didn't invite any sexual act, we didn't talk about sex in that way, no. She continues describing how she closes the door, then realizes that the defendant is still there. The defendant goes from the toilet to her bed and lies down there naked.
Prosecutor:	But don't you ask him to leave?
Complainant:	I texted [witness-friend] 'Come get your fucking mate'. I told [the defendant] if you are going to sleep here, you can sleep in the guest room, and

<table>
<tr><td></td><td>put some clothes on. He asked if he could borrow a pair of sweatpants.</td></tr>
<tr><td>Prosecutor:</td><td>It sounds a bit strange, just like that, when you tell it. You wake up and you've been asleep for 3–4 hours, he tries to kiss you, why didn't you ask him to leave?</td></tr>
<tr><td>Complainant:</td><td>I think how can I solve this? So, I ask my friend to come get him, I try to get him out of my bed; I can't converse with him.</td></tr>
<tr><td>Prosecutor:</td><td>How did you perceive him?</td></tr>
<tr><td>Complainant:</td><td>Drunk, he was slurring his words, bustling around. I wanted to solve the emergency situation, get him out of my room, he was naked in my bed.</td></tr>
</table>

In the excerpt, we observe that the prosecutor's questions clarified that the complainant, despite the video call, had no plans to have sex with the defendant and that she perceived him naked in her bed as an acute situation that had to be solved until witness-friend came to get him. When the opportunity came to the victim counsel, Elvira, she probed further into this situation:

<table>
<tr><td>Victim counsel:</td><td>This sequence of events, from when he comes in until he leaves, do you have any idea how long it was?</td></tr>
<tr><td>Complainant:</td><td>About 30 minutes.</td></tr>
<tr><td>Victim counsel:</td><td>When he has come in, he seemed drunk, but could you reason with him?</td></tr>
<tr><td>Complainant:</td><td>He slurred. We had no real conversation; it was difficult.</td></tr>
<tr><td>Victim counsel:</td><td>You say that you tried to solve the situation? What solutions did you see with a strange man in your flat?</td></tr>
<tr><td>Complainant:</td><td>To get him to sleep, so I have time to solve it, get hold of [witness-friend] to come get him.</td></tr>
<tr><td>Victim counsel:</td><td>So, the fact that he was allowed to stay is because he was so drunk he was going to doze off. (Field notes, Case 11)</td></tr>
</table>

The victim counsel here narrows the temporal boundaries to the 'acute' situation, which we learn lasted 30 minutes. The details of handling the slurring and wasted naked defendant invites to imagine a long time of intensive stress and fear. Elvira then asked about the sex event and the emotive-cognitive state of mind of the complainant:

Victim counsel:	How do you see him, his physical strength?
Complainant:	I see him as strong. I go to the gym myself, but I can't break free.
Victim counsel:	How about your well-being. How do you feel?
Complainant:	Stressed. I feel I need to solve the situation. I had agreed to let them sleep over but then this happened. I tried to stay focused. It was also very difficult.
Victim counsel:	What do you feel during the abuse?
Complainant:	I feel that, now it's going to happen, panic, it made me very sad, now it's happening, now it's happening. I was afraid that it was going to get worse.
Victim counsel:	You were quite verbally tough with him. What were you thinking?
Complainant:	I was upset and angry. Scolding him and wanting him to leave. I was very angry and stressed.
Victim counsel:	So, you managed to stay focused on solutions, that's why you dare to get angry with him.
Complainant:	At first, I felt that I don't want to fight with this person. I want to solve it in a peaceful way before the emotions get out of hand. I stayed calm. Tried to speak out, to avoid and to stop. I was annoyed by [witness-friend's] deceit and lies while trying to get [the defendant] not to attack me but to go to bed and sleep. (Field notes, Case 11)

In this quote, we get an idea of the complainant's fear. It includes the complainant's physical sensation of the defendant's strength, her panic and her fear that 'it was going to get worse'. The victim counsel's questions further illustrates that the complainant did try to 'act tough' before the sex act, but that anger was also to control her own fear, part of staying 'focused on solutions'.

Despite the fact the complainant was not so eloquent, the counsel managed to convey her emotive-cognitive action rationality in 'the situation as whole', which the victim counsel set to the 30 acute minutes. She also asked her about details in the defendant's and witness-friend's statements, to make her explicitly react to (and refute) them, thereby making it more difficult for the defence to use these as *Things*. This is an example of how the victim counsel can extend their role in the examination of the complainant, to include the requisites of the criminal offence (voluntariness and intent) and not just the damage claims (suffering).

In line with this role adaptation, in the examination of the defendant the victim counsel adopted the same strategy as a defence lawyer, namely to highlight *Things* to shed doubts on the credibility of the defendant, pinpointing inexplicable elements. The victim counsel used his own story to demonstrate his irrational behaviour:

Victim counsel:	Why do you need sweatpants?
Defendant:	[The complainant] offers them.
Victim counsel:	But were you going to sleep? You said you were making out? Why did you make out if you were going to sleep? Why did you start making out? (Field notes, Case 11)

In this excerpt, the sweatpants, are transformed to a *Thing* to the prosecution's advantage. They now signify that he realized (and feigned to accept) that the complainant did not want to have sex with him. Next, the victim counsel drew on the lawmaker's intention of the new legislation, that is, to establish norms of mutuality and respect in sex.

Victim counsel:	Did [the complainant] perform any sexual acts on you?
Defendant:	She touched me. He points to his upper body.
Victim counsel:	But you don't say anything concrete, that she touched your penis. Was it one-sided on your part, *you* licked and fucked her? You could have done things to each other?

This is a clever move, as it also serves as a reminder to the court about the norm-changing intention of the new law. Elvira in fact reminds the court about the law's hersensical legal logics. She also shows the defendant's own story to reveal him as selfish and indifferent towards the complainant's wishes, which is crucial for the assessment of intent.

The main witness, the witness-friend, in Case 11 was called by the prosecutor but, in the hearing, turned out to be a prize draw for the defence as his testimony contained several statements regarding the complainant's 'frivolous' sexual behaviour. That night, he did not reply to her calls to come to get the defendant. In the examination of the witness-friend, victim counsel Elvira was confrontative, targeting the credibility of the witness by making a *Thing* of his 'tendency to lie':

Victim counsel:	Do you write true things in your chat conversation to [the complainant]?
Witness-friend:	What do you mean?

Victim counsel:	This evening, do you write things that are true?
Witness-friend:	99 per cent of the time.
Victim counsel: *[referring to the story that he and the defendant were passing through the complainant's town at night and needed somewhere to sleep over. It is clear from previous examinations that this was not true.]*	Is it possible you wrote something not true?
Victim counsel:	Did [the complainant] call you after you were kicked out?
Witness-friend:	Don't remember.
Victim counsel:	There is one missed call on your phone.
Witness-friend:	She may have called me.
Victim counsel:	Do you remember what she wrote in the first text message?
Witness-friend:	That I should throw him out.
Victim counsel *[reads aloud from a copy of a screenshot in the case file.]*:	'Come get your mate, damn it, I didn't think this about you?' You write back, 'What's wrong with you, why do you have such low self-esteem?'. So, what you said before wasn't quite right.
Witness-friend:	That's what I remember. (Field notes, Case 11)

Apart from exposing the lie, in this excerpt we see how victim counsel Elvira prepares for the placement of a pun that also works as an empathy hook. Having established that witness-friend likely saw the messages and the call but ignored them, she reads out loud his one and only arrogant response. The empathy hook consists of imagining the feelings of the complainant, whom we know is trying to handle an 'acute' situation, when she got this answer.

As we reach to the final pleas in Case 11, prosecutor Jesper anticipated one of the *Things* of the defence, namely why the complainant did not simply throw the defendant out right after he came out from the toilet. He tried to empathically translate the rationality of the complainant's action, describing first how she was tired and upset but did not want the complainant to stay:

It's easy for me to sit here and think that I would have gone crazy just kicking him out. But imagine this: she is interested in the

> witness-friend, and the defendant is his friend. We can look at her text message 'pick up your friend'. He doesn't reply. She is stuck in the flat with the defendant. He takes off his clothes. Then she takes a pair of sweatpants and says you can sleep in the guest room. Sits down on a sofa. He follows and then it all happens really fast. (Field notes, Case 11)

The rationality of the complainant's actions does not quite come through in this quote, perhaps because it appears that prosecutor Jesper himself finds it strange – *he* would just have kicked him out. Jesper then lines up the facts, but this does not help to enter in and *feel* the situation (cf Roeser 2012).

In contrast, the victim counsel's final plea probed deeper into the situation and the parts left out by the prosecutor, placing empathy hooks by drawing on *female* action rationality:

> If I had a strange, intoxicated man in my home at night, I would act like [the complainant], with caution. It is not at all certain that you will scream and shout to get someone to leave if you feel that you cannot overpower the person. As a woman, I know that this way of acting makes perfect sense.

Not only does vicitm counsel Elvira identify with the complainant's actions, she also draws on female fear to assert that this action makes perfect sense. This is hersensical reasoning. As discussed in Chapter 3, female fear is likely to be recognized by most women. The empathic imagination is evoked by the image of 'a strange intoxicated man in my home at night'. This is much more powerful than when the prosecutor tried empathic translation from a hissensical perspective: first distancing himself from the complainant, then explaining that the rationale of the complainant might be 'interest' in witness-friend. As a skilled lawyer, Elvira had probably also noted that the presiding DC judge was a woman, and the lay judges were two men and one woman in their 60s.

The victim counsel further anticipated and pre-empted the judges' potential background emotions and thus stereotypical impression of her client's appearance and somewhat frivolous behaviour by identifying it out as an implicit rape myth:

> Does it speak against [the complainant] that she has not fought and kicked? The defence mentioned that she has reported rape before. Can you only be raped once? Of course not! Can you not be raped if you have ever been interested in sex? Is it only the nice girls who can be raped? No.

The argument that one can be raped more than once addressed the witness-friend statement that the complainant had been 'crying rape' before. The interweaved disclaimer regarding 'nice girls' could be primarily directed at the elderly lay judges, to remind them that sexual norms have changed. Women are entitled to their sexuality.

Finally, in the plea the victim counsel forged the *Thing* about witness-friend as notorious liar:

> The text messages provide strong support for what has happened, occurring instantaneously during and after the event. [Witness-friend] is not at all reliable and credible. He obviously lied to the complainant, lied about why they needed to sleep over and lied about the party.

Reminding the judges that the main witness has been proven to lie was to convince them that he could not be credible in his efforts to smear the complainant. Elvira also relentlessly attacked the credibility of the defendant, by means of his own story:

> [The defendant] has a very big overconfidence in his own attractiveness. His story renders a completely unreasonable course of events. 'Making out and snuggling, then smoking, then the intimacy continues on the sofa'. But it is only him doing sexual things on the complainant. If it was mutual, the complainant should have wanted to do something on his body too. It is not mutual.

The victim counsel in Case 11 took an active role, covering the prosecutor's objective back with a partial advocator role throughout the trial. Stepping up this way, she assumed responsibility for the empathy negotiation of the complainant and the construction of *Things* against the defendant, using the same strategy she would have adopted as a defence lawyer.

Interestingly, the defence lawyer in his plea spoke indignantly about 'the reversed process we have seen today' since 'the usual thing is to offend the complainant'. Before that, he had himself argued why the complainant could not be trusted and was not credible, highlighting all *Things* anticipated by the prosecution: the complainant *allowed* the defendant to stay; she video-called with him and the witness-friend *half-naked*; she did *not fight back or shout*; she was *a known 'cry-rape-ist'*. He then added the himpathy cue that both the defendant and the witness-friend were *dead scared of being falsely accused* by the complainant. Ironically, the defence lawyer ended his plea saying that, contrary to the victim counsel, he did not believe in smearing campaigns based on someone's behaviour (the defendant's behaviour at the previous party) before the sex act. To his mind, the trial should be about the 'strength of the evidence'.

In Case 11, the strategy of the victim counsel and the collaboration and workshare between her and the prosecutor can be said to reveal the inherent mechanisms at work in rape trials. Not by reversing the roles, but by drawing on the same tactics as the defence normally does. This includes: 1) loyalty to the client and the client's story, including surreptitious placement of the client's claims as objective facts rather than subjective perspectives; 2) vivid enactment of the court's empathic imagination of the client's understanding and emotive-cognitive action rationality in the situation; 3) relentless undermining of the credibility of the opposed side in the adversarial trial; 4) disputing of the opponent's emotional authenticity and the invocation of the opponent as a liar.

The DC convicted the defendant. It is interesting how the court picked up two points made by the victim counsel, not as objectivity lifebuoys but as an interpretive horizon of the rest of the evidence (the complainant's story, which was deemed credible, and the supporting evidence such as the text messages). From the DC judgment:

> [The complainant and the defendant] have both stated that they had not spoken to each other about anything sexual in the video call they had beforehand. Against this background, it seems completely unlikely that [the complainant] would have voluntarily made out and wanted to have sex with a strange, drunken, naked man after only five or ten minutes. [...]
>
> With regard to [witness-friend], the court further notes that he is also evidently no stranger to lying, which is already evident from his statement on [date] that he was on his way from [Town X] and could not bear to drive all the way home to [Town Y], when in fact he was on his way up from [Town Y] to [complainant's town] to party with other people (DC judgment, Case 11).

Case 11 was appealed by the defence to the AC but, when the defendant was not released after the AC trial, making it clear that the AC would also convict, the defence withdrew the appeal to avoid the risk of a longer prison sentence.

We now turn to our last example of the professional interactional doing of objectivity, Case 15, in which we find a skilled defence lawyer, a consternated prosecutor, and a judge who clings to objectivity lifebuoys.

Doing objectivity as God's eye – Case 15

Case 15 is an example of the combined effect of a prosecutor doing objectivity the standard way, presuming that facts speak for themselves, a judge who refuses to engage with credibility assessments, and a skilled defence lawyer. In addition, the AC in Case 15 offered no information at all about their assessment of the case. The combined effect of a DC judge who appeared to deliberate by his own 'rational mind', a prosecutor who trusted the judge's rational mind, and the AC's non-transparent, *silent* decision, amounts to doing of objectivity as 'a God's eye' perspective akin to Haraway's (1988:581) 'god trick'. It highlights objectivity as a state of 'seeing everything from nowhere'.

The complainant in her 30s had woken up the day after partying with a memory gap. She had pain in her genital area, had a medical examination that showed semen, and reported rape – but did not know who could have assaulted her. Later, a DNA match led to a trial. In the preliminary investigation, the defendant first denied sex – he had just driven the complainant home. She had been severely intoxicated, vomited several times in his car and dozed off on the way. Confronted with the DNA, he changed the story and said that – within the time frame of the 15-minute car ride – the complainant perked up, wanted to have sex and told him what positions she liked. It was voluntary. In fact, she began caressing his penis while driving. Most important for the prosecution was that the defendant still told that the complainant had been extremely drunk, dozing off and vomiting in his car. After the sex act, however, she gave directions to the house and walked steadily when she stepped out. His previous denial, he said, was fear that his, and the complainant's, friend would be jealous. The prosecutor thought she had a really strong rape case as the complainant was clearly in a particularly vulnerable situation. She based this on the defendant's own story and the complainant's memory gap. She also inferred the defendant's own knowledge about the abuse from the fact that he had lied at first. The complainant was not a 'good' complainant in the sense that she was not eloquent; she gave very short answers.

Case 15 differs from the two previous cases in featuring a female defence lawyer who effectively took charge of the trial and directed its focus. To impose doubts about the guilt of the defendant, she made a *Thing* of precisely what the prosecutor thought was obvious; the level of intoxication of the complainant and her long memory gap. We therefore begin with the defence lawyer's strategy.

The defence lawyer

The defence lawyer's strategy was to place as much focus as possible on the complainant. In the examination of the complainant, she began by placing doubts about the memory gap, asking about the last thing the complainant remembered and at what time she left the party. The point the defence lawyer was going to make of this part of the examination was that the complainant woke up at around 11am in her home, which meant, she would argue, that the memory gap lasted an incredible number of hours: 11 or 12 hours. She continued asking about the level of intoxication:

Defence lawyer: How drunk would you say you were?
Complainant: I was drunk.

Defence lawyer:	A lot or just a little?
Complainant *[Irritated]*:	I was drunk.
Defence lawyer:	I get somewhat contradictory pictures of how drunk you were.
	The defence lawyer says that in the case file in the interrogation protocol from the police the complainant said she was 'tipsy' at the party. (Field notes AC, Case 15)

Here, the defence lawyer established that the complainant might not have been so drunk after all. Next, the defence lawyer asked about the telephone call from the complainant to her friend, later that night, in which she asked him to drive her home. He was occupied but asked his friend (the defendant) to do it instead.

Defence lawyer:	Do you remember calling?
Complainant *[chewing gum]*:	I don't as I said, but the day after I could see on my phone that I made the call.

In both this and the previous quote, we see the complainant's short answers. There is little emotional enactment from her part (on the skilled emotion management required by complainants in court, see Chapter 4) and chewing gum gives an arrogant impression. The defence lawyer concluded the examination by summing up her point, that the level of intoxication was unclear, and the memory gap was incredibly long. Combined with the careless impression this complainant made in court, we can infer that the argumentation invoked 'she lies' as a likely scenario.

In her final plea, the defence lawyer argued that the supporting evidence was very poor, again highlighting the drunkenness and now the lack of 'positive evidence' regarding the complainant's state at the time of the sex act. Scrutinizing the evidence presented by the prosecution she continued:

There is a police report, a medical report and some photos showing that there are injuries, but they *cannot explain the origin of the injuries*. Does not prove anything. This raises the question of what has happened and *whether a crime has been committed*. I do not question [the complainant's] concern the next day. What is clarified by journal entries is *what she believes* has happened. There is no legal certificate specifying when the injuries occurred. This leads to an assumption that there may have been an assault. However, it *cannot be ruled out that the injuries were caused by other means*, like falling, kicking. The *memory loss is very long, 10–12 hours. What happened before, or after* he dropped her off? The evidence of the injuries has very low probative value. (Field notes, Case 15, emphasis added)

Here, we see that the defence lawyer now changed the rhetoric (she lies) about the memory gap. She uses it instead to argue that the complainant 'believed' she was raped. This may signal a wish to not smear the complainant. A more obvious reason is that the lawyer could use the memory gap to sow doubt about the origin of the injuries, enabling the argument that the medical report did not prove 'a crime has been committed'.

Further, the evidence of the semen showed that there was an act of sexual intercourse, which the defendant said was voluntary. From the testimony of the complainant's friend, who asked the defendant to drive her home, it could only be concluded that there was a telephone call and, although her friend perceived the complainant as very drunk then, she was still able to make the call and agree to let the defendant drive her home. The lawyer concluded the plea:

The complainant has not been able to describe what happened. On this basis, the value of her information is non-existent. At least it must be judged with great caution, *especially the very long lapse of memory reported by [the complainant] has to be taken into account.* It also has to do with level of intoxication, which is important for assessing particularly vulnerable state and voluntariness. *It is unclear how great the degree of intoxication was. The investigation is flawed in that there is no positive evidence of the memory loss and its causes* [...] The assessment of the degree of intoxication must be based on the persons with whom the complainant had contact during the evening, that is [the defendant] and the witness-friend. The friend says very drunk but able to carry on a conversation. The defendant says intoxicated but that she was lucid, present, determined and conscious in her actions. *We must therefore consider the defendant's story. He has given a detailed account of her signals and expressions of voluntariness, during the part when the incident took place.* (Field notes, Case 15, emphasis added)

Noteworthy here is that the complainant's memory gap was made a 'story gap' – she was 'not [...] able' to describe the sex act. This reopens the possibility that the complainant, for some reason, did not want to remember. Whether amnesia was true or not, the lawyer turned it to her client's advantage; without the complainant's story, the court must rely on the defendant's story. Regarding positive evidence about the level of intoxication, it was important for the lawyer to refute the main charge of abuse of a particularly vulnerable state, as that would overrule any 'signs of voluntariness'.

Looking at this and the previous quote, it is interesting how the lawyer interweaved both the charges (vulnerable state and voluntariness) in her argument and drew on both to refute both: If she had a memory gap, the level of intoxication was still not proven. If she had a memory gap but was *not* in a vulnerable state, we must listen to the defendant's story, If she did *not* have a memory gap, she is lying about rape. If she had a memory gap, forensics about injuries could stem from her falling and tumbling around. The latter point would, arguably, rather speak in favour of a particularly vulnerable state, but the prosecution did not pick this up.

The judge and the prosecutor

Both DC judge Göran and prosecutor Barbro were elderly and very experienced in their legal roles. They shared the opinion that the standard doing of objectivity was the correct and obvious way. This made them strikingly non-responsive to the matter of rape cases.

Judge Göran was cited in Chapter 4 regarding his own hissense experience of memory gaps. According to him, there was no difference at all between the assessment of evidence in rape cases and in other criminal cases. In the interview, it appeared that Judge Göran ascribed the (to him unprofessional) term 'credibility assessment' one-sidedly to the complainant's story. He explained that, instead of evaluating the story, 'If I want to emphasize that I think it makes sense, I usually write that the statement provided by so-and-so gives the impression of reflecting the real course of events'.

The phrasing 'gives the impression', we argue, signifies the feeling of familiarity and the feeling of knowing (Arango-Muñoz 2014; de Sousa 2009). The phrasing 'it makes sense', signifies a feeling of coherence (Barbalet 2011). This is a telling example of how some judges overlook the possibility that their assessments are informed by background emotions. They thereby foreclose the possibility to reflect on, and disentangle, the influence of subjective experiences and gendered common sense on their feelings of familiarity and knowing.

Similarly, when asked about empathy translation and framing the evidence in rape cases, Göran rephrased it as *legal* framing, which allowed him to repeat the conventional doing of objectivity – it all comes down to the prosecutor's framing of the evidence:

Göran:	Yes, it is [the legal professionals] […] who need to translate the stories that the defendant and the complainant are telling, these need to be translated or framed legally.
Researcher:	Yes, so I am curious how that is received by you as a judge.
Göran:	How do I answer that? [*laughs*] … It's a special task as a prosecutor to interrogate people in a way that brings out the full potential of the complainant or witnesses and that … that's it. Skills on that level vary quite a lot.

We observe in this excerpt that framing made sense to Göran in terms of *legal* framing. He connects that, on the one hand, to 'explaining a story' that might suggest a desire for empathic translation; on the other hand, to the prosecutor's 'special skill' to bring out the potential of the complainant or witnesses, which suggest a desire for better testimonies 'to speak for themselves'.

There are similarities between Judge Göran, a confident and experienced judge, and Judge Hans, in Case 2. We observed in Case 2 that building on the understanding of the rule of law as being ultimately established to protect the defendant creates a blind spot where the complainant should be. In rape research, this blind spot is termed herasure (Manne 2018; Smith 2018). In Case 11, herasure was contested by victim counsel Elvira. In Case 15, we notice that herasure is exacerbated by the missing complainant story. Below is an excerpt of the DC judgment, where the ability to make a phone call is made a *Thing*:

> The conversation in question must reasonably have taken place *some considerable time after the complainant may have consumed some alcohol*. In the opinion of the court, the information about this conversation and what has emerged regarding the circumstances of the conversation are such that *it is clear that the complainant was significantly intoxicated* at the time [...]. The fact that she called [friend] in the manner described and participated in such a conversation seems very *difficult to reconcile with the fact that she would then have been particularly vulnerable in such a way that she was not capable of expressing her own will* with regard to sexual intercourse. That she then subsequently, that is during the journey to [her village], would have ended up in such a state does not seem particularly likely either, in view of the assessments described above and *the lack of an investigation into the complainant's alcohol consumption*. (DC judgment, Case 15, emphasis added)

Interesting here is that the judgment first reasons that, at the time of phone call, 'considerable time' had elapsed since the complainant's consumption of alcohol, but then admits that 'it is clear' that she was 'significantly intoxicated'. The judgment then reasons that the telephone call contradicts her being in a particularly vulnerable state, inferring that she was capable of expressing her own will there, and therefore to expressing her own will with regards to sex. Since the complainant did not remember the call, information about her participation in it was based on the defendant's and the witness's (the friend) stories. The judgment used their stories as factual descriptions of the phone call. It is noteworthy that the judgment demonstrates two fascinating examples of hissensical legal reasoning:

First, it states that the complainant was not in a vulnerable state before the journey – therefore it is unlikely that she became in a vulnerable state during the journey (we know the journey takes about 15 minutes). Unsaid but inferred by this assessment is that the defendant's own story (the original and the changed one) is plausible: she was heavily drunk both before and – vomiting and sleeping – during the journey, except for the sex act, where she was lucid and active and in the mood for sex with a person she hardly knew. The hissensical logics is that this scenario makes more sense than the 'particularly vulnerable state' scenario.

Second, while asserting that she was in a 'significantly intoxicated' state when making the phone call, the explicit analogy made between expressing her will in the phone call and expressing her will during the journey does not even consider the scenario that 'significantly intoxicated' she may have been sexually assaulted by a friend of a friend, whom she trusted to drive her home. The analogy effectively forecloses empathic imagination of this situation, in his car, at night, outside town. Hissensical legal logics decouples the free expression of 'one's own will' from the situation.

Turning to prosecutor Barbro, Case 15 was appealed by her, but acquitted also by the AC, which simply referred back to the DC judgment. Barbro expressed consternation and resignation: 'I think [the evaluation of] this case is completely wrong'. She had believed she had a very strong case, considering the DNA match, the defendant's initial lie about the sex act, the defendant's testimony about the complainant's drunkenness. She also believed in the complainant's amnesia. The complainant did not recognize the defendant when she saw him in court. According to Barbro, all these *facts* should speak for themselves. In the interview, she could not understand what she could have done differently:

Researcher:	I wonder, did you think about other possible witnesses?
Barbro:	No. […] For me this was not a strange case. The victim counsel I have, she's really sharp and good, she thinks like me, so I'm not alone in thinking this way. What would be the benefit of hearing the complainant's friends? […] Somewhere you limit the investigation, it would not have advanced the investigation.

We notice that Barbro felt so confident during the preliminary investigation that she decided against more witnesses. Granted that further measures should be taken only if they advance the investigation, prosecutors need to balance reasons of state (taxpayers' money) against their doubt or certainty about a case (Törnqvist and Wettergren 2023). Barbro felt certain about this case, and so did the victim counsel, according to her. The victim counsel in Case 15 was Maria, cited in Chapter 5. We know that she was aware of her potential, but also did not 'want to ruin' the prosecutor's plan. From the analysis below, it appears highly unlikely that Barbro saw any reason for Maria to step up from her minimal role as victim counsel.

When asked to reflect on the strategies of the other legal actors in court, it became clear that Barbro had never considered empathic translation or negotiation. She thought 'the defence pled for a long time' and continued:

Barbro:	In the court I thought, [the defence lawyer] talks and talks … I thought that all that talking she does for nothing because it's not our efforts in the courtroom that determine the outcome of the case. […]
Researcher:	You said that your efforts in the courtroom do not determine the outcome?
Barbro:	I don't think so. I tell my younger colleagues that it takes a lot before I'd leave a trial thinking that the outcome would have been different if I had done this or that instead. Not when they have come so far as to trial, it takes a lot. You present a material, they have to make a judgment of it and, if we happen to say this or that in a plea, I don't think it has any great significance.

This quote reflects prosecutors' conventional doing of objectivity: the trust that judges can make sense of the evidence and thus that the presentation of it, and not the final plea, is what counts. Consequently, she did not see it as a problem that she participated online in the AC (a COVID-19 measure), and that the victim counsel was not there, while the defence lawyer and the defendant were present in the courtroom.

Prosecutor Barbro represents prosecutors who by default insist on the standard doing of objectivity in all criminal cases, regardless of the type of evidence. Barbro, akin to Judge Göran, demonstrated a sort of 'deafness' about the matter of rape cases. She did not grasp the significance for rape cases of defence lawyers' general strategy to spray the courtroom with potential *Things*:

Many defence lawyers, nowadays, they try to pour sand into every moving part, but most of the times it's for nothing … If you have a secure case, it doesn't lead to anything other than making things more complicated and messier. That's my experience. Then there is the fact that they sow doubt.

If Barbro had habituated the professional emotional profile of the confident-to-be-unbeatable prosecutor with a 'secure case', she could still perceive that 'pouring sand' aims to sow doubts. In her view, however, judges should be immune to that strategy. Thus, she displayed consternation with the most successful *Thing* of Case 15, that is, the telephone call:

> I didn't even think it would have any decisive importance that she has called … I can't understand … Just because [the complainant] was able to make this call that … she doesn't remember making this call … that's not so strange? Many people get a blackout and don't remember what they have done, and I think she is credible in this. She won't … she won't make it up. […] It's all quite obvious!

Barbro did not foresee this *Thing*, even as the defence lawyer invested so much effort in the final plea to link the significance of the call to the lack of positive evidence for alcohol intoxication. In sum, the prosecutor and judge in Case 15 shared the lack of adequate insight and understanding of the matter of rape cases and of the necessity to approach the evidence mindful of how it differs from other criminal case evidence. This means that, the memory gap aside, no attempt was made to negotiate empathic imagination of the situation in the car as it might have been experienced from the perspective of the complainant.

Conclusion

In the in-depth analysis of our three cases, we observed that the prosecutor's standard doing of objectivity in combination with standard doing of objectivity of the judge led to acquittals in Cases 2 and 15. The mediating factor in both cases was skilled defence lawyers. In terms of doing objectivity *to be seen*, Case 2 was a failure in how the trial proceedings offended the perspective of the complainant (herasure; see Manne 2018). Case 15 was a failure from both the substantial and procedural aspects of doing objectivity, we argue, regarding the outcome in the DC, which did not consider the situation as a whole in the car and refused to assess voluntariness. The AC acquittal in Case 15 was downright offensive in its lack of transparency, referring its decision to the DC judgment. Cases 2 and 15 demonstrate that, if judges do objectivity the standard way in rape cases, they inevitably and manifestly cement hissensical legal logics and the systematic witness injustice inherent in the rule of law as it is historically and still today put to work by the legal system.

The victim counsels in Cases 2 and 15 failed to enhance their roles, not because they were bad lawyers, but because there was no mutually (adapted) way of collaborating between them and the prosecutors. They maybe were hesitant about their action-space and taking the initiative, or they had limited experience as defence lawyers in rape cases. Some victim counsels, as noted in Chapter 5, are 'juniors' on the law firms. In Case 11, we observed a completely different approach. Victim counsel Elvira shouldered the same responsibility for arguing her client's perspective and negotiating empathy for her action rationality, as she would have done as defence lawyer. In this, she drew on the new rape law's opening to hersensical legal logics. This led to a court trial that did not only *objectively* achieve a balance of strength between the parties, but to the curious *subjective* experience of 'abuse' expressed by the defence. The enhanced performance of the victim counsel role in Case 11 revealed the inherently normalized hissensical emotive-cognitive mechanisms at work in rape trials, namely himpathy and herasure.

Himpathy is structurally facilitated by the rule of law and its protection of the defendant's rights, which takes on a gendered dimension in most rape cases. Himpathy is also the *seen* (by the complainant and third parties, like the researchers) outcome of the standard doing of objectivity, orienting the judge's empathy towards the defendant's perception of the court process; that *he* should see objectivity being done. When power discomfort and himpathy blend, it may lead to over-ambitious pampering of the defendant from the presiding judge (Case 2). Herasure is the flip side of the standard way of doing objectivity in rape trials, the blind spot with respect to the complainant's perspective on procedural justice. The defendant has their rights, but we argue that objectivity, seen as a fair and just process, is not an exclusive privilege of the defendant; it should also embrace the complainant's perception of the proceedings. This is even more important, and obvious, in rape trials in which the complainant is not a marginal figure, sharing her suffering in consequences of the crime, but plays the most prominent role in providing the main evidence – her story. Moreover, defendants are likely to be acquitted in 35 per cent of the cases.

The examples of the successful and failing enactment and interactions of the professional legal roles analysed in this chapter suggest that the doing of objectivity in rape cases requires the judges' sensitivity for both the defendant's and complainant's perspective (cf Smith 2018). They need to accept that rape cases are different, based as they are on a different type of evidence, which requires adaptation of their part in doing objectivity. Examples of judges' adaptation in evaluation and decision-making will be addressed in Part IV. Prosecutors, for their part, need to further enhance their empathic imagination of the crime and put the resulting insights to work by effective empathic translation of the evidence (Bladini et al 2023). They must avoid their habit of revealing the uncertainties of the case, playing into the hands of the defence and take the final plea seriously. Victim counsels, finally, need to step up from their minimal role to the one of active loyal advocators of their client. Enhanced collaboration between prosecutors and skilled victim counsels is crucial to encourage the counsels in this, and ultimately to create a balance between the parties.

PART III

Autonomy and Rationality of Legal Subjects

7

Autonomy and Action Rationality of Non-Voluntariness

Introduction

As we observed in Chapters 5 and 6, the new rape law requires legal professionals to assess and frame the main part of their decisions on 'soft' evidence. This part of the evidence pertains to the issue of voluntariness and intent. The question of voluntariness is directly linked to agency (that is, the ability to express voluntariness) and thereby relies on notions of autonomy. The assessment, in turn, is linked to questions of action rationality, partly concerning whether it was an expression of voluntariness or non-voluntariness, but is also intertwined with questions of credibility and reliability. Approaching this type of question and evidence just like any other criminal case evidence, denying the influence of background emotions and subjective experience, opens up the possibility of the influence of background emotional information to bear on legal interpretations. Leaving this information unscrutinized, there is an obvious risk of importing group-specific (for example, class/gender) values, experiences and common-sense assumptions, often carrying rape myths, into the evaluations (Bitsch 2018; Burman 2010; Smith 2018; Wallin et al 2021; Wegerstad 2015). The present chapter investigates how this ties in with legal professionals' constructions and empathic translations of the complainant's autonomy and action rationality, in their reasoning and argumentation about behavioural expressions of (non-)voluntariness. In Chapters 8 and 9, we shift from the action rationality of the complainant to the subject of the defendant's story in rape cases.

Modern law is based on individual responsibility and presumes that subjects before the law, unless they suffer from severe mental unhealth or intellectual disability, have full access to agency (that is, can assume the role of autonomous individuals, with the abilities of self-reflection, critical thinking and good judgment) regarding their real-life action possibilities and their consequences (Andersson 2011; Berglund 2013; Naffine 2002; Niemi 2010; Mackenzie and Stoljar 2000). In rape legislation, limitations on the autonomy of the complainant are recognized in three situations: use of force (violence or threats), exploitation of a vulnerable situation, or exploitation by someone in a position of power (see Chapter 2). However, the preparatory works also underline that it is of importance to address 'the situation as a whole' when assessing expressed voluntariness. This directs attention to the emotional experiences and expressions of the complainant, encouraging legal professionals to imagine a series of situated actions and interactions temporally sequenced as before, during and after the sex act. Through this imaginative enactment of the complainant's story, they may or may not capture an empathic sense of the complexity of the micro-power relations at work (cf Lloyd 2004; Morton 2013) when addressing questions such as: 1) What is logical behaviour for the complainant in the specific time- and spatial-bound context (action rationality); and 2) what action choices did she, in fact, have (autonomy)?

Contrasting autonomy as disembodied individual deliberation, we argue that individuals are embedded in social and relational contexts; therefore, lived autonomy is distinctively different from the traditional ideal of autonomy in legal knowledge (Svedberg Andersson and Bladini 2021; Nedelsky 2011). While individuals can be held accountable for their actions, the rationality of their action must be understood as situationally bounded by power and status dynamics (Kemper 2011) and emotional exchange (Clark 1990; Hochschild 1983). In the case of sex and rape, power and status dynamics are, we argue, predominantly gendered and historically deep-seated (cf Ahmed 2004; MacKinnon 2016; Young 1990). The presumption of the ideal autonomy obscures such situated experiences and thereby the explanatory relevance of gendered power relations for sexual behaviour, which is of substantial importance for determining whether a complainant's story of their action during the sex act appears 'plausible' and likely true or 'contradictive' and likely false (Bladini et al 2023).

In the following sections, we will first demonstrate how the behaviour of the complainant can be described and understood, in relation to autonomy and action rationality, by legal professionals in our studied rape cases. Legal professionals engage in empathy negotiations and empathic translations about what can be considered emotive-cognitively rational and logical, as well as irrational and illogical, actions of complainants (Bladini et al 2023; Uhnoo et al 2024c). During the trial, prosecutors, victim counsels and defence lawyers could urge judges to take the perspective of the legal subjects, for example to imagine the situation in which potentially ambiguous actions or gaps in the complainant's or defendant's stories make perfect sense.

Legal professionals exhibit varying degrees of engagement and proficiency in these empathy negotiations and empathic translations. In the following, we focus on the legal reasoning and provide examples of how empathy is strengthened or hindered by *Things* and motivated by empathy hooks, to help the judge tune in with the complainant (that is, understand her action rationality or the reverse). The second part of the chapter focuses on the concept and assessment of voluntariness and the empathic translation of fuzzy situated and bounded action into what may pass as variants of the complainant's autonomy and action rationality. We also describe how the legal actors use temporal boundary work to frame the sex act as fragmented and narrow or broader and as a whole (that is, directly connected to their emotive-cognitively logical behaviour in the specific time- and spatial-bound context).

Framing of evidence: empathy negotiation

As observed in Chapter 5, evidence concerning the emotive-cognitively rational and logical conduct of complainants in rape cases does not inherently convey meaning but necessitates active interpretation and contextualization. Legal professionals are confronted with two questions pertaining to the autonomy and action rationality of the complainant: first, understanding their motivations, reasoning and emotional states temporally, that is, prior to, during and after the sex act; second, comprehending the way they communicated afterwards about what happened to various parties, such as friends, family, law enforcement and the judiciary. These questions are in turn closely tied to the legal questions of (non-)voluntariness and the evaluation of the complainant's credibility.

In Chapter 5, it was argued that judges need more knowledge about human behaviour and greater training of their empathic ability in rape cases. Empathic imagination is vital because it is contingent on the specific legal subjects in court and hence counteracts the risks of importing knowledge as a standardized template, applicable to all cases. Consequently, one DC judge reflected on the use of expert knowledge to bolster judicial self-confidence in rape case evaluation, but went on to reject conclusions from general knowledge regarding typical victim behaviours. Contingent upon the specific circumstances, almost any behaviour could be deemed 'normal':

> The more you find out, the more you realize that you can react any way you want. … In an individual case, the reaction doesn't say much … Being completely pacified, well, that's a perfectly reasonable and normal reaction. That you have kicked around like a savage, that is also a perfectly reasonable and normal reaction … Everything! The fact that you have reported immediately is a normal reaction, that you have waited four months is also normal, given the circumstances. So, anything can happen. It's difficult to draw any particularly large conclusions in any individual case, but then you must draw them on

some kind of whole instead and on how it relates to others ... That's what makes it so damn difficult. (DC judge, Group interview)

To evaluate the action rationality of the legal subjects, judges must conduct an overall assessment of the evidence sensitive to each individual case, which is precisely what makes it 'so damn difficult' according to the judge in this excerpt. The empathic ability to accomplish this holistic assessment of her story requires legal professionals to pay attention to the emotional information brought by listening to the complainant's story. The judge continued:

> It is based on the fact that you, sitting there as a human being, as a judge, should get the feeling of this person ... and then you think that [based on] the picture you get of this person, everything appears logical. But if a person then suddenly expresses himself in a way that you think yourself ... does not match the image you have ... And this is what is so strange. Because we're not experts in it, we're lawyers, but that's what we're sitting there doing anyway. That's what it is.

Reflecting on the way that this type of evidence requires a different approach, as this DC judge is doing, is a step away from the more common argument that rape cases are simply difficult due to the 'bad evidence'. The lack of training combined with doubt regarding the usefulness of expert knowledge and the need to draw on empathic ability, and to 'get a feeling' for the individual cases, lucidly argued by the DC judge, is not representative for most judges in our material. There are several examples in which this type of reflexivity is manifestly lacking. As pointed out in Chapter 5, other legal professionals may function as empathic translators, helping judges to empathically imagine the situation of the parties involved in the case.

Case 10 (acquitted) is an example in which this type of reflexivity (empathic ability) is lacking. A crucial question in Case 10 was if the complainant was paralyzed by 'frozen fright' during the sex act, which occurred outside at night (the defendant was a friend). The defence lawyer argued that it was a shortcoming that the prosecutor did not present any evidence to support it (other than the passivity described by the complainant as 'freezing'). The DC judgment reasons on two 'inexplicable elements and contradictions' in the complainant's behaviour during and after the sex act. First, the court examines why the complainant did not cry out for assistance from a third person passing by. Second, the court scrutinizes the timing of the complainant's telephone call made directly after the sex act, juxtaposing this activity with her (alleged) frozen state only minutes before. It is the time elapsed between passivity and activity that particularly puzzles the court:

> One element that is difficult to explain is that [the complainant] did not in any way make herself known to [passer-by] during the sex act [...] the court considers it difficult to explain that [the complainant] had such a freezing reaction that she was unable to call for help when she heard [someone] passing by and only a minute later managed to call [a friend] herself. (DC judgment, Case 10)

This reasoning rests upon two common-sense assumptions regarding emotive-cognitively rational behaviour, which in turn may be impregnated by rape myths about victim-adequate behaviour (see, for example, Estrich 1987). First, it operates on a common-sense understanding of the state of frozen fright, assuming that it would not be possible to go directly from passivity to activity (make a telephone call) when the rape is over. Second, it assumes that in a situation of rape, the normal reaction of a woman would be to cry for help. This assumption implies that a lack of such action could potentially signal a choice not to draw attention to the sexual interaction (and thus the complainant participated voluntary).

Delving into the courtroom proceedings during the trial in Case 10, it is imperative to understand the influence of the inexplicable elements for the decision to acquit. When assessing the action rationality of the complainant, the judges need to empathically imagine the situation from the young woman's own perspective, specifically, why she did not call for help. From the interrogation with the complainant by the victim counsel:

Victim counsel:	Do you remember if you screamed?
Complainant:	No, I couldn't get any sound out of me.
	[*She says that when she heard the passer-by it broke the spell, and she came to life again and managed to get hold of her mobile phone.*] (Field notes, Case 10, DC)

As discussed in Chapter 5, victim counsels and prosecutors do not always realize their roles as empathic translators (that is, in framing the evidence to convey the feeling for the complainant's perspective and thus render insight into their bounded autonomy and action rationality). In Case 10, both the victim counsel and prosecutor believed that 'frozen fright' – which is commonly referred to albeit not always accepted by the courts – would suffice to this effect, a fact that speaks for itself. The telephone call could also have passed as insignificant if it were not for the defence lawyer's skilful elaboration of it as a *Thing* – an inexplicable element that anchors feelings of doubt in the court – by means of tying it in with the behaviour of the complainant *before* the sex act. The complainant had been to a party at the defendant's house. From the defence lawyer's Mattias interrogation with the complainant:

Defence lawyer:	I have to ask you this again. You are having sexual intercourse … Is it because you are frozen that you don't shout? What kind of trousers were you wearing? And how does he get your trousers off? Are you sitting or standing up? During the evening have the two of you made out? French kissed?
Complainant:	Yes, when we played games. Everyone did.
Defence lawyer:	Did you lie in his bed during the evening?
Complainant:	Several times, because the flat was so small. Everyone sat and lay in his bed.
Defence lawyer:	Thank you very much. (Field notes, Case 10, DC)

Once an alternative scenario is successfully planted in the court's imaginary, it increases the demands on the complainant's answers regarding any of the details (like how the jeans came off) that may speak against the alternative scenario of voluntary participation. Particular inexplicable elements thereby become *Things* that prevent or punctuate empathic attunement with the complainant's story and undermine its credibility. Hence, they impose doubts about the guilt of the defendant. Extending the temporality of the import of the sex act to what happened hours before, during the party (temporal boundary work), the lawyer managed to endow the telephone call shortly after the sex act with an alternative meaning; it could signify that the complainant was not frozen, and that she was not frozen because she actually participated voluntarily in 'the intercourse'.

Contrasting *Things* that provide barriers to empathic imagination, during the in-court negotiations, prosecutors, victim counsels and defence lawyers may employ empathy hooks to guide and enhance judges' insights into the emotional experience of the complainant or defendant. For instance, the playback of a complainant's emergency call (referred to as the 112 call) in the courtroom proceedings, as observed in Case 13, can produce a remarkable impact:

The prosecutor begins the presentation of the evidence by playing a 112 call from the 15-year-old complainant. We hear her crying, sobbing and almost unable to speak. She says that she has been raped. 'I was locked up'. Everyone in the courtroom is listening, looking devastated. It is an effective start to the presentation of the case. It is difficult to defend yourself and not think that something very bad has happened to her. This is a young person who is very upset and is out alone in the middle of the night. We hear her say that five minutes have passed since the incident and how she walks towards the bus station in the small town. It is very dramatic and easy to empathize with. She does not know the address of the station and says that her mobile phone is discharging. She sounds very sad but not very drunk, not like she is slurring her words or anything like that. She is asked by the alarm operator to contact someone she meets whose mobile phone number she can give to the person at the alarm centre receiving the call (in case her phone discharges). (Field notes, Case 13)

The interpretation of the observing researcher in the excerpt above was later validated by the judge (Bengt AC): 'It can give a very strong impression, I can say, even if you have very strict requirements for evidence, it makes a very strong impression to listen to these alarm calls'.

Another type of empathy hook utilized by prosecutors, victim counsels and defence lawyers is to convey details of the physical setting (for example, the room, car, bed, garage or park) wherein the sex act occurred, either through verbal descriptions of the space or photographic evidence depicting it. In Case 10, described previously, the defence lawyer demanded a court visit the site of the sex act as a part of the hearing.

Victim counsel Per (Case 3) describes yet another type of empathy hook, in which he encourages his clients to detail their perception of the defendant's demeanour and the situation. In Case 3, his strategy was to prompt the complainant to articulate her thoughts and emotions of being in the small room where the rape took place, particularly what she meant by 'getting a bad feeling':

> [She says that] she gets a bad feeling, and I want her to concretize that. You want the court to understand that she is in a situation where her brain is racing, because I suspect that's how it is, that you don't really [...] 'What the hell do I do now?' [...] Ultimately, I want to build a feeling in the court [by the] picture of what this looks like when you look down into this little room, if you could do it from the outside.

Victim counsel Per's strategy speaks directly to the empathic imagination of the court, akin to a film director and the audience. Just like the court visit to the site was directed by the defence lawyer in Case 10 to obstruct understanding of the complainant, Per directs the court's imagination in Case 3 to reduce the significance of inexplicable elements (one attempt by the defence to make a *Thing* in Case 3 concerned why she stayed in the room). The court gains a feeling of the complainant's bounded action rationality ('her brain is racing', 'what the hell do I do?') of the specific situation, in the specific setting.

Negotiating empathy in court is key to the (de)construction of the complainant's autonomy and action rationality. For the defence, it involves ascribing significance to unexplainable elements in the complainant's story as *Things*. In this way, *Things* may impose reasonable doubts about the guilt of the defendant. One way for victim counsel, and sometimes prosecutors, to counteract the import of doubts, through *Things,* is by elaborating on empathy hooks by which the seemingly irrational behaviour of the complainant appears rational in the situation. Empathy hooks are also sometimes used by the defence to convey the action rationality of the defendant (see Chapters 8 and 9). *Things* are also used by the prosecution against the defence in a variety of ways. However, for *Things* to take on real importance, they need empathic negotiation of a kind that is usually not viewed as the objective prosecutor's task.

The impression of the complainant and how they appear in the courtroom

Prosecutors and lawyers are generally convinced that the appearance and impressions of the complainant inside and outside the courtroom is crucial, especially in rape cases. Prosecutor Nina stated (Case 18):

Researcher:	Who the complainant is and maybe who the defendant is, does it affect you in your work?
Nina:	Oh, yes.
Researcher:	Could it even affect your decision to prosecute or not?
Nina:	I would like to say no, but I think you are affected by … you make a prognosis of what will happen in court later, how will the court perceive the complainant and her story?

Prosecutor Jesper (Case 1) reasoned that judges are only human and, although a judge would never admit it, remained steadfast in his conviction that ideas about typical behaviours of rape victims have a pervasive impact on the judges, demonstrating an awareness about the existence of rape myths. He viewed this as a 'pedagogical challenge' in the courtroom, influencing not only how he presents a case but, notably, how he conducts the interrogations (cf Wettergren and Bergman Blix 2016). Prosecutor Jenny also argued that societal expectations regarding the behaviour of rape victims unintentionally 'spill over' into judges' assessments, noting: 'You don't write anything about that [in a judgment], but we are no more than human beings making these assessments'. Prosecutor Jan (Case 6) provided a concrete example:

Jan:	I think that … even if the judges were to swear that it has absolutely no significance, I am quite convinced that if the complainant had come in with facial piercings and tattoos and looked generally unkempt.

Researcher: Would that have made a difference?

Jan: It would definitely affect the case.

These examples indicate that the legal actors' empathy negotiating strategies at least may be informed by background emotions evoked by the specific complainants: their social identities and appearances. Depending on attributes like age and personal biography of the complainant, prosecutors and victim counsels may try to depict them as 'ideal' or 'typical' victims of rape (cf Christie 1986; Estrich 1987). In this context, it is important to mention that defence lawyers aim to construct their clients as 'Mr Normal' (as opposed to 'a typical rapist') and engage in himpathy brokerage inviting the court to imagine the consequences of conviction for their client's future (Uhnoo et al 2024c).

In our interviews, legal professionals make distinctions between exemplary ('good') and complicated ('bad') complainants in terms of how they appear in court. This is not necessarily connected to myths about the ideal rape victim, but rather communicative abilities, and hence related to epistemic injustice (Fricker 2007). In Case 18, prosecutor Nina described an exemplary complainant as someone with the ability to articulate their experience effectively. For the prosecutor, an exemplary complainant thereby facilitates the task to negotiate empathy in court:

> The complainant was a former victim of sexual abuse and thus when [this rape happened] she got completely paralyzed. She was really good at putting into words why she got paralyzed. It was a pleasure to have her as a complainant. Sometimes we put it that way: 'This is a good complainant'.

In a case prosecuted by Jenny, the complainant was an 'ordinary' and eloquent young woman. Her memory of the evening was somewhat limited due to substantial alcohol consumption, and she was asleep at the beginning of the sex act. Nevertheless, 'at the hearing she was reflecting on choices. Like an ordinary girl who then [...] has the kind of reaction that many people imagine you should have after a rape' (prosecutor Jenny). Besides being an example of how the effective empathy hook of a 112 call can sweep away potential *Things* (that is, aspects that may create doubts), prosecutor Jenny described that the case involved a 'good' complainant; being 'ordinary', eloquent and displaying a common-sense victim-adequate behaviour, calling 112, that is, a behaviour that feels intuitively rational to people who imagine how they would react on a rape. In contrast, Jenny exemplified the 'bad' complainant with another case that was acquitted. Instead of exhibiting passivity and sadness, a complainant displayed anger and cockiness in court, used strong language and responded to some questions with 'no comment'.

Compliance with the ideal victim is not necessarily contingent on victim-adequate behaviour and eloquence; it can also include the category of 'vulnerable women' that closely aligns with the conception of the ideal rape victim. As in Case 6, in which the complainant (under 18 years) gave a strong impression even in the AC, while judges were merely watching the video-recorded DC testimony, as described in the field notes:

[The complainant] seems tense and almost a little scared, or vigilant, because her body is rigidly upright in the same position with her hands under the table, perhaps in her lap, and she looks straight ahead or diagonally down in front of her when she speaks. It doesn't seem to be the prosecutor she is looking at because his voice comes from her left side and it is also clear later that this is the case, but I don't think she is looking across the room at someone else either. The prosecutor's voice is friendly, supportive but matter of fact. According to the hospital records, the complainant weighs just under 40 kg and is 168 cm tall. On examination, she also had relatively recent self-inflicted cuts on her thigh. In a picture shown, we see the bruise on her thigh [from the rape], but also a lot of cuts. (Field notes, AC, Case 6)

It is no coincidence that prosecutor Jan in this case (Case 6) took the opportunity to display information about the complainant's self-harming behaviour, both when reading the text from the medical record and when showing the picture, where the primary objective was to show the rape-related bruise mark. Mentioning the dry facts of her height and weight further adds to the picture of the complainant's state. This way, Jan advanced the impression given by the complainant's own apparition as an empathy hook. Empathy hooks, we argue, are sometimes strong enough to open for unguarded feelings of sympathy, bound by the feeling rules of the emotive-cognitive judicial frame to be managed and contained until the case is closed (Wettergren and Bergman Blix 2016; see also Clark 1997). In the AC's deliberation on Case 6, the effort to contain sympathy became clear in the atmosphere of relief when it surfaced (cf Törnqvist 2021) and was explicitly expressed immediately after the decision to convict was taken. The overall impression of the complainant made the judges conclude that 'this girl, unfortunately, was very typical of a girl who is raped. Who has various ... like, is broken in different ways' (Interview AC judges Jens and Anna, Case 6).[1]

---

[1] We observed the deliberations on Case 6, but the quotation is an excerpt from the follow-up interview with two of the judges. Our ethical agreement with the courts forbids the use of quotations from the deliberations.

However, being 'broken' is not, per se, an empathy hook, according to prosecutor Jan, commenting on Case 6:

> It's a problem in rape cases, we rarely or never have ordinary girls, but often, as in this case, it's girls who have huge problems and have lived a … often have lots of diagnoses, who are … often lack a language, really, and find it very difficult to talk.

In a study by Brå (2019:9), approximately half of the complainants in a sample of Swedish rape cases were found to have some form of 'vulnerability', such as substance abuse issues, cognitive disabilities, or psychosocial difficulties. While not all 'broken girls' may qualify as an ideal victim, categories that have historically been viewed as disqualifying, like women selling sex,[2] may still perform as good complainants in court. In Case 18, the complainant had engaged in selling sex to the defendant. Anticipating and preparing for the defence lawyer's strategy in court, prosecutor Nina was surprised when it was not even mentioned: 'Perhaps it's that [the defence was] too afraid of falling into a kind of cliché or prejudice about the horny whore, "you can't rape a whore"'. Nina ascribed the convicting judgment to the fact that the complainant had been eloquent, clearly articulating the distinction between what she usually agrees to when she sells sex and the behaviour of the defendant: '[The court could] see where she drew the line and that she was so clear about it, I think that helped. "This was okay for me, but not the violence that happened, it was too painful, and I wanted to stop"'. In this way she appeared as an autonomous person, able to clearly communicate yes and no.

The good complainant in terms of the ability to deliver a credible story is the main concern of prosecutors in rape cases. Yet, the story and its supporting evidence require framing and argumentation, facilitating the empathic imagination of the judges, to convey the rationality of the complainant's situated actions and decisions. The *particular* situation of the *particular* complainant can sometimes be effectively transmitted by empathy hooks. However, to identify and draw on these, the prosecutor and the victim counsel must understand the value of negotiating empathy for the complainant, as discussed in Chapter 5. Effective empathy hooks may even sweep away *Things* emphasized by the defence to produce certainty about

---

[2]   This category arguably qualifies for the self-caused accident, which consequently does not deserve sympathy, according to the social-psychological schema called 'belief in a just world' (Clark 1997). In a study of how belief in a just world affects the view of the complainant in criminal cases, Bosma (2019) finds that it has an influence on both lay people and judges, but the latter are better at concealing and to some extent nuancing the effect depending on their educational training.

reasonable doubt in the judges. As we have observed, when the court decides to acquit, it tends to draw on *Things* by echoing the argumentation of the defence lawyers.

Setting stereotypical categories aside, the impression made by the complainant in court seems to be, above all, dependent on good complainant characteristics such as eloquence, a high-quality story, a suitably contained way of talking and answering questions and an absence of victim-inadequate emotional expressions. This may be partly understood in the light of the criteria suggested for evaluating oral testimonies established by the Supreme Court (see Chapter 2). However, sometimes, to pass as a good complainant requires first combatting characteristics that activate stereotypical categories, such as bodily appearance, clothing, ornaments, make-up, movements, gestures and facial expressions. Eloquence given negative characteristics may have the effect of being an unexpected surprise, as it refutes prior expectations. Conversely, if the characteristics give a frail impression, the complainant may be placed in the category of the vulnerable in line with the ideal victim, which may in turn lower the import of eloquence and ease the prosecution's negotiation of empathy. Another element that may be important for the overall effect of typical victim/good complainant characteristics is the interaction effect of the combined impressions made by both the complainant and the defendant (Christie 1986). This all suggests that the influence of background emotional information – and through this the effect of rape myths, prejudice, common sense and personal experience – on judges' discomfort of power and deliberation in rape cases is multilayered and often contingent on the individual case.

In the remaining parts of this chapter, we dig deeper into the empathic translation of the ambiguous choices of fuzzy real-life action into legal expressions of (non-)voluntariness, exploring how legal professionals construct emotive-cognitive rationality though temporal boundary work. This involves where to draw the line of what is relevant for 'the situation as a whole' and the complainant's actions and choices as sequenced before, during and after the sex act. This is closely related to notions of the complainant's autonomy, where the inability to recognize action rationality in a fuzzy world is in line with the traditional view of autonomy, whereas the ability to address and recognize action rationality also in the fuzzy world would align particularly well with *lived* autonomy.

Signs of (non-)voluntariness and temporal boundary work

This section focuses on the autonomy of the complainant in the sense of legal professionals' constructions of complainants' ability to make choices, for example to express voluntariness or non-voluntariness. Swedish rape legislation is based on the legal criterion of voluntariness and the question of voluntariness is closely linked to the legal subject and her autonomy. The concept of voluntariness is based on a presumption that human (sexual) interaction takes place in a vacuum free from affiliations and power relations (for example, Grear 2010; MacKinnon 2016). Although Sweden's advanced consent-based rape legislation attempts to break with a traditional patriarchal heteronormative regime of sexuality, the new legislation still reflects the idea of two equal parties and the view of individuals – not as human bodies embedded in a social context – but as autonomous in a traditional liberal sense, and thus free to make rational choices about sex and to express voluntariness, except if they are in a 'particularly vulnerable situation', subjected to violence or threats, or exploited by someone in a position of power (SCC 6:1). According to Bladini and Svedberg Andersson (2020:124), the problem of the new legislation is the 'inability in law itself to deal with vulnerabilities, structural power imbalances and various forms of situations where the victim cannot use her capability to express her will due to a *demarcated autonomy* in the specific time- and spatial-bound context'. Thus, the new law continues to overlook how agency may be constrained by circumstances arranged in ways that makes submission to implicit relations of power look like free consent to sex. This critique against consent-based rape laws is not new. Smith (2018:66) has discussed this as 'oversimplifying the context of rape', which disregards trauma reactions, fear, coercion and women's actions aimed at avoiding escalation of violence (see also, for example, Andersson 2011; Lacey 1998; MacKinnon 2016).

It is worth noting that the preparatory work emphasizes that voluntariness ought to be interpreted within the context of the situation as a whole, allowing for nuanced contextual interpretations; a few of our cases provide examples of this (see Part IV). However, judges seldom appear to utilize this scope for more contextual interpretations, thereby implicitly rejecting lived (demarked) autonomy.

As the prosecutor has the burden of proof, the focus on the complainant during a rape trial is substantial. There is crucial weight given to their story, their expressions of (non-)voluntariness before and during the sex act and their emotional expressions and behaviour particularly after the sex act (ideally expressing sadness and despair, calling a friend or family or 112).[3] In Sweden, concerns were raised that the new legislation would, contrary to the legislative intent, result in an expanded focus on the complainants and their previous behaviour, as the requirement of voluntariness is suggested to be assessed in the light of what has been expressed 'in word or deed or in

---

[3]   In line with rape myths and gendered stereotypes (for example, Burman 2010; Smith and Skinner 2012; Temkin 2000; Temkin et al 2018).

some other way' (see Chapter 2). According to some of our interviewees, this is also the case, as described by defence lawyer Rikard (Case 7):

> The problem [with the consent law] is that you go in and dig into the complainant. How they have behaved or done or said and so on. But it is not entirely easy to determine what is an expression of [voluntariness] and naturally you then try to scrutinize the complainant's story. Are there elements here that indicate that they are acting or saying something or doing something that signals consent? And that's really quite a difficult area to get into, that kind of interpersonal relationships and how people behave.

AC judge Björn expressed similar concerns, given that the perspective taken to assess voluntariness is the defendant's perspective (Wallin et al 2021); that is, how they understood the complainants' behaviour in terms of indication of voluntariness (crucial for the question of intent):

> It's a bit back to how it was a very long time ago … By looking at the whole picture, how you behave, you behave in a way that gives the perpetrator reason to believe that you want to have sex. This is possibly what I see as a small disadvantage of the new legislation. It is more often now that such discussions come up in the cases.

While defence lawyers like Rikard obviously grasp the opportunity to spend more time pressing the complainant on the issue of expressed voluntariness, judges like Björn feel uneasy about this development, sympathetic with the situation of the complainant. Other judges, like DC judge Therese (Case 10), in contrast, wish that prosecutors would delve more greatly into voluntariness to refute the credibility deficit, when interrogating the complainant: 'There may be no doubt that it was not voluntary, but did she do anything to show it or was it something she came up with afterwards?'. This wish reflects the judicial system's structurally embedded priority of doubt, in line with the principle of innocence, but that contributes to an epistemic injustice, enacted in a sceptical approach to rape complainants.

The encouragement of the law to contextualize the sex act by examining the situation as a whole opens up the opportunity for a broad array of interpretations regarding when and where the situation as a whole begins and ends, urging legal professionals to engage in what we call temporal boundary work. According to prosecutor Jenny, the new law has also shifted emphasis towards a more detailed examination of the sex itself. Thus, complainants must answer inquires by legal professionals that 'break down the sexual intercourse into different parts and just how it has been twisted and turned on a body' (Jenny, prosecutor). This is because the rape law imposes a requirement of voluntariness that needs to be renewed for every new phase or sequence of a sex act.[4] Thus, there is a tension between an overall assessment of circumstances around the sex act and a temporally narrower focus on expressions of voluntariness in each individual sequence of a sex act.

Importantly, considering the situation as a whole implies that anything complainants and defendants have done before, during and after the sex act, might hold relevance, either in terms of credibility or (non-)voluntariness or intent, and is thus possible for legal professionals to address, as *Things* or empathy hooks. Engaging in temporal boundary work, legal professionals delineate the beginning and end of the sex act as well as its broader situational context. Moreover, in this pursuit, they need to explain to the court the rationale behind the relevance ascribed to specific actions occurring within their argued temporal framework. Why is it relevant for a defence lawyer to address a complainant's decision not to leave the defendant's flat before the sex act or her choice to give the defendant a hug after the sex act, given that, from the legal point of view, the core of the trial lies in the voluntariness of each discrete sequence of the sex act?

Defence lawyer Sara (Case 14) noted that actions undertaken by the parties before and after the sex act are increasingly used to substantiate claims about the complainant's expressed (non-)voluntariness. Such surrounding circumstances were accorded great import in the judgment in Case 14, probably because the complainant had only fragmented memories due to intoxication. Admitting that she found the court's reasoning a little peculiar, defence lawyer Sara still argued that an extended time frame, allowing for consideration of actions and other circumstances before and after the sex act, is essential for a thorough examination of expressed and perceived (non-)voluntariness:

> If you read the preparatory works, you should in fact grasp this overall picture, if you can't really understand what has happened. And that's what I think [the judges] have done. They have nothing else to go by, and they must write a judgment. And then it is very natural to look at everything that has gone before … 'What led to this?' There must also be a way for the suspect, who has nothing to protect himself, it must be possible to say 'OK, but did he get the impression that the complainant wanted this?'.

---

[4] In addition, it may also result from how judges interpret the criteria of a credible statement from the Supreme Court, one aspect of which involves specifying details (see also Chapter 2).

The delineation of temporal boundaries constitutes a crucial aspect of empathy negotiations where the legal professionals' (prosecutors, victim counsels and defence lawyers) primary objective is to present reasonable explanations – corresponding either to hissense or hersense – that render the behaviour of the complainant or defendant rational and credible within the given circumstances. They endeavour to craft narratives that effectively frame their respective parties' stories, aiming to establish their credibility before the court. Throughout this process, due to the principle of free admission of evidence (see Chapter 2), legal professionals are given leeway to highlight nearly anything within the defined time-space that might substantiate the claim, that the complainant expressed (non-)voluntariness, or, conversely, that the defendant understood the complainant's participation as voluntary. As argued by defence lawyer Rikard: '[Voluntariness expressed] "in words" is, I dare say, quite straightforward. "In deeds" is more complicated, it is rather ambiguous what all those actions are … And "in other ways" is pure nonsense. It can be everything and nothing'.

Temporal boundary work is illustrated in the following interrogation of the complainant in Case 17, in which defence lawyer Andreas strategically extended the time-space before and after the sex act. The purpose is to advance the apparent irrationality of the complainant's decisions:

Defence lawyer:	I want to talk about this afterparty. The others were leaving, and you really wanted to go home?
Complainant:	Yes, but [girlfriend who was to drive her home] was too tired.
Defence lawyer:	Did you ask if you could come and sleep at her place?
Complainant:	No.
	…
Defence lawyer:	Did you fall asleep on the couch [after the sex]?
Complainant:	No, I dozed off. I was thinking about how to get out of there.
Defence lawyer:	You didn't think about a taxi?
Complainant:	No, I had no wallet. It was with my friend.
Defence lawyer:	Can't you take a taxi and pay when you get home?

(Field notes, observation, Case 17)

The questioning centres on two aspects: first, why the complainant before the sex act chose, as it were, to follow the defendant to an afterparty at his flat, instead of asking if she could accompany a female friend to her house; second, why, after the sex act, she did not rush to call for a taxi, but 'chose' to stay on the couch in the defendant's flat. These types of questions are distinct from the core question of expressed voluntariness during the sex act but serve to place the sex act in the context of the complainant's presumed autonomous action choices before and after the sex act. Such reasoning raises two central questions:

1. What is assumed to be emotive-cognitively logical behaviour for her in the specific time- and spatial-bound context (action rationality)?
2. What action choices did she, in fact, have (autonomy)?

Fuzzy complainants as (ir)rational

Since the rape law requires expressions of voluntariness when every new sequence of a sex act is introduced, a person can participate voluntarily in the first part(s) but change their mind later in a sexual interaction. Obviously, the sequencing of the sex act to establish the change from initial voluntariness to a subsequent involuntariness poses a considerable challenge for prosecutors in terms of evidence.

Assessments of (non-)voluntariness in rape cases involving young people can be messy because the situation to be investigated often involves alcohol consumption and partying; in that context, young people may also explore their sexual identities, as explained by a DC judge (group interview): 'It's not like you're very clear all the time about what you want and don't want ... You may not even know what the hell you want, and wants may change over time'. DC judge Therese also discussed fuzzy young people's tendency to be 'flirting and making out with everyone ... There are parties, they drink a lot, it's typical for this age'. In short, the complex of party, alcohol and sexual inexperience introduces substantial challenges in evaluating expressions of voluntariness, both in the larger temporal and detailed short-term spectrums.

Adding to the complexity, to persuade someone to have sex by repeated nagging, commonly referred to as 'nagging sex', is not illegal under the current legislation. As Lina, an AC judge in Case 7, phrased it, 'If you agree to it, then you have agreed to it even if you didn't really want or feel like it'. Expressed voluntariness is legally valid, irrespective whether it results from 'pressure or persuasion' according to legal preparatory work, but with the reservation that '[t]he decisive factor is whether the person has had the opportunity to freely decide whether to participate in the sexual act' (Prop 2017/18:177, p 78).[5] The formulation 'to freely decide' reflects the

---

[5] The three situations outlined in 6:1 (pp 1–3) are excluded from this type of pressure, namely the use of force (violence or threats), exploitation of their vulnerable situation or exploitation by someone in a position of power.

legal perception of the complainant's autonomy and arguably implies that, if they do not want sex, they should be able to withstand not just verbal nagging or persuasion but also other sorts of 'pressure'. It leaves the fuzzy complainant who does not 'know what the hell you want' or gives in to someone's sustained nagging despite lack of attraction to them, without legal protection. This somewhat contradicts the idea of imposing a responsibility on the active party to assure themselves that the other party participates voluntarily, as it allows for the opposite attitude.

According to the prosecutors and victim counsels interviewed, complainants may express ambivalence and change of mind as long as there is also evidence of their expressed non-voluntariness. A complainant who recounts that she changed her mind about voluntariness is sometimes viewed as a more credible complainant, arguably because, in the eyes of the court, willingness to convey aspects that might not favour their case adds authenticity to their testimony (see also Chapter 4). This was argued by a DC judge (GI) who said: '[The complainant] can also say things that are unfavourable to themselves in some way. Then you can think that the person in question is nuanced'.

In contrast, defence lawyers' strategy in rape cases is to press the notion of the complainant as autonomous and rational with the freedom to make intentional decisions, by advancing fuzzy complainants as non-credible. While, usually, consciously avoiding overt claims that may raise the court's dislike, such as questioning the complainant's sexual character, they push the significance of ambiguous details in complainants' stories (see Chapter 5). If complainants can be constructed as irrational, ambiguous or inconsistent, the defence can argue that the defendant had no chance to understand that they did not want to participate. Thus, defence lawyers often counter the prosecution by questioning why complainants – if they did not desire sexual interactions – chose to (before or after the sex act) engage in actions such as flirting, dancing, hugging, accompanying defendants to their home, lying down in bed next to them, removing their clothes or viewing pornography together. Alternatively, the defence lawyer may argue that the complainant's ambivalent behaviour towards the defendant (before or after the sex act) could reasonably have been perceived by the defendant as an expression of voluntariness, even if she did not want to engage in sexual activity with the defendant. Defence lawyers may argue that even a simple gesture like a hug before the sex act could be interpreted as a signal of voluntary participation (implied consent) or, at the very least, an indication of interest in the defendant (see, for example, Case 11).[6] Giving a hug or anything

---

[6] Furthermore, the defence must also demonstrate how the defendant took measures to ensure the other party's voluntary participation. Simultaneously, in stark contrast to how they portray a credible complainant, defence lawyers construct their clients (the defendants)

like it after a sex act may also signify consensual participation (see Case 8). The underlying rationale is that individuals would be unlikely to extend a gesture of physical intimacy, such as a hug, to someone deemed culpable of perpetrating rape. This also implies that the defence is highlighting indicators that could be interpreted as voluntariness, while simultaneously questioning the complainant's credibility.

Consequently, defence lawyers may strategically explore every possible rationale for why the defendant might have interpreted the complainant's behaviour as voluntary, or at least frame their behaviour as irrational or illogical and hence not credible. Should the defence succeed, the threshold of passing beyond reasonable doubt regarding the defendant's guilt increases. The following analysis of Cases 7 and 8 focuses on legal professionals' constructions of the autonomy of the complainant in the sense of their ability to make choices and to express (non-)voluntariness. Of interest is how empathic imagination affects the assessment of the complainant's emotive-cognitively rational behaviour in the specific time- and spatial-bound context, and hence the credibility of her story.

Irrational and ambivalent behaviour of the complainant – Case 7

Case 7 offers a good example of a fuzzy complainant. The complainant was under 20 years of age and the defendant was her work boss, several years older. After partying, she followed the man, whom she did in fact feel attracted to, to his home. However, she did feel reluctance stemming from not wanting to be alone with him in his flat, nor to have sex with him, described in court in terms of discomfort and pervasive 'bad gut feelings' – in other words, feelings of fear (Barbalet 1998; Ortony et al 2022). In her testimony in the DC, she said that, during the 45-minute sex act, she repeatedly – 'more than ten times' – verbally expressed not wanting to continue. She described that he became irritated, ignored her expressed wishes, physically assaulted her and forced her to perform oral sex against her will.

When she initially articulated a clear 'no' to sex, the defendant reacted with annoyance by saying: 'But why do you come here, you can't make me horny and then just go home'. From the trial:

Prosecutor: 'No, stop, I want to go home', you say that you said. What is he doing then, do you remember that?
Complainant: He wants to have sex with me.

---

as credible despite irrationality, demonstrating ambivalence, committing errors, dishonesty or even encountering memory lapses. This aspect is developed later.

Prosecutor: Are you giving any response here?
Complainant: Yes, when I made out with him … When I can't go
                   home with my friend, then I have to sleep there [at his
                   place] so yes … he makes out and I make out back. Just
                   kissing back (not touching him). (Field notes, Case 7)

It was very late at night and the complainant was concerned about going home alone, not least because public transport was no longer running and she lived in a place outside town. Given these circumstances, she perceived her best option was to stay in his flat, as the alternative of going home was worse in terms of inducing female fear. In addition, and more intuitively (to those who have ever been in similar situations), realizing that this was indeed a bad idea – and a misinterpretation of his intentions with inviting her – her 'making out' with him can be interpreted as an attempt to avoid making him (more) angry. We do not know because the prosecutor adopted a conventionally objective stance during the hearing and never probed the sources and objects of the feelings that led to her emotive-cognitive assessment that she could not simply leave. Rather, the prosecutor's manner of interrogating avoided probing into the emotional information:

Prosecutor: 'A bad gut feeling', how did you view this incident?
                   It is my judgment to decide what [the sex act] is [rape
                   or not], but …
Complainant: I knew from the start that it wasn't right. There was
                   something that wasn't right. I've never experienced
                   anything like this, someone doing it against my will,
                   but it took me a while before I realized it was rape –
                   it was when I told my friends out loud what had
                   happened. They confirmed it.

While the prosecutor may have understood the situation, he did not help the court to do the same by translating the rationality of her feelings to the court, which would have been a way to stimulate empathic imagination. Thus, instead of probing into the roots of her 'bad gut feelings', encouraging her to elaborate on where these came from, the prosecutor asked about her perception of the sex act. This approach introduces spatial and temporal distance, transforming the gut feelings from a potential empathy hook to a fait accompli, jumping to her retrospective understanding of the sex act as a rape. Probing the gut feelings might have clarified her fears by detailing how she perceived the defendant's behaviour, bodily presence, gaze, voice and touch. It might have elucidated why she regretted accompanying him home and why she did not leave. In other words, asking about the rationality of her emotions would be an attempt at empathic translation.

The victim counsel, in contrast, engaged in empathy negotiation by asking questions about how the complainant experienced the situation, what she felt and why she acted the way she did. The victim counsel's interrogation clarified that complainant felt intimidated by the age difference, that she had initially hoped to persuade him to give her a lift home (he drove a car) and that, due to incidents in her suburb, she did not dare to travel home alone at night. The victim counsel then asked what she was thinking about in the defendant's flat. The complainant replied, 'I will have to do my best to make us just go to sleep' (rational problem-solving). When asked why she made out with him, the complainant answered, 'I felt kind of forced, he just did not let go'. She said no 'at least ten times' and at one point she thought he had fallen asleep but then he began touching her again.

A defence lawyer, wanting to make the complainant's expressions appear unintelligible to the court (and the defendant), can try to emphasize a disembedded notion of autonomy, implying freedom of choice and hence the irrationality of the complainant's actions regarding purported non-voluntariness. Defence lawyer Rikard (Case 7) explained:

> The victim's choice may or may not indicate consent, that is in the form of what is communicated externally. It doesn't have to be how it feels inside the body. It is something completely different ... since it's ultimately about how the suspected offender has perceived something, it becomes of interest what has been signalled rather than what has happened, and then [the complainant's] choices set against each other become very interesting.

Hence, in negotiating empathy for his client, defence lawyer Rikard employed a strategy centred on posing leading questions to the complainant, probing the external (as opposed to internal) rationale of her action choices: 'The question itself can be a signal to the court, of course. It is a kind of pleading before I plead. That "look here now, she made this choice". "What does it give you", so to speak, "what conclusions do you draw from it?"'.

Rikard could, by posing leading questions, present an alternative emotive-cognitive interpretation that instead translated the client's action rationality to the court. As demonstrated in the quotation, the questions have an explicit emotive-cognitive value in terms of translation to the court ('what does it give you?'). Thus, by foreclosing the emotional information that might explain the complainant's behaviour, Rikard uses emotional information cues to sway the court.

An illustrative instance wherein the complainant's action rationality is subject to such scrutiny, coupled with a manifestation of temporal boundary work, is when the defence lawyer asks the complainant about what happened earlier that night (before the sex act). Implicit within this line of questioning is the underlying assumption that, by voluntarily engaging in these activities, the complainant may have expressed willingness to engage sexually:

> [*Defence lawyer asks why the complainant met with the defendant in town.*]
>
> Complainant: To get a lift ... I hadn't decided whether to go with him home ... My idea was not that we would have sex. If I'd be too drunk, I wouldn't go with him.
>
> Defence lawyer: So, the idea was that you would ... socialize? At four o'clock in the morning? (Field notes, Case 7)

Rikard continued by presenting alternative scenarios to the court: 'If we just play with the idea: Now my friend is going, so now I'm going too. Could you have done that?'. Yes, she could, he answers himself, and asks her, 'Why didn't you do that?'. Apart from translating the interactions between the parties as perfectly rational in terms of autonomous choices, defence lawyer Rikard expanded the temporality of import to include earlier events that evening and to make these seem highly significant for the actual sex act later. Continuing, he bombarded the complainant with questions with no other aim than to raise these questions in the minds of the court: why did she not tell him to drive her to the nearest bus stop? Why did she not call her parents? Why did she not call someone else? Why did she not take a taxi? Why did she not just leave? He concluded, 'Then we must draw the conclusion that you chose to stay there. Didn't call friends, didn't call parents, chose not to take the tram or bus, didn't call a taxi' (Field notes, Case 7). If this portrayal is not countered, her behaviour appears irrational and hence not credible. However, the prosecutor or victim counsel could counter this with explanations of female fear to be left alone at a bus station or to leave or take a taxi at four o'clock in the morning (cf Gordon and Riger 1991). To call your parents in the middle of the night, drunk and with an older man, may not be an alternative.

In Chapter 6, we observed that skilled defence lawyers make sure to push the sore spots of the legal core value of objectivity as a rational cum unemotional and disembodied state of mind. This is conducive to their goals as a rule reminder that diverts judges' attention to the risks involved in empathic imagination, and, ideally, shuts it down. Meanwhile, defence lawyers also engage in negotiating empathy for their clients, so their strategy works both ways to ensure that acquittal emerges intuitively for the judges as the least uncomfortable, if not the morally most righteous, decision. Regarding the action rationality of the complainant, they use a similar double strategy; by preparing the cross-examination as if the disembedded autonomous subject was a real phenomenon and not an ideal, they confirm the status of this legal core value. Therefore, it is not easy for judges to intervene despite the fact that completely disregarding the context, like Rikard's questions do, is obviously absurd to most people. The questions are, arguably, a strategy to impose doubts about the defendant's guilt. Simultaneously, by completely focusing on the complainant's behaviour and action (ir)rationality, they remove attention from their client's behavioural (ir)rationality, and the question that is central to consent-based rape legislation: did you ask if the complainant wanted to have sex/change position/continue? In some of our cases, this is highlighted by the prosecutor or victim counsel (Cases 3, 9 and 13).

The context-bound rationality of the complaint in Case 7, is both recognizable and intuitive from a gendered perspective. A young woman is romantically in love with her older boss. There has been some flirting; there is curiosity. Love and curiosity are epistemic emotions that encourage wanting to be closer to someone and find out more about that person. At some point the romantic feeling drastically cools because the interaction somehow does not develop according to hopes and expectations, and she wants to leave. This gives rise to shame for disappointing him and fear if he reacts with anger. Fear is highly rational; it drives the identification of threats and the possibilities to avoid them (Barbalet 1998).

In Case 7, the complainant's worry about going home alone late at night (in accordance with hersense) was probably a push factor in her decision to sleep over at his place. However, the explicit reason she stayed in the flat was her fear of his anger. She did not witness that anger erupt, but she sensed it, or at least thought that she did. She was not eloquent in articulating this but simply labelled it bad gut feelings and clarified, 'There was something that wasn't right'. She also said that she had never experienced anything like it before, 'that someone does it against my will'. Taken together with her 'bad gut feelings' and his irritation, she also experienced waning power in the relationship and resultant fear. Finally, fear and low self-confidence concerning physically defending herself if he became violent made her opt for the possibility to manoeuvre the threats by means of damage reduction, that is, by faking calm and normal (Enander 2011; Moussion-Esteve 2022). In the cross-examination, the defence lawyer (Rikard) questioned the complainant's fear reactions:

Defence lawyer:	You say that you were so scared that your body was shaking.
	[*The complainant confirms that she was scared by the way he showed that he wanted to have sex and that the fear lasted until the morning.*]
Defence lawyer:	Why do you take off your trousers then?
Complainant:	Because I don't usually sleep with trousers on.
Defence lawyer:	I don't want to sound 'like that', but you weren't so scared that you wanted to risk your sleep? Had

	the fear passed? Why didn't you call your mum and dad?
Complainant:	No, because we don't have that contact.
Defence lawyer:	If you had told them you were afraid at a guy's house?
Complainant:	Yes, they would have come.
Defence lawyer:	So instead of calling mum and dad, you took off your trousers and stayed in bed.

In the excerpt, we observe how Rikard wilfully ignores the possibility that fear was the reason for her behaving normally, instead arguing that fear would have made her at least call her parents to come and pick her up. Complicated child–parent relationship aside, her intuitive assessment may have been that calling for help would trigger the defendant's anger, just like any action that revealed to him that she was afraid. Continuing, Rikard probed her memory of the sex act and the different positions and accused her of adding new details to her story during the trial, to which she answered that her memory had cleared somewhat and that, even if she did not remember exact details, 'I remember what I felt'. In fact, memory and emotion are deeply intertwined and the feeling of what happened is a way to locate a particular experience in past time-space (Damasio 1994).

After deconstructing her action rationality before and during the sex act, Rikard turned to her behaviour after the sex act. The defence takes an interest in this temporal sequence only if it may undermine the ideal victim-adequate behaviour. Here, Rikard argued again that the rational thing would be to put on the trousers and leave the flat, and not, as she did, wait until daylight and leave when the defendant was asleep. According to the complainant, fear lingered and was so strong that she kept acting normal for weeks back at work and she did not report the rape before she had managed to change workplaces. In effect, belief in the complainant's story boils down to belief in her fear.

In the DC judgment, the defence lawyer's argumentation about the complainant's behaviour was largely embraced:

Before going to the defendant's flat, the complainant had shown an ambivalent attitude towards him and his flirting [...] [It] was reasonable, regardless of the fact that nothing explicit about sex had been mentioned, to expect that the complainant was interested in having an intimate relationship with him. Even just before the parties' intercourse, the complainant, as she put it, 'messed back' by returning kisses, possibly as an attempt to fulfil the expectations of sex that she was probably aware that her attitude may have contributed to creating. (DC judgment, Case 7)

The DC still convicted the defendant of rape, emphasizing the active party's responsibility to assess the other's voluntariness in each phase of the sex act. The evidence of her non-voluntary participation were deemed convincing – substantiated by the complainant's repeated verbal protests and by her refusal to open her mouth when he pressed his penis against it – and therefore the defendant must have realized that she did not participate voluntarily: '[I]t must have been clear to [the defendant] that when the complainant tried to turn her head away and refuse to open her mouth when he wanted her to perform oral sex, there was no voluntary participation' (DC judgment, Case 7). In this judgment, the conviction relied on belief in the complainant's verbal and physical protests as expressions of involuntariness, that a rational person – whom the defendant was assumed to be – could not have passed unnoticed. Unlike the complainant, the defendant was sober. Although the DC judges thus partly followed the reasoning of the defence, they did not use it to excuse the defendant's responsibility. The assessment implies that abilities such as reason and sensitivity can be expected from the defendant, despite him being sexually aroused.

However, when the case was appealed, the AC decided to acquit. It is worth considering the final pleas in the AC to understand this outcome. The prosecutor held on to doing objectivity as in any other criminal case. Hence, the trial taking place during COVID-19, the prosecutor did not consider the value of his presence in court but made his plea on Zoom (see also Chapter 5 in which we argue that prosecutors normally consider final pleas irrelevant). In line with the ordinary way of doing objectivity, the prosecutor trusted that the evidence would suffice and, having emphasized the complainant's credibility concerning the repeat protests, he highlighted 'a couple of points that may call her story into question'. First, she did not remember the exact order of events during the sex act. This was refuted on the grounds that the opposite 'should rather be a warning bell for the court'. The prosecutor here presumed that the court was aware of scientific studies revealing that testimonies that are too consistent can be an indication of fabrication. He added that 'a victim is not always able to defend himself or herself'. As an hersensical attempt to translate the rationality of fear to the court, it is a weak explanation. The prosecutor rounded off by refuting the credibility deficit; 'there is no boyfriend or jealousy or anything else that might cast doubt on her story'. The victim counsel kept her plea short and based it on the DC's assessment, apparently expecting it to hold.

The defence lawyer was the individual who prepared the most for the final plea in the AC. He began saying that the complainant's story must be doubted since her answers when interrogated were evasive and she had changed her story. Confidently taking the position as knowledgeable about memory, he argued, 'That's not how the memory works. New thoughts don't come after several months. It means you have to question the whole memory picture'.

He continued that people have innumerable obscure reasons to lie and, in this case, 'we only know that the sex was not experienced as successful' from the complainant's perspective. The lawyer then pressed the point about the complainant's autonomy, arguing that 'she had plenty of opportunities to go home but [she] makes it sound as if she had none'. Thereafter, he went on to mark her action choices as irrational, listing a range of *Things* that behaviour-wise were 'simply not logical'. Throughout this part, the defence lawyer systematically ridiculed the complainant's recounted fear, juxtaposing it with her choice to go to bed with his client. Finally, he argued that the complainant's behaviour after the sex act was victim-inadequate, an assessment supported by a witness who picked up the complainant in the morning and said the complainant appeared 'a little drunk, whimsy and somewhat light' and that the only things she said was that the sex had been 'skewed'. The defence lawyer reminded the court that it was her friends that made her report rape.

In terms of temporal boundary work, the complainant's credibility was deconstructed by the defence by drawing on *Things* (illogical action choices, particularly those confirmed by the prosecutor) that occurred both before and after the sex act. The before and after were used to frame the situation as a whole, casting new light on the complainant's behaviour during the act itself. This facilitated the counter-interpretation of instances that the prosecutor and victim counsel had interpreted as signs of non-voluntary participation. The defence lawyer questioned whether his client could have moved her around by himself: 'If he asks her to change position and she does it, isn't that manifesting consent through physical action?'. He questioned her resistance to oral sex: 'Why did she eventually open her mouth? Isn't that manifesting consent through action?'. It is important to remember that the aim of the defence strategies is not to champion patriarchal lows but to plant the seeds of doubt in the minds of the judges. Doubt that an alternative scenario cannot be altogether ruled out is key to acquittal.

Like the DC judgment, the AC judgment was influenced by the defence lawyer's argumentation. The judgment reasoned that the complainant, while 'having provided an extensive narrative that is largely coherent', provided 'contradictory information':

> For example, the complainant has stated that she was so scared that she was shaking when she arrived at [the defendant's] flat and that she was scared until she left the flat, but at the same time she has stated that after [the defendant] made clear that he wanted to have sex with her, she took off her trousers to lie down next to him in his bed to sleep. (AC judgment, Case 7)

Unlike in the DC case, the AC judgment spent time on the lack of detail in the complainant's description of the sex act. The judgment exemplified this with *Things* from the defence lawyer's plea, pointing out that she could not describe how they changed positions. The AC wanted greater detail: 'What happened after the defendant, against her will, pushed his penis into her mouth. Did he remain passive, or did he hump and how did she feel about that?'. Besides the absurdity of requiring such level of detail, it is remarkable that the AC judgment stated that the defendant forced himself upon her 'against her will', but still did not find him guilty. Instead, the judgment reasoned that the lack of such details reduces the value of the complainant's story as evidence. Echoing the defence's final plea, the judgment further picked up the *Thing* concerning the complainant's behaviour after the sex act. She did not display typical victim behaviour but, according to one of the witnesses, appeared 'a little drunk, whimsy and somewhat light'.

Finally, in line with the defence's argument that the complainant acquired the understanding of being raped over time and under the influence of friends and family, the AC highlighted the piece of the same witness's testimony, saying that the complainant's feelings of having been violated seemed even stronger now than when it had just happened. It should be noted that there were other witnesses who described the complainant's behaviour afterwards as more victim-typical (in shock, sad and distressed). Contrary to the DC case, the AC judgment ignored these witnesses, as it also ignored the complainant's account of her repeated protests during the sex act. Explaining in an interview why they acquitted, AC judges Petter and Lina described their deliberation in the light of legal logics and underlined the obligation to acquit if doubts remain:

Petter: It was not very detailed, her story in itself was not very strong, and that affects what is required of the other evidence. In addition, she had been quite whimsical and had not at all said the same thing about the offence, directly after it, as she did later … She had talked a lot with her friends.

Lina: It wouldn't have been a problem if … sometimes, there is a reasonable and acceptable explanation for why there is a delay in reporting and then that is no problem. In this context, when considering [this witness's] information, we can't rule out the possibility that a version of what happened emerged, and naturally she believes it's true, but we can't rule out [that it's not] and then … we must be cautious … It must be virtually impossible for it to have happened in any other way than as the prosecutor claims. Then [the evidence] must be enough. There may be a lot of support of the prosecution's version, which of course there are, but it cannot be ruled out that it happened in a different way.

In Case 7, the completely opposite assessment of the evidence in the AC compared with the that of the DC demonstrates how susceptible rape cases are to skilled defence lawyers' ability to highlight selected parts of the evidence while obscuring others. The different outcomes in Case 7 also demonstrate that the new law can be used to either shift the focus from the complainant's action rationality to the defendant's action rationality (as in the DC), or to put so much focus on the complainant's story that every ambiguity and missing detail opens to other possible courses of events.

From voluntariness to non-voluntariness – Case 8

In Case 8, the same set of AC judges as in Case 7 again overturned the DC judgment, but this time they changed it from acquittal to conviction. This case involved two vaguely acquainted persons under 20 years of age. She was sober; he was drunk. When she drove him home, they decided to stop the car to have sex. The sex act lasted 45–60 minutes and, according to the complainant, turned from initially voluntary to non-voluntary. The complainant had agreed to a quick sex act, but the defendant wanted to continue. She agreed at first but then told him she wanted to leave; in the end, she said no. At this point, he forced her to continue by grabbing her hair.

Compared with Case 7, Case 8 displays a temporal boundary that begins when the sex act begins because there was an explicit agreement to have sex. From the DC judgment: 'The question is therefore whether, after a relatively long period of intercourse, the complainant no longer participated voluntarily in vaginal and oral intercourse'. Thus, interesting in Case 8 is how the sex act itself was delineated in distinct ways across the two judicial instances. While DC viewed it as a whole, the AC fragmented the sex act by segmenting it into several constituent parts. Of interest, the judgment from the AC clarified in what phase the non-voluntariness begun and how it was expressed.

Despite this, the DC emphasized the time after the sex act and concluded that it was not beyond reasonable doubt that the complainant had not participated voluntarily. The complainant had told witnesses different versions concerning the non-voluntary parts. The judgment acknowledged that there can be different reasons, like shame, for not offering all details to friends or family, but still concluded 'that the witnesses' testimonies indicate that after the incident the complainant gave false and exaggerated information about her involuntary participation in the sexual activities'. The lack of consistency of the complainant's story after the sex act undermines the value of her story. The DC judgment argued that it does not harmonize with the prosecutor's claims: She 'has not stated that her participation in the vaginal intercourse was a consequence of the violence that the prosecutor has claimed' and she 'has not told that she repeatedly said that it hurts and that she does not want to, but rather expressed it as "no and that she has to leave" and "a no is a no"'. Quite remarkably, the DC acknowledged both an element of violence and the possibility of expressed non-voluntariness. Thus, the decision was motivated by the complainant's assessed low credibility, which was informed by her inconsistent actions after the sex act.

Unsurprisingly, the DC reasoning emphasizing the time after the sex act was influenced by the temporal boundaries set by the defence lawyer and the *Things* he was able to forge as grounds for reasonable doubt due to this strategy. He highlighted her emotive-cognitively irrational behaviour after the sex act. First, the defence lawyer suggested that her distress was attributable to the challenge of finding her way home, rather than to the trauma of rape. Secondly, he contended that her attendance at a subsequent party did not align with the typical behaviour of a victim.

Prosecutor Sandra was upset, calling the DC judgment 'very, very offensive'. She thought it was clear from the start that the complainant had only agreed to a 'quickie'. The DC failed to consider the sex act itself: 'The time aspect [...] and that he, you noticed it, how the sex ended, he didn't come [ejaculate] and that's why this was prolonged. She agreed to have a short intercourse, but she didn't expect it to last for an hour'. The fact that the complainant said that she must go should put responsibility on the defendant to ask if she wanted to stop:

> He should have to ask her 'Do you want us to stop, or should we continue?', according to the new legislation ... But she actually says 'a no is a no' and he doesn't give a shit about that ... It is enough that she says one of these things, according to the new legislation.

In addition, Sandra was convinced that the outcome of the DC trial was influenced by the judge's irritation at the complainant's failure to convey a clear account of her actions and reactions. She recalled that, during the trial, she had a feeling that the judge had made up his mind ('I just felt that no, this will be dismissed'), manifested in his questions to the complainant at the end of her hearing. The judge intervened (which is remarkable in a Swedish court) and asked the complainant if she could summarize how many times and in what way she had expressed non-voluntariness during the sex act. According to Sandra, this revealed a failure to empathically attune with the perspective of the complainant in the court:

> It's difficult for her to talk. Then, when she's been talking for an hour or whatever, in two minutes she is asked to summarize how she said no, and so on. It becomes a completely different situation. It's not good. There's no free narration there at the end; it was as if everything she

had said before was disqualified. So, I think, no, it wasn't good. I felt that [the judge] wanted to find a way to acquit. Just my personal feeling.

In the AC, the defendant was convicted. We recall that the judges ruling in Case 8 also ruled in Case 7 and there were not satisfied with the level of detail in the complainant's story. In Case 8, they dismissed the complainant's claim that she began to express non-voluntariness long before the oral sex – considering this part 'nagging sex' and thereby excluded from the rape law – but deemed that the non-voluntary sequence began when she said no to continued oral sex. To corroborate why they found this part of the story convincing, the AC judgment repeated the (here satisfactory) level of detail conveyed by the complainant:

> The complainant's account shows that after a while she stopped giving [the defendant] oral sex, that [the defendant] then said 'a little more' but that she replied 'no, I don't want to'. She has further stated that she then lifted her head from [the defendant's] penis but that [the defendant] grabbed her hair and pulled it, whereupon she became angry, pushed against his chest and said 'no, a no is a no. I don't want to'. I don't want to'. However, he continued to pull her hair and neck and to push her down towards his penis. He masturbated with the tip of his penis in her mouth until he ejaculated. .... Only then did he release the complainant's head. (AC judgment, Case 8)

The excerpt demonstrates that the judges are stuck on the character of the self-experienced, as based on the criterion of level of detail, to determine the truth value of a story. However, most of all it shows the importance of the violence. The fact that there is both detail and violence motivated them to confidently assess that the complainant did not participate voluntarily. In effect, the defendant was convicted not only because he did not respect the complainant's expressed non-voluntariness (when she said no to continued oral sex) but also because he forced her, which in turn followed upon her expressing an unmistakable 'no' and pushing him. It is worth noting, nonetheless, that the disparities in the verdicts of the two cases are predominantly underpinned by evidentiary considerations, wherein the evidence was deemed insufficiently robust (owing to the testimony of the complainant) in the DC in this case and in the AC in Case 7.

To be fair, the AC judges were not, in Case 8, swayed by the defence lawyer's temporal boundary work, nor by the *Things* advanced by him. In an interview after the court's decision, AC judge Lina felt free to express sympathy for the teenage complainant, calling her 'the girl'. She then commented on why the AC did not find the complainant's behaviour and the different stories told to witnesses after the rape compromising: 'If I have been subject to something horrible, I tell [my friends], but maybe not about the embarrassing things, like, that you first wanted it and then … That's a bit complicated'. Lina clearly displayed empathic imagination engaging with the emotive-cognitive state of the complainant and her experience of the situation. Notably, she slid into the first-person perspective (I), indicating that she placed herself in the complainant's position. When commenting on the AC decision's reasoning about the expressions of non-voluntariness before the violence, Lina conveyed how she felt when she listened to the complainant's story, underscoring our conclusion that her empathic imagination verged on identification with the complainant:

> As I imagine it, and as it is stated in the judgment, she has thought to herself, and in her head clearly articulated it; 'that's when I didn't want to do this anymore, but I couldn't get it out. This is how I got it out, we changed positions, I said okay, a bit of nagging in between, but then it became so clear. I said no'. She probably felt herself, that's at least how I personally understood it, that she was not very clear on this. I felt that's what she expressed when she told her story in court.

That the AC did not find that non-voluntariness was expressed prior to the violence – because, as the judgment stated, the complainant may have been 'thinking it in her head, but it has to come out' – did not affect the decision or the sentence. Even if background emotions sympathetic towards the complainant oriented the AC decision, as it arguably appears in Lina's emotive-cognitive reflections on the case afterwards, their decision was firmly based on 'objective' grounds (a clearly articulated 'no', physical resistance and physical force). However, the fact is that these objective grounds also derived from the complainant's story, which partly explains why the AC avoided following the temporal contextualization of the DC judgment (and the defence) as it might have forged doubts on the same story. Thus, Judge Lina's extensive empathy work reveals both a feeling of similarity (and identification) with the complainant and a need to justify the AC decision by understanding the action rationality of the complainant (hersense).

Conclusion

This chapter demonstrated that judges' challenges to interpret the behaviour and rationality of the complainant are embedded in, and strengthened by, the traditional view of liberal autonomy as it conceals the necessity of reflecting on one's own presumptions and experiences. This in turn allows for unreflected background emotions and inability to deal with the logics of fuzzy complainants. Although this is certainly true for all criminal cases, it is a much larger problem in rape cases in which the credibility of the complainant depends on the way their action choices make sense to the legal actors. The fact that lived autonomy is demarked by micro-power relations means that the complainant's emotive-cognitive evaluation of the situation they were in must be sufficiently understood by judges before they can decide whether the action choices the complainant made seem reasonable or not (in terms of hersense or hissense). Judges, as we observed, may be aware of this but remain puzzled as to how they can do it. Therefore, empathic translation, based on the empathic imagination of the prosecutor and the victim counsel, is needed. To this end, they can employ empathy hooks and empathy negotiation.

The defences' strategy is to deconstruct the complainant's action rationality, emphasize its apparent irrationality and break it into fragments that can be juxtaposed and showcased as contradictive and illogical. When addressing the inexplicable elements of the complainant's story, presenting them as *Things,* they deliberately do it from the standpoint of the legal autonomous subject, as they know that, compared with this, most human behaviour appears irrational. It lies in the defence lawyer's interest, moreover, to keep the focus on the action rationality of the complainant, deflecting attention from the action rationality of the defendant. However, a defence lawyer may also highlight details of her behaviour to illustrate hissence, suggesting that it is not unreasonable that he thought she wanted to have sex since she followed him home, kissed him, and so on.

We have also observed that temporal boundary work is an important part of empathic translation and empathy negotiations. The significance of deciding temporal boundaries of the complainant's story is linked to the legal work's recommendation that the situation as a whole must be considered to shed light on the sex act and the complainant's expressions of (non-)voluntariness. This includes a structurally preset attention on the complainant's actions after the sex act, assuming that there are certain specific signs of victim-adequate behaviour post-rape. However, events before the sex act are also important, particularly to the defence, in the search for behaviours that can be argued to legitimize or delegitimize the sex act. Within the temporal boundaries, invoked by the legal actors, all *Things* that may shed light on why the defendant went on and had sex with someone who claims they did not participate voluntarily are of importance to the defence. The prosecution has the same interest in demonstrating when and how the expressed (non-)voluntariness occurred. As we observed, the sex act itself may be broken down into sequences, often in cases with longer sex acts including change of positions, in which an initially voluntary participation may shift into non-voluntary participation.

Cases 7 and 8 are both cases of fuzzy complainants, sharply contrasting with the legal notion of the autonomous emotive-cognitively rational legal subject. The rape legislation embraces the change of mind and situated emotive-cognitive action rationality in principle but, as we have observed in the contradictive and changed sentences of these cases, it is difficult for legal professionals to operate this legislative flexibility in practice. Consequently, the judges' comprehension of the situation as a whole, and in it the action rationality of the complainant (hersense), depends on the empathic translation abilities of the prosecutor's presentation of the case, and the victim counsel covering the prosecutor's back, and the enfolding empathy negotiations between the parties (see Chapter 5). Once the court has reached a decision, it selects the pieces of the evidence and arguments presented at the trial that make sense of the decision. This is most clearly observed in cases of acquittal, in which the defence lawyers' *Things* are incorporated in the judgment's argumentation on reasonable doubts. In the following quotation, AC judge Petter (Cases 7 and 8) admitted that the application of the law has yet to settle:

Researcher:	I think, on account of expressing hesitation or non-voluntariness, in both of these cases [7 and 8] there were a lot of different ways that you can interpret as a sign that they don't want to, like [Case 7] when she says, 'I'm tired. Can't you drive me home instead?'. In many different ways, these are signals that can be interpreted as … okay, she's younger, she doesn't want to take a taxi, she's never had sex maybe, she doesn't want to bother her parents, she doesn't want to take the bus because she lives on the other side of town. She does everything she can to get out of the situation. She tries: 'Let's watch a movie'. In other words, 'I want to try different ways to make him understand that I don't want this anymore'. This could actually be interpreted as signalling that she does not want to [have sex].
Petter:	Yes, [these evaluations] will become more developed as we test this legislation, more nuanced.

The impression complainants give in court, the way they tell their story, their eloquence and emotional expressions can also influence judges' interpretation of their action rationality, because it is easier to empathize with socially close others; this is more of an effort with those who are socially remote. Together with personal experiences and the collective social identification of the judges, coincidental background emotions of familiarity and recognition or, reversed, background emotions of estrangement and irritation, may emerge in the court hearing. These background emotions either facilitate or complicate empathy with the complainant. In rape cases, in which a wise decision hinges on interest, curiosity and understanding of human complexity and interdependency, unacknowledged background emotions have consequences for the outcomes.

8

The Burden of Explanation

Introduction

Our focus in this chapter and in Chapter 9 shifts from the complainant's story to the subject of the defendant's story in rape cases. Prosecutors commonly make two general statements concerning the rights of the defendant in the rule of law. The first is that that they are allowed to lie and be stupid: 'Sometimes, you ask the defendant: "Are you so incredibly stupid that you didn't understand?" "Yes, I suppose I am", just like that! The problem is that they are *allowed* to be stupid and foolish' (Emilia, prosecutor, Case 4). The second is that defendants should never have to disprove the complainant's story. This is in line with fundamental principles stating that the defendant is innocent until the opposite is proven, that the defendant retains the right to remain silent (ECHR art 6) and that the prosecutor bears the full burden of proof, that is beyond reasonable doubt (Ekelöf 2009). However, since the new rape law requires the active part to detail the steps taken to ensure the other party's voluntariness, it has raised concerns, particularly among defence lawyers, about 'reversing the burden of proof', making the defendant responsible for disproving the (credible) complainant story. We therefore begin this chapter by investigating the meaning of 'the burden of explanation', which has given rise to the 'consent defence' ('I thought she wanted it'). We then examine how legal professionals reason about the criminal intent and rationality of male defendants' actions in cases when they do not initially use a consent defence, but instead deny involvement, claim memory gaps, or shift to a consent defence only after denial has been disproved. In the next chapter (Chapter 9), we will analyse successful (acquittals) and unsuccessful (convictions) cases of the consent defence in our sample. The analysis of the defendants' stories illustrates how the right to remain silent has transformed into the lucrative possibility of the 'consent defence'. Our main point is that, rather than constituting a 'burden of explanation', as defence lawyers suggest, it can be seen as a specific explanatory opportunity, comparable to a self-defence argument that may legitimize an otherwise unlawful act.

The consent defence as an alternative explanation

While the defendant is not required to testify, their stories are not irrelevant in rape cases. The court may examine the defendant's account to determine if a rape has occurred and to assess criminal intent, as explained by a DC judge (GI):

> Even if you take the woman's story as the basis of the assessment, it's not always that it … influences the next step when looking at the man: 'has he realized it or not?'. Because it can indicate that, based on this, he actually hasn't understood [that it was non-voluntary] or should he have understood it? It depends.

Prosecutor Staffan (Case 2) argued that it is more challenging for the prosecutor to prove criminal intent, than to prove (non)-voluntariness. Likewise, the DC judge cited above said that determining criminal intent tends to be the most difficult aspect of rape cases, as it involves empathic attunement, 'getting inside the head of the defendants' and imagining their view of the situation, particularly of the complainants' behaviour:

> What I find most difficult is the next step [intent]. How did this man think about this? Because it's them who should have understood [that it was non-voluntary]. I think that's the most difficult part. Because it could have been a rape for the woman, but the man hasn't perceived it that way.

An explicit intention of the new rape law was to shift focus towards the defendants, requiring them to detail the steps taken to ensure the other party's voluntariness. Although, as demonstrated in Chapter 7, legal professionals also experience the opposite effect of the law, even more focus on the complainant, they also find that the new rape law indeed places higher demands on rape defendants to explain how they ensured voluntary participation. For example, another DC judge (GI) claimed that, with the new law, 'it suddenly becomes more relevant to shift the focus to the defendants and ask, "What led you to believe that consent was given?"'.

However, defence lawyers have criticized the new law for reversing the burden of proof to the defendants, arguing that they must prove their innocence. Prosecutor Jenny defined the new focus on the defendant not as a burden of proof but as a 'burden of explanation'. She stressed that this 'in a way contradicts the right to remain silent'. On the other hand, she continued, 'the legal certainty for the suspect remains intact since [prosecutors] are required to meet the rigorous standard of evidence' (see

Chapter 2). According to DC judge Mårten (Case 1), if the prosecutor has proved that the complainant did not participate voluntarily, it is not enough for the defendant to just disagree. Instead, according to Mårten, 'he must explain how it "really" was', why he got the impression that she participated voluntarily. Similarly, DC judge Jennifer (Case 17) noted that, if the prosecutor presents compelling evidence unaddressed by the defendant, there is no 'alternative explanation' for the court to consider:

> If they [the defendants] can explain how they were thinking in the situation, then it can affect the assessment of intent, providing additional material that must be considered [...] Of course, if they can provide an explanation it can work in their favour.

In fact, to provide an alternative explanation is often easy in rape cases because of the default consent defence ('I thought she wanted it'). If a consent defence is presented, the court must evaluate the reasons, explained by the defendant, to believe sex was voluntary, and assess what he could reasonably have understood in the situation. Based on this, providing an explanation as to why the defendant perceived that the other party participated voluntarily is a more viable defence strategy than remaining silent. According to prosecutor Nina (Case 18), the consent defence is a tactic employed by most rape suspects: 'When we plan to confront a suspect, I talk to the police; "If he's smart, he'll say that he had voluntary sex with the complainant" because I'll never be able to disprove that. Nine times out of ten, they say that'. Since a consent defence is hard – but as we will show in Chapter 9 not impossible – for the prosecutor to counter, Nina was concerned when the new rape law was introduced that suspects would become adept at formulating consent defences: 'we will have a very hard time disproving it. It is enough for the judges to buy that story'. Victim counsel Per (Case 3) also felt frustrated, arguing that, despite the new law's focus on the defendant's awareness of the complainant's voluntariness, the practical impact remains marginal:

> Even as a defendant, if you feel like, 'that didn't go so well that time when we had sex', you could still go into a police interrogation and say, 'What? She wanted it! She didn't say no or do anything that made me think she didn't want this'. Then the burden of proof returns to the prosecutor anyway. You can ask that question as many times as you want. How did you know she wanted this? 'Well, she entered the room, she took off her clothes and lay down on the bed. How am I supposed to interpret that?' he answers. Yes, then we're back to that question again. Sure, you might get more questions as a defendant about consent, but again, it's the same theme.

In this quotation, it appears to be almost impossible to establish the guilt of a defendant who uses a consent defence. The discussion about how difficult it is to disprove consent defences highlights a sense of resignation among legal professionals, shaped by hissensical legal logics regarding male action rationality. However, contrasting the statements of Per and Nina, it is worth noting that, in our study, the consent defence was used in 13 cases, most of them (seven cases) convicted in final instance (see Chapter 9). Clearly, not all defendants who employ a consent defence are acquitted.

This leads to the question of when, if and how legal professionals assess defendants' stories. AC judge Jens (Case 9) pointed out that the standard for evaluating defendants' stories differs from that applied to the complainants' story. Defendants are allowed to 'fabricate, exaggerate and forget'. He explained that 'merely the *potential truthfulness* of a defendant's account can be sufficient to acquit the case, essentially signalling "game over" for the prosecution' (emphasis added). In contrast, prosecutor Sandra (Case 8) argued that the credibility of the defendant's story still holds significance, for example if the defendant provides 'a very poorly detailed story and cannot explain at all why he perceived the interaction as voluntary'.

Consequently, the defendant's right to remain silent, 'fabricate, exaggerate and forget' notwithstanding, after the prosecutor has presented evidence supporting the charge, the court may reject a defendant's explanation of the sex act, suggesting that there are limitations to what courts consider as a plausible alternative scenario (that is, what imposes reasonable doubts about his guilt). In the rest of this chapter, we will analyse the outcome of cases in our data in which the defendants did not provide their own story, which means they did not use the possibility of a consent defence, or changed their story from denial to a consent defence.

Denial or memory gaps: lack of explanation

Denial

In five of our cases, all convicted, defendants did not use a consent defence but either denied the sex act altogether or claimed that they could not remember it. We begin with the 'denial cases', Cases 1, 6 and 12.

In Case 1 (not appealed), the defendant asserted that the sex act did not occur and that he was not even in the complainant's apartment during the alleged offence. According to the DC judge in this case, Mårten, denial used to be typical of rape cases, but the use of the consent defence seemed to increase with the new rape law:

The classic [story] is that it hasn't happened. There hasn't been any assault. If there is no forensic examination of the complainant ... then you just say it hasn't happened ... As a defendant, you may lie, and why shouldn't you if there is no evidence that it has happened? ... If there is sperm or vaginal secretion indicating intercourse or ... DNA or skin scrapings ... then we move on to other questions. [...] most often [the question is] perhaps the subjective circumstances ... did he know? Was it intentional?

In Case 1, the court decided that the complainant's story and the supporting evidence – among others, technical evidence binding him to the place at the specific time – were enough to establish that the defendant was present in the complainant's apartment at the time of the offence. There were also traces of semen proving that a sex act had taken place. The defence failed to present an alternative version that could explain the meaning of this evidence. Judge Mårten noted that the defence in Case 1 could have attempted a consent defence. Instead, the defence clung to the sex act's non-occurrence, resulting in a starkly binary argument. With the court finding that the evidence proved that the sex act had occurred and the defendant's presence at the time, there was little room for disputing intent.

Besides the hard evidence and the lack of explanation, the defendant in Case 1 could appear as 'a typical rapist'. In our field notes from the DC, we noted that the defendant had visible tattoos on his hands and arms and spoke quickly and unclearly. He had a criminal record and in the same trial was charged with several additional offences (to which he confessed). He told the court that he was a drug addict but also stressed that he did the grocery shopping and took care of the complainant when she was intoxicated, as they had a previous sexual relationship. The defence lawyer tried to portray the defendant as credible and virtuous and shift focus onto the credibility of the complainant, who was far from an ideal victim. He highlighted the complainant's mental health and addiction issues, and that she herself had previously been accused of assault. Prosecutor Jesper (Case 1) in the follow-up interview stated that the defendant made a very poor overall impression and was therefore convicted. The defence lawyer's tactics might have been effective in other cases, he argued:

Now, these are my very personal opinions, but I believe that the [defence] strategy works because ... it's people who are judging and ... They may be influenced unconsciously, but if there's someone who ... appears to be ... pleasant and cheerful in court and the complainant looks the opposite, then they're influenced by that. I'm pretty sure about that. And vice versa, if there's a ... uh ... broken Swedish girl sitting there crying, it's easier for them to believe her than if it's a broken drug addict or a prostitute. It sounds terrible, but I actually think it is like that.

Moving on to Case 6, the defendant also denied the prosecutor's allegations, asserting that the sex act did not occur. He insisted that the much younger complainant, whom he treated as his own daughter, was a habitual liar, envious and fixated on sex. He had never had any sexual interest in her. The prosecutor argued that the defendant's general behaviour contradicted his claim of no sexual interest, referring to evidence that he was a habitual consumer of pornography and Viagra, and that he also owned a dildo. The DC judgment stated that the complainant had provided a detailed story that appeared credible, suggesting a strong likelihood of rape, 'if true'. However, the court also emphasized the absence of unreasonable details in the defendant's story: 'His story contains, *if nothing has happened* [that is no rape], no unreasonable details. There is nothing in his story that indicates that, despite his denial, he is guilty. Therefore, it's a matter of *one word against the other*' (DC judgment, Case 6, emphasis added). Ultimately, the court decided to base its judgment on the complainant's story, after assessing the supporting evidence, which was all together found sufficient to establish that rape had occurred. The AC concurred with this assessment, particularly emphasizing the responsibility of the defendant; he was almost like a father to the complainant, the age disparity was significant and, in the complainant's account of the sex act, she was passive and showed no signs of voluntariness. The AC concluded that lack of voluntary participation should have been evident to the defendant.

The third and final denial case, Case 12, shares similarities with Case 6. Both cases involved a very young complainant and a significantly older defendant, who acted like a father in the complainant's life. Like the defendant in Case 1, the defendant had a criminal record and a history of substance abuse. At the time of the rape accusation, he was a respected figure in the community, known for his volunteer work with children in a socio-economically disadvantaged area where the alleged rape had also occurred. Prosecutor Jesper in Case 12 noted that the defendant had a lot to lose if convicted.

The defendant firmly denied the rape allegation, asserting that the young girl had fabricated the entire story. He even filed a counterclaim of defamation. During detention, the defendant appealed the detainment decision and in the courtroom in the AC, he was disruptive by sighing, commenting and whispering loudly to his defence lawyer. The prosecutor spoke up, and the presiding judge intervened, telling the defendant, 'It's best if you don't comment now. Your defence attorney will present your side later, and we will listen to the interview with you from the DC'.[1]

---

[1] Regarding the unruly anger displayed by the defendant in Case 12, it is interesting to note that defendants' moral anger at unjust accusations is most often disliked by judges, but in some white-collar cases, it may pass (cf Bergman Blix and Wettergren 2018) In

The defendant was convicted by the DC, which first established that the complainant's and defendant's stories contradicted each other. They decided to use the complainant's story as a basis for the assessment despite some uncertainties:

> The complainant's spontaneous account has been long and coherent. In some parts it was rich in detail, but not in the parts concerning the indictment itself, where her account can be characterized as rather sparse. However, this can be explained by her age, the fact that she was obviously quite drunk and that it is not comfortable even for an adult to sit in a courtroom and tell intimate details to strangers. (DC judgment, Case 12)

While we can discern that the complainant's story was deemed credible, the DC found she did not 'provide entirely truthful information' but could observe no motive for her to falsely accuse the defendant. The DC judgment also noted that the complainant had suffered social exclusion by reporting the rape. Regarding intent, the judgment concluded that the defendant (according to the complainant's story) had acted indifferently to her non-voluntary participation and as she was 'heavily intoxicated', he unduly abused her 'particularly vulnerable situation' (DC judgment, Case 12). The case was appealed by the defence but withdrawn before the AC verdict.[2]

In in all three of these denial cases, the defendants were convicted of rape. Two of the cases involved defendants with a criminal record (Cases 1 and 12) and all cases involved alcohol or drugs to some degree and socially vulnerable complainants. In Case 1, the court convicted the defendant for violent rape on a socially vulnerable and drunken former girlfriend. In Cases 6 and 12, the courts convicted defendants who had paternal relationships with the much younger and socially vulnerable complainants. The significance given to these aspects in the judgments – the age difference and paternal

---

the interview with judge Bengt regarding rape, he noted that he was surprised at the lack of anger among rape accused who claimed they were innocent (as most do) and said that he would expect expressions of righteous anger to be a sign of innocence. We argue that this apparent discrepancy is explained by the fact that angry expression is a place claim, a marker of status and power, that is denied to socially disadvantaged, previously punished defendants in court (cf Ask and Granhag 2007; Ask and Pina 2011; Wrede 2015; see also Kemper 2011). That said, angry expressions are also viewed as incompatible with adequate victim behaviour (see Chapter 7).

[2] Prosecutors, even if they are satisfied, sometimes respond to defence appeals with a cross-appeal asking for a higher sentence, which is a strategy they use to scare the defence into withdrawing their appeal. This was what occurred in Case 12. At the end of the hearing, the court announced that the defendant would remain in custody until the verdict was decided, indicating the risk of a higher sentence, as requested by the prosecution.

relationship dynamics – indicates that the courts adopted a moral standpoint. As prosecutor Jesper (Case 6) argued, the defendant in Case 6 was 'a person who could not normally be expected to have a sexual relationship with a 15-year-old girl'. Such consideration might have led to conviction of these defendants, even if they had used the consent defence.

The defendants in all cases further exhibited emotive-cognitive behaviours and characteristics consistent with the myth of a 'real rapist' (Estrich 1987). This involved, for example, consumption of pornography, previous criminal records and personal biographies of drug abuse and violence. In Case 1, there were additional charges involved in the same trial, and in Case 12 the defendant acted in an unruly manner in court. We have previously observed that prosecutors and defence lawyers believe that the impressions made by the complainant and defendants in court influence the judges in surreptitious ways (see also Bergman Blix and Wettergren 2018). We argue that the influence of impressions is brought to bear on decision-making by background emotions and common sense. Thus, we suggest that in Cases 1, 6 and 12, the commonsensical 'typical rapist' was activated by: 1) social distance between the legal actors and the legal subjects, which was a hindrance to empathic imagination; and 2) the defendants' behaviours, because of their low social status, characterized by aggression and low morality, which evoked judges' backgrounded antipathy, which in turn harmonizes with the real rapist myth. In other words, in Cases 1, 6 and 12, we are dealing with generally 'condemnable' defendants.

In Chapter 7, we discussed the ideal victim as either associated with complete innocence regarding the predicament (of rape) or, alternatively, as a young and/or vulnerable woman. The complainants in Cases 6 and 12 resembled ideal victims in this respect, while the defendant in Case 1 appeared vulnerable in relation to the defendant. Given the hard evidence supporting the complainant's stories, the attempts by the defence to undermine the complainants' credibility – by depicting them as compulsive liars, envious, violent, mentally unstable and sexually obsessed – arguably boomeranged on the defendants, and likely fuelled the court's background antipathy.

Memory gaps

The second category of cases when defendants did not use a consent defence we refer to as 'memory gap' cases, represented in our data by Cases 3 and 17. Unlike in denial cases, the defendants acknowledged some sexual interaction but claimed not being able to recall the details, attributing this to partial memory loss. Both cases differ from denial cases in that there is a higher likelihood of admitting some mutually voluntary sexual interaction between the parties. In Case 3, the parties had previously had a romantic relationship. In Case 17, the complainant testified to voluntary oral sex with the defendant on the same night. Despite these circumstances, the defendants did not use the consent defence.

In Case 3, the middle-aged defendant, who had a prior sexual relationship with the same-aged complainant, asserted he could not remember the particular sex act under scrutiny. In a follow-up interview, Per, the victim counsel in Case 3, called such memory loss 'a bloody stupid defence'. According to him, the most effective strategic approach would be to say: 'I remember everything, and it was entirely consensual. Period. I was aware of her desires, and she exhibited no signs of reluctance whatsoever'. The DC judgment in Case 3 opined that it was 'highly improbable' that the defendant had no memory of the event during the limited time frame in question. The judgment picked up the prosecutor's empathic translation, calling the lack of memory 'strategic amnesia' with the purpose 'to evade responsibility or, at the very least, to suppress or diminish own responsibility'. The court arrived at this conclusion because he had 'clear and distinct memories' of the evening both before and after the sex act, and the evidence regarding his alcohol consumption did not support intoxication to a level that would likely lead to memory loss.

Regarding criminal intent, the DC judgment in Case 3 argued that it could not be ruled out that the defendant may have 'misinterpreted the complainant's body language at some point during the evening and perceived it as some form of invitation'. Addressing the issue of temporal boundaries, however, the judgment went on to state that it was 'completely irrelevant with regards to the defendant's liability' if such a misinterpretation occurred because it had happened before the sex act. The court concluded that the defendant must have perceived that the complainant did not participate voluntarily, both because she 'expressed that she did not want to participate' and because he then used force. The judgment also clarified that the complainant's limited verbal communication or lack of active resistance was irrelevant because 'a no means no', which the accused should have understood. Finally, the judgment displayed dislike and moral indignation towards the defendant by describing his behaviour as 'blunt, disrespectful, and harsh' and thus indifferent to the complainant's wishes.

Both the DC and AC convicted the defendant in Case 3. Despite memory gaps being termed 'strategic amnesia' or 'a bloody stupid defence' by the legal professionals, AC judge Lina (Case 3) in the follow-up interview asserted that such defence 'happens in so many cases' and that defendants have the right to claim memory gaps; 'it should not burden you, you can of course do that. You have the right to say nothing, you can be completely silent'. Lina also argued for an empathic stance; there may be various plausible reasons for memory gaps, including genuine memory loss due to intoxication or a reluctance to discuss the sex act due to regret or embarrassment. Still, in

Case 3, the AC repeated the DC judgment's 'a no is a no' and argued that there was no evidence in the investigation to suggest that the defendant was unable to discern the rejection.

In Case 17, the defendant also claimed selective memory loss. The alleged rape occurred at an afterparty, during which the complainant stayed overnight with the defendant, a man in his 20s. The complainant reported the incident only a few days later, but it took several months before the accused was arrested. Initially, he denied the accusation, but later he claimed he did not remember the part of the sex act that, according to the complainant, was rape. He admitted engaging in consensual sex earlier that night. In the AC, the defence lawyer pinpointed the various ways in which complainant expressed interest in the defendant throughout the evening; sitting on his lap, staying at his apartment, choosing to sleep in his bed, kissing him and giving him oral sex. The defence lawyer concluded: 'This is what he remembers of the evening. In all these respects, they agree. The defendant remembers nothing else' (field notes, AC, Case 17).

The young defendant in Case 17 was acquitted by a lay judgment in the DC. The judgment deemed the complainant's story credible, describing 'the sex act in a detailed, coherent and emotional manner'. Still, the lay judges considered the time that had passed between the reported rape and when the suspect was first questioned as a reason for the defendant's lack of memory and argued that the defendant's story 'could not be disregarded'. In effect, they juxtaposed the complainant's credible story with the defendant's amnesia as a 'word-against-word' situation. The statement of the dissenting professional judge in the DC instead reasoned that it was unlikely that the defendant lacked memories because he (as in Case 3) otherwise remembered most of what happened on that particular evening and night. Additionally, according to the professional judge, there was forensic evidence in the form of semen traces that provided 'strong support' for the complainant's story.

The defendant was later convicted in the AC, following the reasoning of the dissenting professional DC judge (a credibly story from the complainant supported by forensic evidence). Rather than simply arguing 'word against word', as the DC lay judgment had done, the AC judgment emphasized the discrepancy between the complainant's credible story and the defendant's amnesia (lack of story).

> It can be noted that [the defendant], despite being questioned about the suspicion at a later stage, has provided a relatively detailed account of what happened during the evening, night, and the day after, which broadly corresponds to what the complainant has reported. However, he has explained that he has no memories of the event that the complainant described as an assault. (AC judgment, Case 17)

The AC questioned the defendant's credibility, arguing that his story appeared 'rather general' and was contradicted by technical evidence (semen). They found that the fact that he first denied and later claimed memory loss further diminished his credibility. Regarding the defendant's intent, the judgment argued that it was not beyond reasonable doubt that the defendant had heard when the complainant said 'no' and had observed her waving her hand to signal non-voluntariness. The complainant did not:

> provide any information regarding how loudly she said [no] and whether [he] heard or perceived what she said. Nor does her statement about waving her hand provide any definite conclusion regarding whether [he] perceived this and, if so, he understood that the complainant did not want to engage in sexual activity with him again. (AC judgment, Case 17)

Despite this curious reasoning – presuming that the complainant could determine if the defendant perceived her refusal or simply ignored it – the judgment concluded that it was 'obvious' that the defendant, given the circumstances, must have realized the risk that the complainant did not participate voluntarily. Interestingly, the judgment also pointed out that the absence of the defendant's own story about how he experienced her expression of non-voluntariness was to his disadvantage: 'Proven wrong regarding his performance of the sex act, he lacks his own story of how he perceived the situation which could have affected the assessment of intent. There is also no information indicating that he checked the complainant's attitude toward his actions' (AC judgment, Case 17). This excerpt indicates that the AC judges placed upon the defendant a duty to ensure the voluntary participation of the complainant, in line with the new law's intentions. He used his right to remain silent and, since he did not present a consent defence, his possibility of explanation, he had not provided the court with an alternative explanation to consider.

In summary, in all the five cases analysed in this section on denials and memory gaps, the defendants were convicted. This arguably indicates that, in practice, the defendant has a better chance if they provide an explanation in rape cases. If the court finds the complainant's story and supporting evidence enough to prove the offence, attempting an explanation is necessary for the court to consider the defendant's lack of intent. Without an explanation, it can at least be concluded that the defence faces an uphill struggle, as they do not provide the court with an alternative scenario. From the denial cases investigated, it appears that the hill is likely becoming steeper to climb if the defendant evokes backgrounded antipathy and moral indignation by giving a bad impression or acting arrogantly and unruly. Presuming that courts are more likely to feel sympathetic towards collaborative defendants is another reason why trying to explain is better than remaining silent in rape cases.

As mentioned previously, there is not just a word-against-word situation as often described, but there is also technical evidence. As noted by an interviewed DC judge (GI), denial cases with technical counter-evidence are effectively 'the only time there is functional supporting evidence' in rape cases. This was also the situation in the five cases above; a credible story from the complainant was supported by both oral and technical evidence. However, it also occurs that a denying suspect is confronted with technical evidence, like semen, and then changes their stories. This is the next type of case we will examine.

Altered story: from denial to consent defence

While the burden of explanation holds some significance, it is recurrently argued in our interviews, during trials and in judgments, that defendants may have valid reasons for providing false statements and, therefore, this should not necessarily be held against them. The question in this section is whether, and under what circumstances, a change in the defendant's story can affect their credibility negatively and be held against them, and the role of the legal professionals' empathy negotiations in this.

Cases 18, 15 and 7 were cases in which defendants initially denied sexual interaction but later changed to a consent defence. We call these 'altered story' cases. Since all these cases also included presentations of consent defences from the defendants, they will be further analysed in Chapter 9. In this chapter, we focus on how the fact that the defendants altered their stories was managed by the legal professionals. Nina, the prosecutor in Case 18, was earlier cited saying it is almost impossible to refute a consent defence. However, if the defendant initially denied the sex act and later changed to a consent defence, when contradicted by technical evidence, such as DNA or injuries, it became a different matter. In such cases, Nina said she would present the evidence strategically to make the judges view the defendant's consent defence as a rationalization after the facts.

This was the scenario in Case 18 (earlier analysed in Chapter 7 from the perspective of the complainant) in which the defendant had bought sex from the complainant. Initially, the defendant denied the purchase of sex but, when confronted with technical evidence during the preliminary investigation, he shifted his story to a consent defence. The defendant claimed the sex act was voluntary and did not involve violence or force. He also stated that he purchased sex (which is an offence under Swedish criminal law) because he was under threat.

In the DC, the lay judges (another lay judgment; compare with Case 17) acquitted him, ignoring his initial denial and arguing that the evidence was insufficient to prove rape. The complainant's story, the lay judgment argued, left room for reasonable doubt. The judgment also referred to the defence lawyer's *Thing* regarding uncertainty about exactly how the complainant's head had hit the wall, during the sex act, as important for their decision to acquit.

The AC arrived at a different conclusion more in line with the dissenting opinion of the professional DC judge.[3] In our field notes from Case 18, we noted that Nina's final plea in the AC emphasized the defendant's altered story, highlighting how it changed in response to new and compromising information, a pattern indicative of dishonesty, she argued. He initially denied any involvement in the sex act and later claimed that he was passive, performing under threat. If he was really forced, Nina argued, he would have had no reason to deny when he was interrogated the first time. She also emphasized that even if the purchase of sex was a mutual agreement, voluntariness must be reaffirmed in each subsequent phase of the sex act.

The defence lawyer opened his final plea in the AC with a rule reminder of two fundamental aspects of the rule of law and presumption of innocence: the prosecutor's burden of proof and the defendant's right to silence. He proceeded to outline his client's story, underscoring feelings of shame as motivating the young, previously unpunished man's reluctance to disclose the sex purchase. The defence lawyer sought to normalize the alleged shame reaction of his client by referring to hissensical action rationality: '[Such a reaction] is extremely common'. He further asserted that his client 'had not perceived, or even suspected', that the complainant did not participate voluntarily throughout the sex act (field notes, AC). This defence strategy was unsuccessful, and the defendant was convicted. Unlike in the DC, the AC judgment, unconvinced by the argument that his initial denial stemmed from shame, argued that the altered story 'negatively affects the defendant's credibility'. Moreover, as we will observe in Chapter 9, they found the defendant's consent defence 'implausible' and 'difficult to understand' (AC judgment, Case 18).

Another altered story occurred in Case 7 (analyzed in depth in Chapter 7), in which the defendant initially denied any involvement and maintained that the complainant had never been in his apartment. He changed to a consent defence when confronted with the complainant's detailed description of his apartment. The DC found the defendant guilty, since they deemed the complainant's story credible and well supported by corroborating evidence.

---

[3]   In his dissenting opinion, he categorized the complainant as credible (as a person) and her information as reliable (she had 'recounted the sex act in a detailed, coherent and emotional manner') and that the defendant's story did not 'weaken the value of the evidence presented by the prosecution'.

In contrast, they criticized the defendant's story for its lack of detail (DC judgment, Case 7).

In the AC, the defendant was instead acquitted, with no significance ascribed to the altered story. It irritated prosecutor Staffan (Case 7) that 'the suspect can lie with impunity, without anyone caring'. The defendant's changed story had led Staffan to feel 'reasonably certain' the complainant was telling the truth. He argued that this feeling of knowing was common sense, in line with 'some kind of universal human understanding'. While recognizing the legal logics behind the AC's decision, Staffan said he was still 'a bit irritated' that the defendant's right to lie, as it were, was applied so strictly that they foreclosed consideration of his motives to lie. It should matter, Staffan argued, that the defendant could not give a 'reasonable explanation' for the initial denial.

The defendant had stated that he panicked at the prospect of being accused of rape, thus referring to the hissensical male fear discourse, which, on the contrary, Staffan found partly reasonable: 'Perhaps [you] can't say anything during the first interrogation because you're kind of scared and so on. Then you think "I'll just shut up"'. But the defendant in Case 7 had sternly maintained his denial in several police interrogations and detention hearings, before he was rebutted and changed to the consent defence.

It was arguably important for the final outcome (acquittal in the AC) that defence lawyer Richard (Case 7) was a skilled lawyer with many aces up his sleeve in terms of defence strategies. Given the precarious situation that arises if technical evidence contradicts denial, Richard said he always advices defendants to opt for a consent defence at once: 'If you did have consensual sex, just tell me about it'. If this advice came too late, as in Case 7, Richard was confident that there was still hope. He would plan his defence to deflect the court's focus from his client to the complainant's story. He would also focus on explicating the intense fear experienced by the defendant when he was arrested and faced with a rape accusation: 'a moment of sheer panic'. Richard outlined what we call empathy negotiation, drawing on an empathy hook of hissensical fear (Uhnoo et al 2024c): Suspicion of rape is like a red flag. They panic. They become terrified. And thus, they act as panicky people sometimes do, namely completely irrationally by saying "I've never met this person. I don't even know who this person is. Nothing has ever happened"'. In his final plea in the AC, Rickard consequently developed this empathy hook, arguing that his client was panicking and that 'anyone who has been in a similar situation' could understand why. Like the defence lawyer in Case 18, he also advanced the strategy of rule reminders. First, he emphasized the legal evaluation method of the so-called *Balcony Case* (see Chapters 2 and 10) wherein 'one does not need to consider the defendant's story'. However, 'in the unlikely event' that the AC would come to the evaluation of his client's story, it was 'at least as credible' as the complainant's story, he argued. Second, he emphasized the defendant's right to lie: 'if he denies it, it is of no value. Even if it can be established that he gives false information in court it should not be given importance' (field notes, AC trial, Case 7).

Our final altered story is Case 15, analysed in depth in Chapter 6. It differs from the others since it involves a complainant who had no story of the sex act because of an alcohol-induced memory gap. As we observed in Chapter 6, the defendant when apprehended first denied, then changed to a consent defence when confronted with the counterevidence of his semen. He maintained his story of the drunkenness of the complainant, but confessed the sex act and said it was on the complainant's initiative. Prosecutor Barbro in Case 15 was confident that these circumstances, as reflected by the defendant's own story and its alterations, would be interpreted by the court as supporting the complainant's level of intoxication and, by logical inference, her inability to participate voluntarily in sexual activities. Like prosecutor Staffan in Case 7, Barbro argued that the defendant had no 'reasonable' explanation for why he lied from the outset.

Like the defence lawyers in Cases 18 and 7, the defence lawyer in Case 15 'rule-reminded' the court by referring to the *Balcony Case* model and the defendant's right to lie, arguing that any incorrect statements provided by the defendant should not be accorded significance. She also referred to the defendant's hissensical state of shock as a reason for the initial denial (field notes, AC). The DC judgment did not go by the *Balcony Case* model, however, and, while not finding the prosecution's claim sufficiently proven, did consider the defendant's reason to lie. The judgment instead took the defendant's own hissensical explanation to heart, namely that the defendant 'had the impression' that the complainant and the defendant's friend were in a relationship, and therefore feared the friend's reaction if he found out that defendant and the complainant had sex. The AC in Case 15 also acquitted, but revealed no reasoning of its own. The AC judgment simply referred its assessment back to the DC judgment.

Conclusion

In sum, comparing the defendants' altered stories in Cases 18, 7 and 15 reveals different approaches by the courts. In Cases 7 and 15, the defendants were acquitted in the AC, suggesting that changing their stories from denial to a consent defence does not necessarily lead to negative outcomes for the defendants. In Case 15, neither the DC nor the AC considered the potential significance of the fact that the defendant initially denied the sex act. This case was also complicated since the complainant had no memory of the sex act. In Case 7, the DC considered the evidence presented by the prosecutor as enough and the defendant's story to have low evidential value ('lacking in detail') and convicted him, while the AC acquitted, finding the complainant's story to leave room for reasonable doubts (see analysis in Chapter 7). In both Cases 7 and 15, the prosecutors thought that the defendant's blatant lies would corroborate the evidence presented by the prosecutor and thus support the charges. They expected, in other words, that the lie would 'speak for itself' as evidence against the defendant. In Case 18, the defendant was acquitted in the DC by lay judges, but convicted in the AC, partly because they found his consent defence incredible (see Chapter 9).

With respect to the defence strategies, the empathy hooks drawn upon were the hissensical male fear of being falsely accused of rape, for example the defendant in Case 7 stated that he panicked at the prospect of being accused of rape and therefore denied the sex act. Male fear is arguably the hissense notion most well established as inherent to legal logics (Manne 2018; Uhnoo et al 2024c). Its taken-for-granted rationality is corroborated by the equally hissensical myth that women may lie about rape, which pairs well with, and may be strengthened by, the rule of law, resulting in systematic witness injustice. In addition, an outlier – given that buying sex is illegal in Sweden – in Case 18 was drawing on the male shame of buying sex. In Case 15, we also noted the influence of an apparently successful empathy negotiation drawing on a hissensical assumption about male friendship and fear of jealousy. All these hissense arguments appeared to blend 'naturally' with legal logics.

The way that gendered common sense (hissense or hersense) *cum* the neutral gaze of the law makes its way into the judgments casts light on clever defence lawyers' intuitive understanding of the role of background emotions and the efficiency of activating hissense together with rule reminders. Specific reminders about the prosecutor's burden of proof as an objectivity handrail may prove efficient because, if this is applied, the defendant's story in the best of cases will never be evaluated. In this sense, even a bad story is better than no story. Any story may also give off a good impression, signalling respect for the court by collaboratively taking on the burden of explanation.

In terms of action rationality and criminal intent, it is worth noting that the eight cases analysed so far are marked by what would be the defendant version of 'fuzzy action rationality'. They deny, do not remember, and change their stories. When pitched against fuzzy complainants, who fall into the ideal victim category, fuzzy defendants, particularly of low status, may be convicted. However, when fuzzy complainants meet defence lawyers skilled at empathy negotiations, drawing on legal logics informed by hissense to demonstrate the rationality of their defendants, it is more likely to end up in an acquittal. A contributing factor in this is that hissensical fear is conventionally coded as legally rational, while hersensical fear is conventionally coded as irrational (Åquist 2001; Smith 1987; Wrede 2015).

It also lies within the system, the roles, and the professional work of the legal actors; if hersense is made visible through empathetic translation, the complainants' fear can appear rational (see Chapter 7). In the next chapter we turn to analysing the different constructions of the defendant's action rationality and the complainant's voluntariness in the most rational of all defence strategies: the consent defence.

9

The Making and Breaking of Consent Defences

In this chapter, we will analyse various examples of consent defences used by the defendants in our study (consent defences were employed in 13 cases). The chapter is divided into two sections: one on successful consent defences (resulting in acquittals in the final instance) and another on unsuccessful consent defences (resulting in convictions in the final instance). Although the focus of our analysis is on the role of the consent defence, in all cases there were additional, interacting factors that influenced the outcomes of conviction or acquittal. For instance, the prosecutor's evidence may have been found insufficient to meet the standard of proof beyond a reasonable doubt, or the legal actors may have varied in their success at empathically translating or negotiating the stories presented.

In this chapter, through focusing on the consent defences, we examine if, when and how the defendants' stories are rendered significant by legal actors, highlighting the defence lawyers' empathy negotiation on behalf of the defendant. Defendants' constructions of the complainants' voluntariness in consent defences are examined in detail and how legal professionals present, challenge or assess these consent defences. We also examine closely legal considerations of the degree of defendants' autonomy and rational decision-making capacity, in other words the legal actors' expectations about male defendants' ability to discern expressions of (non-)voluntariness.

The new legal requirement for mutual confirmation of voluntariness before sexual interaction reflects changing societal norms towards reciprocal engagement in sexual interactions. In line with the legal requirement, consent defences thus include descriptions of how the complainant expressed voluntariness in words, deeds or in other ways (see Chapter 2). Thereby, consent defences illustrate constructions of women's emotive-cognitive rational behaviour when they express that they want to have sex or, more precisely, of *perceived* behavioural cues indicative of women's desire for sexual engagement. Moreover, in the defendants' stories detailing the sequence

193

of the sex act, constructions of male sexuality are revealed along with the hissensical rationality of men when establishing signs of voluntariness.

From our interviews and observations, it appears that typical consent defences in rape cases are characterized by brief, vague and underdeveloped responses, lacking in detail. Defendants describe moaning or whimpering noises as signs of voluntariness. DC judge Joel (Case 2) said that defendants referred to 'very small signs' since 'it's not like you sign a contract' before you have sex. It is a recurring – potentially a hissensical – common-sense idea found in our data that people do not communicate with each other during sex. Thus, the consent defence often demonstrates reliance on non-verbal cues, reducing expressed voluntariness to 'signs'. Except sounds, other signs sometimes used by defendants refer to the complainant's vagina being 'wet' (while 'being dry' is sometimes used by complainants as an additional sign of non-voluntariness). Wetness is implicitly, or explicitly, taken as a sign of being 'horny', which is assumed by the defence to signal voluntariness. The absence of objections or silence may also be taken as a sign of voluntariness by defendants, even though passivity should be interpreted as non-voluntariness in general (see Chapter 2).

We begin by analysing successful consent defences that resulted in acquittals (six cases). We thereafter proceed to cases in which the defendants were convicted despite using a consent defence (seven cases). Since many of the rape cases are analysed in detail in other chapters, the level of detail regarding the circumstances framing the consent defences varies across cases.

Acquitted defendants' consent defences

In line with our findings in Chapter 8, we have dived the sections by 'defendant types' to highlight potential patterns regarding the 'ruinable futures' of the defendants.

Consent defences from socially well-adjusted men

In four of the acquitted cases the defendants had 'ruinable futures'; they had no previous convictions and were presented by the defence as socially well-adjusted, with bourgeoning or established careers, or higher education aspirations (Cases 2, 7, 9 and 10).

Case 7 (referred as an altered story in Chapter 8; see also Chapter 7) resulted in acquittal of the defendant after appeal. The defendant, several years older than the young complainant, was her boss at work. At the time, he was sober while she was intoxicated. The defendant's account of perceived voluntariness described that he asked her 'respectfully' if she could perform oral sex on him. He said that *they* cuddled and kissed, implying reciprocity, and that they both undressed. During intercourse she was 'on top' of him, suggesting that she was active. In his final plea in the AC, the prosecutor focused on the defendant's altered story but did not attempt empathic translation or empathy negotiation, nor did he ask how the defendant actively assured himself of the complainant's voluntariness or showed her that he cared about it.

Case 2, analysed in detail in Chapter 6, involved a white, middle-class man in his 30s – a mid-level manager and father of young children. On the night in question, he engaged in sexual activity with three women, each about half his age. The complainant described that she woke up and found the defendant on top of her, having unprotected vaginal sex with her. The prosecutor did not probe the defendant's consent defence. The defendant explained that the interaction between him and the complainant 'sort of transformed into cuddling, touching and kissing. We don't talk much'. During the sex act, 'I was on top, and she strokes my back, holds me around the back … We breathe heavily and moan quietly'. Again, the prosecutor did not challenge these presumably implicit signs of voluntariness by asking how he could be certain that she participated voluntarily.

The DC judgment in Case 2 emphasized the defendant's implicit certainty by rendering the part of his story recounting how he perceived that *they* kissed, *she* was active removing her underwear and 'welcoming him in the missionary position' and caressed his back. Such a description appears to reflect empathic imagination of the defendant's story, while it obscures the defendant's own actions, as if he was passively partaking. The DC judgment concluded that 'the actions described by the defendant are legally considered to be voluntary intercourse' (DC judgment, Case 2). The judgment went on to clarify that, regardless of this fact, the judgment should be based *solely* on the complainant's description of the defendant's behaviour (how he acted towards her), but that her story evoked doubts about crucial details (how her jeans came off and the duration of the sex act). Therefore, the DC did not, at least not in its written judgment, delve further into the reasonableness of the defendant's consent defence. The case was not appealed.

Case 9, analysed in detail in Chapter 11, involved a previously unpunished boy under 18 years accused of raping a girl his own age after a party. Both were drunk. The DC found that, based on his own story, he had not actively ensured that she participated voluntarily. He was convicted for showing a lack of interest in the risk that the sex was non-voluntary (the requirements for intent). In the AC, the court also took interest in the defendant's story but drew the opposite conclusion regarding intent. They found that, from his perspective, it was reasonable to assume she participated voluntarily.

As in Case 7, the defendant in Case 9 had described that he asked the complainant if she could give him oral sex. Otherwise, they did not talk much, he said, but he believed that she wanted to continue with vaginal penetration (field notes, AC, Case 9). The question in Case 9 was if the vaginal intercourse, following the oral sex, was voluntary. The defendant said he went to retrieve a condom and, when returning after a minute or so, her position in the bed signalled that she wanted this. Case 9 had an active victim counsel, Erika, who in her final plea in the DC advanced the rule reminder that 'consent is required in every new phase of the sex act' and rhetorically asked what he had done to confirm this. In the follow-up interview, she argued that the defendant was rightly convicted by the DC on his own story of how he did not confirm voluntary vaginal penetration. Thus, the DC judgment in Case 9 demonstrated an unusual but legally correct focus on the defendant's responsibility and rejected his perception of 'signs' as sufficient explanation of assured voluntariness.

In his final plea in the AC, the defence lawyer deflected the emphasis from his client's responsibility, reminding the judges that 'the legislator says about voluntariness' that it may be expressed 'through words or actions or otherwise'. Thus, the defendant did not need to explicitly ask her. He further engaged in empathy negotiation for his client, inviting the judges to imagine the kissing, followed by voluntary oral sex, and 'only 30 seconds later', she took a position inviting vaginal penetration. Was it then not reasonable that he developed the impression that she wanted this, the defence lawyer rhetorically asked. The AC judgment reasoned that the prosecution had not managed to prove rape, and that 'the course of events described by the defendant *includes such actions that as a rule must be seen as an expression of voluntary participation*. Nothing in the case gives reason to view the situation differently' (AC judgment, Case 9, emphasis added). The AC considered the sex act as one single continuous sequence (hence new consent would not be needed). This was confirmed in the follow-up interview with two of the AC judges: 'dividing this into segments, because we're talking about … a time difference of 30–45 seconds between these two moments, I would say that becomes very strange' (DC judge Bertil, Case 9). The judgment drew on a blend of hissense and implied legal logics about what must typically be viewed as expressions of voluntariness (see further Chapter 11).

One additional aspect of the DC v AC reasoning in Case 9 was the meaning of the parties' previous relationship. They had only been friends and had never had sex before. Evaluating 'the situation as a whole', the DC took this as a further reason why the defendant should have cared to ask the complainant. The AC judgment did not ascribe importance to this circumstance and, in the follow-up interview with the AC judges, they argued that previous relationships, according to the law, should not matter. AC judge Bertil (Case 9) said it was 'a rather odd reasoning [by the DC] … It shouldn't matter whether you've had previous sexual encounters or not'. The new law arguably states that it should not influence the evaluation of voluntariness in rape cases if the legal subjects had previous sexual contact, but nothing about the relevance of no previous sexual interaction. The potential meaning of the latter is obviously dependent on the individual case.

Thus, the AC judges' interpretation of the law on this point illustrates how a male 'objective' perspective benefits a male defendant while disadvantaging a female complainant. In other words, the different judgments in Case 9 highlight how hissense may emphasize one aspect of the new law, while hersense, advanced by DC judge Monika (see Chapter 4), emphasized other aspects.

Case 10 is a consent defence drawing on 'wet and horny' as a sign of voluntariness (see detailed analysis in Chapter 11). A previously unpunished young man with higher education aspirations had, according to him, voluntary sex with a female friend outdoors after a party. Just as in Case 9, both had been drinking. The complainant's story was that the defendant stalked her, persuaded her to stop and have a chat, and then raped her. She was shocked and paralyzed and the prosecution argued 'frozen fright' (see Chapter 7).

In the DC, defence lawyer Mattias extended the temporal boundaries and argued that 'there was sexual tension throughout the evening', in line with the defendant's story about the party, where 'there was a lot of joking about sex', including flirting, kissing and cuddling, on the complainant's initiative. The DC judgment rendered the defendant's story (like the complainant's story) in detail. According to the defendant, outside later that night, they made out again, 'he kissed her neck and she moaned softly'. She suggested to sit down on a bench; she sat on his lap. In short, the judgment's overall representation of the defendant's story includes typical components of consent defences; the complainant did not give any signs of resistance but instead took the initiative, rubbed her buttocks against his penis, moaned and was 'wet'. The defendant also portrayed himself as active, licking her, penetrating her with his fingers, turning her around and penetrating her from behind. The defendant's 'rather passive' story (as in Case 2) or the 'mutually very active story' as in this case, are arguably ways to highlight the complainant's voluntariness, but also to present the defendant as a non-dominant man.

During the trial, the defendant did not detail conversation between them or if he asked her what she wanted. He said, 'the atmosphere was good, and he was completely sure she wanted it', but he also said that she refused him a goodbye kiss after the sex act. After hearing the defendant's story, the defence lawyer looked down at his papers and summarized: 'I wrote down that she was wet and horny'. He also asked the defendant whether it was possible that he could have misunderstood her voluntariness, to which he answered no, and whether she took her panties off herself, to which he answered yes (field notes, DC).

The defendant was acquitted in both the DC and AC. The DC judgment accorded 'low evidential value' to the complainant's story. It was 'not very detailed' and contained 'inexplicable elements and contradictions' (see

Chapter 7). In contrast, the defendant's story was deemed to meet 'all the requirements set by the Supreme Court', which is rare in judgment, as that is not a requirement for defendants' stories (for further analysis, see Chapter 11).

The consent defence as the only story

Our last two acquitted consent defences are Cases 14 and 15, in which the complainants had no or very dim memories of the event due to intoxication. In both cases sober defendants had sex with severely intoxicated complainants (although one of the two defendants in Case 14 claimed that he was intoxicated). While prosecutors may try to advance such cases as 'abuse of a particularly vulnerable state', both prosecutors and judges struggle with the lack of the complainant's story, the question of the level of intoxication and the significance of the defendant's story. When complainants' stories are missing, the objective criteria constituting rape must be assessed without the complainant's story. The defendant's consent defence then stands out as the only story about the sex act, but only really becomes relevant if the particularly vulnerable state cannot be proven, as the intoxication could void a consent if proven (that the defendant improperly exploited her vulnerable state). The crucial question becomes whether her level of intoxication placed her in a particularly vulnerable situation. Prosecutors point out that if the particularly vulnerable state cannot be proven, defendants can describe any sexual activity on behalf of the complainant uncontested, as already observed in Case 15 (see Chapter 6 and later in this chapter).

In Case 14, two defendants (henceforth D1 and D2) were accused of raping a woman during a party. Several other men had also been participating – their semen was secured in and on the body of the complainant – but the two defendants were the only ones identified. D1 and D2 were charged with rape as joint perpetrators, as they carried out the rape 'together and in agreement'[1] with each other and the unidentified men. The prosecution claimed that they unduly exploited that the complainant was in a particularly vulnerable situation due to intoxication. The complainant remembered bits and pieces. She remembered D1 and D2, but only the sex act with one of them. She said she did not participate voluntarily and that she tried to say no and to resist. D1 and D2 admitted having voluntary vaginal intercourse with the complainant. They denied

---

[1] 'Together and in agreement' is a way to forge charges against groups, when the preliminary investigation can only establish that several people were involved in an offence but cannot specify who did what due to the members of the group covering up for each other (Asp et al 2013).

that she was in a particularly vulnerable situation and they denied that they acted 'together and in agreement'.

When questioned by the prosecution during the DC trial, D1 explained that *he* was very intoxicated, so he did not remember much. He did recall that the complainant expressed voluntariness by flirting and talking to him, sitting on his lap, kissing him and voluntarily engaging in vaginal intercourse. He could not remember having oral sex or whether he asked if she wanted to have sex with him. He described the complainant as 'completely intoxicated', but 'very happy, dancing, bumping her hips and smiling'. He also said that, when they entered the room where they had sex, he locked the door, but afterwards he left her naked in the bed and the door wide open.

D2 claimed that he was completely sober. His story was that he simply 'met a girl at the party and we had sex'. As D1 did, he described that she was nice, friendly, happy, sitting in everyone's lap and bumping her hips. Echoing most consent defences, he described the sex as a mechanical sequence of actions; *they* went upstairs, into a room, talked a bit, started kissing and caressing whereupon *she* undressed. He said, 'One odd thing that struck me was that she performed oral sex on me. I didn't ask for it, I didn't initiate it, no gestures, nothing'. When asked how she expressed voluntariness, he said it was clear that she was into sex; 'She kissed me. She was on me, took the initiative, gave me oral sex without me asking, she touched me. Moaning, calling me baby, she grabbed me and said, "keep going"' (Field notes, Case 14). The complainant remembered that D2 had asked her early in the morning whether she had had sex with several people that night, and the prosecutor asked about this. D2 said yes, he asked that question because, if she had given him a spontaneous 'blowjob', she had probably done the same to others. To the question whether he had asked the complainant about intercourse, he answered 'No, and neither did she ask *me* if I wanted'. According to D2, the complainant did nothing to signal resistance. On the contrary, she begged him to go on and reached orgasm.

Noteworthy in Case 14 was the unusual activity of the professional judge (compare with Case 2, Chapter 6). The judge in Case 14 asked D2 about how the complainant undressed, to which he answered that he did not remember that he undressed her. The judge further pressed him on how he concluded 'that she desired to engage in sexual activity'. D2 repeated his consent defence (see above) and added that they also talked: 'It was not simply a matter of going up to the room without talking about it', he clarified. When asked how he perceived her desire for sex when they reached the room, the defendant explained that they 'probably kissed' when going there: 'She had the choice to leave if she wished. I didn't force her, there were other people around'. D2 could not remember specific details like their exact positions during the sex act, but again stressed reciprocal activity. The judge asked about his assessment of a 'hypothetical scenario' with a drunk and passive person. D2 answered that he would still be able to tell the difference between voluntariness and non-voluntariness. When directly asked if he believed she wanted to have sex, D2 answered, 'Yes, 100 per cent sure'.

In a follow-up interview, defence lawyer Sara said it irritated her that the presiding judge asked questions to her client (D2). In her view, the judge departed from the duty to be impartial and 'interfered too much in the proceedings'. Such 'fatal questions' could have serious consequences for the defendant. If the judge was not happy with the prosecution's job, it was not their task to fix it. Sara argued: '[If] it's a deficient preliminary investigation, it falls back on the prosecutor'. Her opinion is in line with the idea that the judge should not intervene and ask questions, so as not to risk tipping the case against the defendant and hence be viewed as compromising impartiality (Bergman Blix and Wettergren 2019; Ekelöf et al. 2016). However, this idea has been challenged, and it is not evident to what extent the judge may and should be active to ensure the best material is presented in court.

In her final plea, prosecutor Julia argued that D1's story was 'lacking in detail', and that both defendants' stories were inconsistent. She dwelled on how they had unduly exploited her particularly vulnerable situation 'together and in agreement'. It 'couldn't have happened without their little assembly line, knocking on doors. People wanted in. Someone was upstairs. They talked and switched places. They knew she was lying there unconscious and exploited that situation'. Victim counsel Sophia, in her final plea, argued that if a person, like the complainant, is very intoxicated, it should at least raise the requirements for certifying voluntariness.

The male defence lawyer representing D1, in his final plea, pointed out that expressions of voluntariness vary greatly and reminded the court that the situation, as a whole, must be considered. In this vein, he set the temporal boundaries of 'the situation' to begin with the 'good atmosphere' at the party before the sex act; 'they danced, she sat on his lap. The complainant seemed to find him nice'. The defence lawyer continued, emphasizing the complainant's action rationality and autonomy. She could have resisted by 'calling for help, especially considering that she had uttered words [earlier that night] and thus was not incapable of talking'. In conclusion, he argued, 'nothing emerged that made D1 believe that she did not participate voluntarily'.

Sara, the defence lawyer of D2, emphasized in her final plea that her client had 'very clear memories' from the party and provided a long and detailed story, without conflicting information. He had been able to account for all central moments. She argued that D2's story was 'more logical and self-experienced' than the complainant's and it was not true that D2 failed to explain how he ensured her voluntariness. They had 'conversations in good spirits' and he had described the sex act; 'During intercourse, both reached climax'. Before that was 'kissing and caressing', the complainant's voluntary oral sex, her 'moaning, asking him to continue'. All this, Sara argued, was 'interpreted by D2 as consent'. If his account of the sex act lacked in detail, it was not so strange, considering that 'it is sensitive to detail information about one's sex life. He is a young man, just turned 18'. The final part of Sara's plea was a carefully placed empathy hook, effectively inviting the court to imagine how the young boy (D2) experienced the trial and the charges:

> So, then you get a feeling, you make [the court] imagine themselves in a situation. 'If *you* had been … how would you have acted?' And of course, then maybe one starts to wonder; 'maybe I would have done … might I have done the same? I haven't even thought about that!'. (Sara, defence lawyer, Case 14, interview)

Both men were acquitted by the DC and the case was not appealed. In a follow-up interview, DC judge Ella explained that it was not proven beyond reasonable doubt that the complainant was in a particularly vulnerable state. It can be noted that the prosecutor's claim that the complainant was incapacitated by alcohol was countered by the defence's expert witness, who argued that the measurements of her level of intoxication did not definitively prove that she was as intoxicated as she claimed. Furthermore, as the complainant had very vague memories of who had done what to her and when, the court could not convict, despite not doubting that she had in fact been raped by one or several individuals that night. The importance ascribed by the court to the temporal sequence of the event was highlighted in the judgment's statement that, 'even if the complainant said "it hurts", it has not been established if she said it *before* [or during the] the vaginal intercourse, nor if he continued *after* this'. It was further 'not established that the complainant stated that she was tired and wanted to sleep *before* the intercourse', or if she said it afterwards. Thus, the problem was that the complainant could not specify *when* she expressed non-voluntariness. Victim counsel Sophia said in the follow-up interview that, while the DC judgment was well written, she disagreed with the assessment of voluntariness since 'consent should be present throughout'. Her feeling was that the DC 'really wanted to acquit' and, as a result, just 'threw in strange things in the judgment'.

Case 15 was another example of a consent defence against a flawed or missing complainant story. The case was analysed in Chapter 6, focusing on the collective doing of objectivity of the prosecutor and the judge, and in Chapter 8 as an example of an 'altered story' case. Here, we will focus on the defence strategy. The prosecutor argued that she was in a 'particularly vulnerable situation' due to intoxication. According to the defendant, the complainant was undeniably very drunk and sick, but then came to life in his car and 'said that I [the defendant] smell good, caressed my body'. He asked her if she wanted to have sex, to which she replied yes. She kissed him on the neck, was excited, tried to touch his 'male organ' and decided the positions (field notes, AC, Case 15). The defence lawyer engaged in temporal boundary work, narrowing the time frame to the sex act in the defendant's car as an isolated event during which no one could know what actually happened. In the absence of a complainant's story, the defence lawyer's strategy was to advance the defendant's consent story and build it up as credible enough for it to be impossible to disregard.

Patterns in acquitted consent defences

In this section we have seen various interacting reasons behind the defendants' acquittals, some of them unrelated to how the consent defences were formulated. In four of the cases (Cases 2, 7, 9 and 10), defendants had 'ruinable futures' (Uhnoo et al 2024c). They were presented by the defence as socially well-adjusted (father, boss, young man), previously unconvicted, with bourgeoning or established careers, or higher education aspirations.

In other cases, the complainants had no story due to memory loss (Cases 14 and 15) and hence could not describe non-voluntariness against the consent defence. A weak presentation of the evidence by the prosecution, coupled with a passive victim counsel, is another factor facilitating consent defences. In cases with flawed complainants' stories (as Cases 14 and 15), the defendants' consent defence becomes the only available story about the sex act only if the particularly vulnerable state cannot be proven by the prosecution, as the intoxication could void a consent if proven (that the defendant improperly exploited her vulnerable state).

All the acquitted rape cases analysed in this section involve alcohol or drugs. While some of the defendants were sober, all complainants had been drinking. Sharp contrasts were observed in Cases 14 and 15, in which sober defendants had sex with severely intoxicated complainants. Regarding the issue of intent in such cases, we noted that the victim counsel in Case 15 argued for elevated requirements on the defendant to ensure consent when he is sober. In Case 14, the victim counsel argued for increased demands on ensuring consent when the complainant is heavily intoxicated. Both these arguments can also be seen as hersensical questioning of legal logics. Conversely, we have observed that intoxication may work as a reason for the court to excuse either the complainant's (see Case 12 in Chapter 8) or the defendant's (in this chapter) less-detailed stories.

Differences aside, in line with the legal requirements (voluntariness expressed through words, deeds or in other ways), the consent defences describe female complainants' actions and initiatives, and men's and women's reciprocal actions (what their bodies did together). The male defendants are described as mostly passively responding or reacting to women's initiatives or, alternatively, the bodily actions are described as entangled, a 'we'. Notably, the descriptions in the consent defences of women as sexually active, even initiative-taking, contradict traditional hissensical assumptions of women as sexually passive, reflected in rape myths and constructions of ideal rape victims (see Chapter 3).

The consent defence typically take the complainant's interest in the defendant as a starting point, the complainants as active, seeking physical contact (touching, making out) and initiating sex. Descriptions of complainants' bodily movements or postures are frequent, as are other 'signs' of wanting sex. Some interactions described by the defendants appear oddly mechanical, as if there was only one way to interpret the other (she lay down) and correspondingly only one way to respond (we had sex).

The question of who removed the complainant's clothes (notably trousers and panties) was addressed in all cases, indicating that the answer would be of legal significance as sign of voluntariness. Consequently, defendants claim that the complainant undressed herself. The underlying hissensical assumption is that undressing (or nakedness) is an unequivocal sign of voluntariness.

Signs of voluntariness through the female body, as it were, were also common in consent defences, like moaning, groaning or being 'wet'. Moaning and groaning, we argue, should be accorded no evidentiary value as these actions can also be signs of unease or pain. 'Wetness' is interesting, as it would correspond to a penis erection being the same as being horny.

Another noteworthy observation is that the consent defences consistently argued passivity, absence of resistance, or absence of taking distance from the defendant, as signs of voluntariness (cf Orrbén 2022). This is a curious argument, as it is based on ignorance or misunderstanding of the new law. It can also be viewed as a diehard remnant of defence strategies pertaining to the previous rape legislation. Sometimes, however, the 'lack of resistance' is still mentioned in judgments.

The presumed legal significance ascribed to these 'signs of voluntariness', in turn, tacitly links to the question of the defendants' action rationality (hissense). In other words, it is rational to pursue sex when desire arises in response to these 'signs'. The question of the defendant's responsibility or care for the complainant's judgment or state of mind is ignored.

So, how can a consent defence be effectively challenged by the prosecutor and victim counsels? What indications might suggest that, despite the consent defence, the defendant ignored the complainant's wishes? In the next section, we turn to consent defences that resulted in convictions.

Convicted defendants' consent defences

In more than half of the cases in our sample, defendants were convicted despite presenting consent defences (Cases 18, 5, 16, 13, 8, 4 and 11). The main contents of these consent defences were the same as those in the acquitted cases, pinpointed in the conclusion of the previous section. Thus, in this section, we focus our analysis on common patterns that help understand how these cases differ from the acquitted defendants' successful consent defences.

Atypical defendants' consent defences

Three cases with convicted consent defences involved legal subjects 'atypical' in rape cases: a female defendant against a male complainant (Case 16), a male defendant against a male complainant (Case 5) and a male defendant buying sex from a female complainant (Case 18). In two of these cases (Cases 16 and 18), the defendants were acquitted by lay judges in the DC but convicted in the AC.

In Case 18 (previously analysed as an altered story in Chapter 8), the interaction began with voluntariness in the form of sex purchase. The defendant described that he was practically forced to participate, while the complainant was the one taking all the initiative to have sex with him. He was almost entirely passive, as recounted in the AC judgment of Case 18: 'she took off his trousers and put on the condom. Then she took his penis and tried to insert it into herself. [The defendant] just stood there with his arms down during this and did not touch her'. Furthermore, the defendant said that, during the sex act, the complainant did not express any signs of non-voluntariness, by telling him to stop or saying that it hurt. Instead, he recalled that she was moaning. He felt ashamed of the purchase of sex (he had a girlfriend) and informed the court that he did not ejaculate; 'the intercourse just ended'.

In their judgment, the AC stated that the defendant's credibility was negatively affected by his altered story (see Chapter 8) and that his new consent defence 'appear[ed] unlikely and difficult to understand'. In a follow-up interview, victim counsel Kattis (Case 18) argued that 'these are typically poor objections from a defendant. If you say these things, we understand that you are guilty. Like "he didn't do anything, and it was just her"'. Regarding intent, the AC judgment considered it proven that the complainant 'repeatedly, both verbally and through actions, expressed that she no longer participated voluntarily'. The judgment put the complainant's story at the base of their assessment and thus followed her story in the judgment. The complainant had described that, when telling him to stop, the defendant had answered, 'I bought you'. The AC judgment picked this up, reinforcing the characterization of the defendant as a young man who purchased sex, used force and violence and demanded his money back because he did not come (and ejaculate). Victim counsel Kattis said that it was clear that the complainant 'suffers abuse at so many levels and this is a constant in her life'. The AC's judgment also considered the broader context beyond the sex act, focusing the defendant's behaviour before and after the act and the asymmetrical power dynamics between the complainant and the defendant.

Case 5 is an atypical case in the sense that it involved two men, where at least one of them was openly homosexual. There was also considerable violence involved. Apart from this, the case does not differ from consent defences in heterosexual rape cases. There are several similarities between Case 18, above, and Case 5. In both cases, the sex act was preceded by an explicit agreement to have sex. In both cases, the defendants altered their stories, expressed shame and described their role during the sex act as almost entirely passive. In Case 5, a consent defence could have followed the complainant's story and the technical evidence, which proved anal penetration. However, according to the prosecutor, the defendant was deeply ashamed and therefore denied anal intercourse. He only admitted brief 'intimate acts of a petting nature'. When confronted with the technical evidence, he changed to a consent defence, but said that the complainant took all the initiatives (asked for oral sex, gave him a massage, put the defendant's penis in his anus and told him to be on top of him). Afterwards, the defendant stated, he dressed, they said farewell and agreed to keep in touch. There was no violence (field notes, Case 5).

The defendant was convicted in the DC based on the complainant's story, which, the judgment wrote, was presented 'in distress' and offered 'a detailed' and 'considerably more credible' story than the defendant's story, which was 'brief and lacking in detail'. The complainant's story was further supported by strong technical evidence in the form of semen and injuries. The judgment stated that it was proven that the defendant had committed rape by non-voluntary anal intercourse and that he had used violence to force the complainant to participate. Case 5 was not appealed.

Like Case 5, Case 16 is atypical, but this time in terms of reversed heterosexual roles. It involved a young male complainant and a young female defendant. The complainant learnt afterward from friends that a young girl had vaginal intercourse with him at a party while he was heavily drunk and almost unconscious. The young woman was charged with rape and abuse of his particularly vulnerable situation. Notable in this case was that two friends of the complainant were eyewitnesses, as they had observed parts of the sex act. The defendant admitted the sex act but claimed she believed it was voluntary. The defence lawyer argued that neither of the two was too intoxicated to give consent; thus, the complainant was not in a particularly vulnerable situation. The male complainant said he was disgusted when he later discovered from friends what had happened. He only remembered that she 'sat on his penis'. The defence lawyer asked the complainant some 'control questions', among these if he had an erection. The commonsensical implication of this is, of course, that men 'cannot be raped' by women unless they 'want it', to be compared with the 'wet and horny' defence.

During the interrogation in the DC the defendant presented a typical consent defence minimizing her own agency, much like the defendant in Cases 18 and 5. She described undressing in a passive voice; 'my pants come off' and 'my bra gets kind of unhooked', as if it happened without her involvement. She also used the entangled bodies figure, discussed in the previous section, describing the sex act in terms like '*we* fool around', '*we* lie down' and '*we* kind of have sex', implying reciprocity. She described the complainant as active and taking initiatives: 'he touches my breasts' and 'he is down there and kind of licks me'. Regarding how his clothes came off, she stated that 'his pants kind of come off, it's not something I've done. I don't take off a guys' pants, you know. They can do that themselves'. Like in Case 15, the defendant also claimed that, although the complainant was so drunk he had passed out, he was awake and active when they had sex. He just 'turned away and pretended to sleep' when the eyewitnesses came by.

When the defence lawyer asked her if the complainant had an erection, she claimed she did not remember, but also said she wondered, could his penis otherwise have penetrated her? The defence lawyer had argued that sexual intercourse with an unconscious man was physically impossible. Since the defendant's answer might undermine this argument (see Flower 2020), he probed further by asking a leading question: 'You said he was searching, what did you mean by that?'. The defendant answered that he was trying to 'direct' his penis 'where it should go'. The defence lawyer asked if the complainant said anything to her during the sex act. The defendant answered that the complainant said that she was 'tight' and 'if you make me come, you're the best'. Her answer thus indicates that he was active and wanting.

It can be noted that, just as in Case 18, according to the defendant it was the complainant who 'directed the penis'. When asked why her story differed so much from that of the complainant, she said that he was either lying or did not remember, and 'I can't help if he regrets it'. In other words, the female defendant in Case 16 refuted the male complainant's rape claims with standard arguments used in most rape cases.

In the DC, the lay judges overruled the professional judge (compare with Cases 17 and 18) and acquitted. The lay judgment argued it was a 'word-against-word' situation regarding the requisite of (non-)voluntariness. The complainant's story was deemed to have low credibility because it could 'hardly be said to contain *all*' of the Supreme Court's criteria for credibility.[2]

---

[2]　All the criteria were listed in the DC lay judgment: 'clear, lengthy, vivid, logical, rich in detail, free from errors, contradictions, exaggerations, inexplicable moments,

Therefore, the lay judgment argued that the defendant's story should be the base for the court's assessment. The charges were not proven beyond reasonable doubt because it could not be ruled out that the complainant '*at some point* participated voluntarily in intercourse' (DC judgment, Case 16).

In a follow-up interview, DC judge Kerstin (Case 16) shared that she believed many legal professionals 'draw upon their own sexual experiences, which one absolutely should not do'. She exemplified with the defence lawyer in Case 16, who argued that it was physically impossible for a heavily intoxicated male complainant in a particularly vulnerable situation to have an erection. Kerstin said: 'That is just nonsense. It is possible. There are studies on it'. Therefore, in her dissenting opinion, she dismissed that argument and stated that it was proven that the defendant 'knowingly and improperly exploited that [the complainant], due to sleep and intoxication, was in a helpless state [that is particularly vulnerable situation]'.

In the final plea in the AC, the prosecutor in Case 16 drew on the evaluation of the dissenting DC judge and emphasized the presence of compelling technical evidence and witness testimonies corroborating the complainant's story. The evidence refuted the defendant's assertion that the complainant was active and conversational. The prosecutor also expressed empathy with both the complainant and the defendant, remarking that 'it was a sad situation for all parties involved'. The victim counsel echoed this feeling of sadness in her final plea in the AC. She also highlighted that the reversed roles in this case added an atypical dimension, possibly necessitating the court to examine their own biases and assess the case with a fresh approach.

The defence lawyer in the AC rule-reminded the court about the principle that the charge should be fully dependent on the quality of the complainant's story, as the prosecutor has the burden of proof. This posed a challenge for the prosecution, he argued, because the complainant's memory was limited due to his alleged state of unconsciousness (compare with Cases 14 and 15). The defence lawyer disputed the quality of the evidence and argued that the technical evidence did not unequivocally support the complainant's version of events. Finally, he portrayed the defendant's story as 'clear, detailed, and devoid of inconsistencies, spanning from the first moment of her arrest to the present' (field notes, AC, Case 16).

---

inconsistencies, poor coherence, or doubt in crucial moments'. This, per se, may be indicative of the lay judges' attempt to follow legal procedure in motivating their decision. While professional judges almost always write the judgment, they usually ask dissenting lay judges, or in this case all the lay judges, to suggest their own motivation. This is one strategy used by professional judges to discourage lay judges from maintaining a decision that clashes with the professional juridical expertise (Bergman Blix and Wettergren 2018).

The AC convicting judgment, like the dissenting professional DC judge, assessed that the complainant 'made a credible impression', 'narrating the parts of the incident he claims to remember in a nuanced and restrained manner. He has in no way given the impression of exaggeration and has been careful to emphasize what he does not remember and which moments he is unsure about' (AC judgment, Case 16). They found the defendant's account of the complainant 'being active and participating' was not in line with the evidence, and regarded her explanation that the complainant 'pretended to be asleep' when the witnesses observed them as 'wholly implausible in light of the circumstances'. Regarding intent, the AC stated:

> It is worth highlighting that voluntary participation must be present throughout the entire sex act. [The defendant] cannot have mistaken [the complainant's] condition and must therefore have consciously exploited it, in a manner deemed inappropriate by the Appeals Court. (AC judgment, Case 16)

Thus, Case 16 illustrates that the consent defence itself must be read in the context of the efforts made by the legal actors in the courtroom in terms of empathic translation and negotiation. Cases 16 and 18 both involve prosecutors and victim counsels working closely together, not assuming that 'evidence speaks for itself'.

Defendants filming or photographing the sex act

In two cases the defendants filmed or photographed the sex act without the complainant's knowledge and shared it with others. In Case 8, a young couple, who were vaguely acquainted, had sex at night (see also previous analysis of this case in Chapter 7). She was sober; he was drunk. When she drove him home, they decided to stop the car to have sex. The complainant had agreed to a 'quickie', but the intercourse lasted for a long time, making her protest and say she wanted to go home. However, he did not let her go and filmed the sex act with his mobile telephone, without her knowledge. The defendant was convicted in the AC, but was previously acquitted in the DC, which stated in the judgment that 'the complainant provided inaccurate and exaggerated information about her involuntary participation'.

Rather unconventionally, the DC judgment began with an account of the defendant's story (cf Chapter 10), stating that, earlier in the evening, the complainant performed oral sex on him and later 'they agreed to have intercourse', indicating verbal mutual agreement for voluntary sex. In the defendant's consent defence, the sex act was described as bodily entangled and mutual ('*they* were having intercourse in various positions for a relatively long time' and '*we* were doing it from behind') and in terms of the defendant's role as being entirely passive. She took all the initiative (she undressed, fetched and put a condom on him, 'sat on his penis' and lay on her back).

The DC judgment concluded the defendant's story: 'It was late, and they were both tired, but both voluntarily participated throughout the sexual interaction, which the complainant demonstrated, among other things, through her body language and moaning'. The DC judgment continued, 'he ejaculated, [and] they parted in good spirits', suggesting that the sex act concluded only after his ejaculation to the satisfaction of both parties. The 'good spirits' phrasing was inferred based on the defendant's statement during the trial that he thought they would meet again; 'It was normal. Especially given the way we parted. It was a cheerful hug and a kiss'. In short, the way the judgment conveyed the defendant's story may be viewed as indicative of the court's assessment that it was more credible than the complainant's story.

Case 8 included interesting attempts by the prosecutor Sandra to use empathic translation and empathy hooks. In the interrogation in the DC trial, she asked the complainant why she believed things unfolded as they did and why defendant 'acted as he did'. The complainant replied: 'He was drunk, and he wanted to have sex and come, and maybe that's why he wanted to continue. And that's why he didn't accept that I didn't want to'. The prosecutor knew the complainant's story and used her own interpretation of the situation to convey the relation between the situation as a whole (drunk, want to come) and the details of the rape. Empathic translation invites the court to *feel* the legal meaning of the story, holistically, instead of merely assessing the story piece by piece and instrumentally. By means of the complainant's situated insights in the defendant's action rationality, the court would both imagine his motivation and relate it to the complainant's perspective, resulting in the image of a drunken man who acted sexually entitled to ejaculate by using the complainant's body as a means to this end.

When prosecutor Sandra interrogated the defendant, he said that, since it was late at night, 'we tried to hurry things along. I suggested that maybe she could give me oral sex, and she agreed, so she did it for a while, but it's not like I forced her into anything'. The defendant also said he had to help himself to ejaculate. Prosecutor Sandra then asked why they needed to rush, to which he answered, 'In the end, I just wanted to finish so that we could go home'. Given the complainant's statements that she repeatedly said stop and that she wanted to go home, the answer portrays a scenario driven by his sexual arousal, with his desire to ejaculate taking precedence over any potential desire or arousal she may have had.

In a follow-up interview, prosecutor Sandra emphasized the defendant's responsibility to ensure voluntariness and stressed that she thought the importance of this responsibility increases if the other party repeatedly says she wants to go home: if the interaction continues for a long time (in this case, 45–60 minutes) and the involved parties have no previous sexual relationship. This reasoning is arguably another example of how the new rape legislation allows space for hersensical interpretations to blend with legal logics.

In her final plea in the AC, prosecutor Sandra emphasized the defendant's callousness towards the complainant's wishes. She advanced the requisite of intent as 'a crucial question', arguing that the defendant must have been aware that the complainant no longer wished to continue because she explicitly told him so. 'He refused to listen to her'. She also underscored the power dynamics (younger complainant, physically superior defendant) and that this made it difficult for the complainant to make herself heard. Prosecutor Sandra further stated that the fact that he filmed her without her knowledge and sent the film to a friend aligned with his disregard for how she experienced the situation. Interesting here is how the prosecutor skilfully utilized the filming as an empathy hook, urging the court to imagine the defendant's lack of care for the young complainant's needs, and his questionable understanding of consensual sex.

In the follow-up interview, Sandra explained that her strategy in the AC – the empathy hook – aimed to convince the judges that the defendant's secret filming of the sexual interaction and the subsequent sharing of the video suggested that he was not the 'regular decent guy' he portrayed himself to be. His behaviour contradicted his claims of valuing mutual respect and portraying their relationship as 'cute' and 'lovey-dovey'. Leaning on common-sense assumptions about how a decent person who values mutual consent *would* behave, the empathy hook served to reveal the defendant as someone of low moral character.

Sandra had been frustrated that the DC did not mention the secret filming in its judgment, arguably because it happened *before* the non-voluntary part, but she thought that it influenced the outcome in the AC. In its convicting judgment, the AC noted that 'one cannot ignore the fact that [the defendant], without the complainant's knowledge, filmed parts of their previous sexual interaction'. The judgment reasoned that this suggests that the defendant 'did not accord much importance to what the complainant wanted or did not want'. In a follow-up interview with two of the AC judges, they explained that they placed crucial weight on the use of force and her verbal refusal, but also on 'his state of mind, which strongly indicates that [what the complainant wanted] didn't matter to him. He wanted to ejaculate'. AC judge Petter added that it appeared that the defendant 'would not care much about what [the complainant] said, considering that he had filmed her'.

In Case 13, the defendant's consent defence revolved around him (he was sober) helping a drunk girl (under 18 years) to find a place to sleep, holding her hand and massaging her arm to help her fall asleep. Case 13 will be analysed in depth in Chapter 11 with regard to the changes made by the AC's convicting judgment. Here, we briefly concentrate on what transpired in the DC. During the hearing, the defendant described the complainant's actions and highlighted the reciprocity of the sex act: 'After a few minutes, *she* said that I was "so damn nice", and *she* kissed my cheek. "You are nice too", I replied. *She* kissed my mouth. And then *we* started kissing and *we* had intercourse. It maybe lasted [max 10] minutes' (Field notes, AC interrogation from the DC, Case 13, emphasis added). The defendant explained that the complainant expressed voluntariness by undressing, touching his penis outside his pants and caressing his neck. He refuted her claim that she was motionless and passive. When asked by the prosecutor if he used a condom, he said no because it was spontaneous and, thus, he had no condoms. Instead, he stated, that he 'withdrew his penis, used his hand and masturbated until ejaculation' (field notes, Case 13). In the trial, he was also charged with photographing her naked without asking. Both these circumstances (ensuring his ejaculation and photographing her without consent) echo elements present in Case 8.

In its judgment, the DC considered 'the situation as a whole' when deciding whether it was reasonable to assume that he perceived that she wanted to have unprotected sex with him. By setting the temporal boundary of import *before* the sex act to the moment the defendant and the complainant met, the DC judgment in Case 13 specifically highlighted that: 1) they had only known each other a few hours; 2) the defendant 'was aware that the complainant had no place to sleep'; and 3) 'There had been no indications of any sexual interest or invitations in the conversation between them'.

Therefore, the judgment concluded there was 'no plausible context to support the defendant's belief that the complainant suddenly desired unprotected intercourse with him'. Interestingly, the DC seemed to accord the fact of unprotected sex great significance in its assessment of voluntariness, unlike in Cases 2, 7, 14 and 15 (acquittals), in which unprotected sex was not mentioned in the courts' judgments. Additionally, the DC considered the short time of their acquaintance – just a few hours – which was not rendered important in, for instance, Cases 2, 14 or 15 (acquittals). The DC judgment in Case 13 relied on hersensical ideas about sexuality, concluding that it is not obvious for a very young drunk girl to want unprotected sex on the garage floor with an older man she has only known for a few hours.

In line with hersensical legal reasoning, the DC judgment further stated that the defendant had failed to ensure voluntariness 'despite being aware of the complainant's intoxicated state' but instead 'acted on his own assumption' regarding voluntariness. Comparisons can be made with other cases (for instance, Cases 14 and 15) in which the complainants' very high degree of intoxication was not considered to put higher demands on the defendants' responsibility to ensure the other party's voluntariness. The DC in Case 13 found the requisite of non-voluntariness beyond reasonable doubt, and convicted for negligent rape ('the complainant's passivity must have raised [the defendant's] suspicions regarding the possibility that she did not participate voluntarily'). He was later convicted of rape in AC (see Chapter 11).

These cases of filming and photographing sex suggest that films and photos can be used as empathy hooks, but also that the mere action to film and take photos can be used to signify a careless defendant.

Consent defences from men with excessive sexual behaviour

In two of the convicted cases (Cases 11 and 4), the defendants were portrayed as individuals who had committed other sexual assaults on women the very same night as the rape. This could be interpreted by the court as indicative of 'bad character'. Both had a minority background. While the defendant in Case 4 was described as a 'very nice guy', the defendant in Case 11 was previously convicted and charged with additional offences. He was heavily intoxicated at the time of the offence.

In the context of the defendants' stories in rape cases, Case 4 stands out as particularly intriguing, given the highly detailed consent defence presented, contrasting against the majority of the convicted consent defence cases. Noteworthy in this case was also the characterization by prosecutor Emilia of the defendant as a 'very nice guy', 'extremely pleasant', remarking that 'he just needs to learn to control himself. He can't go on like this'. By saying that 'he can't go on like this', she alluded to the statements from witnesses that the defendant had been trying to become intimate with other women the same night.

During the trial, neither the prosecutor nor the defence asked the defendant what led him to believe the complainant wanted to have sex, yet the defendant's story was full of indications. The story detailed that the complainant actively participated by willingly undressing, expressing a desire for breast massage, engaging in reciprocal physical contact (rubbing her buttocks, touching his penis and communicating a preference for touching his testicles). The defendant also said that sex had been discussed earlier in the evening. According to our field notes from the AC, the defendant's

> detailed and precise story clearly suggests that the complainant gave the impression of being quite wild and sexually interested, and that even the friend [who was present that evening] pushed in that direction. His detailed story about sex and various indications of willingness made the court embarrassed, as seen in how they became very focused on their 'papers' on the bench [...] The defendant's detailed, drawn-out story about the sex act appears more like a (wet) erotic dream than a story of what actually happened.

In its judgment, the DC acknowledged that the defendant's story was 'relatively long and contained several details' that partly aligned with the complainant's story. They asserted that the story 'was not so improbable as to be disregarded' but concluded that it 'did not diminish the value of the evidence supporting the prosecution'. In the AC, when clarifying the defence's position on the charge, the defence lawyer raised issues of credibility and reliability, emphasizing the quality of details in his client's story. He reiterated the DC judgment that the defendant's story 'was not so improbable as to be disregarded', yet he asserted this was precisely what the DC did when convicting the defendant. In the final plea, the defence lawyer rule-reminded the court about the risk of 'reversing the burden of proof' by forcing the defendant to refute the charges. The field notes illustrate the defence lawyer's tactics in his final plea in the AC:

> The defence lawyer says, 'In here [in the court], we are forced to be psychologists and determine credibility, but it shouldn't be like that'. *He sighs occasionally, quietly dramatic, and one can understand he is somewhat saddened by the state of these cases.* […] He continues to discuss how the new law now requires boys to film interactions with girls to be able to refute rape accusations. […] He talks about the court's perception of the discomfort for the complainant, the consequences of the crime, etc. He continues by asserting that his client's story is the most detailed of the two stories. 'There is nothing to suggest that my client has committed an offence'. […] He concludes 'The defendant doesn't have a video film. You shouldn't have to have a video film [proving your innocence] every time you've spent a night together with someone'. (Field notes, AC, Case 4, researcher's reflection emphasized)

The field notes illustrate that the defence lawyer tried to forge the argument that the only viable defence for an individual accused of rape is to present a video recording of the sex act. He also argued that, despite the defendant being the more credible storyteller, since he provided a long and more detailed story, the court is likely to side with the woman. Additionally, the defence lawyer attempted to prompt reflection on whether the court may harbour prejudice towards his client, who came from a minority background:

> [He] mentions the 'elephant in the room', namely 'the question of whether justice is blind and whether distinctions are made between people' – here he refers to a research study using an identical fabricated case but with different names on the defendant to prove that a foreign name affects the assessment of the defendant's credibility and reliability.

Furthermore, following standard argumentation, the defence lawyer highlighted the complainant's free will and lack of resistance, that she 'could have left [the room] at any time' but chose to stay. This defence tactic failed. Instead, the AC believed the complainant's story and convicted the defendant.

In its judgment, the AC did not explicitly take a position on the credibility of the defendant's story but wrote that both 'have provided long, coherent, and detailed accounts. However, their stories are incompatible, and both cannot correspond with reality'. In other words, the story of the defendant did not appear realistic, at least not in comparison with the story of the complainant. Given the court's reaction to the defendant's detailed story, it appears that too much detail or the wrong (implausible) kind of detail raised suspicion of lying. In Case 4, the apparent desire of the defendant to have sex with someone that night, as testified by witnesses, combined with the very erotic details in his story, made him look like a victim of his fantasies.

Case 11 is our last case of convicted consent defences. It stands out because of the way the prosecution and victim counsel collaborated to make the complainant story appear reasonable, and the victim counsel's efforts to undermine the defendant's story (see Chapter 6). The defendant was a previously convicted and not very eloquent man with a minority background, charged with additional offences at the same trial. At the time of the offence, he was heavily intoxicated. He engaged in what he describes as voluntary oral sex with the complainant, describing how *he* caressed her with her clothes on, then he removed her pants, he gave her oral sex and penetrated her with his fingers. She suddenly stiffened and told him to leave, which he then did. Until then, the complainant expressed voluntariness by touching his chest and appearing to enjoy what was happening. In stating the defence's position on the charge of rape, the defence lawyer was very brief. His client had been 'messing around', which he explained 'means kissing and cuddling', which then led to 'what the defendant has described in the police interrogation'.

In their hearings with the defendant, prosecutor Jesper and victim counsel Elvira inquired about how he knew that she wanted him to perform oral sex on her. The prosecutor questioned whether she signalled voluntariness and if his severe intoxication might have led him to misinterpret her signals. The defendant responded, 'It was consent all the way, when she said stop, I respected it'. Prosecutor Jesper asked whether he removed her clothes. The defendant replied that he took off her pants and that 'she lifted her buttocks when I was taking them off, so it was consent'. Jesper also emphasized the peculiarity of engaging in intimate acts, such as oral sex, with a woman one has known for only half an hour by asking the defendant: 'Don't you find it strange, unknown woman, oral sex, having just met her half an hour ago?', to which the defendant simply responded 'no'. This question exemplifies the way legal professionals navigate common-sense boundaries distinguishing between normal and abnormal sexual behaviour. Also, victim counsel Elvira questioned the plausibility of his consent defence, that it was mutual, by asking him if the complainant was active and performed any sexual acts on him (see Chapter 6). By doing so, she reminded the court of the significance of the new law.

In some of our rape trials, prosecutors and victim counsels pressed the issue that the male defendant had exhibited excessive sexual conduct. This was illustrated by circumstances such as a pattern of recurrent engagement in sexual assaults, notably on the same night as the alleged rape (Cases 4 and 11). Implicit in this argument is the assumption that, if a man displays such behaviour, he may be predisposed to commit rape, suggesting an action rationality inherent of a 'real rapist'. Prosecutors advancing this perspective may be accused by defence lawyers of attempting to discredit the defendant, which transpired in Case 11. In his final plea, prosecutor Jesper underscored that the defendant had been suspected of another rape and sexual assault on the same evening. Reflecting on this, Jesper remarked in a follow-up interview, 'The defence advised against bringing up past incidents, but ... considering that he was suspected of another rape that very night and I've summoned witnesses [pertaining to that], I believe it still has a bearing on intent in this case'.

As for the defendant's consent defence, the prosecutor remarked in his final plea that:

> we hear that he had never met her before, was at a party where he had sex with another girl, then went home to the complainant, whom he had never met. They engage in entirely voluntary sex, including oral sex and petting, within minutes of their encounter. The account lacks detail on how it began, who did what, etc. It lacks credibility. (Field notes, DC, Case 11)

In her final plea, the victim counsel asserted that the defendant maintained excessive confidence in his good looks and specifically highlighted the 'unrealistic sequence of events', including the defendant's wicked perception of reciprocity (see Chapter 6). In his final plea, the defence lawyer in return tried to re-establish hissense ideas about normal sex: 'The prosecutor says that people [do not] have sex immediately. Yes, they do. The situation often invites it. The defendant is not a stranger, a mutual acquaintance with whom [she] has video-talked half-naked'. As we observed in Chapter 6, he also argued that his client had been unfairly smeared due to the reversed roles in this trial, in which the prosecution attacked the credibility of the defendant instead of the other way around.

On account of common-sense normal v abnormal sex, the defence lawyer further pointed out that this would be an 'unusual case of rape – jumping on a girl and performing oral sex on her. Rape often involves penetration, intercourse'. This statement points in the direction of two rape myths; that a real rape includes intercourse and not oral sex and, on the other hand, consequently, that a real rapist would not have stopped at oral sex and petting. He also reminded the court to be objective in terms of 'everyone knows how the evaluation of evidence should proceed' and emphasized that his client's counter-story could not be discarded considering the Supreme Court's requirements of a credibly story (field notes, Case 11). The DC's judgment did not comment on the content of the defendant's story at all but simply stated that the complainant's story was proven beyond reasonable doubt. Regarding his intent, the DC found that 'it must have been obvious to [the defendant] that [the complainant] did not want to have sex with him, a completely unfamiliar person who was also heavily intoxicated'.

When the defence appealed the guilty verdict to the AC, a new defence lawyer took over the case. In his final plea, he presented an elaborate objectivity rule reminder, asserting that the starting point must be that the court 'should assess the circumstances for both parties in a non-prejudiced manner'. He then quoted what he believed to be a prejudiced passage in the DC judgment: 'That [complainant] voluntarily would want to make out and have sex with a stranger, a drunk, nameless man already after five to ten minutes appears completely unlikely in that context'. He argued that such reasoning in a judgment is 'a warning signal' and 'a subjective viewpoint; what is normal or not does not belong in a judgment'. Before a verdict was reached in the AC, when the defendant was not released after the trial, making it clear that the AC would also convict, the defence withdrew the appeal to avoid the risk of a longer prison sentence.

Patterns in convicted consent defences

While the focus of our analysis in Chapter 9 has been on the making and breaking of consent defences, in all cases there were additional and interactive reasons for conviction or acquittal.

In this section on convicted consent defences, three cases involved legal subjects 'atypical' in rape cases: a female defendant and a male complainant (Case 16); a male complainant (Case 5); and a man buying sex from a young woman (Case 18). In two of these cases (Cases 16 and 18), the defendants were acquitted by lay judges in the DC but convicted in the AC. Additionally, in four cases, the action rationality inferred by the defendants' behaviour suggests that they were not particularly interested in the will of the complainant, which indicated that the defendants were negligent if not intentional regarding the (non-)voluntary participation. In two cases (Cases 8 and 13), the defendants filmed or photographed the sex act without the complainants' knowledge and shared it with others. Furthermore, in Cases

11 and 4, the defendants were portrayed as individuals who had previously committed similar sexual assaults on women, which could be interpreted by the court as indicative of 'bad character'.

In the majority of the cases (Cases 4, 5, 11, 13 and 18), the convicted defendants had a foreign or minority background (not the defendants in Cases 8 and 16), while only one of the complainants had a foreign or minority background. A similar pattern emerged in the cases that resulted in acquittals.[3] Previous research on rape myths has demonstrated that a foreign or minority background ties in with the typical rapist myth, as does low social status and a criminal record (Bitsch and Klemetsen 2017). Prosecutors and lawyers in our sample were aware of this. Defence lawyers sometimes tried to counter the effects by adapting their strategies when their clients possessed any of these disadvantages. The strategy to speak out regarding this matter in Case 4 did not influence the outcome, most likely because the defendant's story was highly implausible even if his story was not explicitly assessed in the AC judgment.

The complainants' appearance and character arguably also matter for the outcomes of the cases described in this section. One pattern regarding the complainants refers to the ideal victim myth (Christie 1986) in terms of being socially vulnerable or in a vulnerable situation: a young woman selling sex (Case 18), a highly intoxicated young man who passed out during a party (Case 16), a very drunk young girl without a place to sleep (Case 13) and a slightly drunk young girl who had to share a room with a stranger in a friend's flat (Case 4). Conversely, they did not conform to the ideal victim myth, having placed themselves in vulnerable situations by selling sex (Case 18) or becoming highly intoxicated (Case 16), particularly in the absence of a safe place to stay for the night (Cases 13 and 4). Nor are a young man raped by a woman (Case 16) or a homosexual man dating an unknown man (Case 5) considered typical rape victims, as suggested above.

The other pattern suggests sobriety: a sober woman confronting an intoxicated unknown man (Case 11), a sober young woman consenting to a 'quickie' with an intoxicated man (Case 8), a sober man arranging a meeting with another man on a dating application (Case 5) and a woman selling sex (Case 18). Sobriety may arguably have contributed to the court finding the complainants' stories more credible as compared with the defendants. Additionally, in the convicted cases, two intoxicated complainants were deemed to be in particularly vulnerable situations, according to both the prosecutor and the court (Cases 13 and 16). In contrast to the sober complainants in several of the convicted cases, in the six acquitted consent

---

[3]   Cases 7, 10, 15 and 14 involved defendants with foreign or minority background (not the defendants in Cases 2 and 9). Only the complainant in Case 2 had a minority background

defence cases, *all* complainants were intoxicated, two of them in particularly vulnerable situations, according to the prosecutor, but not according to the court (Cases 14 and 15).

Finally, credibility is not influenced only by the storyteller but also by the story they present (Smith 2018:12), including how the consent defence was formulated by the defence and, to some extent, how it was presented in court. Two main points can be drawn from the analysis of the (convicted) defendants' stories in these cases. First, a story may be self-incriminating if it deviates too much from the complainants' story, either by providing too many details that do not match with the complainant's story (Case 4) or by giving too few details and thus being considered 'brief' and 'lacking in detail' (Cases 5, 8 and 16). The latter makes defendants appear less adept at expressing themselves, highlighting that defendants like complainants who are not very eloquent may be disadvantaged in rape cases. Second, providing too much detail in Case 4 also resulted in the story being deemed implausible by the court, such was the case when defendants portrayed themselves as *very* passive (the complainant did everything: for example, 'directed the penis' case). The credibility of the defendants' stories in this regard also hinges on defence lawyers' ability to translate their clients' action rationality as normal and common (his)sense.

Conclusion

In Chapters 8 and 9 we have explored the defendants' stories, or lack thereof, in the 18 rape cases in our study. Although traditionally the burden of proof rests with the prosecution, the new law has, in line with hersensical reasoning, imposed upon defendants the responsibility to clarify how they ensured voluntariness from the other party. This is sometimes referred to as a 'burden of explanation'. We argue, however, that this can be understood not as an infringement on defendants' rights but as an opportunity to present an explanation, akin to a self-defence claim that can potentially legitimize an otherwise unlawful act. Consent defence provides an opportunity for the defendant to be acquitted even in cases when the prosecutor's evidence is deemed to reach the level of proven beyond reasonable doubt, in line with the *Balcony Case* model. Consequently, defence lawyers strive to convince the court that defendants believed the complainant participated voluntarily, encouraging the defendants to talk about how they perceived the voluntary participation and attempting to negotiate empathy for the defendants' action rationality. In other words, they try to make the defendants' hissensical reasoning coincide with legal logics.

Following linguist Sofia Orrbén (2022), representations of acting bodies in Swedish sex crime judgments draw on acts of intimacy/proximity, distance, assault, violence, resignation, power and emotion. Active/passive bodies are further ascribed meaning with regards to voluntariness. Applying this conceptual framework on the consent defences in our cases, it appears that defendants depicted the women as active through acts of intimacy and emotion. Further, women in consent defences are typically described as active, awake, present, alert and aware, any degree of intoxication set aside (see for example Cases 14 and 15). Together with the described absence of physical distance in consent defences, this implies that, because of the complainants' actions, body language and physical closeness, it is reasonable, from a hissense perspective, for defendants to perceive participation as voluntary. As demonstrated in Chapter 7, since the 'situation as a whole' should be considered in the assessment of voluntariness, everything can be made relevant through temporal boundary work, what happened before, during and after the sex act. In line with this, consent defences often describe the 'good atmosphere', sexual tension, jokes about sex or that the complainant was in a good mood before, or after, the sex act.

Not surprisingly, there is an absence of coercion or violence in men's consent defences, despite supporting evidence in some cases that suggest the opposite. More interestingly, there is a lack of activity from men. Male defendants' agency is often implicit as if they respond or react to women's initiatives but take few initiatives of their own. They receive oral sex, participate courteously in intercourse and accept the complainant's desired positions. This is suggestive of a masculine sexual readiness to serve, as it were, whenever a woman shows interest, seeks physical closeness or initiates sexual activity. This is arguably a version of stereotypical male sexuality as driven by an uncontrollable and unstoppable sexual desire (Hollway 1984). While women are depicted as active in consent defences, details of their activity usually stop at various 'signs', although in some cases are more explicit, like touching the penis or offering oral sex. The notion of male sexuality as an unstoppable force ready to set off in a predictable direction makes it possible to argue that a complainant expressed implicit consent by acting in specific 'inviting' ways. It might be expressed vaguely and ambivalently but still becomes part of 'the situation as a whole', influencing the court's assessment of his perception of her expressions of voluntariness. Consequently, when a man is led to believe that a woman wants to have sex with him, any behaviour before, during and after a sex act can be interpreted as rational behaviour (hissensically normal).

In contrast, to prove intent, prosecutors and victim counsels strive to elucidate the defendants' action rationality as indifferent to the complainant's needs and wants. This can be seen as a hersensical strategy. They do so by encouraging the complainant to detail how they expressed non-voluntariness, or how they did *not* express voluntariness, in words, deeds or other ways, hoping to demonstrate that the defendant should reasonably have realized the absence of voluntariness. In some cases (for example, Case 11), the prosecution also attempts to deflect some of the focus on the complainant by emphasizing and directly probing the defendant's responsibility to ensure voluntariness. We argue that prosecutors could adapt their strategies in line with this to improve their strategic dismantling of the consent defence (see Hohl and Stanko 2024 on suspect-focused preliminary investigation and Rumney and McPhee 2021 on offender-centric policing). To counteract defendants' denial or lies shifting into a consent defence and ensure that the court critically examine altered defence stories (see Chapter 8), they could ask the police to video record early interrogations with rape suspects.

Feminist critique of the legal interpretation of consent-based rape laws highlights that the legal system privileges the subjective perception of male defendants regarding a woman's voluntariness (hissense), rather than considering what is reasonable for her to desire (hersense) (Pineau 1989). Our analysis demonstrates that male hissensical assumptions about sexuality blend easily with legal common sense, but also that the new law forges the possibility of hersensical legal logic. In a few of the cases, we observed that voices were raised or strategies were laid out by the prosecution to turn the tables and state the 'normal' from a woman's perspective. Thus, the analysis in Chapters 8 and 9 raises questions regarding what legal professionals consider reasonable for a man to comprehend about female (non-)voluntariness based on 'the situation as a whole' and the expectations placed on men to ensure voluntariness. Factors such as age disparity, level of intoxication and the nature of previous relationships between the parties were mentioned by legal professionals in our sample as indicators that the defendant should have understood the complainant's lack of voluntariness or the associated risks. It was argued that such factors ought to raise demands of the responsibility of the defendant.

A recurring obvious theme in this chapter is the implicit hissensical notions about male and female sexuality (Muehlenhard et al 2016), embedded in defendants' stories. Actions deemed as 'non-passive' by women such as – depending on the temporal boundary work of the defence – being sexually provocative, performing oral sex, undressing, moaning or not resisting or taking a distance, are interpreted as signs of voluntariness by the defendants. This raises broader questions about lingering but dated societal perceptions of male entitlement to sex and women's responsibility as gatekeepers and for not 'teasing' male sexuality (cf Jozkowski and Peterson 2013). It is noteworthy that courts rarely question the thrust of male desire if they accept his hissensical story about the complainants' signals. It is also worth noting in this context that, in the case of the female defendant (Case 16), the situation was deemed 'tragic' for both the defendant and complainant, possibly suggesting a different view of a female offender's emotive-cognitive action rationality and, thus, of their motives.

We argue throughout this book that legal professional roles need a thorough rethinking to implement the intention of the new law, which we consider to be fundamentally challenging of the male perspective structurally embedded in legal ideals of objectivity, autonomy and rationality, that is hissensical legal logics. Through this chapter, it becomes clear that the adaptation of the roles along with a critical reflexive approach to background emotions and different types of common sense will also be to the advantage of protecting the right of the defendants. Consent defences are the logical development of the defendants' responsibility to clarify how they ensured consent from the other party. Consequently, the consent defence strategy is aptly developed by defence lawyers because they are not bound by the objectivity requirement or by loyalty to the legal system to the same extent as judges and prosecutors. That said, they use it as one more contingent instrument in their strategic toolbox, together with promptly taking on the task to remind the court to remain within the boundaries of legal objectivity.

To guarantee the protection of a complainant's sexual integrity, we argue, judges in rape cases must engage in critical reflection on the plausibility of events as described in consent defences. Instead of wilfully ignoring the role of emotions and common sense, they should engage in *more* critical reflexivity regarding these tacit assumptions and where they come from. Judges may grapple with fear of moral judgment, but when they try to remain objective they are always already leaning on specific types of common sense. It is imperative for legal professionals to do their 'neutral' thinking as many already do impartiality in court, that is, by empathically alternating between perspectives in their emotive-cognitive assessment of the reasonable and the plausible.

PART IV

Rationality and Autonomy in Legal Decision-Making

10

Navigating Reasonable Doubt in the Judgments

Introduction

The legal decision-making process can be simplistically viewed as comprising two distinct forms of interpretation. First, there is the interpretation of the law itself, scrutinizing the meaning and application of legal statutes and principles. Second, there is the interpretation of reality, represented by the evidence presented in the case (Ekelöf 2009; Peczenic 1988), from now on discussed as evaluation of evidence. These interpretative processes are conducted in accordance with foundational legal principles and rules, aligning with the core values of the legal system (Bladini 2013). As illustrated in the quote below, despite the overarching principles of free admission and evaluation of evidence, judges in criminal courts tend to rely on established methods and guiding case law from the Supreme Court to navigate the complexities of cases:

> [A] completely credible statement from the complainant, with supporting evidence consisting of witness information about what the complainant has said and how she behaved in close connection with the incident, may be sufficient to prove the offence (cf the cases NJA 2009 s 447 I-II, NJA 2010 s 671 and NJA 2017 s 361 [sic]). Evidentiary requirements in rape cases and discrepancies with evidentiary requirements for other offences are commented on by Dahlman et al 2018). The Supreme Court has stated a number of criteria that should be considered when assessing witnesses' and parties' statements. These are that if a statement is clear, long and detailed, it is usually a sign that it is true (NJA 2010 s 671 p 8). It is also primarily a matter of assessing the content of a statement, not the reaction of the witness/party. (Judgment, Case 7)

In rape cases, reference to guiding case law is particularly frequent and occurs in most of the judgments in our data. The guidelines suggest that a completely credible statement from the victim combined with supporting evidence may be sufficient proof, and that clarity, length and details are signs of a credible statement. This, per se, is indicative of the level of perceived difficulties associated with decisions in these cases.

This chapter delves into the intricate and contradictory process of legal decision-making within the context of rape cases. We explore how judges appear to navigate this delicate balance to move from the feeling of not knowing to the feeling of knowing (doubt or certainty about guilt) in the written judgments. The legal decision-making process is fundamentally about uncovering what is legally true (that is, proven), a quest that culminates in a verdict of either conviction or acquittal. An acquittal must not be a truth about no guilt, but about guilt not proven beyond reasonable doubt. In terms of emotive-cognitive rationality, this means arriving at certainty about guilt beyond reasonable doubt or at certainty about doubt (certainty about uncertainty, as it were). The judges are, on the one hand, free to decide how to evaluate the evidence, crucial in their autonomy, and expected to be experts both regarding the interpretation of the law and facts. However, rape cases are complicated and many judges frequently rely on guidelines from the Supreme Court.

Embedded in the decision-making process is the element of empathic imagination, and hence the influence of background emotional information, common sense and personal experience. The import from the trial process in terms of empathy hooks, empathic translation and *Things* spins the certainty–doubt spiral (Bladini et al 2023; Törnqvist and Wettergren 2023), as observed in deliberations and in the way the judgments construct the process leading to the decision as *the* rational outcome. Furthermore, empathy in decision-making is interwoven into the judges' sense of autonomy and objectivity. This chapter explores how judges navigate the balance between empathy and objectivity, drawing on insights from an analysis of the written judgments in our 18 rape cases, providing a detailed examination of how legal decision-making unfolds in practice.

The judge as an autonomous expert

In Chapter 2, we explained the legal framework that regulates rape cases. It is important to remember that the burden of proof is placed on the prosecutor and the standard of proof is set at a high level – that is, guilt must be proven beyond reasonable doubt (Ekelöf and Edelstam 2002). The trial is founded on the fundamental principles of free admission and free evaluation of evidence (Ekelöf et al 2009; Fitger 2014). However, the court's evaluation of evidence must not be based on purely subjective opinions but be objectively grounded and justified in a manner that other reasonable persons would find acceptable (NJA II 1943 p 445). Also, the judge may not ground the judgment on the totality of the case but rather an evaluation of every single piece of evidence separately; then, they should be assessed in the light of the totality of the evidence (SOU 1926:32 s 255; SOU 1938:44 s 377 f; and NJA II 1943 s 455; see also Mellqvist (2019/2020). In addition, both legal scholarship and jurisprudence from the Supreme Court have cultivated distinct methodologies and criteria for the process of evaluating evidence. One of the most established methods is the method of alternative hypothesis. In rape cases, the alternative scenario of voluntary intercourse (a consent defence; see Chapters 8 and 9) fits perfectly as an alternative hypothesis. This method, combined with case law from the Supreme Court (NJA 1980 s 725; cf NJA 2010 s 671 and NJA 2017 s 316) establishing that a coherent, clear and detailed testimony of a complainant, combined with lack of reason to believe that the complainant untruthfully would accuse the defendant, paves the way for 'she lies' myths. Moreover, the cases from the Supreme Court that are frequently used in the rape judgments address three questions.

First is the need for corroborating evidence in cases in which there is no hard evidence regarding the questions of voluntariness (and intent). Second are criteria to assess a credible testimony – long, clear and rich in detail. This has also been developed in case law from the Supreme Court and has been modified over time (see above and Chapter 2). The case law underlines that the criteria must be used carefully, because the ability of oral expression varies among people. In addition, the new case law asserts that a lack of consistency is not a sign of lying. Third is how to structure the evidence in the assessment. The Supreme Court has, in the *Balcony Case* (NJA 2015 s 702), suggested starting with the evidence presented by the prosecution, although underlining that it is not a universal method suited to all cases but only to some cases. The model has achieved significant impact and, as will be illustrated and discussed below, was commonly used in our cases.

In criminal cases in general, the question of evaluating evidence is not difficult for judges. Judges are assumed to be experts on evaluating both the law and the evidence, although they are not trained in evaluating the evidence. As described in Chapter 5, legal actors have different views of their roles, including of judges' ability to evaluate evidence. Prosecutors often argue that 'facts speak for themselves' (Bladini et al 2023). As argued by prosecutor Nina when discussing the importance of the complainant being physically present in the AC: 'Maybe you lose the victim's perspective to some extent [if the complainant is not present], but I think, in general, that judges will never deliver a conviction because we [prosecutors] want to apply a victim's perspective, they will always look at the evidence'. In line with this view, outside the courtroom during a coffee break in Case 14, prosecutor Julia discussed the impact of the final plea with two defence lawyers:

Defence lawyer 1 and the prosecutor are discussing the structure for the rest of the day. They wonder whether they will have time to listen to all the witnesses and how the rest of the time should be spent. They both agree that it would be a good idea to plan for the final pleas on an additional day of the trial. Defence lawyer 1 states that it is irresponsible not to plan for your final pleas properly and to plead in the afternoon when everyone is tired. Defence lawyer 2 and the victim counsel join their discission and they all agree to suggest to the court that they make use of another day for pleas. They start to discuss the impact of the final pleas, and if it matters at all. Defence lawyer 2 is convinced that it will have a great impact on the outcome of the case, but the prosecutor disagrees. She [the prosecutor] adds 'they know their things [referring to the judges]'. Defence lawyer 2 insists that it can work, that it may be of great importance. The prosecutor laughs and repeats, 'they are on top of it; they know these things'. (Field notes DC Case 14)

This conversation illustrates how prosecutors assume that judges are experts on evaluating the evidence presented, whereas defence lawyers argue that it matters how the evidence is framed by the legal professionals, for example during their final pleas.

As the evidentiary situation in rape cases differs from many other types of criminal cases with the emphasis on oral statements, it matters how the legal actors frame the evidence during the trial and how judges structure and evaluate the evidence. Some judges hold that these cases are different and more difficult to handle (for example, Chapter 4) whereas others argue that they are just like any criminal case:

For us [judges], it's a routine to sit in the courtroom and handle a trial and even if this is an unusual case, it's a case that we handle according to the procedures we have in the same way as any other case. That's what makes the system work, that we are used to dealing with trials and the fact that there are unusual details doesn't make us start dealing with it differently but even more, when it's different it's even more important. (Interview, AC judge, Case 16)

The structure presented in the *Balcony Case* combined with the case law suggesting that a completely credible story from the complainant with corroborating evidence are commonly used in rape cases, beginning with an evaluation of the story presented by the complainant. However, this structure is only a recommendation from the Supreme Court. The judges are, in fact, free to structure and evaluate the evidence in other rational ways. They can begin with the story as told by the defendant or structure the evaluation around the criminal legal questions. They could also go through all the evidence in a piecemeal way, presented in a way that mixes the prosecutor's and defendant's evidence, or evaluate 'the situation as a whole'.

In effect, the judgments included in this study are structured in various ways, although some structures are more common. Interestingly, the varied attitude among the judges towards the guidelines and criteria from the Supreme Court and the judges' different use of them is interconnected with the way judges embody autonomy, rationality and objectivity. Some judges seem strengthened in their feeling of being autonomous through the use of guidelines and criteria (see, for example, Case 14 below), while others seem to experience the opposite, that the freedom not to use guidelines is crucial for their feeling of autonomy, as will be demonstrated below.

Evaluation of evidence in practice

This section focuses on the process of legal decision-making and the path away from the feeling of not knowing towards the feeling of certainty as presented in written judgments. The legal decision-making process includes the task to find out what is legally true and assess the evidence to decide if the guilt is proven beyond reasonable doubt. Ultimately, the legal truth will end up in either a conviction or an acquittal and will build on the answer about guilt proven beyond reasonable doubt or not. This process includes questions about legal knowledge, rationality and (reasonable) doubts and is intertwined with the feeling of not knowing, the feelings of doubt and certainty and the ability of empathic imagination. In addition, these aspects are intertwined in the judges' feeling of being autonomous and objective.

In rape trials, judges need to establish certainty in relation to the objective criteria of sexual intercourse and non-voluntariness and the subjective criteria of intent or gross negligence. The legal regulation of rape is sometimes interpreted as 'what did she do to communicate voluntariness' and sometimes as 'what did he do to assure himself about her voluntariness'. These different approaches – the focus on her expression *or* his efforts to find out if she was participating voluntarily – are expressed among all legal professionals (see Part III). The methods used by the judges when structuring and evaluating the evidence might lead to different results regarding the focus on her expression or his efforts to find out if she participated voluntarily. As discussed in previous chapters, this may be oriented by background hissense or hersense.

Most of the cases in our study are based on a logic that aligns with the previous rape legislation, focusing on the complainant's expression of (non-)voluntariness. However, as discussed in previous chapters, in some of our cases the court emphasized the defendant's responsibility to assure that the complainant participated voluntarily. One example is the DC judgment in Case 13 (see also the DC judgment in Case 9, discussed in Chapter 11):

Nor has it emerged that the defendant asked the complainant if she wanted to have sexual intercourse with him … Nor has the defendant in any way assured himself of this [that she suddenly wanted to have sexual intercourse with him] … and that the defendant himself did not do anything to ensure that the complainant participated voluntarily – this shows that the defendant acted with deliberate negligence. (DC judgment, Case 13)

The crucial criminal legal questions about voluntariness and *mens rea* (criminal intent, or negligence as in the quote above) are complemented by the evidential issues whether the offence transpired the way the prosecutor states and if the prosecutor has proven this beyond reasonable doubt. As described in the previous section, Swedish judges are entitled to a wide scope of autonomy in legal decision-making.

Rape cases are considered particularly difficult to assess as they usually lack hard evidence concerning voluntariness and intent, which means that the assessment concerning these core questions is often based on (the complainant's) story against (the defendant's) story. The guidelines from the Supreme Court could support judges in these cases and lead them from the feeling of not knowing towards the feeling of knowing, either as certainty about the doubt or certainty that guilt is proven beyond reasonable doubt (certainty about not doubting). A close reading of the judgments reveals if and how judges use the guidelines in practice, both in terms of structure and (descriptions) assessing the evidence.

The rest of this chapter about the evaluation of evidence as presented in the written judgments is divided into three sections. The first section concerns how judgments are structured. This analysis focuses on the structure, use of headings and use of guidelines as a handrail or safety line to find a path from the feeling of not knowing towards some kind of certainty. The second focuses on the evaluation of evidence. This analysis highlights issues of voluntariness, intent/negligence and credibility (see also Part III). The third section addresses doubt, empathy and certainty, how certainty and doubt are expressed, dismissed or nailed down, sometimes through empathic attunement in the background. The writing of judgments is embedded in the semblance of rationality, objectivity and autonomy (Bladini 2013). In this context, empathy appears in two forms: as a full attunement to the perspective of either the complainant or defendant, and as an instrumentally empathetic approach aimed at respecting both parties' positions in the judgment (see Chapter 3). However, genuine empathic attunement is occasionally conveyed even when the judgment ultimately contradicts the interests of the party it empathizes with.

It should be noted that the actual assessment of evidence by judges (for example, during deliberations) may differ from how it is displayed in written judgments. Next, we scrutinize how judges structure judgments, both in terms of adhering to guidelines and in their general structure.

How judges structure judgments

While some judgments adopt a pedagogical structure and tone, others have a more complicated structure and language. In terms of structure, all judgments follow the same structure on an overall level, with headings such as:

- *Parties* – Defendant, defence lawyer, prosecutor, complainant (anonymized in rape cases) and victim counsel. In cases with minor defendants, parents may be part of the case.
- *Verdict* – Acquittal or conviction, the sentence, damages/compensation, confidentiality, reimbursement to legal actors and sometimes a question about custody or deportation.
- *Claims* – Prosecutor's: The description of the offence (the act that constitutes rape) is most often invisible in the judgments, but added in an attachment to the judgment, together with the evidence invoked in the case (complainant's and defendant's).
- *Grounds for the judgment* – This part is structured differently in our cases. Most of them begin with the legal framework, followed by the case as presented by the evidence (complainant's story, defendant's story, witnesses' testimonies and other evidence ending up in a last section, often titled 'the courts assessment/findings') most often beginning with the complainant's story but, in a few cases, starting with the defendant's (see for example, the DC judgment in Case 8).
- *How to appeal.*
- *Signature of the professional judge* (chair of the court) and a list of all the members of the court. This may be read as an autonomous voice, taking ethical responsibility for the judgment (Bladini 2013).
- Where applicable: *dissenting opinion* – if a dissenting opinion is present, it follows after the signature. This section is written in a personal voice, contrasting with the majority opinion, which is impersonal and grounded in *the court's* findings.

The next step of our analysis of the written judgment focuses on how the assessment of the evidence (that is, the 'Grounds of the judgment') is structured, how the legal framework is presented and how this is, or is not, used by the judges as a handrail/lifeline. The so-called *Balcony Case* model does not address the question of how to evaluate, but only how to structure the evidence presented in the case, and in what order to evaluate what parts. According to the model, the evidence presented by the prosecutor should be assessed first. Thus, the courts often begin with the story told by the complainant, followed by the rest of the evidence invoked by the prosecutor. If the court finds that this part of the evidence proves that the defendant has carried out the act as described in the statement of the criminal act as charged, it continues to evaluate the evidence presented by the defendant. If the first step ends in a conclusion that guilt is not proven beyond reasonable doubt, the court will acquit the defendant without evaluating his evidence.

In our study – 30 judgments from the DC or AC related to the 18 rape cases – many judgments began with the *Balcony Case* model. It was used in full in 12 of the judgments and partly in four (more than half of the judgments). Other structures or methods to evaluate evidence were used in 12 judgments, and two AC judgments conveyed no motivation of its own but referred entirely to the judgment from the DC.

An interesting pattern emerges in the 12 cases where the *Balcony Case* model was applied: the vast majority resulted in convictions, with only two ending in acquittals. This contrasts with the majority of acquittal cases, where other methods for structuring judgments and evaluating evidence were employed. The clear predominance of the use of the *Balcony Case* model in cases that resulted in convictions may suggest that some of the critique of the model is relevant, particularly the part that suggests that this way to structure the evaluation of evidence imposes a risk of confirmation bias (see Agnafors 2019/2020; Lidén 2018). From an emotion-sociological perspective, if the judge is convinced of the guilt beyond reasonable doubt (that is, the judge has reached a feeling of certainty regarding the guilt of the defendant), it may be difficult to return to a state of doubt (Bladini 2019; see also Bergman Blix and Minissale 2022). The feeling of certainty may be difficult to release, as the feeling of uncertainty is uncomfortable and may hence be resisted. This implies that judges may experience resistance, to some degree, to readdress the question of guilt with an open mind. Moreover, as demonstrated in previous chapters, many judges regard these cases as notably challenging and uncomfortable from the outset, often commencing their analysis from a place of pervasive and persistent uncertainty (that is, the feeling of not knowing; see Chapter 5).

An example of a pedagogical judgment in general is the DC judgment in Case 7 (conviction). It is also a particularly clear example of how the *Balcony Case* model is used. The court began to explain the criminal regulation of rape and underlined that the person who initiates the sexual activity would be well advised to ensure that the other party maintains his or her preferred level of explicit consent at each new stage. This was followed by an explanation of the structure of the assessment. First, the question of whether the complainant participated voluntarily is examined. If the answer is yes, the charge is dismissed. If not, it is examined whether the defendant committed the criminal act with intent. If the answer is yes, this would result in a conviction; however, if the answer is no, the DC must then, based on the secondary charge of negligent rape, determine whether the offence was committed with gross negligence. If the answer is yes, it will lead to a conviction for negligent rape, but if the answer is no, the court will dismiss the charge.

This explanation of structure in the judgment, revolving around legal questions, is followed by a section on the legal framework on evidence. The court mentions the case law from the Supreme Court, but also includes legal doctrine. Then, the court structures the assessment of the evidence following the model suggested by the *Balcony Case*. In the section in which the court assesses the defendant's criminal intent or negligence, the DC expresses an empathic understanding of the situation, tuning in with the defendant and the complainant, and underlines the fact that:

> she actively contacted the defendant later that evening [after he suggested she could sleep at his place] and chose to accompany him home instead of following her friends, has reasonably, regardless of the fact that whether something explicit about sex was not mentioned, raised expectations in the defendant that the complainant was interested in having an intimate relationship with him. (DC judgment Case 7)

Also, just before 'the parties' intercourse' (cf the previous wording), she returned his kisses, 'possibly as an attempt to fulfil the expectations about sex that she was probably aware that her attitude may have helped to create'. Hence, the court recognizes the hissensical logic of this reasoning but ultimately refutes it as grounds for his legitimate belief in consent. The DC went on to emphasize, however, that this does not detract from the fact that she clearly said no immediately before the intercourse, since it is the responsibility of the 'active' party to ascertain the voluntariness of the other party at every stage of the sexual relationship – an interpretation in line with the preparatory works' hersensical logic.

Besides the *Balcony Case* model, there were other ways to structure the evidence in our judgments. One way was to structure the judgment around the criminal legal questions (that is, if the participation was voluntary or if the defendant was acting intentionally/negligent in relation to the lack of expressed voluntariness; see the DC judgments in Cases 5 and 13, which both resulted in convictions). The DC judgment in Case 8 is unusual, as it begins not with the complainant's story or the prosecutor's evidence but with the defendant's story. It ended in an acquittal. Others based their judgment on the defendant's story, after assessing and rejecting the complainant's story (see the AC judgment in Case 9, discussed in Chapter 11).

The DC judgment in Case 2 is an example of another way to structure the evidence. It also involved a special way of writing. This is the only judgment in our study with a section at the beginning of the judgment on the persons involved, including age, profession and lack of previous criminal record. It begins with facts the parties agree on, followed by the 'alleged offence', then the 'complainant's version' and 'defendant's version'. The legal framework is then set out, both the criminal law on rape and the case law from the Supreme Court on evaluating evidence (NJA 2017 s 316 I), and burden and standard of proof. The DC underlined that even if the court found that the complainant's version was more plausible, it may have to acquit if the standard of proof is not met. The court argued that, since their stories are incompatible, either the complainant or the defendant must be lying, building on an idea about only one truth. The court detailed the supporting evidence, beginning with the evidence corroborating her story, followed by reasons that the court could not use the complainant's story as the basis for the judgment. Then, the DC listed other circumstances that the parties tried to prove but the court rejected as they had no real impact or points in either direction. The court ended its evidence evaluation in a summarized assessment: For a conviction, the court stated that it

> 'must base its judgment only on the complainant's description of the defendant's behaviour, on the complainant's behaviour and statements to witnesses and on information given to relatives and psychologists thereafter. Thus, the prosecution rests essentially on the reliance on a single source'. (DC judgment, Case 2)

This is a special way of describing the supporting evidence as if it came from the complainant instead of writing that it is supporting evidence, which is how it normally appears in rape cases. This is also described as sufficient in case law from the Supreme Court. The DC did not consider that only the complainant's account of the defendant's behaviour [regarding the alleged rape] outweighed what has otherwise emerged. Here, the DC particularly emphasized two *Things* that impose doubts about the prosecution: how the jeans were removed and the time aspect (see a detailed analysis of this case in Chapter 5).[1] In an overall assessment, the DC thus considered that the presented investigation was not sufficient for the evidence requirement in criminal cases (beyond reasonable doubt) to be met.

A clear and pedagogical way to structure the judgment is to follow a structure revolving around the legal questions and either go through all presented evidence or simply assess the parts of the evidence that were evaluated as relevant by the court. In Case 13, the DC began by stating that it was 'undisputed that [the defendant] had sexual intercourse with the complainant'. The court then listed legally relevant questions that structured the rest of the judgment:

---

[1] The complainant had a different idea about how long it took compared with the defendant and witnesses. Although it could be argued that it might be a complicated task to assess time during a trauma and when you are initially asleep.

> A first question is then whether the complainant participated of her own free will. If not, the question is whether [the defendant] knew of the complainant's attitude or, alternatively, that he took undue advantage of the fact that the complainant was in a particularly vulnerable situation due to intoxication. If not, the question is whether he was grossly negligent in relation to the fact that the complainant did not participate voluntarily. (DC judgment Case 13)

Some judgments have headings that pose or answer the legal questions and then explain the assessment that led to that answer. In Case 10, one heading was 'Should the defendant be convicted of a criminal offence [rape]?' and in Case 14, '[name of the defendant] is acquitted of criminal liability'. Sometimes the writings seem to be answers to questions, even if the questions are not explicitly stated in the judgment (for example, the AC judgment in Case 6 and the DC judgment in Cases 8 and 9). The DC judgment in Case 8, after going through the legal settings for evaluation of evidence, stated that the parties had sexual intercourse. It then addressed the next legal question explicitly: 'The question is therefore whether, after the intercourse had lasted for a relatively long time, the complainant no longer participated voluntarily in vaginal and oral intercourse'. This question was answered after assessing the evidence and the court ended in an acquittal, as it argued that it was not proven beyond reasonable doubt that she had not participated voluntary. The situation in Case 6 differed slightly from many of the others, as the defendant denied that sexual intercourse occurred (analysed in Chapter 8). This fact centres the question of sexual intercourse in the legal assessment, together with the hard evidence that supports this fact. The prevalence of such evidence may explain acquittals in several of the denial and memory-loss cases discussed in Chapter 8. So far, we have demonstrated the general structure commonly used in written judgments, noting that the *Balcony Case* model appears more frequently in convictions. We have also explored examples of pedagogical judgments employing the *Balcony Case* model or organizing the judgment around specific legal questions, as well as examined a unique judgment that, in various ways, deviates from the structure typical of most other cases. We now proceed to analyse the assessment of voluntariness, intent/negligence, and credibility in the judgments.

Assessing evidence: guidelines as handrails or as guiding lights

As the *Balcony Case* model does not offer any model for the evaluation itself but only suggests a way to structure the evaluation, many courts used other cases from the Supreme Court as a handrail to hold on to when assessing the evidence. The vast majority of the cases from the Supreme Court that the judgments either referred to or implicitly used deal with the question of how to assess oral testimonies and the standard of proof in cases concerning sexual offences. This includes discussions on what type of evidence is considered sufficient to establish a case beyond reasonable doubt. In this section, we analyse the methods judges employ to determine credibility. As we will demonstrate, some judgments refrain from addressing these questions and are solely focused on voluntariness and criminal intent.

In a majority of the judgments, the court referred to and used case law on evidence and criteria to assess oral testimonies presented by the Supreme Court (see Chapter 2). Most of these judgments were from the DC. In addition, a few more judgments lacked explicit references to case law but used the criteria implicitly. Interestingly, in several cases – a majority of them from the AC – the court did not refer to any legal framework. This might be an expression of a stronger feeling of autonomy in the AC, which consists of three judges who can find their way from not knowing to knowing together, as an experienced collective. Additionally, three judgments only referred to the criminal regulation of rape but did not mention the evidential situation.

However, the courts commonly referred to Supreme Court cases on evaluation of evidence in sexual offences, suggesting that a credible story combined with corroborating evidence may be sufficient proof. To assess an oral statement, the courts used the criteria from the Supreme Court suggesting a credible story is often clear, long and rich in detail, while consistency is not a sign of lack of credibility. The last part on consistency changes previous case law from the Supreme Court, as the research on witness psychology has highlighted this previous problematic use (see also Chapter 4). Yet, some of our judgments still referred to this criterion: for example, the DC in Case 7, which stated that inconsistencies are not signs of lies and can hence be left out of the assessment, but still concluded that 'the complainant's story is long, clear and relatively rich in detail, and without any obvious inconsistencies'. The DC judgment in Case 14 referred to a larger part of the discussion on credible stories from the NJA 2017 s 316 case from the Supreme Court, including the part that complicates it all, namely that 'it should be noted that the criteria may be difficult to use when assessing the statements of people who, for various reasons, have difficulties with oral expression'. This is an unusual way to refer to the case from the Supreme Court because it includes the complexity and challenges in evaluating oral statements. It is interesting to note that, with the exception of this judgment in Case 14, referencing the 2017 case, all other 17 cases included the section on lack of consistency and most shortened the list of criteria in line with the research referred to in the case from 2017. However, they omitted the sentence regarding the challenge of applying the criteria due to individuals' diverse abilities to express themselves orally, even though this sentence directly followed the one on lack of consistency. Hence, in their written judgments, the courts denied the complexity of the task to assess oral statements and only referred to the part that offered them some help. This suggests that the courts hold on to case law as a handrail or a guiding light on the path away from the uncomfortable feeling of not knowing or the feeling of uncertainty towards a feeling of certainty, whether on doubt or certainty about guilt. The complexity introduced by the final convoluted sentence often disrupts this balance, leading to its disregard.

Another interesting exception is the DC judgment in Case 10 (acquittal). It describes the criteria slightly differently from most of the other cases in our data, as it included the longest list of criteria:

> The main emphasis should be on factors relating to the content of the account as such, whether it is clear, vivid, logical, rich in detail, demonstrably truthful in important details and free from errors, contradictions and exaggerations, inexplicable elements, poor coherence or doubt in crucial parts (see for example NJA 2010 p 671) [...] In addition to the above, consideration should also be given to such circumstances that may indicate that the complainant's information is less reliable, for example if there are personal conflicts between the complainant and the defendant or if there are other reasons for the complainant to make untruthful allegations against the defendant. (DC judgment, Case 10)

This last sentence is also connected to older practice from the Supreme Court and in turn directly referred to the 'she lies' myth (see Chapter 4). Another common guideline (case law from the Supreme Court) referred to in a majority of our cases concerns what the complainant has told other people after the event. This is referred to in the DC judgment from Case 14:

> In rape cases, the evidence is often based, in addition to the accounts of the parties, on the fact that the complainant, after the incident, has told other people who have been heard as witnesses. This is not really an investigation into the alleged offence, as the witnesses have not made any personal observations of the event itself. However, such information, together with the witnesses' own observations of, for example, the complainant's behaviour and reactions after the event, may in some cases constitute indirect support for the complainant's story (see NJA 2017 p 316 I and II). (DC judgment, Case 14)

Our main point is that, since rape cases are so complex and often begin with the feeling of not knowing, they challenge judges in their professional role in terms of autonomy, objectivity and rationality. The use of the criteria to assess oral statements and other guidelines from the Supreme Court translates the everyday life represented by oral statements into legal logics (Bladini et al 2023). The transformation from the everyday life into legal logics in turn contributes to the feeling of dealing with facts and logics rather than common sense and everyday life experiences, closely linked to the traditional idea of rationality. This creates an image of an objective procedure, and hence, for judges, a feeling of being objective. This is also an example of the function of the law as an autopoietic system, transforming non-legal facts into legal entities (cf Chapter 3). In addition, the guidelines may be interpreted as supporting the judges to find their way through these complicated questions and embeds the feeling of autonomy. One way to understand why many judges seem to hold on to the methods and guidelines presented by the Supreme Court, within but also outside our rape cases (cf Dahlman 2024), is that it strengthens the judges' feeling of autonomy, as it strengthens the judges in cases in which they must make decisions in complex situations. This may be of particular use and importance for less experienced judges. Simultaneously, it is possible to understand some of the judges' choice not to use the guidelines in their judgment as another type of expression of their autonomy, as the choice not to use the guidelines from the Supreme Court is a way to be independent and capable of making decisions. In our cases, this seems to be more common in the AC, where the court consists of three experienced professional judges who, during deliberations, collectively assess the evidence and make decisions. The role of doubt, empathy and sympathy as expressed in the judgments is to be addressed in the next section.

Doubt, empathy and certainty

The feelings of doubt and certainty, and empathy (not least in terms of himpathy) are expressed, dismissed, held on to or toned down in the judgments. Unsurprisingly, doubt is visible in all acquittals, as the court reaches a decision that the guilt is not proven beyond reasonable doubt. However, questions of doubt are also present in many of the judgments resulting in convictions, as the court needs to conclude that guilt is proven *beyond* reasonable doubt. Doubt may then function as an emotive-cognitive device to hinder premature judgment. In the judgment ending in conviction, the question of false accusations (that is, the 'she lies' myth) is almost always present as the last possible reasonable doubt that needs to be excluded. Noteworthy is that there was no mention of false accusations in judgments from the cases with male complainants (Cases 5 and 16). In the other judgments resulting in convictions, two did not use the 'she lies' myth as the last resort of doubt (that is, certainty of guilt) to feel confident about the decision; see below. The rest did raise the question of false accusation – for example, formulated in the following manner, 'In fact, nothing has emerged to suggest that the complainant has falsely accused the defendant' (DC judgement, Case 12).

As mentioned, only a few cases did not include any questions about false accusations. Interestingly, one was the same case that posed the legal question of what must be proven and who needed to prove what as 'what did he do, to ascertain himself that she wanted to participate?' This concerns the judgments that rejected the common problem of victim blaming and applied the law in line with its motives. The choice to focus on the defendant's responsibility thus opened by the new law arguably demonstrates hersensical reasoning. It should be noted that concerns about false accusations were also present in acquittals, for example in Case 14: 'Nor has there been any motive for the complainant to tell untruths'. In such cases the statement can be seen as empathic writing with the instrumental purpose of alleviate victim blaming.

In some cases, the court held on to the general feeling of doubt, including all aspects in the case that strengthened this feeling. This is a way to secure their uncertainty (or certainty of doubt) and become confident in the decision to acquit the defendant. This is either done continuously throughout the judgment by fragmenting the case or by focusing the judgment on a selection of aspects (how this is done will be illustrated in greater detail later in Chapter 11). Some aspects may be highlighted as particularly strong in the sense of imposing or strengthening the feeling of doubt; those aspects, we call *Things*. The doubt can be anchored and focused on these *Things*. One example of how the court rejects *Things* highlighted and imposed as doubts by the defence lawyer is illustrated in the AC judgment from Case 6. The *Things* that the defence lawyer argued imposed doubts were systematically met and rejected by the court in the judgment. Examples of the opposite, when the court systematically clung to all aspects that may impose doubt, were the DC judgments in Cases 10 (see Chapter 11) and 14. Sometimes the guidelines from the Supreme Court were used in these cases as a magic formula or a lifeline to manage doubts about knowing anything, strengthening or weakening the doubts beyond reason. Again, this is a way to construct an image of objectivity and strengthen the ability to act (that is, to impose a feeling of autonomy).

Furthermore, empathy is used as a tool by the judges to process the evidence presented, in particular the oral statements. Empathy is deployed to tune in with the parties or witnesses. For example, the court in Case 14 wrote, 'we believe [the complainant] has experienced what she describes as a sexual offence [rape]', but decided to acquit the defendants due to lack of evidence that proved that it was the defendants and not others who raped her. In Case 9, the AC wrote that 'the court cannot see any reasons for her to lie intentionally', but it still doubted her story.

Moreover, as discussed in Part III, empathic imagination is closely connected to assessments of the legal subjects' – the complainants', defendants' and witnesses' – rationality. To be able to understand someone's actions as rational, the actions must seem accurate in the situation. Hence, the judgments are full of empathic statements about normality, necessity and the natural way to act in a given situation (Bandes 2009). This is illustrated in the DC judgment in Case 12, in which the complainant's story lacked details about the sex act. The court recognized this as understandable, as it must be inconvenient or troublesome to talk about sex with adult strangers in a trial. Another example is from the DC judgment in Case 3, in which the court highlighted the difficulties in telling close relatives details about sex. Contrarily, judgments may display a non-empathic mode in terms of judgment of actions as unnormal, irrational or unnatural. While all judgments take on a neutral reasoning mode of writing, our analysis demonstrates that judgments are not neutral but informed by hissense, and sometime hersense, evoking himpathy and effectuating herasure (Manne 2018), or suggesting empathic attunement with female fear (Eduards 1997).

Certainty is often related to a certainty of guilt (that is, certain of guilt being proven beyond reasonable doubt) or certainty about uncertainty (that is, certainty about doubt, ending in a conclusion that guilt is not proven beyond reasonable doubt). Also, the reasonableness of the doubt is closely connected to the ability of empathic attunement and the assessment of the rationality of someone's actions. However, certainty can also be more than just certainty or doubt concerning the guilt. It is expressed in various forms in the judgments, such as in different rhetorical expressions: for example, 'it cannot be in any other way', 'it must be evident that ...', 'it is evident that ...' or 'the following facts are established and undisputed'. Some of the judgments were written in a way that one story – the story on which the court based its judgment – was described as an ontological truth, presented as an undisputed objective fact about what actually happened. This fits with the traditional objectivity ideal that permeates the judiciary (cf Bladini 2013). For example, when assessing the story from the complainant in Case 1, the DC judgment ended with 'the following is showed', followed by a long and detailed description based fully on the complainant's story. Another example is from the DC judgment in Case 2, in which the court underlined that either the complainant or the defendant must be lying as their stories were incompatible, also an expression of a belief in the possibility of reaching an ontological truth (certainty about what actually happened rather than what is legally proven).

It is also intriguing how aspects that could have raised doubts are handled when the court is convinced about guilt. This may be done by pointing out all *Things* presented by the defence, only to reject them one by one. In the AC judgment in Case 8, for example, aspects from the complainant's previous statements during the police investigation did not match the story she presented in court. These are met by the court with reference to case law from the Supreme Court, stating that lack of consistency is no longer considered a sign of a lie.

As previously pointed out, another way to manage uncertainties, weaknesses or doubts are to erase them by not addressing or recognizing them at all in the judgment and instead assessing the presented case or evidence as a whole.

Conclusion

Swedish judges, as experts in both legal interpretation and evidence assessment, exercise a broad autonomy and handle the task of writing judgments differently. An analysis of written judgments reveals variations in how cases and evidence are structured: while some judgments fragment the case and/or evidence into isolated components, others employ a more holistic approach, focusing on the overall assessment that informs the conclusion. These differing methods apply both to the interpretation of the offence – particularly with respect to the legal questions of voluntariness, a particularly vulnerable situation and intent – and to the evaluation of evidence. The predominant strategy observed in our cases involves a fragmented treatment of the case or evidence, consistent with Supreme Court guidelines that recommend an initial item-by-item evaluation of evidence, followed by a comprehensive assessment of the situation as a whole.

The legal framework, particularly the guidelines from the Supreme Court, serves two functions in legal decision-making, in addition to being a legal source and guiding the legal decision-making process. The first is as a guiding light and objectivity handrail to follow to leave the feeling of not knowing to reach a feeling of certainty (about doubt or guilt). Through this, the guidelines may paradoxically function to strengthen the feeling of autonomy for some judges. The second is that the guidelines may serve as a transformative formula that translate common sense (both hissense and hersense) and everyday life experiences into legal logics, contributing to the image of objectivity and legal autonomy by upholding the boundaries of the autopoietic system. Conversely, the choice not to use these methods and guidelines may reflect a judge's strong sense of autonomy. This dual possibility highlights the balance between following established recommendations from the Supreme Court and the individual judge's discretion in legal reasoning.

Judges in fact regularly (should) begin a case with the feeling of not knowing (a 'blank slated' mind as it were), as the knowledge will supposedly be introduced to them through the evidence presented during the trial. Rape cases, however, differ from many other types of criminal cases, as the feeling of not knowing in the initial phase appears more genuine and seems to remain longer, not least because it includes the question of *how* to evaluate the evidence concerning voluntariness and intent. Hence, when assessing the evidence, many judges turn to the Supreme Court guideline to be able to leave the feeling of not knowing.

In most of our cases, the court used the method presented in the *Balcony Case* to structure the evidence. Beginning with the evidence presented by the prosecutor, and if the court finds the evidence robust enough to prove that a rape has taken place, the court continues to the evidence presented by the defendant. The frequent application of the *Balcony Case* model in convictions suggests that some criticisms may hold merit. From an emotion-sociological standpoint, once a judge feels certain of a defendant's guilt – reaching a 'beyond reasonable doubt' conclusion – it can be challenging to revert to a state of doubt (Bladini 2019; also discussed in Bergman Blix and Minissale 2022). The discomfort associated with uncertainty may make it difficult for judges to reconsider guilt with an open mind. This resistance to re-evaluating the certainty of guilt suggests that judges may struggle, to an extent, to maintain objectivity in terms of resisting confirmatory bias.

In the process of evaluating evidence, empathic imagination plays a crucial role; judges must be able to understand and weigh testimony and evidence by attunement with different perspectives. This ability to empathetically imagine various situations is essential for making assessments of reasonableness and credibility, evaluating whether something is 'unreasonable' or 'reasonable'. Empathy extends further into judgments about what is normal, reasonable and natural. In this chapter we have seen that judges may adopt 'empathic writing' as a way to soften their assessments of credibility and their verdict. Whether heartfelt or instrumental, empathetic writing addresses the feelings of the lay people (complainant and defendant) involved. Additionally, the chapter recognizes different forms of empathic writing – where empathy is expressed either as sincere or instrumental in relation to the legal subjects. We also argue that, in some judgments, hersense blends with legal logic grounded in the principle of free evaluation and the judge's autonomy.

The different ways to handle the cases matters. The fragmentation or more holistic and hermeneutic approaches, as well as the different ways of handling doubts and lacunas presented above, will be explored and discussed in greater detail in the next chapter, 'Pathways to Knowing', where we dive deep into three of our rape cases.

11

Pathways to Knowing

Introduction

In the previous chapter we analysed the structure and process of evaluation based on all our 18 cases. In this section, we analyse legal decision-making in-depth in three of our rape cases (Cases 9, 10 and 13) to explore how judges' feeling of not knowing turns into knowing, either as certainty about doubt or certainty about guilt. We will also explore the way the courts either assess the situation as a whole or as fragmented pieces. Moreover, empathy hooks, *Things* and the ability of empathic imagination will be analysed, in addition to how the stories of the parties (that is, the complainant and the defendant) are addressed, listened to and assessed in various ways by the legal professionals. Finally, we will address the feeling of autonomy and objectivity in relation to the judges. In terms of data, all three cases were appealed. We attended the trials in both the DC and AC in Cases 9 and 10. In Case 13 we attended the AC trial and watched the DC trial from there. We attended the DC deliberation in Case 10, and the AC deliberations in Cases 9 and 13.

Rejecting rape myths or clinging to doubts – Case 9

This case is interesting to analyse in greater detail since the judgments and outcomes differed between the first and second instance. While the DC found the defendant guilty of rape, the AC delivered an acquittal. The DC ended up in a conclusion in which they examined the situation as a whole after having assessed the pieces of evidence one by one, in accordance with the legal framework. In line with the purpose of the new law, as one of few judgments in our study, the judgment also placed responsibility for ensuring voluntariness on the defendant (that is, rejecting the common method of placing responsibility on the complainant). Conversely, the AC clung to the doubt, worked their way through the evidence and particularly pointed at all the pieces that raised reasonable doubt, a procedure that culminated in the court becoming certain in its feeling of doubt. The court only examined

243

the event in a fragmented manner, deconstructing the case piece by piece, arriving at a conclusion in which a few *Things* were too problematic in its opinion, determining that the chain of evidence did not pass the test. The case also illustrates how the sex act can be viewed as a whole or be fragmented into several phases or activities, leading to different conclusions about when voluntariness needs to be communicated (expressed and ensured) and how.

All legal professionals involved in Case 9 used an empathetic negotiating style in court and the collaboration between the prosecutor and victim counsel seemed to work very well. The defence lawyer was highly professional, engaged and skilled. The victim counsel was present in the AC, but the prosecutor attended via a video link. The defendant's parents were present in both the DC and AC throughout all proceedings. The complainant's family was only present in the DC and were almost more prominent than the defendant's family. Since the complainant was not present in the AC, her family was not there. However, the defendant's parents were there. At that point, the defendant had been subjected to an online witch-hunt, which the court was made aware of, and the mother cried loudly in court. The absence of the prosecutor reflects limited insight into the meaning of empathic translation, whereas the presence of the victim's counsel demonstrates an understanding of empathic negotiation. The defence lawyer likewise exhibited this approach by encouraging parental involvement. This is also discussed in Chapters 5–6.

Most judgments in our study tended to begin with a section in which the court explicitly detailed only the relevant evidence presented in the case or summarized what was established in the case, followed by a summary of what evidence was relevant to assess. In Case 9, the DC did not write anything about what evidence was included/excluded and no section that stated what was established in the case. Instead, the judgment contained a summary of all statements in the case, beginning with the complainant, followed by the defendant and then witness testimonies. Thus, the background of the case was presented in the DC judgment as pieces of evidence, rather than to establish a background story. It provided a summary of the parties' stories. This way of writing may be a sign of an autonomous judge who feels safe to write the judgment in a way that suits her and the case.

According to the DC judgment, the complainant had told the court that she and the defendant have known each other for a relatively long time, being friends with no previous sexual relationship. The defendant arranged a party in her honour. She was not planning to sleep at his place but had no way to return home. She had been drinking but was not out of control. They laid down in his bed to watch television before they slept, they took off their pants and shared a duvet. She often spent time with her friends like this, but not previously with the defendant. He began to be physical, which she did not like so she stood up, put her pants back on and asked him to call a friend to pick her up. While waiting for her friend, she laid down in bed again and fell asleep. When she woke up, he was having vaginal intercourse with her. She left the bed and dressed. She had no memory of her underwear being removed. She had not kissed him, as far as she could remember, and she was sure that they did not discuss or engage in oral sex. She did not remember how her tampon (a *Thing* in this case) was removed or what she told the police about it.

The defendant, on the other side, used a consent defence and described a scenario in which the complainant also took initiative in the intimate contact. He arranged a party to celebrate her; he had been drinking but was not very drunk. He described how they began to kiss when watching television, then she engaged in oral sex on his request. They did not discuss vaginal intercourse, but he believes they both expected it. He went to retrieve a condom and she made herself ready by taking a position inviting him to penetrate her (later in the AC, the position was illustrated by the defendant in a reconstruction photograph). He removed her panties and began to have sex with her. At first, she did not do anything, but then when he had started, she said stop and he stopped. The DC judgment's representation of their stories also included descriptions of what happened afterwards, their reactions and emotions. However, that is left out by us here, as are the witness statements. Of interest is the next section in the judgment, after the last witness statement, about the court's assessment of the evidence.

The criminal legal questions in Case 9 concern whether the complainant was in a particularly vulnerable state due to sleep or whether she participated voluntarily, and if the defendant acted with intent or negligence. The DC began with a conclusion that 'the complainant has given her testimony in a way that gives no reason to question her credibility' and continued:

> However, she was intoxicated on the occasion in question and a relatively long time has passed since the incident occurred. Furthermore, she has in the District Court provided information, which was partly contradictory and which, with regard to certain details, does not correspond to what she told [two witnesses] immediately after the incident.
>
> Therefore, it cannot be ruled out that she was awake when the defendant penetrated her vaginally. The prosecutor's claim that the complainant participated in the sexual intercourse as a result of the defendant taking undue advantage of the fact that the complainant was in a particularly vulnerable situation due to sleep, is therefore not proven. (DC judgment, Case 9)

In this section, the court began by establishing its trust in her story, although simultaneously accepting that all of it may not be proven beyond reasonable doubt. As she was drunk and a long time had passed since the event, we can read between the lines that she is still credible, and it is understandable that her memory is not perfect regarding these facts. This offers the court a possibility to continue to listen to her story:

> It is, however, clear that the defendant initiated vaginal intercourse with the complainant, and that this was immediately interrupted by the complainant. The parties had no previous sexual relation, and they were both intoxicated. It has therefore – regardless of whether they had oral sex just before this during the same night, and/or the complainant had changed her position in bed – there was a significant risk that the complainant did not want to have vaginal intercourse with the defendant. (DC judgment, Case 9)

At this point, the court no longer assessed the parties' stories as reliable and credible. Instead, it used both their stories and stated that, regardless of what they did before the vaginal intercourse, he should have been more careful and checked with her to determine if she wanted to proceed or not. In a majority of our cases, the actions performed by the complainant just before the event were interpreted as a sign of voluntariness for other sex acts, maybe not as the complainant's real inner will, but as expressions that the defendant was allowed to take as a basis for assuming that she also wanted to take part in other sex acts (see Part III). In this case – in line with the aim of the new legislation – the court argued differently:

> The defendant has neither through eye contact, verbally or in any other way checked whether the complainant had fallen asleep or whether she really wanted him to penetrate her vaginally. This fact – but also through the way in which the defendant reacted and expressed himself immediately after the incident – it is shown that he was aware of the risk that the complainant did not want to be penetrated vaginally. Despite this, he penetrated her. He thereby showed indifference to the fact that she did not participate voluntarily in the intercourse. He therefore committed the offence with intent. (DC judgment, Case 9)

Hence, the court placed full responsibility on the defendant to communicate carefully with the complainant to assure himself that she wanted to have sex with him in the way he wanted. In addition, the court noted that it took into consideration his actions following the incident. For example, he sent a text message apologizing to the complainant, which the court interpreted as an indication that he recognized he had disregarded her will.

The AC took a very different approach to this case. The defence invoked new evidence in the AC, namely photographs of the defendant's room where the sex act took place. The defence argued that they wanted to show the court that his bed was smaller than the complainant had stated. The image pictured the defendant as a sad boy in his bed in his boy's room. Combined with the defendant's family members' presence in the AC and the absence of the complainant, the photograph constituted a strong empathy hook that embedded strongly, not only for empathic attunement but also for himpathy. In addition, a second photograph was invoked in which the defendant was placed in the room by the bed to illustrate the position of the complainant when he initiated the vaginal intercourse that should be interpreted as an expression of voluntariness. It should be noted that the defendant in the photograph was illustrating the complainant's position to help the court understand *his* perspective (that is, another clear empathy hook). Hence, this was a kind of empathy negotiation (successfully) performed by the defence.

The AC judgment presented the parties' stories and began by arguing: 'The complainant and the defendant have given consistent accounts of what happened during the evening and night leading up to the sex act but they have given different accounts of what happened just before and during the sexual intercourse.' The judgment then presented differences in their stories:

> The complainant has stated that she got out of bed and put on her clothes after the defendant initiated some sexual behaviours. She also stated that it was decided that she would be picked up by a friend, that she then went back to bed and fell asleep with her clothes on and woke up when the defendant had vaginal intercourse with her.
>
> The defendant has stated that he thought the complainant was awake and that she wanted to have sexual intercourse. According to him, this was evident from the fact that they first kissed, that they had some oral sex and from the position that the complainant took after he went to get a condom. (DC judgment, Case 9)

When the AC imagined the position, they probably had help from the picture shown by the defendant of his room and how she was waiting for him in a certain position. After this presentation of the stories from the parties, the court assessed the complainant's story:

> The story given by the complainant has been clear, coherent and relatively detailed. Nothing has emerged that indicates that she would deliberately give false information about what happened. The AC therefore agrees with the DC's assessment that the complainant is credible. In order for her story to form the basis of the assessment, however, it is required that it appears to be reliable and is sufficiently

supported by the rest of the investigation (see for example the case NJA 2017 p 316). In this respect, the AC makes the following assessment. (DC judgment, Case 9)

Thus, the court considered her story credible, including the assessment that she would not 'deliberately give false information' (the 'she lies' myth) but continued to evaluate her story in relation to what she had previously told others:

> That the complainant experienced the event in the way she has described is strongly supported by what witness (W) 1, 3 and 4 have stated about her reaction after the incident. However, it has emerged that the complainant, to both W1 and W2, has described the course of events in a way that deviates in central parts from what she later described in the District Court. (AC judgment, Case 9)

As previously described, inconsistencies were initially suggested by the Supreme Court to be assessed as a sign of a story that is not true, but this was later changed. However, in Case 9, we argue that the inconsistencies were implicitly viewed as a reason for the AC to hold on to the feeling of doubt:

> Furthermore, the complainant has not been able to clearly remember whether or not she and the defendant kissed when they were in bed. There have also been different accounts of what happened to the complainant's tampon. This casts some doubt on the reliability of the complainant's recollections of the incident. It also appears to be somewhat contradictory that the complainant would have gone back to bed and fallen asleep, after she got up and dressed to be picked up by [W1]. (AC judgment, Case 9)

This excerpt from the AC judgment illustrates how the court clung to the feeling of doubt.

We observe how the tampon became a *Thing* and how this, in combination with the unclear recollection of whether they kissed or not, according to the court, cast explicit doubts about the reliability of her story. This conclusion also implicitly builds on an idea of normal behaviour. According to the judges, it is not realistic, when drunk and tired, to react strongly to unwanted sexual invitations, prepare to be able to leave his house, only to fall asleep again while waiting for a friend to pick her up. The AC proceeded by presenting other details that it found not really in line with her story: 'Furthermore, [W1]'s information about when she arrived at the defendant's is more consistent with the defendant's version of the events than with the complainant's'. In general, the court placed significant emphasis on questions of time. The court continued the assessment of the parties' stories, focusing on the story presented by the defendant. They continued, although explicitly, to discuss normalities, rationalities and what is reasonable to do in a specific situation:

> Regarding the message sent by the defendant to the complainant during the night, his explanation – that he panicked about what W1 was accusing him of and wanted to apologize to the complainant because she was sad – does not seem *unreasonable*. The message thus provides no direct support for the offence allegation. (AC judgment, Case 9, emphasis added)

Furthermore, the AC concluded that 'All in all, the AC, like the DC, is of the opinion that the complainant's account is not supported by the rest of the evidence so strongly that it can be used as a basis for the judgment'. They continued: 'This means, as the DC found, that it has not been established beyond reasonable doubt that the complainant was asleep during the sexual intercourse and that for that reason alone her participation would not have been voluntary. Interestingly, the AC formulation indicates that it nevertheless listened to her attentively and favourably until that point – although it seemed to have had strong doubts from the outset – and only then dismissed her story as insufficiently strong to be used as a basis for assessment. Moreover, it is also intriguing that, akin to the DC, it made an evaluation of the cumulative value of the prosecutor's evidence, reaching the conclusion that it did not hold in relation to a particular issue (if the complainant was asleep), but still chose to proceed in its examination. The DC also argued that it was not proven that she was asleep, but they nonetheless opted to believe her, conducting an amalgamated assessment of the situation. In the next step, the AC asked 'whether it has been shown that the complainant did not participate voluntarily anyway. In this assessment, the AC has to rely on the defendant's story'. However, it should be noted that the DC chose another solution. It is therefore not evident that the AC actually 'has to' rely on his story at this point. Although not explicitly, it is clear that the DC used both their stories to form a basis for its legal judgment. In the AC, the court stressed that it had no other choice, an assumption strengthening their certainty of doubt, meaning that they could hold only to the defendant's version of the event. Hence, the court evaluated *her* voluntariness through *his* story: 'The course of events described by the defendant includes such actions that as a rule must be seen as an expression of voluntary participation. Nothing in the case gives reason to view the situation in question differently'. The wording is somewhat unclear since the court did not explicitly state what 'such actions' refers to, that they mean 'as a rule must be seen as an expression of voluntary participation'. In other words, the AC did not formulate a clear assumption that voluntariness in the case of making out and other forms of sex automatically implies signals of interest also in vaginal intercourse. Moreover, it is interesting to note that the court chose to use his story to assess her voluntariness instead of focusing on the question of his intent based on the facts he presented. The court's choice granted the defendant's interpretation of the situation an ontological truth value, implying that the complainant's story about non-voluntariness was not true. Hence, she must be lying. This approach, basing its judgment of the complainant's expressed voluntariness solely on the defendant's account, differs from many other judgments in our study, where the court rather centred its assessment on the defendant's intent. The latter approach allows her story to be taken seriously, in that the court does not question her statement about not participating voluntarily, while also considering his perspective, which can ultimately result in a conviction due to lack of intent. This method allows the court to take her account seriously without questioning her statement about not participating voluntarily, while also recognizing his belief that she wished to participate. Such handling offers a more empathic writing in relation to the parties' stories, unlike the approach taken by the AC in Case 9 that only recognized the defendant's story. The interpretation of the AC can be read as an expression of herasure and himpathy, in which her way of acting, according to the AC, cannot be interpreted in any other way than as an expression for voluntary sex. Note that the defence has presented a picture of the defendant himself showing *her* position, functioning as an empathy hook. Hence, all members of the court have been invited to see what he saw. This exemplifies the impressive empathic negotiation (successfully) performed by the defence lawyer, as clearly captured in our observation notes.

The construction of the sex act is another significant difference from the DC's way of dealing with the question of (non-)voluntariness. The DC interpreted the progression of events, from kisses and oral intercourse to vaginal intercourse, as a series of individual sex acts, each requiring a renewed expression of voluntariness. Additionally, the DC assigned the responsibility of ensuring voluntary participation to the defendant. Conversely, the AC did not address this question in the judgment but held that 'such actions […] as a rule must be seen as an expression of voluntary participation'. Hence, the AC did not address the question of voluntariness in relation to each new sex act. As we attended the deliberations in this case, we know that the AC discussed the issue back and forth and finally decided to define the sequence as one (that is, the oral sex and vaginal intercourse). Instead of regarding it as a series of separate acts, they argued that it should be viewed 'as a continuum', making it one single sex act. Moreover, when the verdict was decided, based on the defendant's version, we experienced a wave of sympathy for the defendant. This relates to the fact that he had been exposed to a hate campaign on social media after the suspected rape. The choice to build the question of voluntariness on his version, implicitly suggesting that she lied, thus facilitated the ushering of himpathy without concern for the complainant, as this way of handling the case suggests that she lied.

In conclusion, the AC here adopted a fragmented way to structure the evidence. The court could thereby describe the weaknesses in the complainant's story and the evidence presented by the prosecutor in a way that allows doubts about the defendant's guilt to be maintained throughout the whole assessment of the case. Regarding the assessment of intent, the AC concluded:

> The fact that the complainant and the defendant did not know each other in a sexual sense does not change that assessment. The prosecution has therefore not proven that the complainant did not participate voluntarily in the sexual intercourse. There is therefore no reason to go on to examine the question of what the defendant realized or should have realized. What has now been said means that the defendant shall be acquitted. (AC judgment, Case 9)

Paths to certainty about doubt – Case 10

Case 10 ended in acquittals in both legal instances, but the two courts arrived at their conclusions in different ways. The DC clung to the feeling of doubt about guilt throughout the whole assessment, similar to what the AC did in Case 9. The descriptions of the complainant's story and the rest of the evidence presented by the prosecutor built on what the DC considered inexplicable elements and other shortcomings and inconsistencies (*Things*). Piece by piece, the case as presented by the prosecutor was fragmented and anchored to the criteria suggested by the Supreme Court. Just like the AC in Case 9, the DC thus based its judgment on the defendant's story. The AC took a similar approach to the case, but applied a more explicit empathic mode in relation to the complainant's story.

In terms of the legal professionals involved in Case 10, it could be noted that the prosecutor in the DC was given the case from a colleague at a late stage, and they switched place in the AC, which may have resulted in less-engaged role performance. Contrary to this, the defence lawyer was very driven and active. He shifted the focus of the trial onto *Things*, a focus that the judge and prosecutor followed. In fact, within the limits of the legal regulation, he influenced the trial by pushing through certain activities. One such activity was embedding empathy hooks through which the judges would effectively imagine the situation from the defendant's perspective. In the DC, the complainant had wanted her close family members to attend the trial, but the defence lawyer objected to this and argued that, if this were allowed, his client's relatives should also be allowed to attend too. Because the victim's counsel and prosecutor protested letting the defendant's family members attend the trial, the DC decided to deny attendance to both parties' relatives. In the AC, neither the complainant nor the victim counsel attended the trial and the prosecutor was only present via a video link from the prosecution office. In this setting, the defendant entered the courtroom surrounded by his family members, who gave him hugs and expressed love in front of the AC judges before the doors closed and his family had to leave. This was staged by the defence lawyer and functioned as an empathy hook, possibly picturing the defendant as a loved son, far from the 'real rapist'. Below, we will focus on the DC judgment as particularly illustrative of maintenance of doubt.

The DC judgment listed the evidence presented in the case, beginning with the evidence invoked by the prosecutor. This included the complainant's story, hearings involving three witnesses and written evidence such as photographs of telephone calls, messages, images of the crime scene, a map and screenshots from Google Maps. On behalf of the defence, the evidence included a hearing with a fourth witness and the defendant's story. The court explained that the stories presented by the complainant and the defendant were summarized in a separate section, whereas witness statements were only represented when relevant. In addition, on the request of the defence, the court held a visit at the site. Such measures are very rare in these cases, and it was subject to intense discussions before being granted.

The grounds for the judgment began with a section of what is commonly known (facts stated in the case). The complainant and the defendant knew each other from school. This particular night, they were having a party with school mates. The party took place at the defendant's place and outdoors (at the scene of the sex act). Witness 1 passed by not too far away at the time of the crime. Witness 2 was a friend of the complainant and met her the day after and helped her with reporting to the police.

The judgment then continued with a description of the complainant's story. She described the close relations the students had in school, which had also led to many 'intrigues'. She had an intense spring semester with many things affecting her personal life. The defendant had been a great support during this period; they had a beautiful friendship and helped each other. She described the evening of the party. They were all playing games, being intimate with kisses and hugs. Everyone was involved, but in a playful and friendly way. After the party, she was planning to sleep at a friend's place. The complainant talked to the defendant during the evening. She noticed that he flirted with her, and she tried to joke to neutralize the situation. She kissed him during the night, but only during the games. She asked Witness 3 to keep an eye on her as she experienced that the defendant was after her. At the end of the evening, she was left alone in the apartment with the defendant and another person. She left the party and contacted a friend on the way. As she walked home, the defendant called her and wanted to meet. She rejected him, but he ran after her and said he wanted to talk. As she heard him coming, she sent a text message to her friend (W3) 'Help, he [the defendant] is following me'. She thought he wanted to share something, and they sat down to talk. He immediately became intimate. She tried to back off and showed him that she was not interested. She did not kiss him back and she thinks she said: 'I don't want to do this' and she believes that the defendant said: 'yes you do, come on' (DC judgment, Case 10). The defendant grabbed her, he unbuttoned her trousers and continued to kiss her. He started to touch her in private areas, and she tried to find all sorts of excuses to move away. The complainant said that it was cold, that a friend was on his way and that she was tired. She explained that she tried to reject the defendant in a polite way. She did not understand what was happening and went into shock as the defendant, who used to be her friend, was not listening to her objections and efforts to reject him. She describes how she experienced the sex act:

> When he started to penetrate her, she gave up, thinking that there was no point in resisting because he grabbed her harder when she resisted. She didn't scream but just gave up […] Everything stopped and she felt sick. The intercourse was quick but it felt like an eternity. Afterwards, everything was empty, and she had switched off completely. She just wanted to throw herself into the water [in front of her] and get away. (DC judgment, Case 10)

With the details about entering into shock, feeling sick and wanting to disappear in the water (signs of frozen fright), the complainant's description of the sex act could clearly be interpreted as a depiction of lived experience. However, as we will observe, the courts did not seem so think so. The complainant described how she, after the sex act ended, called her friend (W3) who was close by, who helped her home. W3 asked her how she was, and she told him what had happened but said that she did not want to report it. However, the next day she decided to report and visited a doctor. The complainant also described that she had been emotionally affected after the event and had to quit her job.

The judgment thereafter turned to the defendant's story. The defendant presented a consent defence. He said that they were flirting and made out during the evening; the complainant was the one taking the initiative. At the end of the evening, she left to go home. He asked if he could meet her, but he had no thoughts about having sex with her. (He provided no explanation for why he wanted to meet her when she had left, and he was not asked about it during the trial.) He met the complainant, they talked and then began to make out again. They went to the place of the event to be in privacy; it was her suggestion. According to the DC judgment '[h]e never noticed that she was trying to get away from him or tried to escape him'. The DC could have interpreted this as an acknowledgment that she indeed attempted to escape, but that he failed to understand her actions as such ('[h]e never noticed that[…]'). The defendant described her as the active party, being intimate and beginning to undress. The complainant was the one who initiated sex. He added that she sounded like she enjoyed it. 'There was a good atmosphere, and he is rather sure that she wanted to'. The expression 'rather sure', could be interpreted as him implicitly saying that he was not all sure. He added 'it was easy; she was wet', using the 'wet and horny defence' as discussed in Chapter 9.

Suddenly, the defendant heard someone calling the complainant's name. The complainant reacted to this, and they stopped what they were doing. The defendant asked for a kiss but was rejected by the complainant. He said they could do this again, that it would be better when he was sober. He kissed her – despite her rejection just a minute ago, perhaps indicating that he did not care about what she wanted – and they went separate ways. He described the day after, when the police came to interrogate him, as frightening, humiliating and surprising. His expression of strong negative feelings invited the court to feel himpathy. He stated that he believed the complainant reported him because she wanted to hide the sex from her friend. Moreover, she had told him about being raped before, and she had also been involved in many intrigues. He supported her through all this. Depicting the complainant as cunning and intriguing and himself as somewhat naïve, the defendant's story indicates that the complainant had reasons to lie and might be capable of falsely accusing innocent young men. One can ask why this part of the defendant's story was relevant to include in the judgment. The judgment also recognized what the defendant had told the court about his dreams for his future – to achieve his dream job, he needed an impeccable record. This, we argue, constructed another empathy hook in terms of a 'ruinable future' (Uhnoo et al 2024c). In short, the defendant argued that he was never sexually interested in her – it was only that night, on her initiative. He had been really depressed after being accused of rape. He had not attended school and withdrew from his friends – except one evening, when he met the complainant and 'she was dancing close to him, as if nothing had happened'. He was in shock – how could she do this to him?

The ensuing part of the DC judgment presented the court's assessment and reasons. It is clearly entangled with strong feelings of himpathy with the defendant, which in turn enabled holding on to the feeling of doubt about his guilt. In a separate section, the judgment began by stating the legal grounds concerning standard of proof and evaluation of evidence. As in all criminal cases, the standard of proof in sexual cases demands that the court finds it proven beyond reasonable doubt that the defendant is guilty as described by the prosecutor. 'It must therefore *not* be ruled out', the court continued, 'that it happened in a different way than what the prosecutor has claimed'.

This wording – 'it must therefore not be ruled out' – possibly indicates that the DC imposes a higher threshold than beyond reasonable doubt. Moreover, it is stated that the evidence in rape cases mainly consists of the stories told by the complainant and the defendant and that the DC must assess the value of these stories. Drawing on the Supreme Court, the judgment then provided the longest list of credibility criteria of all the judgments in our study, including outdated case law. The court referred to and assessed potential reasons for the complainant to falsely accuse the defendant of rape, by stating that 'consideration should also be given to such circumstances that may indicate that the complainant's information is less reliable, for example, that there are personal conflicts between the complainant and the defendant or if there are other reasons for the complainant to make untruthful allegations against the defendant' (cf NJA 1980 s 725). Thereafter, the court explained that the standard of proof for sexual offences is the same as in other criminal cases:

> A prosecution is not proven by just weighing the statements of the complainant and the defendant, and the complainant's story is found to be more credible. The Supreme Court has stated that a credible account in combination with the other evidence presented in the case – for example about the complainant's behaviour afterwards or technical supporting evidence – may however be sufficient for a conviction.
>
> It is common in this type of case that, in addition to the parties' statements, it is based on the fact that the complainant has told others, heard as witnesses in the case, about the incident. If these are deemed credible and reliable, they can, together with information about the witnesses' observations of the complainant's behaviour and reactions after the incident, in some cases provide indirect support for the victim's story. (DC judgment, Case 10)

After this presentation of the legal setting for the assessment, the DC judgment turned to the evaluation of the facts presented in the case. The court stated that it is established that the complainant and the defendant met at the time and place specified by the prosecutor, and that the sex act described took place between them. The court returned to the legal setting and explained that the first question is whether it is proven beyond reasonable doubt that the complainant did not participate voluntarily in the sexual activity. If the court finds that she did not, the court must assess whether the act should be classified as rape or negligent rape. The court explained the legal requisites for negligent rape and stated that the border between legal and illegal is the voluntariness, and ended it by stating that, if the court finds that the complainant participated voluntary, the court should dismiss the prosecution, and the defendant be acquitted of the charges.

The DC's assessment of the parties' stories began by stating that the complainant's story is 'of crucial importance' and 'when examining the account on the basis of the criteria set out by the Supreme Court', the DC found the following:

> The account [from the complainant] is certainly clear, vivid, and reasonably detailed in several parts. However, when it comes to crucial parts of the sex act, the complainant has hesitated, and the account is not particularly detailed. She said that she doesn't remember, [and] that she switched off and suffered a so-called frozen fright. She has not been able to describe what happened immediately afterwards, when W1 arrived at the scene. Nor has she been able to explain whether she told W1 that she had been raped or whether it was W1 who asked her. (DC judgment, Case 10)

This extract from the judgment shows that, on the one hand, the court found that her testimony met many of the credibility criteria. On the other hand, they argued that too many things were questionable, and hence raised doubts. It should be noted that it is a well-known phenomenon for victims to have difficulty remembering details from a sexual trauma (see Vrij et al 2015). Although the complainant in Case 10 described clear signs of frozen fright, how she wanted to sink into the water and disappear, the court did not seem to consider this an explanation for the lack of detail in her story about the sex act. The court continued to point out *Things* that they defined as 'inexplicable elements and contradictions', among them that she did not call for help (from W1 passing by) during the sex act (see also Chapter 7). Regarding the prosecution's assertion of frozen fright, the DC noted that no evidence had been invoked to prove this. This arguably indicates that the DC did not empathetically listen to the complainant's description of her experiences. Her story, if taken seriously, clearly described that she was shocked and paralyzed by the sudden assault from someone she held as a trusted friend. The DC instead focused on the time frame and telephone calls and stated that it 'finds it difficult to explain that the complainant had such a freezing reaction that she was unable to call for help when she heard W1 call and only a minute later managed to call W1 herself and in that call failed to call for help'. This passage does not reveal the fact that the sex act was over when the complainant finally managed to call W1. This omission, however, facilitated making the time of the phone call a *Thing* – an objective reason for doubt. Knowing that the defence lawyer successfully invested great effort into this *Thing*, it is not surprising it appears in the judgment. From our observations and interviews we also know that the prosecutor and victim counsel failed to withstand the defence lawyer's focus shift, just as they failed to empathically translate and negotiate the perspective of the complainant.

The DC judgment continued to identify what they considered inconsistencies linked to some of the witness testimonies, for example what W3 (complainant's friend) and W4 (defendant's friend) said about the games that had taken place during the party. W3 did not remember observing the complainant and defendant kissing during any games and could not remember any games being played at all. However, W3 had left the party early. This fact was later discussed by the court (see below). W4 was sure that neither the defendant nor the complainant was involved in any games but stated that some others may have played games, implying that the kissing and cuddling were mutual. The weight of his statement depends on whether he had in fact observed the two during the whole evening. It could be noted that W4 admitted he was very drunk at the time – but that was not something that the court took into account.

This shows how the DC used the Supreme Court criteria throughout the assessment of the complainant's story, fragmenting and dividing it into pieces. Select pieces of other evidence (the witness stories) are highlighted in support of doubting her story. For example, the court highlighted parts of the witness statements that seemed inconsistent with her story, but toned down, or excluded, evidence that supported her story, such as the text message she wrote to W3 ('Help, he [the defendant] is following me'). This procedure resulted in her story appearing inconsistent, especially from the perspective of legal logics blended with hissense. In this perspective, the complainant's alleged flirting, kissing and 'active initiative' could not be mistaken for anything but wanting to have sex. Accordingly, the defendant's action to pursue sex was natural and rational. Interestingly, the DC judgment also used the Supreme Court credibility criteria in support of the defendant's story:

> In the opinion of the court, *the defendant's story fulfils all the requirements set by the Supreme Court.* The DC has not found it to be contradicted by any of the witnesses. W3 has indeed stated that the complainant thought that the defendant behaved in an unpleasant way towards her and therefore asked W3 to be present so that she would not be left alone with him. However, W3 was only partly attendant during the evening. His testimony is also inconsistent with W4's, who says that they were alone, which is also stated by the complainant and the defendant. The defendant has also stated that the complainant showed naked pictures of herself and was flirting with him. This has not been questioned by the prosecutor. (DC judgment, Case 10, emphasis added)

This quote clearly illustrates how the use of the credibility criteria by means of select pieces of supporting evidence makes the defendant's story into a whole, while the complainant's story falls apart. W3's testimony was used to highlight that, contrary to the story of the complainant, the defendant and the complainant had not participated in any games together. The part of W3's statement that supported the complainant's story (the defendant's unpleasant behaviour) was implicitly doubted on the grounds that W3 was not attending the party the whole evening. Doubt (in a version supporting the complainant's story) is then strengthened by the statement of the defendant's friend (W4) and finally settled by the statement of the defendant himself (flirting and naked pictures). The DC concluded: 'In view of the above, the court considers that the complainant's story has a relatively low evidential value and that it is the defendant's story that must form the basis of the court's judgment. A conviction therefore requires other evidence of considerable strength that refutes the defendant's story'.

Towards the meaning of voluntariness – Case 13

Case 13 is interesting because it is one of two cases in our study that fully addressed the question of voluntariness in rape cases in line with the preparatory works (that is, that the new legislation aims to shift the responsibility for the sexual offence from the complainant to the defendant; see Chapter 8 about the burden and/or possibility of explanation depending on perspective). In addition, Case 13 considers the new crime of negligent rape. Negligent rape is a less serious offence than rape and consists of the same objective criteria (sexual intercourse and non-voluntariness or, for example, use of force or undue exploitation of a particularly vulnerable state or serious abuse of a position of dependence) but requires only gross negligence instead of intent – explained in Chapter 2. Both instances end in convictions: the DC in negligent rape and the AC in rape. Although all rape cases are defined as challenging, the judges found this case particularly difficult to decide. A sign of the complexity of this case is that the judgment from the AC included two dissenting opinions, one arguing for negligent rape and the other for an acquittal.

Just like Case 9, Case 13 addresses the legal prerequisite of whether the complainant was in a particularly vulnerable situation. Hence, the focus of the judgments lies on the question of voluntariness or whether the complainant was in a particularly vulnerable situation that the defendant unduly exploited. The situation is evaluated and assessed in context, rather than being fragmented and deconstructed into pieces. The complainant and the defendant were both vulnerable and easy to sympathize with, and both were carefully dealt with in the judgments through what we call empathic writing.

In the AC, besides the researcher, the five judges, the defendant and the defence lawyer were present in the courtroom, whereas the prosecutor participated via video link. The complainant and her victim council were not present in the AC.

At a general level, it could be noted that the DC judgment in Case 13 did not structure the evaluation of evidence in line with the *Balcony Case* model, nor make any reference to case law or other legal sources. It did not include any general explanations of the criminal legal regulation or principles for evaluating evidence or standard of proof, one of the few DC judgments that lacked these parts. Rather, it unfolded the assessment around legal questions and used what is sometimes called 'woven grounds'.[1] The judge in the DC had extensive experience, and this may be read as an expression of her confidence and feeling of autonomy.

The DC judgment began with the 'undisputed facts' in the case and described that the two parties met for the first time, outside in the city centre, the same evening as the sex act. The complainant and her friend invited the defendant to chat, and the complainant spent a large part of the evening talking to the defendant. Her plan was to stay at a friend's place but, at a late stage of the evening, she found that this was no longer an option. She could not return home at that time of the evening and asked her other friends about a place to stay for the night; but they did not help her. In the end, and at her request, the defendant offered her to sleep in a garage on his property. The two of them went there and spent some time there before she was about to sleep. It is also undisputed and supported by technical evidence that the defendant carried out vaginal intercourse with the complainant. Then, the judgment outlined legally relevant questions:

> A first question is then whether the complainant participated of her own free will. If not, the question is whether the defendant knew about it or whether he took undue advantage of the fact that the complainant was in a vulnerable situation due to intoxication. If this is not the case, the question is whether he was grossly negligent in relation to the circumstances that the complainant did not participate voluntarily. (DC judgment, Case 13)

Regarding the question of voluntariness, the court's judgment began with a telephone call from the complainant to the emergency response centre (112) and stated that the call showed that she was very sad in close proximity to the sex act and related that she had been raped. This is an example of temporal boundary work by the DC (see Chapter 7). In general, telephone

---

[1]   Until about 15 years ago, the writing technique in judgments involved presenting each oral statement separately. Recently, however, a method known as 'woven grounds' has been developed, in which multiple statements are combined and integrated in the presentation. Nonetheless, the traditional technique is still frequently used, especially in rape cases.

calls to the emergency response centre work as an empathy hook. It can demonstrate 'adequate' victim behaviour from the complainant – for instance that she sounded devastated and promptly reported the incident to the police. In accordance with this, the DC wrote that the telephone call in Case 13 strongly suggested that the complainant did not participate voluntarily. The telephone call constituted a part of the hard evidence and thus contributed to the construction and feeling of objective decision-making. The court noted that no facts indicated violence, threats or other pressure from the defendant.

Moreover, the court found both parties credible, although they both deviated to some extent from their previous statements in police hearings. Deviations in the case of the defendant did not concern any details of relevance for the case, the court underlined, and deviations from the complainant concerned her level of intoxication. The court stressed that her statement regarding the intoxication thus should be considered carefully. On the other hand, the court added, there was also other information regarding her level of intoxication.

Contrary to the story from the defendant, the complainant told the court that she did not participate voluntarily, that she was heavily drunk and that she froze and became paralyzed when the defendant began to touch her. The complainant explained that she did not do or say anything to stop him, but that the defendant undressed her and carried out sexual intercourse with her. The defendant explained that she kissed him and said he was kind. He stated that they began to make out, took off their clothes and had sexual intercourse. In one part of their statements, the one about the sexual intercourse, their stories differed. As there was technical evidence supporting her version, the court stated that it based their decision on her version in this part.

As the indictment included an allegation that she was in a particularly vulnerable situation, her level of intoxication was relevant for the legal assessment of the case. She said she had been drinking a lot, and that she fell several times during the evening. Blood analyses confirmed that she was drunk. The defendant described that she was somewhat affected by alcohol, that she was happy, laughing a great deal and lost her balance a few times. Her friends also witnessed to the court that she was drunk, but not too drunk, and that she laughed and was a bit wobbly. This situation appeared in several cases in our study. Female friends abandoned the complainant drunk in the middle of the night and later, when asked about the complainant's state when they left her, the friends denied that she was heavily intoxicated (for example, Cases 10 and 14). A possible aspect to empathically imagine when assessing such witness statements is that it may be difficult to admit to yourself and others that you abandoned your friend, drunk in the middle of the night with strangers – and, implicitly, admit your own level of drinking.

The DC ended the assessment of the complainant's intoxication with a statement from a male officer who met her just after the event. Thus, the court returned to the point at which they began (the 112 call), in which she sounded extremely sad, that she could hardly answer any questions. The police officer described that she was possibly a bit drunk, but hardly noticeable. She described to the police what she had been through, and they defined it as a rape. The court summed up regarding the question of voluntariness and reflected upon her ability to express her (non-)voluntariness:

> [P]articularly in considering what is shown in the alarm call and the police's testimony – the court considers that the investigation shows that the complainant did not participate voluntarily, hence the sexual intercourse was carried out against her will. The question is then whether this was expressed or whether she was unable to make such an expression or otherwise defend herself due to intoxication. (DC judgment, Case 13)

A possible interpretation of this quote is that the court framed the inquiry as a question of whether and how the complainant expressed her non-voluntariness, rather than focusing on the defendant's intentions and his care about her will. At this stage, the court was articulating old ideas about her rejection. However, later in its judgment, the DC sought for expressions of 'yes' instead of searching for expressions of 'no': 'There has been nothing presented in the case that suggests that the complainant has expressed a desire to have sexual intercourse with the defendant'.

Regarding her situation and condition, the court found that the investigation did not prove that she was intoxicated to such a degree that she was in a particularly vulnerable situation. That she was tired and tried to sleep was not investigated in the case; hence, the court found that it was not proven that the defendant unduly exploited a situation in which the complainant was so particularly vulnerable that he could be convicted of intentional rape on that basis.

The next legal question for the court to assess is whether the defendant was intentional or grossly negligent in relation to the fact that the complainant did not participate voluntarily. The DC stated that the case was 'word against word' and that neither of them was more credible than the other. Still, there was reason to assess their stories in relation to the rest of the evidence presented in the case. The court framed the assessment of their stories in an empathetic tone, explaining that, on the one hand, they did not find reason to immediately reject his story, but continued to conclude that his description of the sex act (his consent defence) was unlikely:

> The District Court also considers that the sequence of events described by the defendant – that the complainant went from lying down to sleep

fully dressed to suddenly kissing the defendant in a way that invited sexual intercourse – appears to be very poorly described. Nor has it been shown that the defendant asked the complainant if she wanted to have sexual intercourse with him and if so, whether he would use protection, which the court considers to be very remarkable. The defendant himself has expressed that he perceived that the complainant participated voluntarily, which somewhat contradicts that this would have been completely clear to him. In an overall assessment, the court finds that the defendant's statement that the complainant at some stage acted clearly and actively to have sexual intercourse with him does not deserve any credibility. (DC Judgment, Case 13)

To assess his story, the court then went on to base its stance on an understanding of the law that assumes that it was his responsibility to assure himself that she participated voluntarily:

In the light of what has been shown about the complainant's and the defendant's previous contacts – that they had only known each other for a few hours, that the defendant was aware that the complainant had ended up in a situation that meant that she no longer had a place to sleep, and that nothing has been found to indicate that the conversation between the complainant and the defendant included any expressions of sexual interest or invitations – the court finds that there was no explanatory context for the defendant's view that the complainant suddenly wanted to have unprotected sexual intercourse with him. Nor has the defendant in any way assured himself of this, but only – and despite knowing that the complainant was intoxicated – acted on his own opinion. The court has dismissed the defendant's information that the complainant acted actively in a way that gave reason for this belief. According to the court, this in turn speaks in favour of the complainant's statements that she had become paralyzed and was unable to do anything at all. (DC Judgment, Case 13)

In this extract we observe the court's temporal boundary work and its construction of the situational context as a means to shed light on the sex act. By framing the events within a timeline of limited prior contact and recognizing the complainant's precarious position (having nowhere to sleep and being intoxicated), the court underscores a lack of mutual intent or prior interest. This careful contextualization serves to question the defendant's perspective on consent, contrasting it with the complainant's account of paralysis and inability to resist. Also, the DC reiterated that it was his responsibility to ensure that she wanted to participate in the sexual activities, yet the court to some extent believed his story and found that he was not acting intentionally. It ended in a conclusion that he had been grossly negligent:

> Despite this, the court considers that it has not been shown that the defendant was aware of the complainant's involuntariness. However, the court considers that the complainant's passivity must have led him to suspect that there was a risk that the complainant would not participate voluntarily. However, no circumstances have emerged that show with sufficient strength that he was indifferent to the fact that the complainant did not participate voluntarily. The defendant is thus deemed not to have had intent for the offence. The court considers instead – particularly in light of the fact that the complainant was intoxicated and had gone to sleep and that the complainant did not express in a word a desire for sexual intercourse or even an interest in the defendant, and that the defendant himself did not do anything to ensure that the complainant participated voluntarily – it has been shown that the defendant acted with deliberate negligence in a way that means that he should be judged to have been grossly negligent in relation to the fact that the complainant did not participate voluntarily. Consequently, he shall be sentenced to liability for negligent rape. (DC Judgment, Case 13)

It should be noted that the defendant in this case was also easy to perceive as vulnerable, and that he gave a sympathetic impression in court. In conclusion, the court based its judgment on the complainant's story, in most parts, and explicitly placed the responsibility on the defendant regarding the question of reassuring himself about her voluntary participation. Yet, the court assessed his story concerning his intent in an empathetic way, as the court seemed to take his view seriously and did not believe he had been acting indifferently towards her will.

The AC, in contrast convicted the defendant of rape instead of negligent rape. In the appeal the prosecutor requested that the defendant be convicted for rape, and the defendant requested an acquittal, or at least a milder sentence. The prosecutor adjusted the statement of the criminal act as charged and added some factors that contributed to the vulnerable state: 'the defendant took undue advantage of the fact that the complainant, due to drunkenness, severe fear, fatigue and vulnerability, was in a particularly vulnerable situation'. The same evidence was presented in the AC as in the DC. The AC set out its reasons for the judgment under the heading 'Grounds for the judgment': 'As the DC concluded, and as the parties agree, it is proven that the defendant had sexual intercourse with the complainant at the time and place specified in the indictment. The question then is whether the intercourse constituted rape'. The court began with the legal regulation of rape and what it means, and ended with:

A person can never, as far as is now of interest, be considered to participate voluntarily if the offender takes undue advantage of the fact that the person is in a particularly vulnerable situation due to unconsciousness, sleep, serious fear, intoxication or other drug influence, illness, bodily injury, mental disorder or otherwise in view of the circumstances. (AC judgment, Case 13)

This was followed by a clarifying section:

The circumstances set out in the criminal provision may, *individually or in combination,* lead to the complainant being considered to have been in a particularly vulnerable situation. For example, a person's level of intoxication combined with the fact that the person is young and is in a strange place with an offender who is not previously known to the person may mean that the person is in such a vulnerable situation. The assessment of whether a complainant is in a particularly vulnerable situation should be based on the situation as a whole. The circumstances can be related to both the complainant's person and to external circumstances. A particularly vulnerable situation is characterized by the fact that the complainant then lacks or at least has clearly limited opportunities to protect her sexual integrity. (AC judgment, Case 13, emphasis added)

It should be noted that most of the judgments in our study did not take this approach to the prerequisite of a vulnerable state, that is, assessing the circumstances 'in combination' or based on 'the situation as a whole'. More common in similar cases (for example, Cases 9, 14 and 15) was to assess whether any of the circumstances (unconsciousness, sleep, serious fear, intoxication or other drug influence, illness, bodily injury, mental disorder or otherwise) are at hand, that is, what we call a fragmented approach. The AC examined the specific circumstances in Case 13 and wrote: '[T]he prosecution invoked that the complainant was drunk, seriously frightened, tired and hence in a vulnerable situation. The allegation of a vulnerable situation includes the age of the complainant and the external circumstances that led to the interaction between the defendant and the complainant'. Hence, the court presented a view of the regulation that allowed for contextualization of the event. The provision, in their view, must not be read as either drunk or afraid, but allows for a combination of these aspects. However, on the way to the conclusion, in which the court interprets the situation as a whole, it must first assess each aspect separately.

Thus, first the court began with her age. The complainant was young, but the question is what the defendant may have understood about it. Both the complainant and the witnesses' statements stated that they thought that she talked about their age with him, but they were not completely sure and their statements differed. The AC found that the information presented in the case all together left them with the conclusion that the defendant understood she was young, although he did not know her exact age.

Second, the court continued with the level of intoxication, stating that she was not intoxicated to a degree that automatically placed her in a vulnerable situation, but from the evidence presented (her story, his story and blood analyses), the court drew the conclusion that her judgment was clearly compromised, and that the defendant must have realized that.

Third, the complainant said she was afraid of the defendant during and after the sexual intercourse, but she was the one suggesting that he arranged somewhere to sleep, and she went with him. Hence, according to the AC, the fear should not be considered in the assessment of the particularly vulnerable situation. This consideration demonstrates how the court allowed for a more nuanced interpretation of the parties' stories than just whether they were credible or not, whether they told a lie or a truth, which is more often the case (Smith 2018).

Fourth, the complainant was very tired and in search of somewhere to sleep, and the defendant told the court that she tried to sleep. The AC thus assumed that she was very tired. The court then assessed the circumstances together:

> In sum: The complainant was [young]. Her judgment was impaired due to intoxication. It was the middle of the night, and she was tired, but she had no place to sleep other than the [garage] offered to her by an adult male stranger. The fact that the circumstances were such that she had clearly limited opportunities to protect her sexual integrity is strongly supported by the fact that shortly after the sexual intercourse she called 112 [SOS] in despair and told them that she had been raped. The AC's conclusion is that the prosecutor has proved his claim that the complainant was in a particularly vulnerable situation and that the defendant had insight into all the circumstances that form the basis for this assessment and unduly exploited these circumstances. The defendant should therefore be convicted of rape. (AC judgment, Case 13)

Although the evidence presented was assessed and contributed to the findings, this judgment differed from many others in the sense that it focused primarily on the criminal legal questions, rather than on the evidential aspects. This may be explained by the need to establish if she was in a *particularly vulnerable* state.

The AC judgment was accompanied by two dissenting opinions, suggesting that the case was particularly difficult to assess. The first dissenting opinion was made by a young female professional judge, who reached the same conclusion as the DC that the defendant should be convicted for negligent rape. This judge took a similar approach as the majority, assessing each aspect that may constitute a particularly vulnerable situation all together and processing them one by one. She agreed with the majority that it was not proven that she was afraid (doubt about fear). She continued to the intoxication and underlined that neither the friends, the police or the telephone call to the alarm central showed that she was very drunk (doubt about drunkenness). The opinion continued by stating that, although it was late and the complainant was tired, it is not clear how this would affect her possibilities to protect her sexual integrity:

> The fact that the complainant was [young] and was in a garage with a man several years older than her, whom she had only known for a short time, does indeed mean that she was in a vulnerable situation, but that circumstance is not in itself sufficient to assess the situation as *particularly* vulnerable. (AC judgment, Case 13, emphasis added)

Hence, this dissenting judge reached other conclusions regarding the different aspects (age, intoxication, tiredness, fear) than the majority of the court, and found that the complainant was not in a particularly vulnerable situation. In other words, she expressed certainty about doubt about the 'particularly vulnerable situation'. However, the judge underlined that the telephone call to the emergency response centre strongly suggested that she did not participate voluntarily. This was supported by the statement by the police about the complainant's devastated state of mind. Hence, the judge argued that it was objectively proven that she did not participate voluntarily. The question was then whether he acted intentionally or with gross negligence regarding her non-voluntariness. The judge used his story and not her story to argue that it was not proven that he knew or understood that she did not want to have sexual intercourse with him: 'He has described how he saw her face, how she told him personal things, he tried to comfort her. She said he was nice and kissed him on the cheek and they started kissing. He has described how she touched him and that they undressed and had sexual intercourse'. The judge highlighted that the complainant did not describe what happened in detail (this was a conclusion after listening to the witnesses), and that her claims that she was completely passive contradicted the defendant's perception of the situation. From this, the judge drew the conclusion: 'It is therefore not proven that the defendant realized that there was a significant risk that the complainant would not participate voluntarily. The first element of indifference is therefore not fulfilled'. The question then becomes whether the defendant was negligent and whether the negligence can be judged as gross negligence:

> In my opinion, the circumstances regarding the complainant's vulnerable position mean that the defendant must have realized that

there was a certain risk that the complainant would not participate voluntarily and that he should have acquired knowledge of this. The circumstances were such that the negligence cannot be judged as anything other than gross. The offence was not less serious. I would therefore, like the District Court, convict the defendant of negligent rape. Outvoted in this part, I otherwise agree with the majority. (AC judgment, Case 13)

The second dissenting opinion was made by a male lay judge, who concluded that the defendant should be acquitted. Like the other dissenting judge, he argued that the complainant was not in a particularly vulnerable situation. He considered that the defendant's information about the course of events negated the value of the evidence invoked by the prosecution, and thereby it was 'not established beyond reasonable doubt that the complainant did not participate voluntarily'. This (lay) judge was the only one, out of the three in the DC plus four in the AC, that remained with the feeling of doubt about the defendant's guilt. Four judges ended in certainty about negligent rape, and three in certainty about rape, suggesting that this was a really difficult case for the judges.

Case 13 stands out in several ways from the other cases in our study. First, it exemplifies a judicial approach where the majority of judges actively rejected the common 'she lies' myth, instead placing responsibility for ensuring voluntary participation on the defendant, the active party. This reflects a shift towards accountability aligned with the new legislation's aims. Second, Case 13 demonstrates a holistic assessment, evaluating the situation in its entirety rather than fragmenting the evidence – a perspective that allows the court to consider the broader context of consent and agency. Third, it highlights the inherent complexity in addressing rape cases through legal frameworks, underscoring the multiple judicial pathways and interpretations possible when dealing with such sensitive matters.

Ultimately, Case 13 illustrates the tension within judicial reasoning between applying empathetic, hersensical logic that aligns with the law's intent to protect the complainant's autonomy, and the more traditional, hissensical approach focused on scepticism and evidence fragmentation. While the majority in the AC reached a conviction, the dissenting opinion reveals how a fragmented view of the complainant's particularly vulnerable situation can perpetuate a sense of doubt. This divergence underscores the challenges courts face in balancing a holistic understanding of vulnerability with the rigorous standards of legal certainty required in criminal cases.

Conclusion

This chapter illustrated different pathways to knowing in judicial decision-making, showcasing how courts navigate between fragmented and holistic approaches to evidence in rape cases. In Case 9, we observe two contrasting judicial approaches: the DC's rejection of rape myths and the AC's way of clinging on to doubt. The DC took an active stance against traditional biases, assigning responsibility for ensuring consent to the defendant and reframing the evaluation of voluntariness to align with legislative intentions, thus challenging the assumption that the burden lies with the complainant. This approach reflects a hersensical logic, consistent with the aims of the new legislation and preparatory works, which prioritize the complainant's autonomy and shift the responsibility for voluntary participation to the defendant.

Conversely, the AC's reasoning follows a hissensical logic, rooted in a traditional framework that centres on cultivating doubt. By fragmenting the evidence and identifying uncertainties, the AC upheld a strict standard of reasonable doubt. These judgments illustrate a judicial tension between addressing stereotypes, as in the hersensical approach of the DC, and maintaining a rigorous standard of doubt, as exemplified by the hissensical reasoning of the AC. While the DC judgment shows how hersensical logics can integrate with legal principles under the new rape legislation, aligning with the statutory emphasis on autonomy and responsibility, the AC judgment demonstrates how procedural legal logics easily incorporate hissensical reasoning, reinforcing scepticism.

In Case 10, both the DC and the AC reached acquittals, yet through different paths to certainty about doubt. The DC maintained a sense of doubt by fragmenting the prosecutor's case into inexplicable elements and perceived inconsistencies (*Things*) in the complainant's account. The DC clung to the feeling of doubt about guilt throughout the whole assessment, similar to what the AC did in Case 9. Piece by piece, the case as presented by the prosecutor was fragmented and anchored to the criteria suggested by the Supreme Court. Just like the AC in Case 9, the DC thus based its judgment on the defendant's story. The AC in Case 10 applied a similar strategy, but with a more explicit use of empathetic writing to engage with the complainant's story.

It was largely thanks to the defence's strategic focus on *Things* that these elements became central in both courts' assessments. The prosecutor, who joined the case at a late stage, appeared less engaged, while the defence lawyer took a proactive role, steering attention to specific *Things* and embedding empathy hooks that encouraged judges to view the situation from the defendant's perspective. In both courts, these empathy hooks – such as orchestrating family support for the defendant in the AC – may have influenced perceptions, subtly framing him as a loved family member rather than a 'real rapist'.

Case 13 differs from many other cases in our study by its distinctive judicial approach. First, it provides a clear example of the majority of judges rejecting the 'she lies' myth and placing the responsibility to ensure voluntary participation on the active party – the defendant. This approach reflects a hersensical logic, aligning with the intent of recent legislation and preparatory works by emphasizing the complainant's autonomy and shifting responsibility onto the defendant. Second, Case 13 demonstrates a holistic evaluation of the situation, examining events as a cohesive whole rather than fragmenting them into isolated elements. This hersensical reasoning resonates with the legislative emphasis on understanding the complainant's experience in context, rather than dissecting specific actions.

At the same time, Case 13 highlights the inherent difficulties and diverse approaches in legally addressing rape cases. The AC ruling in particular illustrates how fundamental procedural logics can sometimes be infused with hissensical reasoning, focusing more on traditional scepticism and detailed dissection of evidence. This case exemplifies the challenges inherent in handling this type of case, ultimately resulting in multiple judgments, including two dissenting opinions in the AC. The differing conclusions highlight the complexity judges face in interpreting evidence and legal responsibility in cases of this nature.

In conclusion, Cases 9, 10 and 13 each demonstrate the varied judicial approaches to rape cases, highlighting a spectrum from hersensical reasoning that supports legislative aims to hissensical approaches grounded in evidentiary doubt. These cases also illustrate how focusing on *Things* – fragmented, isolated elements of evidence – can contribute to a sense of certainty about doubt, often reinforcing hissensical reasoning. Conversely, a more holistic approach aligns more closely with the law's intent, supporting hersensical reasoning that shifts responsibility to the defendant while respecting the complainant's autonomy.

PART V

Conclusion

12

Legal Core Values and Beyond

Introduction

In this book we aimed to demonstrate how the implementation of the 2018 Swedish rape law challenges core legal values. Parts II–IV presented empirically grounded analyses, based on our study, showing how legal practice sometimes realized, but more often counteracted, the intentions of the new law. This outcome we argue is rooted in the autopoietic inertia of a modern legal system originally conceived in nineteenth-century patriarchy (cf Smart 1995).

According to Teubner (1993), autonomy is a central function of autopoietic systems. By reference to 'fixed points', among them what we call core legal values, the Law reproduces itself 'in such a way that it corresponds to [its] self-description' (Teubner 1993:15), making it partly immune to change in the surrounding society. This idea of the legal system's autonomy is built into the constitution of modern democratic societies to protect it from political volatility or authoritarianism, but also brings the risk of the Law becoming dysfunctional to an evolving social environment.

Our analyses showed how the legal concept of autonomy resists the intentions of the new law at the micro level both in terms of 'the free will' of legal subjects, and in terms of the (rational mind of) 'the autonomous judge' to whom the prosecutor needs merely to 'present the evidence'. In line with this critique of the concept of autonomy, we see that the structural 'legal autonomy' illustrates the legal system's *ideal* autopoiesis, while the Law is, and always will be, part of social life. The social embedding of the legal system is seen in its own concern about democratic legitimacy. This is linked to the fact that the autopoiesis of the legal system is made and maintained by humans, who every day cross the border between the Law and its environment and take pride in safeguarding legitimacy. Furthermore, humans import social norms, values, classed, and gendered perspectives, common sense, and morality into the legal system even when they assume their habituated system-shaped roles. Finally, legislation has its origins in

273

society; it is created and amended on the initiative of democratically elected legislators (that is, politicians).

What makes the concept of the law as an autopoietic system interesting and relevant to us is that it accounts for how, in the process of making new laws, proposed legislation must be translated into juridical terminology and, through this, the end-product is moulded into a shape determined by an autopoietic logic, that is, social norms and values become 'subject to legal reformulation. As soon as they are in dispute, a decision has to be made about them according to criteria established by the law itself. In some cases it may be necessary to redefine them' (Teubner 1993:35–36, see also Tilly 2008). In this process, it may appear that 'meaning' is an actant in itself – bits of 'communication' circulate detached from humans – while empirical analysis, like ours, demonstrates that the meaning and communication of the legal system is ultimately sustained by emotive-cognitively reflexive human beings whose professional identity is contingent on it. The 'fixed points' are maintained and reproduced because they anchor the shared collective identity of legal professionals in meaningful ways and generate comforting and pleasant emotions of knowing and sense (Hochschild 1990).

In our terminology the meaning-making of the legal system is part of the emotive-cognitive judicial frame, addressing the everyday 'emotional practice' (Scheer 2021) of doing law as a collaborative and habituated achievement. The frame can be seen as a versatile practice-oriented sub-system of the legal system, providing professional scripts for the concrete doing of abstract values and sustaining the power of these to define meaning. Because internal referentiality thus depends on practice, changed practice impacts on the meaning of the values.

The case investigated in this book, the new rape law, demonstrates how changing norms in the social environment give rise to a new law – thus from the *outside* of the legal system – fundamentally challenging the core legal values of autonomy, rationality and objectivity in terms of their taken-for-granted meaning *inside* the legal system. The law does not directly criticize the meaning of those values, but meaning gets destabilized because the law poses real obstacles to the habituated doing of them, forcing legal actors to reflect on how they do them and why. At the level of society, the law also forges reconsideration of the legal system's role (in society) and its relation to changing social norms, and thus the very meaning of legal autonomy. Again, we emphasize that we do not argue for rationality, autonomy and objectivity to be discarded as core legal values, but that their meaning, particularly for practice, must be scrutinized in a society that no longer endorses patriarchy as a social order.

Presuming that social systems are never entirely closed to the environment, the theory of the law as an autopoietic system further proposes an interesting theory of change (Teubner 1993). This occurs in the emergence of *variations*, which may be selected for practice based on their compatibility with the system's identity and 'fixed points'. The rape law's radical potential, we argue, lies in legitimizing hersensical legal logics. Destabilising the privileged male gaze on the world, behind the 'neutral' core values, the new law opens up the opportunity for change but retains the values.

Variations are reflected in the concerns and adaptations of legal professionals as they try to meet the lawmakers' intentions, although this challenges the way they are used to think. The retaining function of the concept of *legal autonomy* is evident in how legal professionals, practising the new law, struggle to translate fuzzy intimate interactions to fit the legal assumption of individual autonomy and free will, to understand the credibility and intent of legal subjects. *Legal rationality*, conceived as the ideal instrumentally goal-oriented autonomous action, resists recognition of the emotional drives and orientations of human action, just as the legal conception of autonomy resists recognition of the legal subjects' 'free' will as bounded and relational. The two concepts are closely linked and constitutive of the third core legal value, objectivity, which is conceived as a disembodied, autonomous state of pure rationality. Elsewhere, we have demonstrated how the legal notion of the rational autonomous subject is central to the self-description of 'the objective judge' or 'the objective prosecutor' and thus for the doing of objectivity as legal practice (cf Bergman Blix and Wettergren 2019; Bladini 2013).

In short, the concepts of rationality, autonomy and objectivity as core judicial values constitute 'fixed points' that, through the emotive-cognitive judicial frame, orient legal professional actors in their different roles within the legal system. When the core judicial values are put to practice, they are endowed with flesh and blood and the five senses and can never reach the 'purity' of the abstract ideals but merely attempt to approximate them, which, in itself, opens up the possibility of variations. Thus, embodied and embedded, in legal practice (like in social life in general), rationality is informed by emotion, autonomy is structurally and relationally bounded, and objectivity is continuously done by means of situated empathic imagination and professional collaboration. Since the laws, just decades ago, were made only by men, and the legal system was inhabited only by male legal professionals sharing their emotive-cognitive perspective on the world from their privileged standpoint, hissense of this particular group shaped lawmaking and legal practice. The new law, opening for female perspectives and hersense(s), reveals just how deeply entwined the 'neutrality' of the core legal values has been with one particular perspective. By the simple placing of responsibility on the active party to confirm the voluntary participation of the other party, the new law legitimizes hersensical legal logics, which we have seen gives rise to a plethora of more or less remarkable variations that are compatible with the 'fixed points' but may also, eventually, change how these are done in practice.

In the rest of this chapter, we summarize and discuss our findings in light of the fields of law and emotion and feminist legal research. We then proceed to discuss the concrete implications of our results for legal practice in terms of professional role adaptations.

The new rape law and legal practice

In Part II, 'The Making of Legal Objectivity', we argued that the legal handling of rape cases under the new law is haunted by a pervasive feeling of not knowing referring to the handling of rape cases. Professional frustration boils down to the 'bad' evidence, compared with other criminal cases. Under the new law the complainant's story of non-voluntary participation is emphasized as the main evidence and, while supporting evidence (witness testimonies and hard evidence) is usually required, its meaning and strength is contingent on the credibility of the complainant's story. Fragments of witness testimonies appear to be retrospectively cherry-picked to support or refute the complainant's story. Hard evidence, although it may function as objectivity lifebuoys in support of the 'subjective' story of the complainant, can be dismissed as irrelevant by a successful consent defence. In support of the evaluation of stories, the Supreme Court has issued criteria that are routinely used to 'objectify' the evaluation of the complainant's story. Any which way the legal professionals choose to approach the complainant's story as main evidence, they cannot escape handling, through the lens of their different professional roles, soft evidence; subjective stories, eloquence, emotional expressions and personal impressions. This means that the new rape law instils fundamental disturbances to the autopoiesis of the legal system in terms of what counts as legitimate evidence.

Disturbance is sensed by legal professionals as irritation, signalling irrelevance (Barbalet 1998), but in the context of the new law it reveals a feeling of not knowing and the need to acquire new knowledge (cf de Sousa 2008; Törnqvist and Bergman Blix 2023). The feeling of not knowing and the focus on oral testimony opens up the opportunity for background emotions, through the tools of individual and shared experience (and 'notorious facts'; see Chapter 2) to evaluate the evidence. This is seen not least in legal professionals' reflections on the new law, where it appears that they approach its meaning from different common-sense perspectives. Through this, rape myths become activated as familiar tropes, most notably the 'she lies' myth. The latter is already inherent in the legal logical need to foreclose the 'alternative hypothesis' that the complainant has a motive to falsely accuse the defendant. This, in turn, is tied to the standard of proof (beyond reasonable doubt).

The she lies myth lingers throughout the legal process of dealing with rape. We argued that this is comparable to what Fricker (2007) calls a credibility deficit inherent to epistemic injustice directed at specific social groups. In our discussion, epistemic injustice pertains to the identitarian power exercised by the Law against (primarily) women who report rape. Epistemic injustice dispossesses complainants from privileged knowledge of what they themselves did (not) do, and from knowing the offence (rape) as an ontological premise of the trial.

We differentiate between her- and hissense and legal logics and argue that the latter blends easily with hissense. On the other hand, the law opens up the opportunity of moving some of the attention from the complainant to the defendant's story, in search for intent as explicit neglect to ensure voluntariness. Interest is then redirected from the complainant's action rationality to the defendant's action rationality (Part III). In this move the law opens up the opportunity for, and indeed legitimizes, hersense to blend with legal logics.

The legal logics of the principle of legal certainty and the presumption of innocence places the burden of proof on the prosecutor, who must demonstrate guilt beyond reasonable doubt. In rape cases, when hissense informs legal logics, it determines what constitutes reasonable doubt. It recognizes 'male fear' (of being falsely accused) as rational, while 'female fear' (of sexual violence) is doubted. Male fear aligns well with the principles of legal certainty, while female fear underlies the new legislation, aiming to strengthen the protection for sexual integrity and assure the sex act is mutual. In short, both irritation and the opening of legal logics to hersense may prompt legal professionals' search for new ways of practising autonomy, rationality and objectivity.

We have demonstrated how the default doing of objectivity as a collaborative achievement, falls short in the handling of rape cases. Judges who refuse to confront the irritation caused by dealing with soft evidence become susceptible to background power discomfort. Within the parameters of the principle of free evaluation, judges may come to rather unpredictable conclusions through rather irrational (hissensical) paths of reasoning. Prosecutors who act by their default doing of objectivity, trusting that 'the evidence speaks for itself', do not realize that in rape cases judges may really not know what to make of the evidence presented. Moreover, their default display of prosecutorial certainty and confidence, by highlighting weaknesses in the evidence, provides defence lawyers with clues as to which particular *Things* – among all the potential ones anticipated by the defence – are most salient for their purpose to sow doubt about the charges.

We coined the notion of *Things* to conceptualize how some particular inexplicable elements of the complainant's (and sometimes the defendant's) stories transform into quasi-objective reasons for alternative hypothesis: 'How *the jeans* came off' (Case 2) or 'the *phone call*' (Cases 10 and 15) are examples from our data, tipping certainty *beyond* reasonable doubt to certainty *about* reasonable doubt. We have shown that *Things* can be prevented or defused if the prosecution instead engages in empathic translation and negotiation, essentially intensifying the adversarial dimension of the trial.

In the work of thus inviting the judges' empathic imagination of the offence, we suggest the prosecutors, who have an objectivity requirement, may draw on the experience and emotive-cognitive know-how of the victim counsels (who often have experience as defence lawyers), who can step up from their minimal role as care-takers, to active advocators of the complainant's perspective. An interesting consequence when such collaboration was put into practice was seen in Case 11 where it managed to equalize the power balance between prosecution and defence. Case 11 also effectively illuminated the offensive and humiliating mechanisms of the rape trial proceedings, to which the complainant is routinely subjected, and how these are considered neutral and necessary until they also affect the defendant.

In Part III, 'Autonomy and Rationality of Legal Subjects', we investigated the projection of the legal notion of autonomous action rationality onto the legal subjects. Because rape trials are most often manifestly *not* accompanied by proper empathic translation, judges are at pains to understand the ordinary and in most cases fuzzy behaviour of young or drunken complainants. And since many rapes occur by someone whom the complainant knows or trusts, or trusts by proxy (as a person trusted by someone they trust), many complainants, at the time of the rape, found themselves in the intricate situation of simultaneously managing their own consternation and fear and their regard for the relationships involved. For this reason, they may try to soothe, humour, or just generally recognize the perpetrator's definition of the situation, both before, during and after the rape. This bounded, or lived, autonomy (cf Bladini & Svedberg Andersson 2020), without empathic translation from a hersense perspective, appears incomprehensible to legal logics. Some judges indeed expressed frustration about the lack of empathic translation from prosecutors.

While empathic translation requires the prosecutor's empathic insight in the action rationality of the complainant already in the preliminary investigation, it might also draw on own experience and gendered common sense but must be based on statements explicitly made by the complainant. An eloquent complainant with the capacity to tell the story 'spontaneously' and with appropriate emotional expressions is helpful, but the prosecutor's feeling of knowing and collaboration with the victim counsel is more important. Equipped with a shared understanding of how the event unfolded and why the complainant acted as they did, it is easier for the prosecutor to determine the adequate temporal boundaries (of the situation as a whole), and place empathy hooks in the presentation of evidence, without deviating from the objectivity requirement. Moreover, there is also some space for speculation and empathy negotiation for the prosecutor in the final plea. The importance of the final plea is conventionally downplayed by prosecutors, who argue that the evidence speaks for itself and that their most important part in the trial is the presentation of the evidence. Our findings suggest also that the prosecutors could spend more time on the final plea, not least to repeat the point of the empathic translation. The victim counsel, however, may legitimately engage in empathic negotiation for their client, both by asking leading question when examining the complainant, by placing *Things* against the defendant, and by engaging in vivid empathic negotiation in the final pleas.

Empathic translation and negotiation for the complainant's perspective is all the more important in cases where the complainant is not 'good'. The impression complainants give in court, the way they tell their story, their eloquence and emotional expressions may influence judges' interpretation of their action rationality. It is also easier to empathize with similar others, while more of an effort is required with those who are socially remote (Clark 1997). Together with personal experiences and the collective social identification of the judges, coincidental background emotions of familiarity and recognition or, reversed, background emotions of estrangement and irritation, may emerge in the court hearing. These background emotions either facilitate or complicate empathy with the complainant. In rape cases in which a wise decision hinges on interest, curiosity and understanding of human complexity and interdependency, unacknowledged background emotions have consequences for the outcomes.

As demonstrated in Part III, the defences' strategy is to keep the court's interest firmly fixed on the complainant's action rationality and fragment it to showcase *Things* that emphasize its apparent irrationality. This is done to advance the, in rape cases, always present alternative hypothesis that the sex act was no rape (she lies) or, at least, the action rationality of the complainant was just as impossible to read as a sign of non-voluntariness as it may appear to the court (no intent). Explicitly arguing that the complainant's behaviour before the sex act was 'sexually provocative' or 'seductive' is said to go against the legal norms of contemporary rape trials (Uhnoo et al 2024c). Yet a skilled defence may excel in insinuations and temporal boundary work in the search for interactions between the parties that support a consent defence.

The proposition often advanced by defence lawyers, that the burden of proof is reversed in rape cases, is refuted by judges and prosecutors. However, the defendant's right to remain silent is important to scrutinize when the evidence consists of stories. Missing stories on either side of the case – whether it is the complainant's missing story or the defendant's missing story– inevitably makes the court inclined to lean on the one story presented to determine what has happened. Consequently, based on our sample of cases, we demonstrated that denial or silence from the defendant accords crucial weight to the supporting hard evidence and usually results in conviction. However, it should be noted that prosecutors in these cases refrain from pressing charges unless they believe they have exceptionally strong evidence and are themselves convinced beyond reasonable doubt.

The new law provides the defence with an obvious alternative hypothesis, namely that the complainant participated voluntarily, shifting focus from the defendant's right to remain silent to their *possibility of explanation*, which then takes the form of a consent defence. While this is termed a *burden* of explanation by legal professionals, we argue it may be understood as a possibility of explanation, comparable to the self-defence argument in assault cases, which may justify an otherwise illegal act. This becomes particularly evident in light of the frequent use of the so-called *Balcony Case* model (see later).

In the consent defence, the lawyers engage in empathic negotiation for the defendant's (innocent) action rationality, often vividly so by drawing on hissense. It reveals the fine line between the acceptable and the unacceptable in terms of positioning the complainant's action rationality as both irrational (with regards to non-voluntariness) and intentionally seductive (from the point of view of the defendant's action rationality). Noteworthy in most consent defences is, within the temporal boundaries asserted by the defence, the description of the complainants as intimate and emotional, active, alert and aware, taking different sorts of initiatives. Faced with these 'signs' of voluntariness, the defendants are rendered kind and passive, but ready to respond as presumably expected by any 'rational' observer. If the action rationality of the defendant was scrutinized on a par with the complainant, a stunningly tragicomic image appears, revealing male sexuality as a 'rationally' unstoppable force once it has been set off in a predictable direction by means of the complainant's active 'invitations' (implicit consent).

Part IV, 'Rationality and Autonomy in Legal Decision-Making', dwells on judges' evaluation of the evidence and writing of the sentences. We demonstrate the unpredictability of the verdicts, given the free evaluation of evidence. While the feeling of not knowing is an inherent and important tool of the certainty/doubt spiral as a means for judges to remain objective until all the evidence is presented and properly treated, our analysis suggests that the feeling of not knowing lingers in rape cases because it includes not knowing how to evaluate the evidence.

In 12 judgments, the court used the method presented in the Supreme Court assessment of the *Balcony Case* to structure the evidence. Beginning with the evidence presented by the prosecutor, and if finding the evidence robust enough to prove that a rape has taken place, the court continues to the evidence presented by the defendant. If they do not find the evidence proven beyond reasonable doubt, they may acquit without assessing the defendant's story. The defendant is nevertheless allowed to tell their story in the trial. Moreover, the defendant is present in the trial both in the DC and, usually contrary to the complainant, in the AC. This means the *Balcony Case* model presupposes that the judges can disregard both the impression made and the story told by the defendant when, at the deliberations after the trial, they begin by assessing the robustness of the prosecution's evidence.

From the point of view of our argument in this book regarding the import of background emotions when arriving at a feeling of knowing, it is unlikely that the impression of the defendant would not influence the assessment, when using the *Balcony Case* model, if some doubt about the complainant's story remains when it comes to hearing the defendant. On the other hand, the reverse can be said if certainty about the defendant's guilt is reached when evaluating the evidence of the prosecution. In the 12 judgments in which the *Balcony Case* model was used, ten led to convictions. In contrast, acquittals were the majority when other ways to structure the judgment and its evaluation of evidence were used. This suggests that some of the critique regarding confirmation bias (see Agnafors 2019/2020; Lidén 2018) when using the model is motivated. From an emotion-sociological perspective, the feeling of certainty (guilt or doubt) derives from comfort in sense. To venture out in uncertainty, as in staying open to the possibility that the assessment of the defendant's story may change the certainty arrived at by evaluating the complainant's story and the supporting evidence, is thus associated with background reluctance against undoing certainty (Bladini 2019; see also Bergman Blix and Minissale 2022; Törnqvist and Wettergren 2023).

Faced with the pervasive feeling of not knowing, the guidelines from the Supreme Court are often referenced in judgments, serving the function of an objectivity handrail to transport the common sense and everyday life experiences informing the feeling of knowing, into 'objective' legal reasoning.

Changing society, changing legal institutions

We argued earlier that the theory of autopoietic systems helps conceptualize the mechanisms of the legal system's self-referentiality and resistance to change but understates the force of changed norms introduced through the making of new laws. Granted that autopoietic systems evolve through variations (Teubner 1993), which may occur in multiple ways, it is noteworthy that in our empirical analysis they are seen in the active or passive sometimes highly reflexive adaptation of legal professional roles to the new rape law.

As laid out in Chapter 3, the emotive-cognitive judicial frame is a tacit set of norms, habituated along with work-life experience as 'the evident' way of performing, for instance, the prosecutor's role (Wettergren and Bergman Blix 2021). As a collectively *felt* frame defining professional conduct, it is co-producing of the professional common sense we call legal logics. The frame is understood and learnt through practice, by imitating senior colleagues, and by feeling the (shame of) transgressing the norms. This also means it is versatile, interactionally negotiated, and open to situated variations. Change, however, occurs when a sufficient number of colleagues pick up on, for instance, new ways of performing the professional role, arguably because it is sensed as a better way in relation to specific legal goals.

We have seen that some of the most promising role adaptations in the implementation of the new rape law are based on shifting from a hissense perspective to a hersense perspective. The examples we have seen can be discussed in terms of just how they advance the legal doing of rationality, autonomy and objectivity. The example of the judge (Case 9) who adopted hersense reasoning (normally functioning men can tell the difference between voluntary and non-voluntary participation) as a ground for conviction is arguably indicative of a privileged (hersense) perspective. Other examples, like the victim counsel in Case 11 drawing on female fear, cut across social categories. The corresponding hissense is the much more common drawing on male fear, which, in some of our cases, outweigh the potential negative stereotyping of the defendant's social identity markers. Hersense, as we have argued, is in line with the intention of the rape law *and* blends with legal logics, which makes it a variation prone to introduce change if enough legal professionals adopt it.

Here it may be objected that what is at stake is a feminist worldview replacing a patriarchal one as 'the neutral' perspective. Against this can be argued, first, that patriarchy is not just a worldview but a social emotive-cognitive structure lingering in autopoietic institutions, such as the law. It will not disappear easily, Second, feminism does not strive for 'matriarchy' (whatever that means) but drives analysis, critique and deconstruction of patriarchy, thus opening up the possibility of diversity, reflexivity and accountability.

If the law is taken seriously for what it is, an attempt to get rid of the patriarchal perspective as the *only* and the *neutral* way to define the core legal values and legal logics, the aim is not to simply reverse the power balance between men and women, but to obtain fair and equal treatment of the parties in rape cases, regardless of gender and other identity markers. If nothing else, it will improve procedural justice. Without changing the fact that the prosecution has the full burden of proof, when the procedure in rape trials is allowed to involve routine humiliation of the complainant, fair and equal treatment demands similar treatment of the defendant. This is, after all, the idea of the adversarial trial procedure. This includes inquiring into the (personal) motives of the defendant for not securing consent – or for lying about consent – for as long as inquiring into the (personal) motives of the complainant for lying about rape prevails in legal practice.

Put differently, if the credibility deficit is argued by legal professionals to be reasonable because of the complex nature of intimate and sexual relations, routine distrust should be ascribed equally to both parties and their stories should be equally scrutinized. While the defendant is allowed to lie, the lie should be considered in the overall assessment (Part IV).

Given that hissense emanates from the patriarchal structure of the law and is thus part of the emotive-cognitive judicial frame informing the conduct of both female and male legal professionals, both sexes are likely to adopt hissensical reasoning, which, we have seen, is also the dominant pattern in our study (see also Dixon 2010). In Sweden, the professions of both judge and prosecutor are gender-equal – at least 40 per cent of judges and almost 60 per cent of prosecutors are women. When women are introduced in a male-dominated profession, the first thing they need to do is to prove that being a woman does not disqualify them. This makes them rather prone to emphasize the given emotive-cognitive professional frame (cf Tracy and Tretheway 2005). In judging, this may in fact lead them to over-compensate for any potentially positive bias (for example, Bergman Blix and Wettergren 2018:140). Our point with hersensical legal logics instead resonates with Hessler (2021) arguing that 'feminist judging' (by women *and* men) is normatively legitimate and consistent with unbiased judging, and that 'calling for judges to be feminist, especially in their judging of cases involving issues of gender justice, is calling for judges to examine the contextual values they inevitably bring to the bench, and to ensure that those values enable them to be appropriately responsive to women's rights and interests' (Hessler 2021:468) As should be clear from our argumentation, hersensical reasoning cannot be made 'a policy', or a checklist, to be applied to the stories of female complainants to understand their action rationality in situations of sexual abuse. Empathic imagination can never be reduced to a readymade template but will require the time and effort of listening, inquiring, imagining and feeling, in each and every individual case.

We have highlighted the workings of background emotions, common sense, and personal experience as sources of the feeling of knowing in the rape cases investigated in this book, and how such sources (notably hersense) can actually facilitate the implementation of the law. Our main point is that *emotions, common sense and personal experience always need to be rendered transparent by submitting them to conscious and critical reflection.* We see how this is done in the research interview situation, in which we prompt participants to do it. However, the emotive-cognitive judicial frame includes, as one of its retaining functions, that it may be controversial to reflect openly on these sources of knowing with colleagues. Given the habitual separation of emotion and reason in law, it is always involved with the risk of 'disclosing' lack of professionalism (Bergman Blix and Wettergren 2018).

Implications for practice: reflexive adaptation of professional legal roles

In Chapter 4 we argued that systematic witness injustice is based on negative prejudiced stereotypes held by the group of legal professionals exerting identitarian power (Fricker 2007). If we think of the legal system as a remnant of a patriarchal power order, it is easy to see how such epistemic injustice makes women and their narratives less credible than those of men. This explains why women's stories about rape suffer from a credibility deficit (she lies) from the report to the trial. Interestingly, the relatively harsh Swedish rape legislation originates in a society characterized by a general, widely accepted, critique of patriarchy, and by numerous political policy initiatives targeting gender equality. That the law remains a patriarchal institution in this context is arguably due to its autonomy being highly valued in democratic society.

Therefore, we argue, when a law aims at a general shift in societal norms, professional training is required. For the implementation of the 2018 rape law to be legally sound and avoid risking the protection of the defendant's rights, as well as the right to fairness and integrity of the complainant, there must be a shared understanding of the law's intentions and how to implement them, across the legal professions. Training is also necessary to reflect on the meaning of the core judicial values, making them guiding lights, not obstacles, to change.

We have argued that autonomy in rape cases must be understood as bounded by situated micro-relations of power and status and that action rationality must be understood as gendered when it comes to gendered crimes (Part III). We have also argued that the routine doing of objectivity and the rule of law unjustly privileges the defendant's perspective in rape cases, because these cases are primarily based on stories as evidence. To address these problems, and drawing on the findings in our analysis, we want to end by suggesting several adaptations to the professional roles that could be made to better the legal practice in rape cases. An overview of these adaptations are represented in Figure 2.

The prosecutor – enhanced empathic imagination

We observed in Chapters 5 and 6 that prosecutors' professional emotional profile when they act in the adversarial trial in court is two-dimensional: they should display confidence and certainty as a party *and* remain aware of their objectivity requirement. In the former lies knowing that the preliminary investigation reached the conclusion of the defendant's guilt and in the latter taking seriously new evidence concerning the defendant's innocence that might emerge during the hearing. The conventional way of dealing

Figure 2: Adapted professional roles

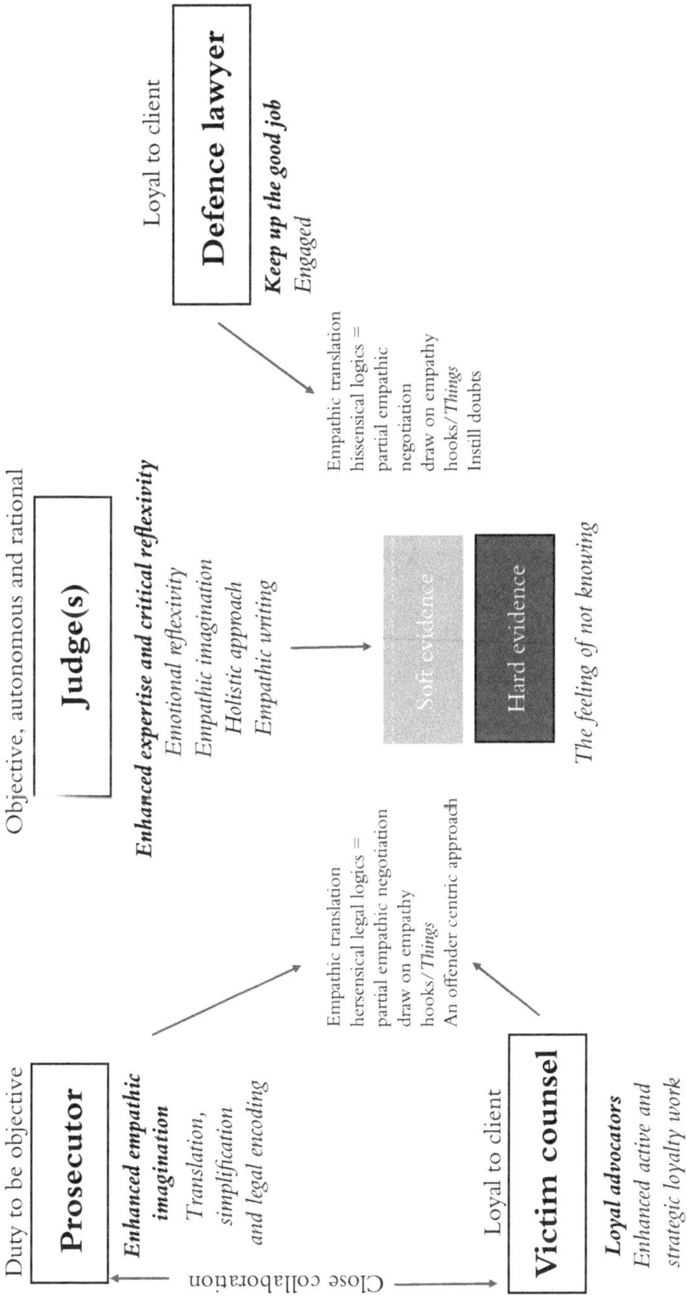

with this somewhat schizophrenic task of reconciling dual roles is to give priority to the role as party but remain ready to summon the objective representative within. To convince both judges and the defence about their certainty, a common strategy is to highlight the potential uncertainties in the evidence and then demonstrate why these have low significance compared to the rest of the evidence. We question this strategy in rape cases for the following reasons.

Firstly, in rape cases prosecutors must realize that judges are no more experts on rape than they are – rather the opposite. Prosecutors are allowed to specialize on types of offences, judges are not. In all cases, the judge is much further removed from fuzzy real life than any other legal actor. The judge depends on the prosecution's translation, simplification and legal encoding, of real events to apply their legal expertise in deliberation and decision-making. Consequently, if prosecutors trust the evidence to 'speak for itself' to the judge's rational mind, it is because they have a done a good job translating the evidence. In rape cases, there is already resistance from the court (the irritation of not knowing what to make of stories) that poses extra challenge for prosecutors. They have no reason at all to trust judges' legal expertise, nor that the evidence speaks for itself, in such cases.

Secondly, stories are 'subjective' in the sense that they narrate an event from a particular perspective. The interpretation of the story as an intersubjectively valid source of information of what (really) happened must be conveyed to the court. Prosecutors attempt to do so with the help of supportive evidence. Since this also consists of stories and the hard evidence is interpreted through the stories, prosecutors cannot escape from the fact that they themselves must be convinced of the truth value of the complainant's story. This in turn requires that prosecutors, in the preliminary investigation engage in *enhancing* their own empathic imagination of the criminal event to the point where they feel that the story makes sense not just to them but to other 'reasonable beings'. Only then can it be convincingly translated in terms of hersensical legal logics, which here means within the boundaries of the new law. In other words, prosecutors must advance the complainant's story as virtually independent of the supporting evidence; as reliable evidence first and foremost in and of itself.

Thirdly, prosecutors' task is then to convey this professional judgment of the story as main evidence by means of empathic translation. The goal can be set to evoke a 'feeling of knowing' in judges, counteracting potential power discomfort and himpathy. Empathic translation involves drawing on empathy hooks and partial empathic negotiation. The latter will remain restricted for prosecutors due to their objectivity requirement – although they could, and we argue they should, engage more in it as part of their final plea. The most effective parts of the empathic negotiation, along with the more aggressive examination of the defendant, can be left to the victim counsel.

As we have seen in our empirical chapter, the role of emotions in legal decision-making gets foregrounded in rape cases. This is not, yet, an effect of increased professional interest in emotional reflexivity or of suddenly granting the information brought by emotion new status as legitimate for decision-making, but of the pressing feeling of not knowing how to deal with stories as evidence. This feeling is encapsulated in the common expression of the 'bad' evidence in rape cases. If instead the evidence is taken seriously, ascribing to it a status as *different* but *equally legitimate* as compared with the evidence in other offences, the problem shifts from the matter of the evidence to finding the right tools to translate it. We believe prosecutors, in collaboration with victim counsels, must pioneer this adaptation to the new law.

Fourthly, prosecutors' strategy to pinpoint weaknesses in the complainant's story is most often counterproductive in rape cases. Prosecutors may here lean on the defence; trust that they will do this for them. Prosecutors should focus on rendering the meaning of the complainant's story, their experiences in and interpretation of the situation, in support of the complainant's privileged access to their own feelings and knowing, This prevents that the prosecution contributes to the defence's construction of *Things*. *Things*, as we have demonstrated, are co-products of the prosecution and the defence, an unintentional consequence of the prosecutor's conventional doing of objectivity. *Things* are furthermore used by judges primarily when they have decided to acquit based on the feeling of not knowing and the need (and comfort) to argue certainty about doubt.

Finally, our results suggest that, as carefully prepared consent defences are increasingly common, the preliminary investigation should strive to secure the defendant's story early in the process The investigation often starts with a focus on, and a thorough investigation of, the complainant's story and its supporting evidence, delaying the arrest of the accused until later. If instead the accused is detained directly after the reported rape, they will not have time to prepare a consent defence and their stories will 'neither be directed by their lawyer nor [will the suspect be] very thoughtful of "what am I saying here"', as prosecutor Johan put it in our study. Similarly, prosecutor Nina (Case 18) argued for video recording the defendants' very first 'spontaneous story' in the police interrogation 'so we can see it in the courtroom, to show not *what* he said but *how* he said it'. These thoughts gain support in recent rape research on suspect/offender-centric policing. Hohl and Stanko (2024) argue that a suspect-focused preliminary investigation will achieve more 'fair and effective rape investigations':

Suspect-focused investigations examine the suspect's offending behaviour as the primary site of interest. They impartially follow relevant and proportionate lines of enquiry to gather evidentiary material that points away or towards the suspect [...]. Practically, this means asking questions about what happened before, during, and after the rape in a manner that centres on the suspect's behaviour, not that of the victim-survivor. (Hohl and Stanko 2024:48)

If such a strategy is implemented, it would counter and probably diminish the credibility deficit attached to the 'she lies' hypothesis at the start of the investigation. It would even out the power asymmetry between the parties in rape cases by putting much more emphasis on the unvarnished story of the defendant. We have argued that a hersensical reasoning of judges in line with the new law is to direct attention to the defendant's responsibility to ensure voluntariness. Through a suspect-focused approach this could be done early in the investigation, 'focusing the attention of investigators on what steps were taken by a suspect to ascertain the complainant's consent' (Rumney and McPhee 2021:425).

The victim counsel – assuming the role as loyal advocators

In rape cases, prosecutors do wisely to invite close collaboration with the victim counsel, and to listen and learn from their experience. Victim counsels' task in rape cases is to step up from the minimal role of carer and formal advocator of damage claims and do the same active and strategic loyalty work as defence lawyers do. Provided that the victim counsel has experience of defence lawyering, which makes them an optimal resource in rape cases, collaboration between the prosecutor and victim counsel can increase the chances of anticipating, navigating and defusing the defence's strategy. As we have demonstrated, the victim counsel can help the prosecutor avoid the unintentional marking of inexplicable elements as *Things* for the defence. The victim counsel taking the role of the complainant's loyal advocator in the examinations of the defendant will also contribute to a more defendant-focused court procedure, alleviating some of the presently disproportionate weight and time put on examining the complainant's story. It might result in a trial in which the complainant and defendant, for good and for bad, truly receive equal treatment in the adversarial procedure.

The victim counsel and prosecutor should work closely in the preliminary investigation with the goal to reach an intersubjective empathic understanding of the complainant's story, a shared feeling of knowing their action rationality, and plan together how to convey it to the judges by means of temporal boundary work and empathy hooks, and by identifying *Things* against the defendant's story. While both the prosecutor and the victim counsel can adopt hersensical legal logics in the investigation, the victim counsel's task is to take this empathic translation of the evidence further into loyalty with the complainant's story – pressing it as the true story – in court, posing leading questions to help less eloquent complainants, and examining the defendant's story as strategically and thoroughly as the defence does with the complainant. Finally, but not least, the victim counsel's task is to maximize empathic negotiation in the final plea, facilitating judges' imagination of the situation as a whole and the character of the situated micro-politics of emotions in the interaction between the defendant and the complainant. The complainant's action rationality should be made to make perfect (her) sense. Lawyers in their role as loyal legal actors typically have insights in, and frequently draw on, stereotypes and common sense, and try to play on judge's background emotions of power discomfort, antipathy and sympathy. Victim counsels can use these insights to articulate and thus pre-empt common rape myths that might otherwise be put to work based on the impression made by the complainant in court.

An additional and very important argument in this context is the vital importance, when cases are appealed, of the victim counsel's presence and final plea in the AC. The reasons for this are the same as in the DC; final pleas facilitate the empathic imagination of the judges and pleading in vivo is necessary to attract and monitor the judges' attention and interest. As we have seen, prosecutors, while they do not need the victim counsel to repeat the damage claims, cannot and do not take the place of the missing victim counsel in the AC pleading. Finally, given the surreptitious effect of impressions in the courtroom, we also argue that the complainant should be encouraged by their victim counsel to be present in the AC (as in, for example, Norway). That judges see the complainant on screen from the video-recorded DC trial is not the same as if they saw and sensed their physical presence 'in flesh and blood' (Carline et al 2021), like they do with the defendant. While sparing the complainant from the trial in the AC might be sensible in other criminal cases, in rape cases this procedure instead risks resulting in herasure (Manne 2018).

The defence lawyer – keep up the good work

In our empirical analysis we have had the opportunity to observe many engaged and skilled defence lawyers, revealing how they think about the new law, their concerns about it and their defence strategies. As also observed, many lawyers alternate between the role as victim counsel and defence lawyer in rape cases. One of their concerns with the new law is that it reinforces the focus on the complainant's behaviour before, during, and after the event rather than the opposite. We argue that this is by no means a consequence of the new rape law but of the way it is implemented. Particularly, this is an effect of the conventional doing of loyalty of defence lawyers, who try to deflect the focus from their client to the complainant, and from the sex act itself to unrelated, often irrelevant aspects. They do this to 'pour sand into every moving part', as prosecutor Barbro (Case 15) expressed it. They are well motivated to do it in rape cases, as this may result in a *Thing* decisive for acquittal. The strategy is facilitated in consent defences if the prosecution does not understand the salience of *Things* and has no plan to balance and counter them. In other words, the concern with the 'increased focus on the complainant's story', as it were, may be revealing of background guilt and shame among lawyers because they find the strategy to rip the complainant's story into pieces relatively successful and therefore often also use it.

It should be noted that this is a strategy adopted by both male and female skilled defence lawyers, illustrative of the hissensical legal logics of their emotive-cognitive professional profile. It should also be noted that the defence lawyers are wary of not crossing the line between the acceptable and unacceptable when adopting this strategy. By means of the self-reinforcing logic of their legal professional role, however, if the strategy is successful, it will prevail and expand and continue to push the limits.

We would like to call defence lawyers' attention to this development and the need to critically reflect on whether this is something they desire. They might also want to step back and look at how they risk cementing stereotypical views on male sexuality. Often, male sexual action rationality is depicted in the defence's argument as governed by what we may call 'a penis privilege' that frees the defendant from any responsibility for failing to empathically attune with the complainant's perspective. It is arguably not helpful for the advancement of gender equality, nor for the implementation of the new law, which almost all defence lawyers say they basically agree with, to reproduce their clients' view of male sexuality this way. That said, if the problematic aspects and inherent reproduction of stereotyped male sexuality in rape cases became emphasized by a more defendant-focused court procedure – through the optimization of the victim counsel's role suggested earlier – it would arguably contribute to defence lawyers' enhanced reflexivity on their own role and its consequences.

We note that many defence lawyers believe they are engaged in a heroic defence of a client whose chances are bleak, because the 'rapist stigma' is likely to stick to them merely by their being accused of rape. In line with this, defence lawyers in our study believe they are engaged in an uphill struggle because the court's sympathies are always initially on the side of the complainant, and thus the new law reverses the burden of proof (Uhnoo et al 2024c). As we have demonstrated throughout this book, there are very weak grounds for these beliefs. On the contrary, the complainant is the one submitted to systematic epistemic injustice, beginning with the taken-for-granted assumption that they might lie about rape. The defendant is gifted the possibility of explanation (consent defence), and enjoys the protection of the rule of law, especially if they are previously unpunished, white and middle class, with a 'ruinable future'. In these cases, they benefit from the himpathy and power discomfort of judges.

Although lawyers are not bound by the objectivity requirement, they ought to see their role in the collective achievement of doing objectivity and thus in safeguarding the legitimacy of the legal system. They are also responsible for reproducing respect for the law, in the eyes of their clients, the complainants and the public. We would encourage defence lawyers to be less convinced and, above all, less sentimental about the injustice done to their clients when they are accused of rape, and instead consider how they can defend their clients in a dignified way, without pushing the button of himpathy and without producing herasure.

A final note on the adaptation of the role of defence lawyers is that they need to develop their strategies when working with clients who are more prone to get convicted in rape cases, namely minority groups, foreigners and men of low socio-economic status. It may not be as easy or as fun to work with these clients as it is with similar others, but if there is a risk that people get innocently sentenced for rape the risk is arguably higher for these groups. We have not elaborated on this dimension in our analysis, but we have seen tendencies that we think are worth investigating in future research (cf Bitsch and Klemetsen 2017; Lovett and Kelly 2009).

It is interesting to note that, in some of our observed rape cases, some very skilled defence lawyers seem to take an active and engaged interest in this type of offence, while intimate partner violence and similar crimes would otherwise have relatively low status for them. This may be because in rape cases their habituated strategies to affect the court, drawing on background emotions, pay off more often than in criminal cases where the evidence is not considered as 'bad'. In other words, defence lawyers can here take pride in 'winning' cases.

The judge – enhanced expertise and critical reflexivity

We end this discussion of the different roles with the judge, simply because, in legal practice, judges are on top of the hierarchy. The presiding judge rules in court and should do so; but as the passive arbiter in the adversarial trial they also rely on all the matters of relevance to the case being presented in court. Matters that must be legally encoded and presented in a way that renders it significant as evidence. Therefore, the role adaptations discussed above, particularly those of the prosecution (including both the prosecutor and the victim counsel) would, as indicated in our study, be very helpful for judges' deliberation in rape cases. This presumes that judges allow the adaptations, as these can challenge their conventional way of proceeding in significant ways.

Judges already accept their dependence on the prosecutor as these have 'the full burden of proof'. Their failure to prove the case is thus a default excuse for acquitting. Judges are *not* used to seeing the victim counsel taking an active adversarial role, and they may react nervously on the prosecutor's empathic translation. They may feel that norms of the emotive-cognitive judicial frame are breached. In previous research (for example, Bergman Blix and Wettergren 2018; Wettergren and Bergman Blix 2016) we demonstrated that judges generally dislike the use of empathy hooks, for instance when prosecutors project photos of a murdered victim when still alive, or child pornography videos. In the present study, perhaps significant for rape case types of evidence, we have not come across any complaints from judges regarding this. On the contrary, we have seen that some judges find empathy hooks elucidating and even expect the prosecutors to do empathic translation. We have, however, also seen that judges may interrupt the prosecutor, ban what they consider irrelevant evidence, or interfere with the prosecution's examinations. They may also downright refuse the idea that rape case evidence requires a different approach than other criminal cases. If judges care about the intentions of the new law and want to move ahead from the pervasive feeling of not knowing, this is not the right way. Besides destroying the prosecution's planned course of trial and ruining their own chances of learning about the case, they risk appearing biased to the legal subjects in court. Thereby they fail to do objectivity and justice as 'seen to be done', which is one of their key functions in the courtroom.

Regarding the evaluation of the evidence, we argue that judges need training in critical theory of science. Through this they would gain insight into the relational and embodied character of knowledge and, not least, in the embodied and situated doing of objectivity, rationality and autonomy. It would open up the possibility to insights about the entwined emotional *and* cognitive character of rational action, advancing their ability to engage in critical emotional reflexivity. Further, training in social scientific qualitative methods might contribute to raise the status of the evidence provided in rape cases. Hands-on training in the craft of analysing and interpreting qualitative data, notably hermeneutic analysis, would enable judges to evaluate soft evidence in terms of parts (details in the story) and wholes (context or the situation as a whole). Equipped this way, they could feel confident to test different variants of evaluating soft evidence, taking into account the intentions of the new law and without being afraid of betraying core legal values.

Besides this, we argue that judges, instead of protecting the idea that legal autonomy and objectivity equals lack of insights in 'real life' behind the legally encoded offence, would be better served by knowing as much as possible. Some judges argue for more use of expert witnesses (for instance regarding freezing, fright and trauma in rape cases), but to understand an expert also requires knowledge. In Sweden judges are not allowed to specialize in different crimes, but we believe it would be a good idea to allow judges to specialize in particular offences (for example, sexual crimes, domestic violence, white-collar crime). The specialized prosecutors would appreciate specialized judges, as it would relieve them from some of the strenuous and time-consuming translation and explanation work.

In the absence of such training, judges must respect the knowledge of prosecutors and allow the space they need to explain the evidence, as with empathic translation in rape cases. It is not per se controversial that different types of criminal evidence, pertaining to different types of crime, require different translation techniques.

In rape cases, judges' apprehension of the rule of law must be expanded from priority concern for the defendants' rights to include concern for the protection of the complainant's integrity, with the aim to achieve a balance between these to create a process experienced by both as impartial and fair. This includes giving space for enhancing the prosecution's adversarial component through the victim counsel's enhanced role. Just as the defendants' perception of a fair trial targets their acceptance of a conviction, the complainant's perception of a fair trial targets their perception of receiving redress despite an acquittal. It is noteworthy that judges try to achieve the latter by empathic writing in acquitting judgments, when stating that the court does not question the complainant's experience, but the prosecutor's proof does not reach the standard 'beyond reasonable doubt' (Part IV). In contrast, they seem to overlook empathy with the complainant's perception of the trial process.

Finally, judges must recognize that emotions cannot and should not be silenced in rape cases. Common sense and personal experience are routinely drawn on in the evaluations, and background emotions of power discomfort and himpathy are skilfully used by defence lawyers. The need for empathic imagination to understand the legal subject's action rationality is partly recognized by judges. This all highlights that emotions must be recognized for how they inform evaluation in rape cases. This can be done, for instance, by reference to the legal concept of 'notorious facts', and 'individual and collective experience in aid of the interpretation of the evidence' (Chapter 2), through which emotional information and common sense can be rendered transparent and submitted to intersubjective scrutiny. The process might reflect the one in social science, where analysis, interpretation and conclusions are routinely discussed and criticized in seminars and peer reviews.

Lay judges could also be used for the purpose of judges' emotional reflexivity. The reason for having a system with lay judges is arguably to counter autopoietic closure. In this capacity they could be involved in workshops scrutinizing the legal evaluations. More directly, professional judges could use discussion with lay judges in the deliberations to gain knowledge of popular rape myths and stereotypes inherent in different common senses, and this way get a view of their own backgrounded emotional information.

The recommendations for judges laid out here would considerably decrease their vulnerability to objectivity rule reminders and benefit their sense of judicial autonomy in rape cases. We recall that the rule reminder strategy of the defence addresses judges' power discomfort and feeling of not knowing. Its effectiveness relies on, and serves to retain, hissense legal logics and its marking of rape case evidence as 'bad'. Our recommendations, opening up the possibility of a more versatile apprehension of the legal core values, would enable different types of evidence to be properly assessed without compromising the rule of law and the legitimacy of the legal system in contemporary democratic societies.

Conclusion

In this final chapter we have discussed the legal system in terms of a slow-changing autopoietic system. Autopoiesis, as a kind of autonomy, arguable functions as both protective of core judicial values and an obstacle to their evolving in line with societal values of diversity, inclusion, equality and justice. We argue that the new rape law is transformative of the legal system due to its introduction of hersense to legal logics. It destabilizes the dominance of hissensical legal logics in practice, rooted in the patriarchal perspective structurally embedded in the legal system.

We used the theory of the autopoietic system to explain how the legal system changes, arguing that change is introduced through social influence both from the top (in the form of the law) and from the bottom (in the form of adaptations to the law). Legal professionals interpret and understand the law differently resulting in various and contradictory ways of implementing it. That the law poses challenges to habituated ways of doing objectivity, rationality and autonomy in practice, is seen in the way it evokes irritation and uncertainty and sometimes curiosity and creativity. This gives rise to the variations we call role adaptations, which may bring about long-term and potentially substantial change if they spread and become part of a new legal practice of rape cases – especially as these adaptations, along with hersense, are legitimized by the new law.

The chapter has summarized and discussed the result of our study in the light of this, and we ended with a thorough description of how the different legal roles can disseminate the promising adaptations we have seen in our study. We also suggested a few more adaptations, especially for presiding judges and defence lawyers, to accomplish a fair trial in both the DC and the AC. Of vital importance for a successful path towards a more fair and just procedure is, we argue, that the evidence is respected for what it is, namely soft evidence, and that methods are developed to translate, negotiate and evaluate the meaning of such evidence. In essence, the changes suggested address the default separation of emotion and reason, still strong in the legal system. The emotive-cognitive nature of all human reason and action is arguably not just a new way of thinking for legal professionals but also for professionals in other social institutions. In the legal system, rape cases highlight the impossibility of this separation, due to the nature of the evidence and the necessity to engage with it, which consequently engages the legal professionals' lived experience and common sense.

Based on our findings, we have discussed the adaptations that introduce variation in the legal system's doing, in practice, of the core judicial values. We choose to see these as promising signs of continued change of the legal system, making it better adapted to contemporary society. Having core legal values as ideals to strive for is central to the democratic rule of law. Understanding these values as versatile and open to interpretation can also prevent them from being used as allegedly neutral instruments of governments taking an authoritarian turn. Increased critical insight and emotional reflexivity, we argue, will make the legal system better equipped to protect liberal values.

References

Adler Z (2022) *Rape on trial*, Routledge, London.

Agnafors M (2019/2020) 'Bevisprövningsmetoden i Balkongmålet – en kritik', *Juridisk Tidskrift*:358–373.

Ahmed S (2004) *The cultural politics of emotion*, Edinburgh University Press, Edinburgh.

Alvesson M and Sköldberg K (2009) *Reflexive methodology: New vistas for qualitative research*, Sage, London.

Anderberg A, Martinsson D and Svensson E (2022) *Teori och politik. Straffrätt I omvandling*. Iustus förlag, Stockholm.

Andersson U (2004) *Hans (ord) eller hennes*, Bokbox Förlag, Malmö.

Andersson U (2011) 'Våld mot kvinnor och straffrätt', in Svensson, E-M (ed) *På vei: Kjønn og rett i Norden*, Makadam Förlag, Malmö.

Andersson U, Edgren M, Karlsson L and Nilsson G (eds) (2019) *Rape narratives in motion*, Palgrave Macmillan, Basingstoke.

Antonsdottir F (2020) *Decentring criminal law: understandings of justice by victim-survivors of sexual violence and their implications of different justice strategies*, Lund University, Lund.

Antonsdóttir HF and Laugerud S (2024) 'The Norwegian victim lawyer in a Nordic Context: Professional boundaries, legal hierarchies and purification processes, *International Criminology*, 4(1):79–92.

Anwar S, Bayer P and Hjalmarsson R (2015) *Politics in the courtroom: Political ideology and jury decision making*, University of Gothenburg, Gothenburg, http://hdl.handle.net/2077/38863.

Åquist A-C (2001) *Den motsägelsefulla staden*, Studentlitteratur, Malmö.

Arango-Muñoz S (2014) 'The nature of epistemic feelings', *Philosophical Psychology*, 27(2):193–211.

Ask K and Granhag PA (2007) 'Hot cognition in investigative judgments: The differential influence of anger and sadness', *Law and Human Behavior*, 31(6):537–551.

Ask K and Landström S (2010) 'Why emotions matter: expectancy violation and affective response mediate the emotional victim effect', *Law and Human Behavior*, 34(5):392–401.

Ask K and Pina A (2011) 'On being angry and punitive: How anger alters perception of criminal intent', *Social Psychological and Personality Science*, 2(5):494–499.

Asp P, Ulväng M and Jareborg N (2013) *Svensk straffrätt*, Iustus Förlag, Uppsala.

Asplund J (2022) *Människan som samhällsvarelse: tid, rum, individ och kollektiv*, Arkiv Förlag, Lund.

Bandes SA (2006) 'Loyalty to one's convictions: the prosecutor and tunnel vision', *Howard Law Journal*, 49(2):475–494.

Bandes SA (2009) 'Empathetic judging and the rule of law', *Cardozo Law Review*, 133–148.

Barbalet J (1998) *Emotion, social theory, and social structure – a macrosociological approach*, Cambridge University Press, Cambridge.

Barbalet J (2011) 'Emotions beyond regulation: Backgrounded emotions in science and trust', *Emotion Review*, 3(1):36–43.

Berglund K (2013) 'Samtycke eller ej?', in Nordlöf K (ed) *Argumentation i nordisk straffrätt*, Nordstedts juridik, Stockholm.

Bergman Blix S (2019) 'Different roads to empathy: stage actors and judges as polar cases', *Emotions & Society*, 1(2):163–180.

Bergman Blix S (2022) 'Making independent decisions together: rational emotions in legal adjudication', *Symbolic Interaction*, 45(1):50–71.

Bergman Blix S and Minissale A (2022) '(Dis)passionate law stories: the emotional processes of encoding narratives in court', *Journal of Law and Society*, 49:245–262.

Bergman Blix S and Wettergren Å (2016) 'A sociological perspective on emotions in the judiciary', *Emotion Review*, 8(1):32–37.

Bergman Blix S and Wettergren Å (2018) *Professional emotions in court: A sociological perspective*, Routledge, London.

Bergman Blix S and Wettergren, Å (2019) 'The emotional interaction of judicial objectivity', *Oñati Socio-Legal Series*, 9(5):726–746.

Bergman Blix S and Wettergren Å (2024) 'Integrating rationality and emotion in legal institutions', in Flam H (ed) *Research handbook on the sociology of emotion, institutions and emotional rule regimes*, Edward Elgar, Cheltenham.

Bitsch A (2018) 'The micro-politics of emotions in legal space: an autoethnography about sexual violence and displacement in Norway', *Gender, Place & Culture*, 25(10):1514–1532.

Bitsch A (2019) 'The geography of rape: Shaming narratives in Norwegian rape cases', *Signs*, 44(4).

Bitsch A and Klemetsen ME (2017) 'The legal grading of sexual citizenship: Sentencing practices in Norwegian rape cases', *Gender, Place & Culture*, 24(2):174–188.

Björling E (2017) 'Rättstillämpningens tystnad. En rättsvetenskaplig narratologisk studie om argumentation och rättsliga uttryck inom civilprocessen' (Doctoral dissertation, Gothenburg University).

Bladini M (2013) *I objektivitetens sken: en kritisk granskning av objektivitetsideal, objektivitetsanspråk och legitimeringsstrategier i diskurser om dömande i brottmål* [*In the semblance of objectivity – a critical review of objectivity claims and legitimation strategies in criminal trial discourses*], Makadam Förlag, Göteborg.

Bladini M (2019) 'Om emotioners vara eller icke vara – ett exempel från processrätten', *Juridisk Publication*, 2:489–509.

Bladini M and Svedberg Andersson WS (2020) 'Swedish rape legislation from use of force to voluntariness – critical reflections from an everyday life perspective', *Bergen Journal of Criminal Law & Criminal Justice*, 8(2):95–125.

Bladini M and Bergman Blix S (2022) 'The judge under pressure. fostering objectivity by leaving the myth of dispassion', in Giannoupoulos D and McDermott Rees Y (eds) 'Challenges to judicial independence in times of crisis', in *Proceedings of the British Academy* volume on *Judicial Independence*.

Bladini M, Uhnoo S and Wettergren Å (2023) '"It sounds like lived experience" – on empathy in rape trials', *International Journal of Law, Crime and Justice*, 72:100575.

Bolding P-O (1989) *Går det att bevisa? Perspektiv på domstolsprocessen*, Norstedt, Stockholm.

Booth T (2012) ' "Cooling out" victims of crime: Managing victim participation in the sentencing process in a superior sentencing court', *Australian & New Zealand Journal of Criminology*, 45(2):214–230.

Bosma A (2019) *Emotive justice: laypersons' and legal professionals' evaluations of victims within the just world paradigm*, Wolf Legal Publishers, Tilburg.

Boyle K (2019) 'What's in a name? Theorizing the inter-relationships of gender and violence', *Feminist Theory*, 20(1):19–36.

Brienen MEI and Hoegen EH (2000) *Victims of crime in 22 European criminal justice systems*, WPL, Nijmegen.

Brooks O and Burman M (2017) 'Reporting rape: Victim perspectives on advocacy support in the criminal justice process', *Criminology & Criminal Justice*, 17(2):209–225.

Brå (2019) 'Våldtäkt från anmälan till dom. En studie av rättsväsendets arbete med våldtäktsärenden', https://bra.se/publikationer/arkiv/publik ationer/2019-05-27-valdtakt-fran-anmalan-till-dom.html [Accessed 30 March 2023].

Brå (2020) 'The new consent law in practice: an updated review of the changes in 2018 to the legal rules concerning rape', https://bra.se/bra-in-english/home/publications/archive/publications/2020-07-01-the-new-consent-law-in-practice.html [Accessed 30 March 2023].

Burkitt I (2012) 'Emotional reflexivity: Feeling, emotion and imagination in reflexive dialogues', *Sociology*, 46(3):458–472.

Burman M (2007) *Straffrätt och mäns våld mot kvinnor: om straffrättens förmåga att producera jämställdhe*, IUSTUS Förlag, Uppsala.

Burman M (2009) 'Evidencing sexual assault: Women in the witness box', *Probation Journal*, 56(4):379–398.

Burman M (2010) *Rethinking rape law in Sweden: Coercion, consent or non-voluntariness?*, Routledge, London.

Burt MR (1980) 'Cultural myths and supports for rape', *Journal of Personality and Social Psychology*, 38(2):217.

Cahill AJ (2001) *Rethinking rape*, Cornell University Press, Ithica.

Carline A, Gunby C and Murray J (2021) '"And that's why street-wise complainants now always give evidence behind screens, live": exploring the intensive affects of the courtroom', in *Courthouse Architecture, Design and Social Justice*, Routledge, London.

Carroll CP (2021) 'The "lottery" of rape reporting: secondary victimization and Swedish criminal justice professionals', *Nordic Journal of Criminology*, 22(1):22–41.

Carroll CP (2022) 'Accessing rights and mitigating revictimization: The role of the victim's legal counsel in the Swedish criminal justice system', *Violence Against Women*, 28(1):255–276.

Christie N (1986) 'The ideal victim', in Fattah EA (ed) *From crime policy to victim policy: Reorienting the justice system*, Palgrave Macmillan, London.

Clark C (1990) 'Emotions and micropolitics in everyday life: Some patterns and paradoxes of "place"', in Kemper TD (ed) *Research agendas in the sociology of emotions*, State University of New York Press, New York.

Clark C (1997) *Misery and company: Sympathy in everyday life*, University of Chicago Press, Chicago.

Cuff BM, Brown SJ and Taylor L (2016) 'Empathy: A review of the concept', *Emotion Review*, 144–153.

Czarniawska B (2007) *Shadowing and other techniques for doing fieldwork in modern societies*, Liber, Malmö.

Dahlman C (2018) *Beviskraft: metod för bevisvärdering i brottmål*, Norstedts Juridik, Stockholm.

Dahlman C (2024) '"Balkongmålet" erbjuder ingen bevisvärderingsmetod', *Dagens Juridik*, https://www.dagensjuridik.se/nyheter/christian-dahlman-balkongmalet-erbjuder-ingen-bevisvarderingsmetod/ [Accessed 1 November 2024].

Dahlman C and Korths Aspegren A (2018) Varför är bevisning som uppfyller beviskravet i våldtäktsmål inte tillräcklig i mål om olaga hot? *Svensk juristtidning*:327–342.

Daly E (2022) *Rape, gender and class: Intersections in courtroom narratives*, Springer Nature, London.

Damasio A (1994) *Descartes' error, emotion, reason and the human brain*, Avon Books, New York.

Darbyshire P (2011) *Sitting in judgment: The working lives of judges*, Hart Publishing, Oxford.

de Sousa R (1987) *The rationality of emotion*, MIT Press, Cambridge.

de Sousa R (2008) 'Epistemic feelings', in Brun G, Doğuoğlu U and Kuenzle D (eds) *Epistemology and emotions*, Ashgate Publishing, Farnham.

de Sousa R (2009) 'Epistemic feelings', *Mind and Matter*, 7(2):139–161.

Diesen C (1996) *Lekmän som domare*, Juristförlaget, Stockholm.

Diesen C (2011/2012) 'För och emot nämndemän', *Juridisk Tidskrift*, 3:531–546.

Diesen C (2015) *Bevisprövning i brottmål*. Norstedts Juridik, Stockholm.

Dixon R (2010) 'Female justices, feminism, and the politics of judicial appointment: A re-examination', *Yale Journal of Law and Feminism*, 21:297–338.

Dowds E and Agnew E (2022) *Rape law and policy. Persistent challenges and future directions*, Routledge, London.

Dudek M and Stepien M (2021) *Courtroom power distance dynamics*, Springer, New York.

Durkheim E (1997) *The division of labor in society*, Free Press, New York.

Edelstam H (2001) *Offentlighet och sekretess i rättegång: principen om förhandlingsoffentlighet*, Norstedts juridic, Stockholm.

Eduards M (1997) 'Den förbjudna handlingen', *Tidskrift för Politisk Filosofi*, 3:17–36.

Ekelöf P-O and Edelstam H (2002) *Rättegång I*, Norstedts juridik, Stockholm.

Ekelöf P-O et al (2016) *Rättegång IV* (8th ed), Norstedts Juridik, Stockholm.

Elias N (2007 [1987]) *An essay on time*, University College Dublin Press, Dublin.

Ellison L and Munro VE (2009) 'Reacting to rape: Exploring mock jurors' assessments of complainant credibility', *British Journal of Criminology*, 49(2):202–219.

Enander V (2010) '"A fool to keep staying": Battered women labeling themselves stupid as an expression of gendered shame', *Violence Against Women*, 16(1):5–31.

Enander V (2011) 'Leaving Jekyll and Hyde: Emotion work in the context of intimate partner violence', *Feminism & Psychology*, 21(1):29–48.

Estrich S (1987) *Real rape*, Harvard University Press, Cambridge.

Feldman Barrett L (2017) *How emotions are made: The secret life of the brain*, MacMillan, London.

Fitger P (2014) *Rättegångsbalken*, Norstedts Juridik, Stockholm.

Flam H (1990) 'Emotional "man": I. The emotional man and the problem of collective action', *International Sociology*, 5(1):39–56.

Flam, H. (2000) *The emotional "man" and the problem of collective action*. Lang, Frankfurt am Main.

Flower L (2018) 'Doing loyalty: Defense lawyers' subtle dramas in the courtroom', *Journal of Contemporary Ethnography*, 47(2):226–254.

Flower L (2020) *Interactional justice: The role of emotions in the performance of loyalty*. Routledge, Abingdon.

Fricker M (2007) *Epistemic injustice: Power and the ethics of knowing*, Oxford University Press, Oxford.

Gagnon JH and Simon W (1973) *Sexual conduct: The social sources of human sexuality*, Aldine Books, Chicago.

Giddens A (1991) *The consequences of modernity*, Stanford University Press, Stanford.

Glynn AN and Sen M (2015) 'Identifying judicial empathy: Does having daughters cause judges to rule for women's issues?', *American Journal of Political Science*, 59(1):37–54.

Goffman E (1959) *The presentation of self in everyday life*, Doubleday, New York.

Goffman E (1990) *Stigma: Notes on the management of spoiled identity*, Penguin Books, Harmondsworth.

Goodrum S (2013) 'Bridging the gap between prosecutors' cases and victims' biographies in the criminal justice system through shared emotions', *Law and Social Inquiry*, 38(2):257–287.

Goodrum S and Stafford MC (2003) 'The management of emotions in the criminal justice system', *Sociological Focus*, 36(3):179–196.

Gordon MT and Riger S (1991) *The female fear: The social cost of rape*, University of Illinois Press, Champaign.

Grear A (2010) *Redirecting human rights: Facing the challenge of corporate legal humanity*, Palgrave Macmillan, Basingstoke.

Gunby C and Carline A (2020) 'The emotional particulars of working on rape cases: Doing dirty work, managing emotional dirt and conceptualizing "tempered indifference"', *British Journal of Criminology*, 60(2):343–362.

Gunnarsson Å and Svensson E-M (2009) *Genusrättsvetenskap*, Studentlitteratur, Lund.

Gustafsson H (2011) *Dissens. Om det rättsliga vetandet*, Juridiska institutionens skriftserie, Handelshögskolan vid Göteborgs universitet, Göteborg.

Halkier B (2011) 'Methodological practicalities in analytical generalization', *Qualitative Inquiry*, 17(9):787–797.

Haraway D (1988) 'Situated knowledges: The science question in feminism and the privilege of partial perspective', *Feminist Studies*, 14(3):575–599.

Haraway D (1992) 'Otherworldly conversations; terran topics; local terms', *Science as Culture*, 3(1):64–98.

Hauch V, Masip J, Sporer SL and Blandón-Gitlin I (2017) 'Can credibility criteria be assessed reliably? A meta-analysis of criteria-based content analysis', *Psychological Assessment*, 29(6):819–834.

Heinskou MB, Skilbrei M-L and Stefansen K (eds) (2020) *Rape in the Nordic countries: Continuity and change*, Routledge, London.

Helm BW (2009) 'Emotions as evaluative feelings', *Emotion Review*, 1(3):248–255.

Hessler K (2021) 'Women judges or feminist judges?: Gender representation and feminist values in international courts', *Journal of Social Philosophy*, 52:59–472.

Hlavka HR and Mulla S (2021) *Bodies in evidence: Race, gender, and science in sexual assault adjudication*, New York University Press, New York.

Hochschild AR (1979) 'Emotion work, feeling rules, and social structure', *American Journal of Sociology*, 85(3):551–575.

Hochschild AR (1983) *The managed heart – commercialization of human feeling*, University of California Press, Los Angeles.

Hochschild, AR (1990) 'Ideology and emotion management: A perspective and path for future research', in Kemper TD (ed) *Research Agendas in the Sociology of Emotions*, State University of New York Press, New York, pp 117–142.

Hohl, K and Stanko EA (2024) *Policing rape: The way forward*, Taylor & Francis, London.

Hollway W (1984) 'Women's power in heterosexual sex', *Women's Studies International Forum*, 7(1):63–68.

Holmes M (2010) 'The emotionalization of reflexivity', *Sociology*, 44(1):139–154.

Holmgård L (2019) *Bevisning i brottmål*, Norstedts Juridik, Stockholm.

Hörnle T (2017) 'The new German law on sexual assault and sexual harassment', *German Law Journal*, 18(6):1309–1330.

Horvath M and Brown J (2023) *Rape: Challenging contemporary thinking*, Routledge, London.

Houge AB and Laugerud S (2023) '"Unconscious or for other reasons incapable of resisting":(Un) protected sexual assault under Norwegian criminal law', *Violence Against Women*, DOI: 10778012231181048.

Houge AB and Laugerud S (2024) '"Unconscious or for other reasons incapable of resisting": (Un)protected sexual assault under Norwegian Criminal Law', *Violence Against Women*, 30(14):3676–3703.

Jacobsen J and Skilbrei M-L (2020) 'Reforming the rape offence in Norwegian criminal law', *Bergen Journal of Criminal Law and Criminal Justice*, 8(2):28–94.

Jakobsson K (2008) "We can't just do it any which way" – objectivity work among Swedish prosecutors', *Qualitative Sociology*, 4(1):46–68.

Jeuland E (2020) *Judge and emotion in civil law countries, the French example'*, Hal, hal-03003272.

Jordan J (2022) *Women, rape and justice, unravelling the rape conundrum*, Routledge, London.

Jorgensen MW and Phillips LJ (2002) *Discourse analysis as theory and method*, SAGE, London.

Jozkowski KN and Peterson ZD (2013) 'College students and sexual consent: Unique insights', *The Journal of Sex Research*, 50(6):517–523.

Kemper T (1978) 'Toward a sociology of emotions: Some problems and some solutions', *The American Sociologist*, 13(1):30–41.

Kemper TD (2001) 'A structural approach to social movement emotions', in Goodwin J, Jasper JM and Polletta F (eds) *Passionate politics – emotions and social movements*, University of Chicago Press, Chicago.

Kemper TD (2006) 'Power and status and the power-status theory of emotions', in Stets JE and Turner JH (eds) *Handbook of the sociology of emotions*, Springer, New York.

Kemper TD (2011) *Status, power and ritual interaction – a relational reading of Durkheim, Goffman and Collins*, Ashgate, Farnham.

Kleres J (2009) 'Preface: notes on the sociology of emotions in Europe', in Hopkins D, Kleres J, Flam H and Kuzmics H (eds) *Theorizing emotions: Sociological explorations and applications*, University of Chicago Press, Chicago.

Kleres J (2011) 'Emotion and narrative analysis: a methodological approach', *Journal for the Theory of Social Behaviour*, 41(2):182–202.

Koriat A (2000) 'The feeling of knowing: Some metatheoretical implications for consciousness and control', *Consciousness and Cognition*, 9:149–171.

Koselleck R (2004) *Futures past: On the semantics of historical time*, Columbia University Press, New York.

Lacey N (1998) 'Unspeakable subjects, impossible rights: Sexuality, integrity and criminal law', *Canadian Journal of Law & Jurisprudence*, 11(1):47–68.

Laclau E and Mouffe C (1985) *Hegemony and socialist strategy – towards a radical democratic politics*, The Thetford Press, Thetford.

Lange B (2002) 'The emotional dimension in legal regulation', *Journal of Law and Society*, 29(1):197–225.

Lantz PMV (2021) 'Affecting argumentative action: The temporality of decisive emotion', *Argumentation*, DOI: 10.1007/s10503-021-09546-2.

Larsson B (2014) 'Emotional professionalism in a bureaucratic context: emotion management in case handling at the Swedish Enforcement Authority', *International Journal of Work Organisation and Emotion*, 6(3):281–294.

Latour B (2010) *The making of law. An ethnography of the Conseil d'Etat*, Polity Press, Cambridge.

Le Bon G (2010 [1895]) *The crowd: A study of the popular mind*, Benediction Classics, Oxford.

Lees S (1996) *Carnal knowledge: Rape on trial*, Hamish Hamilton Gunnarsson, London.

Leijonhufvud M (2015) *Svensk sexualbrottslag: En framåtsyftande tillbakablick*, Norstedts Juridik, Stockholm.

Lidén M (2018) *Confirmation bias in criminal cases*, Uppsala University, Uppsala.

Lively K (2008) 'Emotional segues and the management of emotion by women and men', *Social Forces*, 87(2):911–936.

Lovett J and Kelly L (2009) *Different systems, similar outcomes? Tracking attrition in reported rape cases across Europe*, London Metropolitan University, Child & Woman Abuse Studies Unit, London.

Lloyd G (2004) *The man of reason: 'Male' and 'female' in western philosophy*. London: Routledge.

Luhmann N (1996) *Social systems*, Stanford University Press, Stanford.

Mack K and Roach Anleu S (2010) 'Performing impartiality: Judicial demeanor and legitimacy', *Law and Social Inquiry – Journal of the American Bar Foundation*, 35(1):137–173.

Mackenzie C and Stoljar E (2000) *Relational autonomy: Feminist perspectives on autonomy, agency and the social self*, Oxford University Press, New York.

MacKinnon CA (1989) *Toward a feminist theory of the state*, Harvard University Press, Cambridge.

MacKinnon CA (2016) 'Rape redefined general essays', *Harvard Law & Policy Review*, 10(2):431–478.

Maier S (2014) *Rape, victims, and investigations*, Routledge, London.

Manne K (2018) *Down girl: The logic of misogyny*, Oxford University Press, New York.

Mardorossian CM (2014) *Framing the rape victim: Gender and agency reconsidered*, Rutgers University Press, New Brunswick.

Maroney TA (2011) 'The persistent cultural script of judicial dispassion', *California Law Review*, 99:629–681.

Maroney TA (2012) 'Angry judges', *Vanderbilt Law Review*, 65(5):1207–1286.

Maroney TA and Gross JJ (2014) 'The ideal of the dispassionate judge: An emotion regulation perspective', *Emotion Review*, 6(2):142–151.

Martin PY (2005) *Rape work: Victims, gender, and emotions in organization and community context*, Routledge, New York.

McDonald S (2005) 'Studying actions in context: a qualitative shadowing method for organizational research', *Qualitative research*, 5(4):455–473.

McGlynn C (2010) 'Feminist activism and rape law reforms in England and Wales: A Sisyphean struggle?', in McGlynn C and Munro VE (eds) *Rethinking rape law: An introduction*, Routledge, London.

McGlynn C (2022) 'Challenging anti-carceral feminism: criminalisation, justice and continuum thinking', *Women's Studies International Forum* 93.

McGlynn C and Munro VE (2010) *Rethinking rape law: An introduction*, Routledge, London.

Mellqvist M (2019/2020) 'Balkongmetoden – några kommentarer till visa kommentarer', *Juridisk Tidskrift*:776–781.

Minissale A (2023a) *Emotions in legal decisions: The construction of objective narratives in italian criminal trials*, Uppsala University, Uppsala.

Minissale A (2023b) 'Scrutinising gut feelings: Emotional reflexive practices in Italian courts', *Emotions and Society*:1–19.

Morton A (2013) *Emotion and imagination*, Polity Press, Cambridge.

Mouffe C (1999) 'Deliberative democracy or agonistic pluralism?', *Social Research*, 66(3).

Moussion-Esteve A (2022) 'Domestic fear beyond traumatic terror: Understanding mothers' everyday experiences of recurring fear in the context of domestic violence', *Emotions and Society*, 4(3):341–357.

Muehlenhard CL, Humphreys TP, Jozkowski KN and Peterson ZD (2016) 'The complexities of sexual consent among college students: A conceptual and empirical review', *The Journal of Sex Research*, 53(4–5):457–487.

Naffine N (2002) 'Can women be legal persons?', in James S and Palmer S (eds) *Visible women*, Hart Publishing, Oxford, pp 69–90.

Nedelsky J (2011) *Law's Relations. A relational theory of self, autonomy and law*, Oxford: Oxford University Press.

Niemi J (2010) 'What we talk about when we talk about buying sex', *Violence Against women*, 16(2):159–172.

Oatley K (2009) 'An emotion's emergence, unfolding, and potential for empathy: a study of resentment by the "Psychologist of Avon"', *Emotion Review*, 1(1):24–30.

Orrbén S (2022) '"Han hade sin penis i henne" – representationer av agerande kroppar i sexualbrottsdomar', *Tidskrift för Genusvetenskap*, 43(2–3).

Ortony A, Clore GL and Collins A (2022) *The cognitive structure of emotions*, Cambridge University Press, Cambridge.

Påhlsson R (2005) *Hunden klockan tre och fjorton. Rapport från juridikens tankevärld*, Iustus förlag, Stockholm.

Pineau L (1989) 'Date rape: A feminist analysis', *Law and Philosophy*, 8(2):217–243.

Pratt J (2008) 'Scandinavian exceptionalism in an era of penal excess. Part I: the nature and roots of Scandinavian exceptionalism', *British Journal of Criminology*, 48(2):119–137.

Randall M (2010) 'Sexual assault law, credibility, and "ideal victims": Consent, resistance, and victim blaming', *Canadian Journal of Women and the Law*, 22:397.

Reddy WM (2001) *The navigation of feeling – a framework for the history of emotions*, Cambridge University Press, Cambridge.

Rifkin J (1980) 'Toward a theory of law and patriarchy', *Harvard Women's Law Journal*, 3:83–95.

Roach Anleu S and Mack K (2017) *Performing judicial authority in the lower courts*, Palgrave Socio-Legal Studies, London.

Rose M, Nadler J and Clark J (2006) 'Appropriately upset? Emotion norms and perceptions of crime victims', *Law and Human Behavior*, 30(2):203–219.

Roeser S (2012) 'Risk communication, public engagement, and climate change: A role for emotions', *Risk Analysis*, 32:1033–1040.

Rumney PN and McPhee D (2021) 'Offender-centric policing in cases of rape', *Journal of Criminal Law*, 85(6):425–440.

Ryan KM (2011) 'The relationship between rape myths and sexual scripts: The social construction of rape', *Sex Roles*, 65:774–782.

Saunders CL (2018) 'Rape as "one person's word against another's": Challenging the conventional wisdom', *International Journal of Evidence & Proof*, 22(2):161–181.

Scarduzio JA (2011) 'Maintaining order through deviance? The emotional deviance, power, and professional work of municipal court judges', *Management Communication Quarterly*, 25(2):283–310.

Scheer M (2021) *Enthusiasm: Emotional practices of conviction in modern Germany*, Oxford University Press, Oxford.

Scheff TJ (1988) 'Shame and conformity: The deference-emotion system', *American Sociological Review*, 53(3):395–406.

Scheff TJ (1990) *Microsociology. Discourse, emotion, and social structure*, Chicago: University of Chicago Press.

Scheff TJ (1997) *Emotions, the social bond, and human reality. Part/whole analysis*, Cambridge University Press, Cambridge.

von Scheve C and Ismer S (2013) 'Towards a theory of collective emotions', *Emotion Review*, 5(4):406–413.

Schuster ML and Propen A (2010) 'Degrees of emotion: Judicial responses to victim impact statements', *Law, Culture and the Humanities*, 6(1):75–104.

Shields SA (2002) *Speaking from the heart: Gender and the social meaning of emotion*, Cambridge University Press, Cambridge.

Simmel G (1971) 'The metropolis and mental life', in Levine DN (ed) *Georg Simmel, on individuality and social forms*, University of Chicago Press, Chicago.

Smart C (1995) *Law, crime and sexuality: Essays in feminism*, SAGE, London.

Smith DE (1987) *The everyday world as problematic: A feminist sociology*, Northeastern University Press, Boston.

Smith O (2018) *Rape trials in England and Wales: Observing justice and rethinking rape myths*, Palgrave Macmillan, London.

Smith O and Skinner T (2012) 'Observing court responses to victims of rape and sexual assault', *Feminist Criminology*, 7(4):298–326.

Smith O and Skinner T (2017) 'How rape myths are used and challenged in rape and sexual assault trials', *Social & Legal Studies*, 26(4):441–466.

Spohn C and Horney J (1992) *Rape law reform: A grassroots revolution and its impact*, Plenum Press, New York.

Stearns PN (1994) *American cool – constructing a twentieth-century emotional style* (Vol. 3) New York University Press, New York.

Stefansen K (2020) 'Understanding unwanted sexual touching: A situational approach', in Heinskou MB, Skilbrei ML and Stefansen K (eds) *Rape in the Nordic countries*, Routledge, London, pp 49–65.

Sterzel F (ed) (2001) R*ättsstaten – rätt, politik och moral*, Rättsfonden, Stockholm.

Strindlöv (2024) 'Sprickan i samtyckeslagen – så olika döms våldtäktsfall', *Expressen*, 19 May, https://www.expressen.se/nyheter/sverige/sprickan-i-samtyckeslagen-sa-olika-doms-valdtaktsfall [Accessed 1 November 2024].

Strömwall L and Granhag PA (2003) 'How to detect deception? Arresting the beliefs of police officers, prosecutors and judges', *Psychology, Crime and Law*, 9(1):19–36.

Sutorius H and Kaldal A (2003) *Bevisprövning vid sexualbrott*, Norstedts Juridik, Stockholm.

Svedberg W (2016) *Nya och gamla perspektiv på ansvar? En rättsvetenskaplig studie om ansvar i en straffrättslig kontext gällande självkörande/uppkopplade fordon*, VTI, Göteborg.

Svedberg Andersson W and Bladini M (2021) 'Autonomy and beyond: Voluntariness in the light of lived autonomy', *Nordic Journal of Law and Justice*, 3:35–49.

Svensson E-M (1997) *Genus och rätt: EN problematisering av föreställningen om rätten*, Iustus Förlag, Uppsala.

Sveriges Domstolar (2010) *Bemötandestrategi för Sveriges domstolar*, Dnr. 783.

Temkin J (2000) 'Prosecuting and defending rape: Perspectives from the bar', *Journal of Law and Society*, 27(2):219–248.

Temkin J, Gray JM and Barret J (2018) 'Different functions of rape myth use in court: Findings from a trial observation study', *Feminist Criminology*, 13(2):205–226.

Terwiel A (2020) 'What is carceral feminism?', *Political Theory*, 48(4):421–442.

Teubner G (1993) *Law as an autopoietic system*, Blackwell, Oxford.

Tilly C (2008) *Why?* Princeton University Press, Princeton.

Törnqvist N (2017) *Att göra rätt. En studie om professionell respektabilitet, emotioner och narrativa linjer bland relationsvåldsspecialiserade åklagare*, Stockholm University, Stockholm.

Törnqvist N (2021) 'Drizzling sympathy: Ideal victims and flows of sympathy in Swedish courts', *International Review of Victimology*, 28(3):263–285.

Törnqvist N and Wettergren Å (2023) 'Epistemic emotions in prosecutorial decision-making', *Journal of Law and Society*, 50:208–230.

Tracy SJ and Tretheway A (2005) 'Fracturing the real-self↔fake-self dichotomy: Moving toward "crystallized" organizational discourses and identities', *Communication Theory*:168–195.

Träskman P-O and Wennberg S (2019) *Brottsbalken: En kommentar. Del 1 (1–12 kap.) brotten mot person och förmögenhetsbrotten*, Norstedts Juridik, Stockholm.

Tyler TR (2003) 'Procedural justice, legitimacy, and the effective rule of law', *Crime and Justice*, 30:283–357.

Uhnoo S, Bladini M and Wettergren Å (2024a) 'Negotiating access', in Flower L and Klosterkamp S (eds) *Courtroom ethnography. Exploring contemporary approaches, fieldwork and challenges*, Palgrave Macmillan, Cham, pp 33–46.

Uhnoo S, Erixon S and Bladini M (2024b) 'The wave of consent-based rape laws in Europe', *International Journal of Law, Crime and Justice*, 77:100668.

Uhnoo S, Wettergren Å and Bladini M (2024c) ' "It could have been my son!" "Himpathy" and the male fear defence in rape trials', *Journal of Law and Society*, 51(4), https://onlinelibrary.wiley.com/doi/10.1111/jols.12508.

Vermeule A (2001) 'Veil of ignorance rules in constitutional law', *Yale Law Journal*, 111(2):399–434.

Vrij A, Verschuere B and Granhag PA (2015) *Deception detection: Current challenges and cognitive approaches*, Wiley Blackwell, Chichester.

Wallin L, Uhnoo S, Wettergren Å and Bladini M (2021) 'Capricious credibility – legal assessments of voluntariness in Swedish negligent rape judgements', *Nordic Journal of Criminology*, 22(1):3–22.

Weber M (1978) 'The types of legitimate domination', in Roth G and Wittich C (eds) *Economy and society – an outline of interpretive sociology* (Vol 1), University of California, Berkeley.

Weber M (1998) 'Bureaucracy', in Gerth HH and Mills CW (eds) *From Max Weber: essays in sociology*, Routledge, London.

Wegerstad L (2015) 'Skyddsvärda intressen & straffvärda kränkningar. Om sexualbrotten i det straffrättsliga systemet med utgångspunkt i brottet sexuellt ofredande' (Doctoral dissertation, Lund University).

Wegerstad L (2021) 'Sex must be voluntary: Sexual communication and the new definition of rape in Sweden', *German Law Journal*, 22(5):734–752.

Wendt-Höjer M (2002) *Rädslans politik: våld och sexualitet i den svenska demokratin*, PhD thesis, Stockholms Universitet.

Wennberg S (2018/19) 'Befogad kritik av det nya våldtäktsbrottet?' *Juridisk tidskrift*, 298.

Wettergren Å (2010) 'Managing unlawful feelings: The emotional regime of the Swedish migration board', *International Journal for Work, Organisation and Emotion*, 3(4):400–419.

Wettergren Å (2019) 'Emotive-cognitive rationality, background emotions and emotion work', in Bellocchi A, Khorana S, McKenzie J, Olson R, Patulny R and Peterie M (eds) *Emotions in late modernity*, Routledge, London.

Wettergren Å (2024) 'Emotionalising hope in times of climate crisis', *Emotions and Society*, 1:1–19.

Wettergren Å and Bergman Blix S (2016) 'Empathy and objectivity in the legal process: The case of Swedish prosecutors', *Journal of Scandinavian Studies in Criminology and Crime Prevention*, 17(1):19–35.

Wettergren Å and Bergman Blix S (2021) 'Comparing culturally embedded frames of judicial dispassion', in Bandes S, Madeira JL, Temple K and Kidd White E (eds) *Research handbook on law and emotion*, Edward Elgar Publishing, Cheltenham.

Wettergren Å and Bergman Blix S (2022) 'Prosecutors' habituation of emotion management in Swedish courts', *Law & Social Inquiry*, 47(3):971–995.

Wheatcroft JM and Walklate S (2014) 'Thinking differently about "false allegation" in cases of rape: The search for truth', *International Journal of Criminology and Sociology*, 3:239–248.

Willén RM and Strömwall LA (2012) 'Offenders' lies and truths: an evaluation of the Supreme Court of Sweden's criteria for credibility assessment', *Psychology, Crime & Law*, 18(8):745–758.

Wolcott HF (1994) *Transforming qualitative data: Description, analysis, and interpretation*, Sage, London.

Wong C (2012) 'Sweden', in L. Ligeti (ed) *Towards a prosecutor for the European Union*, 742–778, Hart Publishing Ltd.

Wrede O (2015) *The role of emotions in judgements of crime victims*, University of Gothenburg, Gothenburg.

Young IM (1990) *Throwing like a girl and other essays in feminist philosophy and social theory*, Indiana University Press, Bloomington.

Zizek S (1989) *The sublime object of ideology*, Verso, London.

Case law

NJA 1980 s 725.

NJA 2005 s 712.

NJA 2009 s 447 I–II.

NJA 2010 s 671.

NJA 2015 s 702 (*Balcony Case*).

NJA 2017 s 316 I–II.

NJA 2019 s 668.

NJA 2023 s 29 I–II.

NJA II 1943 s 445.

Swedish public documents

Bill [Prop] 2012/13:111 *En skärpt sexualbrottslagstiftning*.

Bill [Prop] 2017/18:177 *En ny sexualbrottslagstiftning byggd på frivillighet*.

SOU 2001:14.

SOU 2010:71.

SOU 2016:60.

SOU 2016:78 'Ordning och reda i välfärden'.

SOU 2017:7 Straffprocessens ramar och domstolens beslutsunderlag i brottmål – en bättre hantering av stora mål.

SOU 2023:12 Förstärkt skydd för demokratin och domstolarnas oberoende.

SOU series 1926:32 *Processkommissionens betänkande angående rättegångsväsendets ombildning, del II*.

SOU series 1938:44 *Processlagberedningens förslag till rättegångsbalk, II, Motiv. m. m.*

Index

References to figures appear in *italic* type. References to notes show
both the page number and the note number (9n10).